MICROCOMPUTER APPLICATIONS

Using
WordPerfect 5.1,®
Lotus 1-2-3®/
Version 2.2,
and dBASE IV®

Using
WordPerfect 5.1®,
Lotus 1-2-3®/
Version 2.2,
and dBASE IV®

Fritz H. Grupe

University of Nevada — Reno

Kerry J. Chase

Wm. C. Brown Publishers

Book Team

Editor *Kathy Shields*
Software Hotline and Developmental Support Technician *Lisa Schonhoff*
Production Coordinator *Deborah Donner*

 Wm. C. Brown Publishers
President *G. Franklin Lewis*
Vice President, Publisher *George Wm. Bergquist*
Vice President, Publisher *Thomas E. Doran*
Vice President, Operations and Production *Beverly Kolz*
National Sales Manager *Virginia S. Moffat*
Advertising and Marketing Manager *Ann M. Knepper*
Editor-in-Chief *Edward G. Jaffe*
Managing Editor, Production *Colleen A. Yonda*
Production Editorial Manager *Julie A. Kennedy*
Production Editorial Manager *Ann Fuerste*
Publishing Services Manager *Karen J. Slaght*
Manager of Visuals and Design *Faye M. Shilling*

Cover design by Sailer & Cook Creative Services

MS-DOS ® is a registered trademark of Microsoft Corporation

WordPerfect ® is a registered trademark of WordPerfect Corporation

Lotus 1-2-3 ® is a registered trademark of Lotus Development Corporation

dBASE IV ® is a registered trademark of Aston-Tate

Printed in the United States of America by Wm. C. Brown Publishers, 2460 Kerper Boulevard,
Dubuque, IA 52001

10 9 8 7 6 5 4 3 2 1

Contents

Chapter 1

Introduction To Microcomputing

Chapter Outline

COMPUTERS IN SOCIETY

The Mirrors of Man

Computers have become the mirrors of mankind. We describe their functions in human terms. They are depicted as thinking, expecting, breaking down, and solving problems. Humans are portrayed as crashing, computing, and programmed. A sentence like, "The word processor isn't working," is ambiguous as to whether the word processor is a person or a machine. In the cinema we are fascinated by the degree to which we see computers and computerized robots that act as though they were people. In *Star Wars*, R2D2 and 3CPO endear themselves to us in much the same way that a puppy might. They are equal to us in intelligence but lack the emotion we expect from people. In the film *Short Circuit*, Number 5 becomes a robot with emotions: a robot who has become indistinguishable from a human. Computers like these are believable because we see computers at work every day that are maintaining our health, enabling our businesses to operate, creating new music and art, and expanding our scientific horizons. Computers make a positive contribution to society.

In *War Games*, however, the computer is clearly out of control. This computer is symbolic of our ambivilence to computers. The science fiction writer Issac Assimov once wrote that the first rule for robots was that they should do no harm to mankind. Situations we have heard about and experienced support our distrust of computers. We assume that they are capable of getting out of control and taking on a life of their own. It is of little comfort to say that computers and robots are created and programmed by people; that they are simply doing what they have been instructed to do. If they can issue checks for $1 million when the amount was supposed to have been $1.25, we are not surprised when they call the armed forces to strategic alert when the moon rises, or when the fail-safe mechanisms of nuclear power plants seem to compound, rather than simplify, the operation of the plant at times of crisis.

HAL, the advanced computer system in the film *2001*, is not only out of control, but is affected by a seemingly psychological disorder. Its intent is to control its own destiny. Even HAL's malevolent behavior is clearly within the realm of technological feasibility. HAL sets its own objectives and takes on a life that is scarcely distinguishable from our own.

The computers with which we come in contact, the computers we see on the screen, and the computers we read about in magazines and literature give us contradictory messages. We read about people with computer phobia--the fear of computers. An estimated 9 million microcomputers are being sold annually, but one study estimated that half of the computers purchased for home usage were unused. How many computers sit idle in business or are greatly under-utilized?

Our society's ambivalence is due in large measure to a lack of understanding about how computers work, about their limitations and about their potential contributions toward the resolution of problems that have beset mankind for centuries. Improving your knowledge of computer systems can make you a more intelligent consumer of computerized goods, a more informed user of computer systems, and a more concerned citizen whose private and public life is ever more affected by computers.

Computer Proficiency

This book has been written to assist its user in becoming proficient in the use of computers. The so-called computer revolution has just begun. The computers of today's cinema will, in fifty years, seem as primitive to us as Gutenberg's printing press does now. The computer revolution will change the workplace, the home, and our recreational pursuits. Sophisticated knowledge of computer applications will be as important to the doctor as to the computer scientist, as valuable to the artist as to the president of a company, as critical to a politician as to a computer manufacturer, and as neccessary to a student as to the treasurer of a large corporation.

Computers are and will remain an integral part of your life. They will not only not go away, they will affect you more and more every day. You will have to make decisions about their purchase and about how to use them. You will have to interpret their conclusions. There will always be a great demand for people to operate and program them. Yes, you will probably have to continue to fight with them every now and again. Beyond simply being familiar with computers you must be computer proficient. Computer proficiency requires you to be:

1. Psychologically comfortable with computers. This comfort comes from working with computers at a level where you begin to understand how they work and what they can do.
2. Competent to work effectively with a computer. For some people, computer proficiency will entail computer programming--a skill not taught in this book. For many others, computer proficiency will require technical knowledge of how to use computers effectively in work and other situations. The specific requirements for computer proficiency for any specific vocation will vary, but some knowledge of using computers advantageously is common to most modern professions and to many semi-professional vocations.
3. Knowledgeable of how computers work. They are not black boxes that operate in mysterious ways. They operate within known constraints and limits. Knowledge of what they can do and what they cannot do is essential for the citizen and the worker, for the employer and the employee,

for the family member and the consumer.

4. Aware of the impact of the computer on society. Computers can and will change the ways in which we live. For good or ill, computers will have an impact on our lives. You have a role to play in defining what computers should be allowed to do and what they should not be allowed to do. An informed awareness of the social implications computers have for the future is part of computer proficiency.

5. Competent to apply computers to problems that affect you. Perceiving which problems are susceptible to solution with the use of computers, and actually using computers to solve those problems is critical. No person can master all of the potential uses of computers. This does not excuse anyone from mastering some of its capabilities. Skills learned in this book--operating system usage, word processing, spreadsheet development, database management and communications--are the most commonly needed skills. They are not, however, the universe of applications. Be prepared for others.

TYPES OF COMPUTERS

The pervasive influence of computers on our society is partially due to the variety of computers that are produced by uncounted numbers of vendors that sell such systems. Not only do computers come in a spectrum of sizes, but so too do printers, graphics plotters, magnetic storage devices, and other computer-related equipment. Some computers are designed to optimize the handling of specialized problems, while others are general purpose machines. Categorizing computers has become increasingly difficult as the capacities of the computers overlap with one another.

Supercomputers are the largest computers available. These machines carry purchase costs that are measured in the tens of millions of dollars. They can carry out hundreds of computer instructions every second, serve hundreds of users simultaneously, support a wide range of types of software, generally of a scientific nature, and are very expensive to maintain and operate. They operate in a highly controlled environment in which air conditioning, electrical power stabilization, fire control, and other securities are taken to insure that the computer can function even though external problems arise. Because of their expense, most companies and universities cannot buy their own super computers. Therefore, most super computers are shared by users from around the country who must use software that require fast processor speeds to make many computations before the program finishes.

Mainframe computers are large computer systems that cost between 1 and 5 million dollars to purchase. Their computational speeds are rated at from 5 to 20 million computer instructions per second. These systems also operate in a carefully controlled environment. Professionally trained computer support staff are needed to keep the computer running. Most mainframe computers are used to support entire companies or large divisions of a company. Some mainframes are dedicated to a function like computer-assisted design or transaction processing, but most mainframes are general purpose computers that support many aspects of a business.

Mini and super minicomputers, once thought of as a distinct class of machines, now rival mainframes in speed and accuracy. Their cost, though, is considerably lower, often between 100 thousand and 1 million dollars. These machines, as a rule, require less professional support and less environmental control than would a mainframe. Many of these computers function well in an office environment that has air conditioning adequate for people. Super minicomputers may be the primary computer system for a small to medium size company, or for a single department within a company. Many super minicomputers are dedicated to carrying out a small number of related tasks for the organization. They are generally supported by a system administrator and a small support staff of programmers.

Micro and super microcomputers are generally thought of as single-user systems and are operated by persons who have no formal training in computer programming or computer operations. Costing from several hundred to 50 thousand dollars, these systems will fit into an office easily. Most such systems will carry out from 100 **thousand to 3 million** computer instructions per second. The computers will function well without **professional support** staff, although users may need assistance from time to time. Super microcomputers **acting as multi-user** systems are typically capable of supporting up to fifty users.

Microcomputers come in a variety of sizes. **Portable** and lap top computers are especially **light to** make them easy to transport. Desktop computers are **larger and** generally have larger screens. Recreational computers are inexpensive **computers that are** limited to running games, instructional programs, and some limited capability business **software.**

The classification of a particular computer **into** one of these categories is often difficult because the capabilities of machines in each **range often overlap.** Even single vendors may sell computers that appear to provide competing levels of computing services.

FIVE COMPONENTS OF A MICROCOMPUTER SYSTEM

A microcomputer can be viewed **as a system of five interacting** components: hardware, software, **data,** procedures, and users. Figure 1-1 **illustrates some examples** of these components.

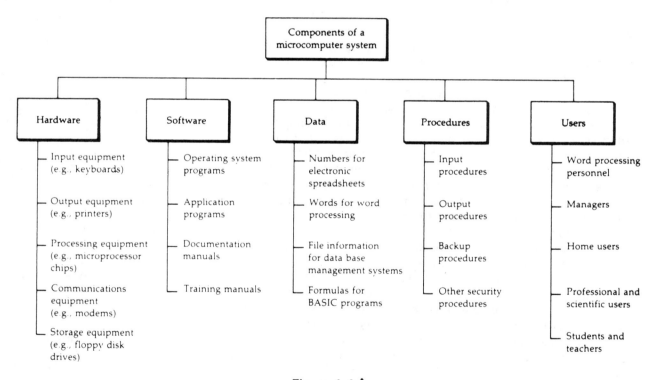

Figure 1-1. [*]

[*]From M. Simkin and R. Dependahl, **Jr.** *Microcomputer Principles and Applications.* Copyright 1988 **Wm.** C. Brown Publishers, Dubuque, Iowa. All **Rights Reserved.** Reprinted by permission.

Figure 1-2 illustrates some **examples of these** components in a typical setting. Although the **power** of a microcomputer is often attributed to the **technical capabilities** of its hardware and software, it is more often a function of how well **these components work** together as a system.

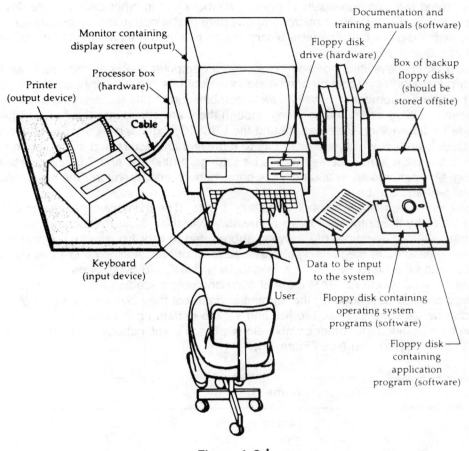

Figure 1-2.*

*From M. Simkin and R. Dependahl, Jr. *Microcomputer Principles and Applications*. Copyright 1988 Wm. C. Brown Publishers, Dubuque, Iowa. All Rights Reserved. Reprinted by permission.

Microcomputer hardware is the physical equipment of the system. The most obvious hardware is the equipment that is visible, such as the floppy disk drive. Some of this equipment, for example, the keyboard, is primarily used to provide data to the microcomputer and is therefore called input equipment. Other equipment, for example, the monitor screen, is primarily designed for preparing outputs from the microcomputer and is therefore called output equipment. Hardware components that are located outside of the processor box are referred to as peripheral equipment.

Software consists of data and programs. Data consists of the information that is to be stored in the computer and operated on by programs. Programs are the instructions stored in the computer that can be executed by the computer to manipulate the data in some way.

The user is the person using the system. Procedures are the methods by which the user and the user's organization collect, input, arrange, output, analyze, save, backup, and utilize the data and software in the computer. Procedures coordinate the usage of data to convert it to useful information.

REPRESENTING DATA

Information is stored electromagnetically in primary memory and in other data storage devices in either of two states: zeros and ones. Most microcomputers are digital computers whose fundamental unit storage is the binary digit or bit. The term binary means two, and a binary digit is therefore a digit with only two settings, 0 and 1.

By itself, a bit conveys little meaning. However, a computer is able to represent our familiar letters, numbers, and punctuation symbols by combining individual bits into a binary code. This is a code composed of a specific number of bits, with each combination of bits representing a different character. The most common binary codes in use today, though there are others, are the ASCII (American Standard Code for Information Interchange) and the EBCDIC (Extended Binary Coded Decimal Interchange Code), both of which use eight bits to represent characters and symbols. In ASCII, for example, the character A is represented by the bit settings, 11000001, and Z is represented by 11011010. Eight-bit patterns allow 256 possible combinations and, therefore, the representation of 256 different characters and symbols.

Eight bits, one character or symbol, constitute 1 byte. The memory capacities of computers are generally described by the number of bytes of memory available. Most microcomputers have their memories measured in the number of kilobytes, abbreviated to K or Kb, although newer microcomputers offer RAM sizes measured in megabytes, abbreviated to M or Mb. A kilobyte is 1,024 bytes of data (2^{10}), roughly 1,000, hence the prefix kilo, while a megabyte is 1,048,576 bytes of data (2^{20}), roughly 1 million, hence the prefix mega. Common RAM sizes of microcomputers are 256 Kb (Kilobytes), 512 Kb, and 640 Kb. Disk drives are also described by the amount of data that they can store on a single diskette. Commonly, disk drives store 360 Kb, 720 Kb, and 1.2 Mb of data on the diskette.

Bits can be combined into other combinations. These combinations are named based on the number of bits that they contain (see Figure 1-3).

No. Bytes	No. Bits	Name
1	4	Nibble
1	8	Byte
2	16	Half word
4	32	Word
8	64	Double word

Figure 1-3. Bit Pattern Naming Conventions

The prefixes giga and tera are also used to denote billions and trillions of elements. Each of the four prefixes can be combined with bits, as in kilobits, with bytes, as in gigabytes, and with words, as in megawords.

MICROCOMPUTER HARDWARE

Central Processing Unit

The processing heart of a microcomputer is its central processing unit, or CPU. The CPU is a microprocessor chip that consists of several integrated components: 1) a control unit; 2) an arithmetic/logic unit; and 3) primary memory. The functions of a microprocessor are:

1. To control the processing and movement of data among components of the system, and to control the order and speed at which program instructions are executed. This control is exercised by a portion of the microprocessor called the control unit.
2. To manipulate data in arithmetic operations, for example, addition, subtraction, division, and multiplication; and in logical operations, for example, determining whether a given number is the number 10 or not.
3. To store data and programs that are in active use. The ability of computers to store programs in memory while they are being worked on is the key feature that separates computers from mechanical calculating devices. The stored program concept is implemented in primary memory. Primary memory is also called random access memory, or RAM.

Random Access Memory (RAM)

It has been mentioned that primary memory is also called RAM, random access memory. The computer has the ability to locate necessary data in RAM randomly (by address and not by exhaustive search), and change it. RAM holds the operating system that controls the computer's hardware and supplies the user with commands that can be carried out. RAM is free of programs and data when the computer is first turned on. When the system is turned on, part of the operating system is loaded into memory. When a program like a word processor is started, it is loaded into RAM also. The document that is created with the word processor is also contained in RAM. The size of RAM for your computer may determine what programs can be run, and the size of user-created documents, worksheets, databases, and other files.

RAM stores information only while the computer is turned on. If power is lost the information it contains is lost and cannot be recaptured. For this reason RAM is said to be volatile.

Secondary Storage

Storage devices like disk drives and tape drives are called secondary storage units. Data that is written into files on diskettes or tape are permanently stored. In order to remove the saved files from secondary storage, the user must either give an explicit command to erase it, or must commit some error, like overwriting the file or damaging the storage medium.

The capacity of floppy disk drives has already been mentioned. Hard disk drive capacities are typically rated at 10 Mb, 20 Mb, and 40 Mb, although they can be considerably larger. Drives larger than 32 Mb operated under MS-DOS must be subdivided into partitions. Each partition will be treated as a separate disk drive even though all of these logical drives reside on the same physical disk.

Tape drives are frequently used for backing up data on hard drives. They are rated in the number of Mb per minute that they can transfer, as well as on the number of bytes that they can store on one tape.

Read Only Memory (ROM)

Read only memory, or ROM, is found in a ROM chip. This memory stores instructions that the computer uses to begin to operate, and to load the operating system. The instructions are permanently stored in the chip by the manufacturer and cannot be over-written. Nor will they be lost when the system is turned off. For this reason ROM is said to be static.

ROM is also found on some additional cards that may be added to some microcomputers. This ROM may store a complete program like Lotus 1-2-3, a language like BASIC, or a game. If ROM instructions are not available, software of this type has to be provided on a diskette from which the instructions can be read.

Microprocessors

The central control unit of a microcomputer is called the microprocessor. Some computers are described in terms of the bit size of the microprocessor's registers--special, very high-speed, storage locations where data is being actively manipulated. 8-bit computers are less accurate than 16-bit computers. 32 and 64-bit computers are still more accurate.

There are many microprocessors that have been installed in microcomputers. They differ in the speed at which they operate and in the number of bits they can operate on for arithmetic operations and for transmission onto the data bus. The characteristics of four of the more popular microprocessor chips that are produced by the Intel Corporation and that are used by manufacturers of MS-DOS compatible microcomputers are summarized in Figure 1-4. The figure also shows which model of IBM computer introduced this chip. The same chips are used by many other companies, some of which have adapted the chip to run at a higher clock speed.

Intel Chip	Processor Clock Speed	Processor Type	Data Bus	Introduced With IBM Model
8088	4.77 Megahertz	16 bit	8 bit	PC
8086	8 Megahertz	16 bit	16 bit	PC XT
80286	12 Megahertz	16 bit	16 bit	PC AT
80386	16 Megahertz	32 bit	32 bit	PS/2 Model 80
80486	25 Megahertz	32 bit	32 bit	PS/2 Model 70

Figure 1-4. Selected Microprocessors.

As a rule, the faster the clock speed of a processor, and the greater the number of bits that can be handled, the more powerful is the processor.

The Data Bus

The data bus of a microcomputer is the pathway of circuits that connects the CPU with the major hardware components: the CPU, the disks, primary memory, and the add-in cards that are inserted into expansion slots within the central processor cabinet. A data bus is like a street with 8, 16, or 32 lanes in each direction. The 8 bits that constitute a character are transported along the data bus to major components. An 8-bit bus can transport one character's bits simultaneously. A 16-bit bus can transport two characters simultaneously. And a 32-bit bus can transport 4 characters simultaneously.

Expansion Slots

Microcomputers are built with expansion slots into which the add-in cards can be placed. The add-in cards, also informally called boards, extend the microcomputer's functions. Some add-in cards can expand the primary memory into the multi-megabyte range, while others enable the user to connect joysticks and mouses to the system. Other cards can enable the computer to receive and output sound, connect to real-time data gathering devices like thermometers and geiger counters, and hold a clock with a battery so the computer can keep its own calendar and clock for system usage.

Ports

Externally connected devices like a mouse or a data communications modem communicate with the bus through a port. There are ports through which data is sent or received sequentially, one bit at a time. Such ports are called serial ports and RS-232-C ports. Other ports send and receive data along pathways which carry 8, 16, or 32 bits simultaneously. These ports are called parallel ports since the bits move along in parallel with one another. Printers typically use parallel ports to receive data, while a mouse, a modem, and a joystick typically use serial ports to send and receive data.

MICROCOMPUTER SOFTWARE

Operating Systems

Operating systems software is the software that controls the hardware components of the computer. It also provides the user with interface commands that permit the creation and manipulation of files that contain programs, documents, worksheets, and databases. Different computer systems use different operating systems. This book focuses on the operating system produced by Microsoft called **MS-DOS**, for Microsoft Disk Operating System. Originally developed for the first IBM personal computers, this operating system has been used by numerous other manufacturers of computers who wished to maintain compatibility of software with the IBM line of computers. Compatibility is a measure of the ability of a computer to run programs and to share files that run on another computer. The large number of MS-DOS compatible machines has greatly enhanced the ability of software developers to create software for computers produced by many manufacturing companies, while facilitating the ability of users within companies to share files.

OS/2 is a relatively new operating system that is designed to run on microcomputers that in the past would have run MS-DOS. It is being produced to allow microcomputers to serve as multi-user systems and to support the concurrent running and displaying of several programs simultaneously. OS/2 is being developed by Microsoft.

The **UNIX** operating system is produced by AT&T and is used on computers of all types: microcomputer through super computer. Originally designed to support multi-user, interactive computer systems, UNIX has only recently become popular on larger micro and super microcomputers. Although there are several versions of UNIX available, users making a transition from one system running UNIX to another system will not encounter major problems in switching environments. Also, companies that use UNIX will find it easier to incrementally add new computers without multiplying the number of operating systems that must be supported by computer staff.

There are many microcomputer manufacturers that produce their own, **proprietary**, operating systems along with their own hardware. Apple computers and Atari, for instance, produce their own operating systems. Due to the central role operating systems play in determining how computers will function, the operating system often constrains the level of compatibility one computer will have with another.

Some microcomputers can support multiple operating systems. These computers allow the user to select from among these systems and to choose which system will control the computer at any point in time.

Programming Languages

People who need to develop programs that are unique to their situations have to prepare their own software to use. These programs are frequently written in programming languages that allow them to have great flexibility and control over how the application program will function and how it will look to the users. There are hundreds of programming languages. The most popular languages are:

1.   **COBOL**, an abbreviation for <u>Co</u>mmon <u>B</u>usiness <u>O</u>riented <u>L</u>anguage, a language that is heavily used in business and industry.
2.   **FORTRAN**, an abbreviation for <u>FOR</u>mula <u>TRAN</u>slator, a language that is designed to support scientific and engineering applications.
3.   **BASIC**, a relatively easy to learn language that is especially used in education for instruction and the production of computer-assisted-instruction, and in business for small projects.
4.   **Pascal**, a language that is used in instruction.
5.   **C**, an increasingly popular language for writing operating systems and for instructional purposes.
6.   **LISP**, for <u>Lis</u>t <u>P</u>rocessing, and **Prolog**, for <u>Pro</u>gramming in <u>Log</u>ic, that are being employed in the area of artificial intelligence.
7.   **ADA**, a new, multipurpose language introduced to standardize the language for defense and other governmental programming projects.

Essential Applications Development Software

Most users of microcomputers do not write completely original programs using the languages listed above. There was a time when programming was the only avenue by which a company or an individual could produce a usable product. But programming takes a considerable amount of time even when the programmer is well trained. Most novices found it considerably beyond their skill and their interest to produce a satisfactory program that was adequate to a real world task. Fortunately, one does not have to write one's own word processor in order to use one. The same is true for other types of programs. Software can be purchased that addresses users needs without users having to become involved in the intricacies of programming, though comprehension of the fundamentals of programming will certainly reinforce one's ability to use some software at the most productive levels possible. The majority of computers purchased for home or for business use are acquired to make use of software that is written in a language like assembler or Pascal, but which functions in such a way as to eliminate any need to have any knowledge of this language.

   Word Processing software is used to make the production of documents more efficient. Common tasks carried out by word processors are preparing mailing labels, creating form letters for personalized communications, supporting the movement of information between documents and between the word processor and some other type of program, and the development of documents with demanding technical requirements such as multiple columns, the formatting of equations, and the use of special type styles. Word processors encourage the use of laser printers, graphic images, and spell checkers that lead to higher quality documents than would be possible if typewriters were the only technology present. This book focuses on the use of WordPerfect, one of the most widely used word processors.

   Worksheet Programs are programs that ease the preparation of financial and other quantitative reports and analyses. Such programs are used to analyze complex business problems, to keep checkbooks balanced, to study the financial desirability of pursuing alternative courses of action, to project future expenses, and to test the impact of options for action. Lotus 1-2-3, the standard worksheet processor for industry, is used in this book to illustrate how this type of software can be applied.

   Database software is used to record, track, modify, and organize information about people, events, activities, and objects that are of interest to the computer user. Inventories of cars on a car lot, personnel files, lists of Supreme Court jurists votes, and parts listings are examples of databases. Records (a record is all of the information about one entity in the database) can be edited when information changes, sorted into an order that is appropriate for some function, deleted when the information is no longer needed, or printed in a report format that is of use to decision makers. The most popular database software, dBASE III Plus, is used in this book to illustrate how databases function. Although this text does not cover programming, dBASE III Plus provides a command language that offers the same types of programming statements that are contained in traditional languages like FORTRAN and Pascal.

Communications software is software that can be employed in appropriately configured microcomputers to communicate with larger computers. Communications capabilities are needed to make the transfer of documents between users possible and to use programs and data that are found on the larger computer but not on the microcomputer. Access to electronic mail and electronic bulletin boards is also important. Software called Kermit is used to illustrate how communications software operates.

Increasingly Important Software Packages

The four types of applications development software noted above are the most commonly purchased types of software. They do not constitute the universe of software available, however. As the microcomputer industry has matured, other types of software are being acquired and are having their own impact. These types of software are not covered in this book.

Graphics software comes in various types. Business presentation graphics, bar charts, and pie charts can be produced by Lotus 1-2-3, and higher caliber graphics can be created with packages intended to serve this purpose. Free-form art software allows you to paint objects and pictures in much the same way that you would if you were using a paint brush and an easel. Computer-assisted-design (CAD) software enables architects, engineers, and designers to plot out complex pieces of machinery, houses, circuit boards, and computers.

Project Management software is used to plan definable projects more effectively. A project manager displays when the various phases of a project should begin and end, what resources will be needed, and what the costs for the project should be. Project managers help to organize the activities that go into a major project and will help to identify ways by which economies can be realized.

Desktop publishing software improves on word processing software by enabling users to produce documents at levels that are indistinguishable from documents typeset by a professional printer. Going beyond the traditional capabilities of word processors, desktop publishing software enables users to integrate high quality graphics into text, to draw on ornate type styles, to obtain expensive looking output from laser printers, and to format complex documents that use serpentine columns and elaborate tables and charts.

Decision support software strengthens the ability of managers to reach decisions with a multitude of factors to consider. This software goes beyond worksheet programs by supplying complex statistical and financial functions to analyze, forecast, and interpret data.

Expert system shells are software packages that expedite the process of programming a computer to evaluate problems in the same way that a human expert would evaluate the same problem. Expert systems are used for trouble shooting technical problems, diagnosing diseases, prescribing remedies to problems, recommending configurations for computers sufficient to meet a customer's needs, and to evaluate battle field manuevers in a specific war-time situation.

Computer-based instructional software can be used to teach students basic concepts, to provide drill and practice experiences, and to augment other educational practices with instructional techniques that reinforce, extend, and strengthen a learner's capacity to deal with new concepts and relationships.

Integrated software packages are programs that combine the capabilities of several, single purpose software packages. For instance, many integrated software packages assemble a word processor, a database manager, a worksheet, business presentation graphics, and a communications package into one program. The advantage of integrated software is that the user can carry out many functions that have a familiar, unified set of commands and operations.

Turn-Key Applications

The production of computer programs to solve problems is an essential activity for many companies and organizations. Writing and then maintaining the programs is often an expensive undertaking, even when the user is employing applications development software and not a programming language. Many companies do not have the staff or budget to do this. To address problems that they have in common with other organizations, they may choose to buy or lease software that is capable of being used immediately. This software is called **turn-key** or **ready-to-go** software since it can be used with minimal company involvement. They simply supply the data that is to be processed.

Turn-key applications are readily purchased for microcomputers to deal with problems such as billing, mailing list production, accounts payable and accounts receivable, and customer records maintenance. Some of these applications are specifically developed for a particular industry or profession, while others are more generic and can be used by companies with very different objectives.

BUYING A MICROCOMPUTER

Taking a course on computing? Read a book about computers? Know anyone who has a computer? You are already on the road to becoming a recognized computer consultant. Before you know it people will be asking you what kind of a computer they should buy. There is no doubt that as your knowledge of how to use a computer grows, you will want to acquire your own computer. What will you recommend or choose? What do you need to think about before buying a computer?

Which Software is Going to be Used?

This chapter has listed four basic and seven increasingly popular categories of microcomputer software. Before buying a computer, the purchaser must make as accurate an assessment of the software that will be used as possible. To utilize many packages you will have to have specific types of hardware to use, or to make full use of, the software. Without adequate consideration, a user may find that a newly purchased computer cannot satisfy the objectives for which the computer was acquired.

For instance, if you plan to use computer assisted design software you will need a computer with high processor speed, a color monitor, and probably a math co-processor that increases the speed by which certain types of calculations can be completed. If you plan to generate large spreadsheets your computer might need more memory than is typically found on microcomputers. The use of desktop publishing implies the need for a high-resolution graphics monitor, a hard disk drive, and a mouse for cursor movements. Even this superficial list of examples illustrates how the software you use should determine how a microcomputer should be configured before it is purchased. Don't let the hardware determine which software you can run. The more specific you can be in identifying software you want to use, the more clearly you can define what computer you want and what add-ons will be needed.

How will you know what software you will want to use? What software fits your courses and the business or industry you work or intend to work in? Do you know, or do you have friends who know, which software products are the leaders for their types of applications? Do you have access to free software libraries that can augment your commercial software purchases to give your computer more functionality? In many cases you will need to go beyond, "I think that I'll be doing word processing and programming." Figure out which products you will purchase. Check with knowledgeable people to find out what kind of hardware is required by the software, and which additional hardware purchases will optimize your use of the system.

Which Operating System Will Be Used?

Just as hardware can constrain which programs you can run, so too will the operating system limit which software will be available to you. There are significant differences between Apple and MS-DOS computers. UNIX systems are notably different from both of these. Not only do the commands change from system to system, but the software available to each type of system is quite different. Generally, you can find the same types of products in each environment, but the brand names and their capabilities will be quite different. Very few products manage to run in more than one operating environment. Try out computers by different manufacturers to get a feel for how they work. Ask users of the computers you are interested in how they feel about their system after they have grown accustomed to it. Find out whether you need to buy a computer that can run the same software you use at school or at work. These factors will help you screen out the computers you can't use as much as others.

What Hardware is Needed?

Although there are many opportunities for making an incorrect purchase, most beginning users of computers who have made an effort to define their software needs will not make decisions that cannot be corrected easily if they find that they under-bought their hardware. The primary decisions you will have to make about hardware are the following:

1. **How much RAM is needed?** Many manufacturers do not provide the maximum amount of RAM that your software may need to run or to build adequate sized files. Read the manuals of the software you plan to run and see what size RAM, and other hardware, is required. Main memory has become sufficiently inexpensive to make it desirable to acquire as much as you can afford so that you need not worry about whether you have enough.
2. **Which processor is needed?** How much speed and power do you need? The various models increase in cost in direct relation to the processor they use. If you plan to use statistical, computer-assisted design, or expert systems software that use the processor heavily, you will need a faster processor than you would use for word processing or spreadsheet development.
3. **Do I need a hard disk?** Many persons can save money and be quite satisfied using floppy disk systems. A hard disk adds several hundred dollars to a computer purchase and is more expensive to repair and replace if it fails. To some extent a hard disk requires you to know more about organizing your files. It also permits you to run some programs that are delivered on multiple diskettes. It reads and writes files faster than a floppy diskette and it enables you to switch between programs rapidly and conveniently. There are some programs, programs like desk managers, that can be loaded from the hard disk automatically when the system is booted.
4. **Do I need a color monitor?** Again, several hundred dollars can be saved by using a monochrome monitor. Will you be dissatisfied when you are unable to use color for games, computer art and drawing, or even for enhancing the appearance of your word processor? For many programs color is not essential, but it can improve the appearance of the screen none-the-less.
5. **Do I need a co-processor?** Programs which must carry out numerous floating point calculations, programs like statistical and computer-assisted design programs, will be speeded up by the addition of a co-processor chip. Co-processor chips augment and speed up the basic microprocessor, but may not have any effect on some types of computer operations.
6. **Do I need expanded memory?** Persons who expect to build large spreadsheets or expert systems, or who expect to run multiple programs simultaneously will need more primary memory than is normally provided. Additional memory can be added with an add-in board.
7. **What level of graphics support is required?** Most microcomputers provide a low level of graphics. Will the programs you expect to run require very clear graphics output? Enhanced graphics may require the addition of an add-in board and the acquisition of a monitor that is consistent with the level of graphics provided.
8. **What peripherals are needed?** You will have to think about what quality printer you will need. Do you want a plotter? A mouse? Any of hundreds of other peripherals? These needs may not become evident until you have worked with a computer for some time.

EXERCISES

A.   Think about your computing needs as a student and, perhaps, as professional. What are your computing needs? Using popular computing magazines, price a system that will meet your needs.

B.   What are the functions of a CPU?

C.   From a popular computing magazine, compare the respective capabilities of a low cost ($600) computer, and a high-speed, high-productivity desktop computer costing above $3,000. Compare the systems in terms of such features as CPU, hard disk capacities, monitor type, floppy disk options, and other components.

D.   Pick one of the types of software categories mentioned earlier in the chapter. Examine popular computing magazines and identify: 1) five important features that can be used in evaluating the products that are available; and 2) compare three products on these features.

Glossary

A   **Ada** A programming language sponsored by the Department of Defense.

Adapter cards A printed circuit card that controls a device, such as a display or a printer and makes it compatible with the computer's data bus.

Application The product of a generalized application program such as a document from a word processor, a budget projection from a spreadsheet, or an inventory from a database manager.

Application program A program that allows users to produce specific applications of the computer to a particular area or need.

Arithmetic/logic unit The portion of the central processing unit that conducts calculations and logical comparisons.

ASCII American Standard Code for Information Interchange; the coding scheme whereby every character, number, or symbol is represented by an integer code between 0 and 255.

ASCII files (Text) Files saved in a format specified by the American Standard Code for Information Interchange. Files saved in this format often can be used by other programs or transmitted by modem because they have a standard format.

B   **BASIC** (Beginner's All-Purpose Symbolic Instruction Code) A relatively easy to use third-generation language.

Binary Base-two numbering with the digits 0 and 1.

Binary file A file created with an applications program that contains non-ASCII codes specific to that program.

Bit Binary digit. The unit for constructing larger representational items such as bytes and words. Bits have two states, 0 and 1.

Byte A unit of representation constructed from 8 bits. One byte represents a single character.

C   **C** A third-generation language primarily used by recreational, scientific, and operating systems programmers.

COBOL (Common Business-Oriented Language) A third-generation language primarily used for business data processing.

Compiler A computer program that converts an entire source code program into machine executable form.

Co-processor A processing chip that carries out specialized operations for the processor such as graphics or mathematical data processing.

CPU Central processing unit. The unit that processes data and supports random access memory (RAM).

D   **Data** Alphanumeric and graphic input or output.

Data bus The pathway along which data is passed from one computer component to another.

Diskette A secondary storage medium for a computer. Diskettes come in floppy, rigid, and semirigid cases.

Double word Sixty-four bits.

E **EBCDIC** (Extended Binary Coded Decimal Interchange Code) An IBM-created method of representing data.

Expansion slot An electrical socket into which adapter boards are inserted to control communications with peripherals or to increase RAM.

F **Filename** The identifier that uniquely describes a file. Consists of from one to eight characters.

Floppy disk Diskettes which allow some physical flexibility, especially of the 3 1/2" and 5 1/4" size.

FORTRAN (Formula Translation) A third-generation language primarily used by engineers, scientists, and mathematicians.

H **Half-word** Sixteen bits.

Hard disk Secondary storage devices with a rigid disk(s).

Hardware The physically tangible components of a computer.

I **IBM compatible computer** A computer capable of executing identically to an IBM computer. Also called a "clone."

Information Data to which meaning has been assigned.

Integrated circuit Electronic devices that connect thousands of transistors on a silicon chip. Also referred to as an IC and as a chip.

K **Kilo (K)** A prefix approximately equal to one thousand (1,024).

L **LISP** (List Processor) A third-generation language primarily used in programming robots and artificially intelligent machines.

M **Mainframe** A large computer capable of supporting a large business, typically for transaction processing

Mega A prefix meaning approximately 1 million.

Megahertz (MHz) A frequency measurement. One megahertz equals 1 million cycles-per-second.

Microcomputer Small, lower-power desktop and recreational computers.

Microprocessor The central processor chip in a microcomputer.

Minicomputer Medium size, typically office-environment computers capable of supporting a department or small company.

Modem Modulator/Demodulator. A device that permits the transmission of computer data over telephone lines and other media.

MS-DOS Abbreviation for Microsoft - Disk Operating System. The operating system used on IBM PC compatible computers.

N   **Nibble** Four bits.

O   **Object code** A program that has been converted into a computer executable form.

Operating System A program that coordinates the operation of all parts of a computer system.

OS/2 An multitasking operating system seen by some as a replacement for MS-DOS.

Output Data transferred to an output device.

Output device Any device receiving data from a computer. Common output devices are the monitors, printers, and plotters.

P   **Pascal** A programming language that is primarily used for teaching structured programming.

PC Abbreviation for personal computer.

Peripheral device Devices such as printers and modems connected to the system unit and communicating through an adapter card.

Plotter An output device that produces high-quality graphics, often by drawing the lines.

Port The electrical connector on a computer through which communication with other devices or other computers are maintained.

Primary memory See Random access memory.

Printer An output device that produces characters, numbers and other symbols.

Procedure A method by which data is stored in a computer.

Program A sequence of instructions that a computer can execute to accomplish a task.

Proprietary operating system An operating system that is limited to use on the computers of single manufacturer.

R   **Random Access Memory (RAM)** The portion of the computer's memory which stores the internal DOS commands, programs, and data. Also called main memory or primary memory.

Read-Only Memory (ROM) A computer component that can be read but not written (changed). One type of ROM chip contains the initial instructions for booting a computer.

S   **Secondary storage** Disk drives, tape drives, and other units capable of permanently storing data and programs.

Software Programs that are used with a computer system. In contrast to hardware.

Source code Original program code which is to be processed by a programming language compiler or interpreter.

Superminicomputers Computers with power midway between a minicomputer and a mainframe computer.

Supercomputer The largest, fastest computers available.

Stored program The ability of a computer to retain a binary program that it is executing in primary memory.

System unit The component of a microcomputer system that contains the microprocessor, the data bus and expansion slots.

T   **Tape drive** A device that stores computer data on electromagnetic tape.

Turnkey application An application program requiring little or no modification by the user.

U   **UNIX** An operating system developed by AT&T and used on a variety of computer systems.

User A person who utilizes a computer system.

W   **Word** Thirty-two bits.

INDEX

Contents

Preface

This book has been written to teach introductory readers to use the Microsoft Disk Operating System software effectively. It offers practical, hands on instruction in the use of a highly successful, commercial quality worksheet program. This operating system is widely used in business and education.

Intended to meet several needs, *Microsoft Disk Operating System* can be useful in many settings. It can be used as a supplemental laboratory manual for courses that introduce students to computers and their applications, such as Introduction to Computing in Business, Computer Literacy, and Introduction to Microcomputer Software.

This book can also be used as a stand-alone text for short courses that focus on educating students in the main uses of microcomputers. The tutorial orientation of this book allows it to be used by a learner who wishes to work independently. The instructional approach utilized is entirely hands-on and step-by-step.

Each chapter concludes with a group of exercises that reinforce the techniques learned in that chapter. A summary of MS-DOS commands is included for instructors who wish to cover material beyond the scope of this book. A glossary of terminology is also provided.

Fritz H. Grupe

Chapter 1

Meet Your Microcomputer System

The microcomputer you use to complete the exercises in this book is small in size, but large in power. It is capable of many operations that were unheard of a decade ago. You will find that its primary limitation is what you, the user, don't know about the system and its software. The more you know, the more the microcomputer can do. The less you know, the more difficult it is to make it produce what you want to create.

 In this chapter you obtain a general understanding of microcomputer hardware. You learn

1. What the primary components of the system are;
2. How the keyboard is designed and how the keys are used;
3. What floppy disks are and how they should be handled;
4. How to name files that store programs and data;

5. What DOS is;
6. Which disk operating system commands are present to help you manage files and disks;
7. How to deal with some common DOS problems.

SYSTEM HARDWARE COMPONENTS

There are many types of microcomputers. This book uses a personal computer (PC) with one floppy disk drive and a hard drive to illustrate the primary components of a microcomputer system. Other brands and models of computers exhibit differences in appearance and operation. An illustration of the type of computer discussed is shown in Figure 1-1. The primary hardware components of a microcomputer are the system unit, the monitor, the keyboard, and any peripherals such as disk drives, printers, plotters, and monitors. Peripherals are devices that connected to the system unit.

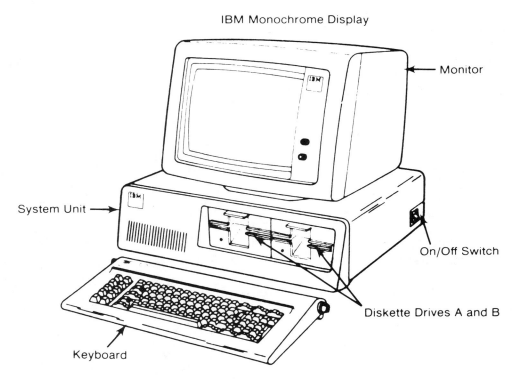

Figure 1-1. A Standard Microcomputer System

The System Unit

The system unit is the heart of the microcomputer system. This box contains the processor, a computer chip that controls the major operations of the computer. The processor chip controls the input of data from the keyboard, output of data to the monitor, manipulation of mathematical data, and the reading and writing of data to disk. The processor is physically located on a board that is known either as the processor board or as the mother board.

Inside the system unit are located random access memory (RAM) chips, the computer's main memory. The amount of RAM determines the maximum size of programs and files that the microcomputer can accept. Common RAM sizes of microcomputers are 128 Kb (kilobytes, or 1,024 characters), 256 Kb, and 640 Kb.

An on/off switch, often located to the right rear of the system unit, must be switched on to operate the microcomputer. This switch may or may not also turn on the monitor. If the monitor does not come on automatically, look for an on/off switch on the monitor with which to turn on the monitor.

The Monitor

The monitor displays what the user is typing, what the system is prompting the user to enter next, or what the output of a computer program is. Monitors, also called video displays or cathode-ray tubes (CRTs), can display characters and graphic presentations. The display may be in color or in monochrome (one color against a black background).

The Keyboard

The detachable keyboard is similar to, but not identical with, a typewriter keyboard. A typical keyboard is displayed in Figure 1-2. The standard keys are found in the center of the keyboard.
Several additional keys and groups of keys are also present.

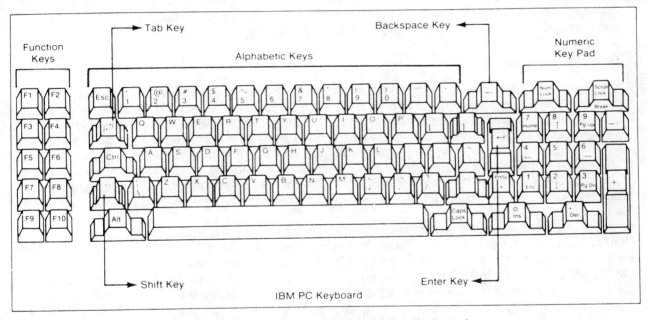

Figure 1-2. A Typical Microcomputer Keyboard

To the left of the standard keys are the function keys, labeled F1 through F10, or F12. Function keys are typically assigned to carry out complex operations. The exact nature of each function key varies from one software program to another.

There are five keys located in a vertical line between the function keys and the standard keys. The Escape key, marked Esc, normally is used to escape from commands and menus that have not yet been completed, allowing the user to avoid taking actions that would be undesirable.

The Tab key, which on some older MS-DOS computers is marked only with left and right arrows pointing to vertical lines, moves the cursor in steps larger than one character at a time. The cursor is a flashing underscore character that is typically used to show a user where data is to be entered or commands executed. The movement caused by the Tab key depends on the program in which the tab is issued. Pressing the Tab key moves the cursor to the right. Simultaneously pressing the Shift (uppercase) key and the Tab key moves the cursor to the left. Movements of five spaces are common, but this can be changed by the user.

The Shift keys are simply marked with a broad, upward pointing arrow (they may have Shift printed on them). The Shift keys put alphabetic, operator (e.g. comma, period, etc.), and numerical character keys into their uppercase value. The Shift keys may, in some programs, give alternative meanings to function keys also.

The Ctrl (Control) key and the Alt(ernate) key are used in conjunction with other keys. As with the Shift keys, these keys are held down and another key is pressed simultaneously. Pressing these keys alone has no effect. Pressing these keys along with another standard or function key gives the second key a new or alternate meaning. The alternate meaning assigned depends almost entirely on the software in use.

The Backspace key, marked only with a left-pointing arrow and located to the right of the equal sign key, is used to erase characters to the left of the cursor. The Del(ete) key erases characters immediately above the cursor.

The Return key, also called the Enter key, is used like a carriage return on a typewriter. The Enter key is marked with a broken left-pointing arrow.

Caps Lock is pressed to place the alphabetic characters into uppercase. The Caps Lock key is said to be toggled on and off. Pressing it once turns the Caps Lock on. Pressing it again turns the Caps Lock off. Turning Caps Lock on has no effect on the function, numerical, or operator keys. To type a dollar sign you have to press the Shift key even though Caps Lock is still on.

The Keypad

The keypad to the right of the standard keys can be used to enter numbers. However, the lowercase values of the key pad are directional keys: arrows, PgUp, PgDn, Home, and End. These keys are used to move rapidly around a file. The precise movement is defined by the software they are used in.

An Ins(ert) key is generally, but not always, used to insert characters into the middle of a line of text. Pressing Insert a second time often exits you from insertion. Because of the Insert key's ability to be turned on and off, it is said to be toggled. When Insert is on toggled on characters typed are entered at the location of the cursor and the characters to the right are pushed over further to the right. When insert is toggled off, overwrite of text is started in which characters typed replace the characters above the cursor.

Two keys having limited functions are the Num(ber) Lock key and the Scroll Lock key. The Number Lock key places the keypad values into uppercase. The Scroll Lock key has few functions in the software discussed in this book. The Scroll Lock key is, however, also called the Break key. Used with the Control key, most currently active programs is terminated. For instance, if you are printing a file and discover an error, you can often stop printing by simultaneously pressing the Control and Break keys.

The key marked with an asterisk and PrtSc is the Print Screen key. The asterisk is used in programming as the symbol for multiplication. This is identical with the 8 as the uppercase character. Shift and PrtSc prints the image of the monitor screen.

On the far right are the grey plus and grey minus signs. Usually these keys are used to enter the mathematical operators. In WordPerfect they are used to move the cursor.

Extended keyboards, keyboards with 101 keys rather than with the traditional 80 keys, carry the arrow keys, Insert, Delete, Home, End, Page Up, and Page Down keys in separated groupings to permit their use when Num Lock makes these keys unavailable from the keypad.

Other Peripherals

The term peripheral refers to devices that are outside of the processing portion of the system unit. The monitor is one peripheral. The disk drives are peripherals even though they are inside of the cabinet containing the microprocessor. Other peripherals include external hard disks, printers and plotters, mouse devices, and sound generation devices.

Disk Drives

Some computers have two disk drives, drive A on the left, drive B on the right, to accept floppy diskettes. Some computers have the drive doors placed in a vertical position with drive A continuing to be placed to the left of drive B. Other computers may stack the drives on top of one another. In this case, drive A is usually in the top position. Floppy diskettes that are inserted in the two drives are used as secondary memory. Secondary memory is, by comparison to RAM, relatively stable. If data is saved on a disk, the data remains there until it is explicitly erased by the user. On the other hand, the contents of RAM memory is lost if the machine is turned off and the data were not stored on disk. Diskettes are placed in the disk drives with the labels at the front of the disk drive, facing up.

Some computers use fully self-contained hard drives that store much more data than does a floppy drive. The hard drives are normally referred to as drive C.

Printers and Plotters

To use the software discussed in this book, the only peripherals required are the disk drives, the monitor, and a printer. A dot matrix printer is a printer that produces its letters with a column of wires in the print head. The wires produce blocks of dots and spaces that can be identified as letters. Although dot matrix printers are usually quite fast and can create reasonably good type, they are often considered to be draft quality printers.

Letter quality printers create a letter from the impact of a printer ball or daisy wheel which has completely formed letters on them. Letter quality printers are generally slower than dot matrix printers, but they create sharper letters. Some newer, high-quality dot matrix printers can produce output equivalent to letter quality printers. Laser printers produce the highest quality print copy.

Plotters are devices that draw images, including the images of characters on paper.

FLOPPY DISKETTES

Computer users, even computer users whose machines have hard disk drives, must use floppy diskettes. Software is delivered on floppy disks and backup copies of files are usually stored on this medium. Although diskettes have a lengthy life when they are treated well, they can be rendered useless by an act of carelessness.

The Structure of a Floppy Diskette

Floppy diskettes get their name from their flexibility. Diskettes are generally sold in protective boxes and removable sleeves, or envelopes. Both of these forms of protection should be used as much as possible.

Many microcomputers use floppy diskettes that are 5 1/4" in diameter. Others are 3 1/2". Figures 1-3A and 1-3B show both types of diskettes.

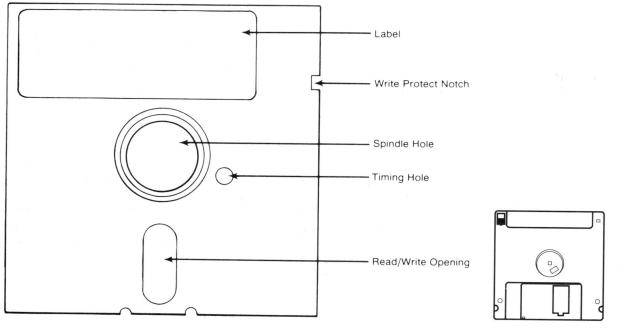

Figure 1-3A. 5 1/4" Diskette   **Figure 1-3B.** 3 1/2" Diskette

The circular diskette is covered by another protective device, the surrounding nonremovable jacket. The envelope has a manufacturer's label and space on the same side for a user's label which can be used to identify the files that are stored on the diskette. When handling the diskette place your fingers on the label edge of the diskette and carefully avoid contact with the shiny recording surface of the diskette.

A write-protect notch in one side of the envelope is used by the microcomputer to determine whether the user wishes to allow files on that diskette to be modified. When diskettes are purchased, the manufacturer provides adhesive tabs that covers the write-protect notch. If a tab is present, the machine detects this and prevent the user from adding a file or from changing a file on the diskette. If no tab is present the machine writes to the diskette as the user instructs it to do so. The tab can be removed and replaced as is necessary.

Oval openings on opposite sides of the diskette are used by the computer for reading and writing operations. Access to the recording surface is made through these read/write openings. A device in the computer called a read/write head electronically places data on the diskette by moving back and forth over the diskette.

Timing holes on opposite sides of the jacket allow light to pass through whenever a hole in the diskette passes between them. The microcomputer uses the timing hole to determine the starting location for addresses of files stored on the diskette.

The broad circular opening in the center of the diskette is the spindle hole. When the diskette is placed in the drive and the drive door is closed, the spindle of the disk drive is placed in the hole and is tightened. The spindle rotates the diskette under the read/write head of the disk drive.

The diskette that is largely hidden from view is circular in appearance. When a diskette is formatted (prepared to receive data), the diskette is written to by the computer in a pattern that allows the computer to identify, read from, and write to specific sets of sectors and tracks. It has a top and bottom recording surface, hence it is said to be double-sided. Each surface has forty concentric tracks on which data can be written. Each diskette is divided into nine pie-wedge-shaped sectors. Directories stored on diskettes provide information about where the contents of files are found on the diskette. The user of the computer is generally unaware of the precise locations of the files.

Many microcomputers use 5 1/4" floppy disk drives that store data in a format called double density. Double density diskettes can store 360 Kb of data, twice as much data as a single density diskette found in older computers. Newer computers utilize a quad-density, or high density diskette, that increases the amount of storage by another factor of four (1.2 megabytes). Depending on the computer in use, 3 1/2" diskettes may store 720 Kb or 1.44 Mb of data.

It is increasingly common that computers use hard disk drives which store significantly greater amounts of data. Generally, the size of hard disks is measured in megabytes (millions of bytes) storage capacity. Common sizes are 20, and 40 megabytes. Some microcomputers are networked so that a central system called a file server provides a hard disk that is shared by the attached workstations.

Nine Rules for Handling and Storing Diskettes

The cost of a diskette is minimal when compared to the cost of the data stored on it. A diskette's value may be less than $1, but a file containing a document of twenty pages requires a minimum investment of around $100 when one figures out the cost of the time involved in typing it. This cost is rapidly increased when the document contains data or formulas that cannot be easily recaptured from a hardcopy of the file. For instance, a spreadsheet might contain one hundred formulas, formatting commands, and even data that, if it were lost, must be reconstructed at considerable cost. To make the cost even more substantial, each diskette may contain multiple files. A diskette with thirty files could have a replacement value of several hundred dollars for each file. Equally important, there is an inevitable time loss in reconstructing a file that can mean a failure to meet deadlines.

The point is clear and unarguable: Be careful in your use and handling of diskettes. Follow these rules:

1. *Only touch the envelope or jacket of the diskette--never the recording surfaces.* Dirt and oil on your fingers destroys the recording surface. Severe dirt on the diskette can damage the read/write head of the disk drive. Store diskettes in their envelopes and protective boxes.
2. *Don't subject the diskette to other contaminating factors.* Soda, food, tabletop dirt, dust, and a host of other contaminants may scratch, mar, or coat the recording surface, making the diskette useless.
3. *Avoid bringing the diskette in contact or even in close proximity with any magnetically charged objects.* Many electronic devices produce as much magnetism as magnetized objects. Some copy holders which are placed next to computers to hold pages of text being entered use magnets. The information stored on diskettes is stored in a magnetic pattern that is easily destroyed by an external magnetic field, rendering the contents of the diskette undecipherable.
4. *Write on the diskette label with a felt tip pen, not with a ballpoint pen or pencil.* The label for filenames, if it is not already on the diskette, is placed on the same side and edge of the diskette as the manufacturer's label. The recording surface of the diskette is sensitive to pressure. Hard-pointed writing implements can produce such pressure. Used lightly, a felt tip pen can be used to retitle the label without harming the data. If you can, write on the label before it is attached to the diskette's jacket.
5. *Store diskettes vertically in hard boxes.* A hard box protects the diskettes from pressure when being transported. Storage in a vertical position keeps them from warping.
6. *Store diskettes in the envelope.* Don't rely on the diskette's jacket to protect the exposed portions of the recording surface. Place the diskette in the removable envelope whenever the diskette is not in use.
7. *Don't bend or crease the diskettes.* Even though the diskettes are somewhat flexible, they are not indestructible. Distortions of the surfaces destroys the diskette's usefulness.
8. *Don't remove the diskette from the disk drive when the red light is on.* Many programs, and the operating system itself, displays a message on the monitor noting that operations requiring writing to the diskette have been completed before the drive is actually finished. The write is completed when the red light on the front of the disk drive goes out, not before. Premature removal of the

diskette causes the file and the directory of the diskette to be incomplete. This almost always means that the corrupted file cannot be recovered.

9.   *Make backup (duplicate) copies of your diskettes.* If you work extensively with microcomputers, you occasionally lose some of the files that you have created. The discipline of making backup files saves you hours of work in recreating these files if a diskette is lost or damaged.

SOFTWARE VERSUS HARDWARE

The hardware components alone are incapable of carrying out many useful operations. To provide word processing or database capabilities, for example, the hardware needs programs and data. The instructions and data contained in programs that are stored on diskettes are called software. You can see the diskette, but you cannot directly see the programs and data stored on it. Software may be stored in a text form that can easily be read by the computer to produce screens understandable by humans, or it can be stored in a binary form composed of machine-readable zeros and ones, which are less easily translated into a form that can be read by humans.

USING THE DISK OPERATING SYSTEM (MS-DOS)

IBM and IBM-compatible computers, as well as some noncompatible microcomputers, use the Microsoft Disk Operating System (MS-DOS). An operating system is an important type of software that carries out a variety of tasks. Among these are:

1.   Providing the structure with which to create, store, and retrieve files you have constructed;
2.   Providing the means by which diskettes are formatted;
3.   Providing communications among the several hardware components. For example, letters typed at the keyboard must be associated with specific commands, entered into files being modified, etc. Directories of files must be kept up to date on the diskettes being used so the integrity of data and programs is protected;
4.   Providing the coordination between different processing tasks--printing, keyboard entry, program processing--so that coherence among these activities is preserved.

These and many other functions are carried out by the software known as the Disk Operating System (DOS).

Booting the Microcomputer

A microcomputer with a hard drive can generally be activated by simply turning the system on. On some networked computers (computers that communicate with one another), and on all dual drive microcomputers, this is accomplished by putting the DOS diskette into drive A. Hold the disk with the label up and slide the diskette into the drive with the recording oval entering first. Close the disk drive door and turn the machine on. After the computer completes its procedures for checking its circuits and memory, it seeks to load DOS from drive A. Part of DOS is loaded and this part helps to load more of DOS. This process of loading more and more of the operating system until the system is up and running is called booting. The term booting is an abbreviated form of pulling oneself up by one's bootstraps.
    The final stage of the booting procedure is the appearance of DOS prompts for the date and time. The prompts and examples of the responses that you might type appear in Figure 1-4.

```
A>date
Current date is Tue  1-01-80
Enter new date:  6-15-86

A>time
Current time is  0:00:15:87
Enter new time:  10:30
```

Figure 1-4. Time and Date Prompts

It is not required that you type in either the date or time, but it is generally a good idea to enter this information. If you press the Enter key without entering the date and time, DOS uses the date and time originally displayed. DOS uses this information to date the last change that was made to a file.

Booting the system by turning the system on is called a cold boot. Cold is used because the system is booted from a completely powered-down state.

At times, when a program freezes or when you simply want to return to DOS from a program that permits ungraceful exits, you can reboot the system without turning off the computer, or powering down. Total powering down causes the system to go through all of its internal rechecking before the date and time prompts appear. This is unnecessarily time-consuming. By simultaneously holding down the Control, Alternate, and Delete keys, the system reboots and returns the date and time prompts. This is called a warm boot.

Files, Filenames, and Filename Extensions

As you create programs, documents, databases, and worksheets with a computer you need to store these groups of data on hard disks or on diskettes. When a letter is created, for instance, with WordPerfect, it is initially created in the RAM, or main, memory of the computer. You must save the letter on the diskette. When the letter is written to the diskette, DOS reserves portions of the diskette specifically for that document in a space called a file. The directory that DOS maintains on the diskette is a listing of the names of files that are currently accessible and information about those files. Some of this information is visible to you, but some of it is not. The starting location of the file on the diskette is not available to you. Neither is a listing of the tracks and sectors where the file is found. Usually, the absence of this information is unimportant.

Rules for Filenames

Just as you need to have a correctly spelled word to look up a word in the dictionary, you must use correctly formed filenames to have DOS save, manipulate, and retrieve files on the diskette.

Filenames are normally assigned by the user of the computer, not by the computer. Sometimes filenames are modified or created by a particular software package. When you are asked by the computer to name a file you are saving, these are the rules you must follow:

1. The filename can have no more than eight characters;
2. An extension to the filename can have no more than three characters. An extension is used by typing the filename, a period, and the extension characters (e.g., MYFILE.DOC). An extension is optional.

3. The characters in a filename are limited to:
    a. The upper and lowercase alphabetic characters,
    b. The numbers 0 through 9,
    c. The special characters: / ! @ # $ % & ( ) - _ { } ' '
       Although you can use these characters, you should avoid doing so since they make filenames unreadable;
4. Periods (except to separate the filename from the extension), commas, and spaces are among the characters which cannot be part of a filename.

Here are five examples of valid filenames you could assign to a file:

Filename	Comment
D	Single letter filenames are alright.
MYFILE	Extensions are not required.
86LEDGER	Numbers can be in a filename.
FEB13.LTR	Extensions can be added.
ACCOUNTS.D86	Numbers can be used in an extension.

Here are five examples of invalid or incorrectly constructed filenames:

Filename	Comment
	At least one valid character must be in a filename.
CHAPTER12	Not illegal, but the 2 is dropped by DOS since only eight characters are permitted. This means that a file named CHAPTER1, if it exists, is replaced by the CHAPTER12 since DOS can only use CHAPTER1 and drops the 2.
.BAS	An extension must also have a preceding filename.
SALE ACCT.FIN	Spaces are not allowed in the filename.
1,385BUD.FIN	Commas are not allowed in the filename.

By looking at filenames and their extensions you can frequently tell what their contents are and which programs use them. You can tell this if the filenames which have been assigned to files are meaningful and if you know which programs assign particular extensions. You will come to recognize that the filename CHAP1 is a user-created file, while files having extensions of .COM or .EXE are DOS files, and files with extensions of .DBF and .PRG belong to dBASE IV.

Prompts and Default Drives

Assuming that you are using a hard drive with DOS added on it, after you have typed in the date and time, DOS responds by placing

    C >

on a new line. This is called the DOS prompt. A dual drive system may respond with an A> while a networked computer may respond with a different letter and other information as well. A prompt from DOS or from a software package requires you to type a valid command or to enter information of the type the program expects to receive. In this instance the prompt tells you that you are expected to type a valid DOS command and that the computer is using disk drive C as its default drive. A default value is a value that the computer uses if you do not explicitly tell it to use some other comparable value. In this instance, if you ask it to print a file, DOS looks to drive C for the file first and usually no further. WordPerfect, to cite another default value, gives you automatic margins at columns 1 inch on either side, but you can change these if that is desirable. If you wish, you can change the default drive by typing.

a:

which changes the default drive to A. The letter designating the drive (or any DOS command) can be typed in either upper or lowercase. After execution of this change you receive the prompt

A>

meaning that the default drive is now drive A and commands are interpreted based on the contents of that drive and not on those of drive C.

Basic DOS Commands

To use DOS effectively you must learn some of its commands. There are many options that can be used with these commands that are not be described here, but that are described in the DOS manual. The following commands are fundamental to using your microcomputer to achieve productive results. Failure to use these commands appropriately can lead to confusion at minimum and to a loss of your files at the extreme.

The use of upper or lowercase in the typing of commands and filenames is of no consequence to DOS. DOS automatically translates lowercase characters to uppercase.

DIR(ectory)

Entering the command

dir

produces a directory listing of the default drive, a columnar listing of filenames, and other information about the files on a disk. Sample output for the dir command is shown in Figure 1-5.

```
DOCUMENT TXT    10440    10-20-86   12:00p
PAPER           10070     1-01-80   12:26a
MEMORAND BAK    87876    10-29-86    3:44a
APPENDIX        10115    11-05-86    1:13a

       4 Files(s)    242688 bytes free
```

Figure 1-5. Response to the DOS Command

This listing shows the filename, the extension (no period, only a space is displayed), the number of characters in the file, the date the file was created, and the time the file was created. If the DOS diskette is in drive A and the A> prompt is showing, you would see a listing of files that compose the operating system. A directory listing on drive C, will vary the resulting filenames from system to system.

Since a diskette can have many more files stored on it than can appear on one screen, the DIR command has two useful options. Typing and entering

dir/w

produces a wide listing that only shows the filenames and their extensions. The extensions are shown in separate columns. The period separating the filename from the extension does not appear. The command

dir/p

produces the complete information provided by DIR but the listing pauses with every screen of data to allow you to find files you are looking for.

If you wish to display the directory for drive C even though the default drive is drive A, you must type

dir   c:

Any drive reference can be typed after the DIR command.

FORMAT

Before you can use a diskette for saving files, the diskette must be formatted; that is, made ready to receive the files. If you wish to format a disk, and assuming that DOS is on drive C, place your unformatted diskette in drive A, and type the command

C > format   a:

You then receive a prompt

Insert new diskette in drive A:
Strike any key when ready

If you have not already done so, place the diskette to be formatted in drive A and press Enter. If the diskette was already in the drive, just press Enter and the formatting of the diskette begins. A diskette need only be formatted once in order to store many files on it. You must be very careful in issuing FORMAT since it destroys all data that was already on the disk. DOS allows you to format a diskette that has already been formatted and used. No warning is given that data may be lost. When in doubt, use the DIR command to make sure that there are no files on the diskette that are still useful to you.

When the formatting is completed, you receive a message **Format another? (Y/N)** to which you can respond with upper or lowercase Y if you wish to format additional diskettes, or with upper or lowercase N if you do not.

Make sure that you always have several formatted diskettes before you begin to create files. If you do not have a formatted diskette at hand, a program may force you to exit the program to format a diskette. This means that the file(s) you are working on will be lost because you may not be able to save them. Some programs allow you to format diskettes from within the program but it is foolish to rely on this option.

FORMAT is an extenal command that must be retrieved from the disk storing DOS. On a dual drive system, this requires the presence of the DOS disk in drive A before the command can be executed.

COPY

COPY is used to make a duplicate or a backup of a file. The backup copy is needed in case the original file, or the diskette it is found on, is erased, lost, or damaged. One common method of making backup files is to use COPY. The command

        C > copy   memo3.txt   a:

copies the file named MEMO3.TXT on drive C because the prompt C> shows drive C to be the default drive, to the diskette in drive A. The file is assumed by DOS to be on drive C because C is the default drive, and that the copy of the file being placed on drive A has the same name on drive A as it did on drive C. If you wish to change the name you could type

        C > copy   memo3.txt   a:memo3.bak

which keeps the old filename, but changes the extension. The original file on drive A is still there. In either command, the file being copied replaces any existing files with the same name without giving a warning. The command

        A > copy   c:memo3.txt   a:

copies a file on drive C to drive A even if the default drive is drive A.
        In these and in other examples in this section, the inclusion of the extension to the filename is required if the file has an extension. If you had three files with the names MEMO3 and MEMO3.TXT and MEMO3.BAK on the same diskette, the extension would distinguish among them. If your diskette only had the file MEMO3.TXT on it, DOS would not assume that the command

        C > copy   memo3   c:

referred to the file MEMO3.TXT since the extension is missing.

ERASE and *DELETE*

You can selectively remove files from your diskette with either ERASE or DELETE. They are the same command. DELETE can be abbreviated to DEL.
For either command to be properly executed, complete identification of the file is required. The command

        C > erase   memo3.txt

removes the file MEMO3.TXT from drive C. If a file with the same filename existed on drive A, the file on drive A would not be removed. DOS removed the file on drive C because the prompt showed drive C to be the default drive. If you wished to remove a file of the same name on drive A you would type either

        C > a:
        A > erase   memo3.txt

    or

        C > erase   a:memo3.txt

TYPE and PRINT

The TYPE command allows you to view the contents of some files on the screen while PRINT prints those files on the printer. The command

    C>type   a:memo3.txt

lists the file MEMO3.TXT found on drive A to your screen, if it exists and if the file only contains normal text characters (ASCII files). Neither TYPE nor the PRINT command lists files that contain embedded characters or that consist of non-printable characters. Often, they do not print word processor, worksheet, or database files, for instance. To print the file on the printer, make sure the printer is turned on and paper is available, and that the C> prompt is displaying. For example, the command

    C>print   a:memo3.txt

would print MEMO3.TXT if it was an ASCII file. Like FORMAT, both TYPE and PRINT, are external commands that only function correctly if DOS can retrieve the commands from the DOS diskette. Thus, on a dual drive system, the DOS diskette must be in drive A when the command is issued.

RENAME

The RENAME command changes the name of a file. RENAME does not produce a second copy of the file. This command is often used to alter a filename to make the name more descriptive of the file's contents. For instance

    C>rename   23xyz.txt   chap1.txt

gives the file 23XYZ.TXT the new name, CHAP1.TXT.

DISKCOPY versus COPY   *.*

Files can be copied from one diskette to another or from a hard drive to a diskette with COPY. Periodically, there is a need to copy all files from one diskette to another. This is accomplished most easily with a dual drive system. One variation of COPY involves the use of the asterisk. The asterisk is a wild card character. An asterisk matches any string of characters in a filename. The filename *.TXT matches all files that have the extension .TXT, and the filename XYZ.* matches all the files that have the name XYZ regardless of the extension. To copy files from one diskette to another with the prompt A> showing, one might type

    A>copy   *.*   c:

which copies all files from drive A to drive C. This procedure replaces any files on drive C which have the same name as those on drive A with the version on drive A. Files on drive C that are not duplicated by name on drive A are left alone.
    DISKCOPY causes DOS to make the diskette on the destination drive an exact copy of the diskette on the source drive. DISKCOPY can only be executed on a dual drive system in which both drives support the same size and types of disks. To execute DISKCOPY on a dual drive system, the DOS disk must be in the default drive, most likely drive A. With DOS in drive A, the command

    A>diskcopy   a: b:

causes DOS to prompt you to place the disk you wish to duplicate, the source disk, in drive A and then to place a diskette in drive B to receive the contents of the disk in drive A. DOS formats the diskette in drive B destroying its previous contents and duplicates the contents of the A drive diskette on the B drive diskette.

Common Error Messages

Bad Command or File Name

In executing the commands cited above, you may receive the error message, **Bad command or file name.** There are several possible causes for this message to appear. One reason is that you may have misspelled a command. The command

    dri

is not be recognized as the DIR(ectory) command. A second possible cause for this error message is the misspelling of the filename. The command

    type   memo13.txt

illustrates the misspelling of MEMO3.TXT. A third possibility is that the extension is omitted. The command

    type   memo3

does not send the file MEMO3.TXT to the screen. Another possibility is that the file does not exist on the default drive. Perhaps the command should be altered to address a different drive. The command

    type   memo3.txt

may fail because MEMO3.TXT is on drive A. The correct command is

    type   a:memo3.txt

If you receive the bad command or filename error message you can determine what files are actually on the disk with the DIR command.

Abort, Retry, Ignore

A second common error message is **Abort, Retry, Ignore.** This error message generally appears because a disk drive is not ready for reading or writing because the printer is not ready for printing or because a diskette has been damaged or is unformatted. When you receive this message check to see that

1.   There is a diskette in the drive involved;
2.   The diskette is properly inserted in the drive;
3.   The drive door is closed properly;
4.   The diskette is not write protected;
5.   The diskette is not damaged or unformatted;
6.   The printer is plugged in and turned on;
7.   The printer has the Select (or on-line) button turned on;

8.   The printer has paper in it and that the paper is not jammed;
9.   The printer's cables are tightly connected.

Once the error condition is corrected, press R for retry and printing proceeds. If you cannot correct the condition, press A for abort. Aborting an operation may exit you from a program and return you to DOS. Only press A if you cannot correct the condition causing the error. Do not press I for ignore since this may cause the machine to attempt operations that causes a loss of data.

BACKING UP FILES

One point cannot be stressed often enough: Back up your files! Backup files can be created in several ways:

1.   Use the DISKCOPY or COPY command to duplicate files from an original to a backup disk;
2.   From within a program that has a file saving procedure, first save your file on the original files diskette. Then use the file save command to save the file again on another diskette, the backup diskette;
3.   Save or copy the file a second time to the same diskette, but save it under a different filename. This procedure protects against inadvertent erasure of one of the files. It does not protect against diskette damage, formatting errors, or diskette loss.

Valuable files should be stored on diskettes that are in physically separated locations. Originals and backups may both be lost if the diskettes are in the same box.

COPYRIGHT VERSUS COPY PROTECTION

Much commerically available software is copyrighted. Copyrighted programs have been protected by federal law as the intellectual properties of the companies that possess software copyrights. It is illegal to make unauthorized copies of this software. Up to $50,000 in fines can be levied against persons who violate the copyrights applied to these software packages *for each violation*. The copyright protection extended to these packages is the same as it is for textbooks, sheet music, and other printed materials.
Some programs are copy protected. These programs require either that you have the key, or system disk in drive A in order to load the program properly, or the software must be installed on drive C. When copy protected software is installed on a hard drive, the key disk cannot be used on another computer, nor can copies of the key disks be made and have the software load and run properly. The programs are restricted to one user at a time. Modification of these diskettes to behave differently is, again, a violation of copyright law.
The software discussed in this book is not copy protected. The diskettes are capable of being copied and installed on multiple machines. The companies that copyrighted this software did not copy protect their software so that purchasers of the software would be able to make backup copies easily. In no way does the philosophical decision not to copy protect the diskettes signify that the copyright laws do not apply to these software packages. Alteration of the program and/or copying of the diskette for use on multiple machines is still illegal. No university, corporation, individual, or entity other than the WordPerfect Corporation, which has copyrighted these programs, can alter the restricted nature of its use. Users of this text should be certain that they are using fully licensed and properly paid for versions of the three packages. Personal liability is not reduced by the assumption that because someone else did the copying, the user is not also responsible.

EXERCISES

A. Write out the DOS commands you would use to:
1. Change the name of a file BOOK.001 to CHAPT.01.
2. Delete all of the files on disk drive A with the prompt displaying C>.
3. Copy a file named FIRST.DOC on drive A to drive C, giving it the name FIRST.BAK.
4. Display only the names of the files on a disk without displaying any other information about the files.
5. Display the names of files on a disk that end with the extension .BAK.
6. Display the contents of a file named GOODSTUF on the monitor.
7. Send the contents of the file named GOODSTUF to the printer.
8. See the names of all of the files on an unlabelled disk.

B. Indicate whether the following filenames are acceptable or unacceptable to DOS as they are shown.
1. @E
2. WRONG.!#-
3. RIGHTRIGHT.RIG
4. 1,200.SYS
5. ().
6. A3.PART.NME
7. .PAS
8. 123.456
9. goodone.txt
10. *.*
11. -----.---

C. With MS-DOS on drive C and a blank diskette in drive A, execute the following commands. Use the DIR command to confirm that the commands you issue are executed correctly.
1. Format the disk in drive A.
2. Copy all files on drive A that begin with the letter C to drive B.
3. Change the default from drive C to drive A.
4. Delete the file COMMAND.COM from the disk in drive A.
5. Remove all files on drive A that begin with C and end with .COM.
6. Remove all files from drive A.
7. On a dual drive system, carry out a diskcopy reproducing DOS on the disk in drive A.

D. If you have access to the shareware diskette *Computer Tutorial* (PC-SIG disk 403) from Computer Knowledge, place it in drive A and enter "tutor" to start the program. Work your way through the following modules:
1. Description of the IBM-PC computer keyboard and special keys.
2. A short history of computers.

Chapter 2:

Hard Disk Management

Chapter Outline

ADVANTAGES TO USING HARD DISKS

As the purchase price of microcomputers has dropped, the number of persons and organizations that have acquired microcomputers with hard disks has increased noticeably. In chapter 1 you were introduced to the Disk Operating System (DOS) and to some of the commands that DOS provides. All of the commands described in that chapter assumed that you were using a two disk drive microcomputer system. In this chapter you are introduced to new commands and options of commands that you already know, which enables you to work effectively on another common type of computer: a computer with both a floppy disk system and a hard disk system. There are many reasons why hard disk systems are preferable to floppy disk systems, including:

1. ***To avoid handling floppy disks.*** There are literally thousands of computer programs available to the computer user. The average user obtains three or four programs that are used regularly and perhaps another ten or twenty that are used only occasionally. In addition to these, most programs expect the user to create files that will be saved. In a very short period of time the typical computer user has a significant number of diskettes with which to deal. Keeping track of where needed files reside, what the files were called, and whose files are whose can become an onerous task. A hard disk replaces many floppy disks, something on the order of thirty floppies to

one ten-megabyte hard disk. This consolidation reduces the necessity for physically handling, and possibly damaging, the floppy disks.

2. *To increase access speed.* Hard disks spin rapidly, so the speed with which programs can be loaded into memory is faster than is true of programs that reside on floppy disks. Data, documents, and worksheets can also be obtained more quickly.

3. *Some programs require a hard disk or are made more convenient with one.* A program like WordPerfect has important components like the Speller and the Thesaurus that come on several diskettes. It is possible to use these by switching the diskettes while you are creating a document, but when all of the programs have been installed on a hard drive, the access to these subprograms is greatly facilitated. There are some programs that are so large that they simply cannot work without all of the diskettes having been loaded onto a hard drive.

4. *To organize files.* Generally, one organizes files on floppy disks by storing those that belong together on the same diskettes. On a hard drive, files can be organized in hierarchical manner (similar to a family tree), so files that belong together, are together logically.

DISADVANTAGES TO HARD DISKS

As the price of hard disks has decreased, the number of people acquiring them has increased substantially. The hard disk, desirable as it is, has drawbacks.

1. *Cost.* The addition of a hard disk increases the cost of a microcomputer $300 or more, depending on the size of the disk.

2. *Effects of failure or damage.* A ten megabyte hard disk holds the equivalent of thirty floppy diskettes. Damage to the hard disk or unintentional formatting of the hard disk leads to a total loss of data on that disk--a situation too painful to think about. If you have not been conscientious about keeping backup files, your panic is justified, even if the cause is excusable.

3. *Complexity even with organization.* Hard disks can store large numbers of files. In this chapter you will learn about hard disk directories, which can help to organize your programs, documents, worksheets, databases, and other files. Even with a good method of organization, however, you can find it confusing to deal with the obstacles that a hard disk presents.

4. *Organizing information hierarchically.* Directories that are used to organize hard disk files cannot be dealt with effectively without a change in the way you conceptualize what a disk is like. You cannot see anything but the outside case of the hard disk, yet you must think about files being organized in an upside down tree, and about yourself moving up and down on the tree to locate files. You have to use some commands that are unnecessary on a floppy drive system. Similarly, other commands require you to use options that you would not otherwise need.

5. *Sharing your disk.* With a computer that uses floppy diskettes, sharing is seldom a problem. Several people might use the same program disk, but generally they use their own disks for storing files. Whose file is whose is rarely debated. A hard disk computer is typically a shared machine. This means that the people sharing the computer must adopt certain conventions and courtesies, otherwise each person can significantly affect the other users. The security on a personal computer is often so limited that you must assume that someone else can read, copy, destroy, or alter your files. Don't rely on the microcomputer to be more reliable than it is.

A SAMPLE HIERARCHY OF FILES AND DIRECTORIES

When using a microcomputer with two floppy drives, you implicitly organized your files by diskette. Your files were on your diskettes and other people stored their files on their own diskettes. Further, most active computer users store logically related groups of files on the same diskettes: document files on one diskette, spreadsheet files on another, and so on. If you were especially active, you might subdivide your diskettes so that all of the files related to one activity, such as a course or an organization, are stored on one diskette and those related to another activities on other diskettes. Retrieval of a file involves physical location of the appropriate diskette.

This method of organization would be inappropriate for a hard drive. You cannot install and un-install hard drives like you can insert and remove floppy diskettes. Also, if you didn't arrange your files effectively, you would have a morass of filenames to deal with when you tried to locate or retrieve files. The DIR command, for instance, might list hundreds of filenames. Programs using the same filenames for different files would interfere with one another. Actually, since a filename can only be used once in a directory, the last file entered would replace the previous file.

Consequently, the method of organization on a hard disk is substantially different. It is comparable to organizing information in a large company. Different offices maintain their own files so that the president's correspondence is in the president's office, financial records are in the controller's office and so forth. If a person named Jack Jones wanted to inquire about a bill he had received, he might look up the address of the company in a telephone directory, which was arranged alphabetically. He would go to that location, which is numerically organized on a street, and, assuming that more than one company was located in the building, he would check the building directory to locate which floor the company was on. The building directory is based on physical location. Upon arrival at the correct floor, he would check the floor directory to see where the billing office was located. When he arrived at that office, the clerk would know that billings were found in a particular set of file cabinets. The clerk would go to the room that those file cabinets were found in, locate the cabinet that had bills for people whose last names began with the letters H through K, find the drawer for persons whose names were James through Jyzk, open the drawer and find the area where the Jones files were, and finally, find the folder for Jack Jones. The billing should be one of the entries in the folder, which is then retrieved for discussion.

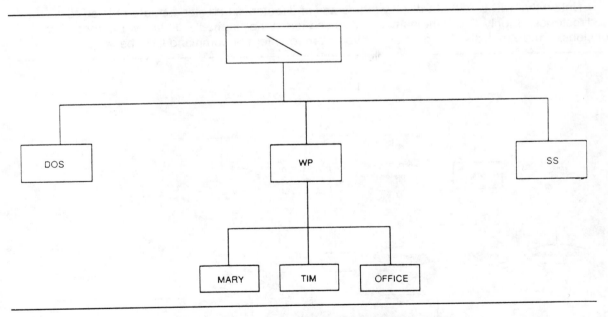

Figure 2-1. A Hypothetical Directory Structure

On hard disks, a network of directories that parallels the distribution of pointers to the bill of Jack Jones can, and should, be used. Figure 2-1 describes the organization of a hypothetical hard disk. The tree, upside down--don't ask why, that's just the way computer types like to display them--begins with the location called root. Root is represented in DOS commands as the Backslash, \. Root is a directory, and like all directories, it can point to files or it can point to other directories. Directories that are beneath other directories can be referred to as subdirectories.

A newly formatted disk has only one directory, the root directory. Other directories are created, and destroyed, by the users. They decide how the disk is best organized. In the hypothetical directory structure displayed, the root directory points to three directories, represented by rectangles, which have the names DOS, WP, and SS, acronyms for Disk Operating System, word processor, and spreadsheet. Unlike the directories DOS and SS, which are empty, WP has subdirectories called MARY, TIM, and OFFICE. Figure 2-1 displays only the names of the directories in the hypothetical tree. Each directory can also point to files that contain programs, data, documents, or spreadsheets. Unlike directories, files do not point to anything. They are called leaves of the tree. Figure 2-2 shows the same directory structure with files. The files are represented by ovals. In this structure, the directory DOS points to three files--COMMAND.COM, PRINT.COM, AND DISKCOPY.COM--but does not have any subdirectories. WP points to three subdirectories as well as two files, perhaps those that contain the word processing program. SS is an empty directory: it has no files and does not point to any directories.

If the user entered this directory structure at the level of root, as is normal when a hard drive system is booted, the DIR command might display

```
.               <DIR>
..              <DIR>
DOS             <DIR>
AUTOEXEC BAT   FILE  283      1-12-90    11:00a
CONFIG   SYS   FILE  145      1-12-90    11:20a
WP              <DIR>         2-14-90     4:14p
SS              <DIR>         4-22-90    10:23a
```

Notice that DIR would not display the names of directories and files that are pointed to by the subdirectories. It only "sees" the names of files and directories immediately below the root. The notations, . and .. are discussed below. If you were to enter the command CD, the resulting

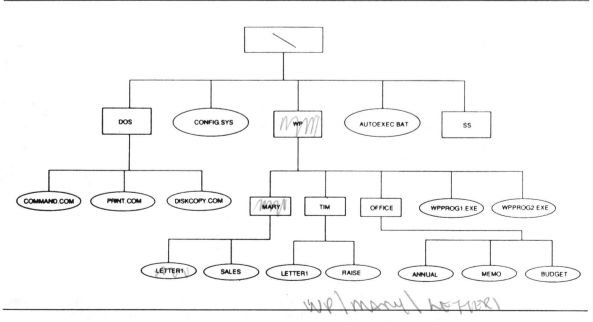

WP \ MARY \ LETTER1

Figure 2-2. Hypothetical Directory Structure With Files

response from DOS would be \, to indicate that the directory currently active is the root.

If the currently active directory was SS, the response to the DIR command would only be . and ..,
then the C> prompt would return. This is because SS does not contain any files. If WP was the active
directory the response by DOS would be   C1) dir wp

```
.                    <DIR>
..                   <DIR>
MARY          <DIR>
WPPROG1 EXE      123283    1-20-90   11:00a
WPPROG2 EXE      344145    1=20-90   11:30a
TIM           <DIR>        6-24-90    3:43p
OFFICE        <DIR>        7-25-90   10:12A
```

The DOS response to CD would be, \WP, which indicates that the pathway to the active directory
is from root, through to WP. Look at Figure 2-2. What would the responses to DIR and CD be if the
active directory was MARY? DOS?

Directory Rationales

The use of directories is preferred over flat file methods of displaying filenames because files that
logically belong together can be grouped together. There would make little point in creating directories
in which the files bore no relationship to one another, and there was no way of using directory names to
determine where needed files could be located. There are several common bases on which to consider
building and naming directories to make them useful.

1. *By language or package.* Directories named PASCAL, WP (Word Processor), FORTRAN, and DB
    (Database) can be recognized as containing specific types of files. A search for a needed file or
    package can be reduced quickly to a few likely candidates.

2. *By user name.* Similarly, directories named JOHN, CAROL, MARKTING, and STAFF offer
    substantial insight into whose files are stored where on the disk.

3. *By topic or applications area.* Another common naming convention is to give directories names
    like MARKTING, PLANING, TRAVEL, or PROJECT1. These directories could each contain files that
    originate with a common package like a word processor or spreadsheet, or they could cluster files
    that originate with many different packages, but that all relate to the function described.

4. *By path name.* Most people use a relatively informal method of naming their directories and files.
    Since most people have relatively simple organizational needs, an informal approach is
    appropriate. Some organizations, which produce extensive numbers of files, allow many users to
    access a disk, or have a large hard disk, may need more rigorous organizational techniques. Such
    organizations might be well-advised to adopt an approach in which each directory with a common
    parent directory is assigned a name with a unique first letter. Each file within a directory is given a
    name that begins with an acronym, which summarizes the path to the directory, along with a
    sequential number that identifies the file within the directory.

    For instance, a filename such as WMP011 might signify that the file is located along the
    pathway that starts with WP and moves through MARKTING and PROJECTS, and among the files,
    it was the eleventh file created. If the filename is included at the base of the document, its retrieval
    location is determined rapidly.

5. *By using a combination of techniques.* As the above example illustrates, the naming of
    subdirectories rarely has a single organizing theme. Unless one restricts the tree to one level, it is
    virtually impossible to use a single organizing principle to set up the hierarchy. A combination of
    organizing techniques are appropriate at different branches of the tree.

Path Names

There are two files in the hypothetical tree structure named LETTER1. Within the root or any single subdirectory, DOS does not permit the creation of two files with the same name. DOS does permit reuse of a filename if the files are created in different subdirectories. By default, DOS considers a filename to be prefaced by the path of subdirectories that lead up to the file. Therefore, the file that is designated with the path name \WP\MARY\LETTER1 can be distinguished from the file with the path name \WP\TIM\LETTER1. The latter path name is understood to mean, "Find the file LETTER1 by beginning at root, proceed through the subdirectory WP, and find the file in the subdirectory TIM."

Filenames that are used without path names are assumed by DOS to be in the active directory. Path names can be used to unambiguously specify where a file is to be found, or as in the case of the COPY command, where a file is to be placed.

Path names can include reference to the disk drive on which a file is to be found. The path name C:\WP\TIM\LETTER1 specifies that the file is to be found on drive C, as well as the subdirectories that must be traversed in order to locate the file.

Some examples of commands using path names include the following:

type c:\letters\mary\march\mr15

This displays the contents of the file MR15 (it must be a file for the command to execute successfully since the command type operates only on files, not on directories), which is found by successively traversing the directories on drive C from root, to LETTERS, to MARY, to MARCH.

del b:\doc*.*

deletes all files in the subdirectory DOC under the root of drive B.

cd wp\frank

changes the active directory from the currently active directory to WP and then to FRANK. In this example, it is only known that the directory WP is beneath the currently active directory. It is not known where that directory, or the currently active directory are located in the hierarchy. In

cd \wp\helen

because the path name begins with a Backslash, it starts at root with WP immediately beneath root, and HELEN immediately below WP.

When constructing path names, keep the following rules in mind:

1.   Path names cannot exceed 63 characters in length.
2.   Directory names are separated from one another by Backslashes. If a file is named at the end of the path name, it is separated from the preceding directory by a Backslash.
3.   A drive name may precede a path name.
4.   When a path name begins with a Backslash, it begins at the root of the tree's hierarchy.
5.   When no leading Backslash is present, the path name begins at the currently active directory.

Default Path Names in Memory

The disk operating system retains knowledge of the currently active directory even though the active drive has been changed. For instance, suppose that the active drive was C, and the active directory was \WP\TOM. At the C> prompt, if you entered a: the prompt would be changed to A>. DOS retains the knowledge of the active directory on drive C. If you switched back to C with c:, you would be returned to \WP\TOM, not to root. If you entered

A > copy *.* c:

all files on drive A would be copied to the currently active directory, \WP\TOM, and not to the root directory.

HARD DISK-RELATED COMMANDS AND OPTIONS

DOS possesses many commands and options. This chapter is designed to offer you some insight into the commands and command options that are most commonly used with hard disk drives. It is not a compendium of all of the important and useful commands available. Consult the DOS manual for more detailed information.

CD (Change Directory)

The CD command is used to make another directory the active directory. Only one directory is active at a time. If the active directory was root and you typed

cd wp

the active directory would become \WP. By typing

cd

DOS responds with the pathway to the active directory: possibly a pathway as long as

\wp\tim\personal\secret

that shows the active directory is SECRET, which can be located by starting at root and progressing through TIM and PERSONAL.
        The **CD** command can be used to make a directory other than one below the current directory active. The command

cd wp\tim

finds the directory WP and makes its subdirectory TIM the active directory. In this example, the pair of directories must be immediately beneath the currently active directory. As applied to Figure 2-2, the active directory would have had to have been root. You can also issue the command

cd \wp\tim

which forces the search for the new active directory to begin at the root and continue until the desired directory is made active. This command can be issued anywhere in the hierarchy since DOS always begins with the root of the tree. The command

cd \

makes the root the active directory, regardless of where in the hierarchy the command is issued.

When the DIR command is issued, the notations . and .. always appear. The . symbolizes the current directory pathway, while .. symbolizes the directory which is the pathway to the parent of the currently active directory. Assume that the currently active directory is MARY. Typing the command

cd ..

makes the parent directory of MARY active. This is the directory WP. A subdirectory can have only one parent. Root is its own parent. The command

cd .

keep the current directory active. Although this command is legal, it is seldom used, for an obvious reason.
 CD is the abbreviated form of CHDIR, which is also an acceptable DOS command.

MD (Make Directory)

Both hard and floppy disks have a root directory created as part of the formatting process. Other directories must be created by the user with the MD command. Typically, you should be in the directory under which the new subdirectory is to be placed. Again, referring to Figure 2-2, if the active directory was OFFICE and the commands

md personnl

and

md personnl\policies

were issued, the first command would create a directory PERSONNL that was a subdirectory of OFFICE. The second command would indicate that from OFFICE a subdirectory PERSONNL could be found and that a new subdirectory, POLICIES, should be created under it. If these commands were issued, the hierarchy resulting would look like Figure 2-3.
 MD is an abbreviated form of the command MKDIR that is longer to type.

RD (Remove Directory)

Once created, a directory need not be saved forever. It can be removed with the RD command. Before the RD command can be issued successfully, however, the directory being removed must be empty. Any files that are pointed to by the directory to be removed must be erased first. Any directories that are pointed to by the directory to be removed must be removed first. To determine whether a directory

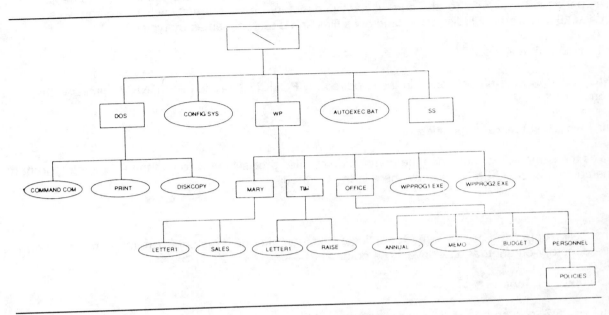

Figure 2-3. Sample Hierarchy

is empty, enter the DIR command. If the response shows any filenames, or any directory names other than

```
.                <DIR>
..               <DIR>
```

the directory is not empty. Be aware that there is a significant difference between the erase (or delete) command and the RD command.

rd policies

removes a directory, POLICIES, which must be empty.

erase policies

gives you the warning, "Are you sure (Y/N)_" because ERASE deletes files. Even though you named a directory, the command deletes all of the files immediately beneath the directory POLICIES. POLICIES is not be removed by ERASE.

DIR (Directory)

The DIR command has already been used to illustrate how it can be used to display the names of files and directories that are pointed to by the currently active directory. The command

dir

lists these names because DOS, by default, assumes that the directory whose files are to be listed is . The period is the symbol for the currently active directory. If the currently active directory was \WP\OFFICE, you could list a subdirectory's files and directory names by typing

dir personnl\policies

which lists only the names found in the subdirectory POLICIES, not in PERSONNL. Similarly, the command

dir \wp\office\personnl\policies

gives the same listing, but since the command specifies precisely how to find the subdirectory from root, the command could be issued anywhere in the hierarchy.

COPY

The COPY command can be used to replicate files found in one directory in another directory, perhaps in a directory on another disk drive. The command

A > copy   b:\doc*.*   c:\wp

causes DOS to override the default path name . which would be used to locate the files to be copied with the disk drive designation of B. Although ***.*** indicates that all files are to be copied, the path name \DOC specifies that only the files found in the DOC subdirectory are to be copied. Any files found at the root directory level or in any subdirectory are not be copied. The files that are copied from B:\DOC are placed in the WP subdirectory of root on drive C. Similarly

A > copy   b:*.*   c:\wp

copies any files found on drive B at the root directory level. It does not replicate any files that are found in subdirectories on drive B.

Unless otherwise specified by a drive designation and a path name, DOS uses the default of . as the active directory for both the source file, the file being copied, and the destination file, the second copy of the file. The command

C > copy a:myfile.doc

causes DOS to assume that the copy of the file MYFILE.DOC, which is to be created, will be placed in the currently active directory. The destination is assumed to be . . In this example, since an adequate designation for the drive and filename were given, DOS assumed that this file was the source file.

FORMAT

The FORMAT command is a command you should always be cautious about using. It destroys all data on the disk when it is being used to reformat a disk, as opposed to formatting it for the first time. Most hard drive microcomputers have only one floppy drive, so the only legitimate FORMAT command that should be issued 99.999% of the time is

format a:

The command

C > format

causes DOS to assume that you wished to format . , the currently active drive/directory. FORMAT cannot be restricted to the current directory, so the entire hard disk is formatted, wiping out all of the files, programs, subdirectories, documents, and worksheets stored on that drive. Some programs that are formally installed on the hard drive use hidden files, which, when destroyed, cannot be recaptured in any way. The only way to obtain these files is to buy a replacement disk from the software manufacturer.

FORMAT does issue a warning that data will be destroyed. Consider this warning seriously.

It is a rare occasion that should require the formatting of the hard disk! Never do so unless you are absolutely certain that this is required. If the microcomputer you are working on is not your computer, do not format the hard disk.

BACKUP

COPY and the file saving procedures of applications programs that save files to disks other than the hard drive are generally adequate for ensuring users that their files can be recovered if the hard disk is damaged. Persons who are responsible for ensuring the security of data on a hard disk, as well as many users with extensive numbers of files, should consider using BACKUP also because of the limitations of the COPY command. COPY is awkward to use since a directory may contain more files than the floppy disk can hold. In fact, a single large file may be too big to fit on one floppy disk. COPY does not allow a single file to overlap diskettes.

BACKUP saves files in a different form than does COPY. BACKUP can overlap files to different diskettes. It does, however, require that all of the backup diskettes must be kept in the same sequential order that the files are backed up. An error in the labeling of the diskettes can cause data that is backed up to become inaccessible. An example of the use of the BACKUP is

backup c:\ a:

which backs up all files at the root level and only at the root level, of drive C. The backup files are sent to the diskettes on drive A. The /s option used in

backup c:\ a: /s

backs up all of the subdirectories under the root of the drive C.

backup   c:\wp*.doc   a:

only backs up files with the extension .DOC in the WP subdirectory of the C drive. No other files are backed up. Selective backups are desirable since a complete backup takes a long period of time and requires a substantial number of diskettes. Also, many files, for example your word processor and your spreadsheet program files, do not change, as opposed to your document and worksheet files. You should have the original program diskettes in a secure location, so there is no reason to back them up.

BACKUP has options that allow you to selectively back up only those files that have been changed since the last backup was made, or only those files that changed after a specific date. In addition, many hard disk owners have acquired tape backup units that speed up and simplify the process. Owners of such devices may use other commands and options.

RESTORE

Files that have been created with BACKUP are retrieved with RESTORE. It can restore one file, an entire disk drive, or all files in specific subdirectories.

restore   a: c:\   /s

restores from drive A all files that were backed up to drive C. All subdirectories are also backed up, since the \s option was used. If this option was not used, only the files immediately under root would be backed up.

restore   a: c:\   /p

uses the \p option. This option prompts the user before each file is backed up to determine whether the file is to be restored.

restore   a: c:\wp*.txt

restores from drive A only the files that belong under subdirectory WP that have the extension .TXT.
      Commercial programs that are copy protected often create hidden files on the hard disk that cannot be backed up. If a hard disk is damaged, it may not be possible to completely restore the program since these files cannot be restored. In these circumstances, the manufacturer of the program must provide replacement disks.

PROMPT

The usual DOS prompt identifies the default drive and that is all. The prompt, C>, for instance, designates drive C as the default drive. This prompt does not fully reflect the default value held by DOS, however, since DOS keeps track of the default directory as well as the default drive. If you were using the subdirectory WP, the prompt would not display this assumed default directory. DOS provides users with some control over the display of the prompt to make the prompt more informative. Two options are of particular value. The command

prompt pg

uses the $p option to display the pathway to the current directory, while the $g option displays the greater than sign. After executing the command, you would see prompts like those in Figure 2-4.

PROMPT	DEFAULT
C:\>	Drive is C, Directory is root.
C:\WP>	Drive is C, Directory is WP, a subdirectory of root.
C:\WP\PERSONAL	Drive is C, Directory is PERSONAL a subdirectory of WP which is a subdirectory of root.

Figure 2-4. Sample Prompts With PG Option

By using the $p option you receive a reminder about the current drive and directory with the completion of each DOS operation. Remember which defaults are in use when you switch drives because DOS doesn't forget even though you may switch default drives. Suppose you were using the default prompt and DOS simply displayed, C>, but you were in the subdirectory WP. If you issue the DOS commands

C>a:
A>copy myfile c:

where would the copy of MYFILE be sent? To the root level of drive C? To the subdirectory WP? To somewhere else? Actually, the copy is placed in the subdirectory WP because DOS remembers the default directory you were in when you switched drives. Similarly, if you were to issue these commands and then entered

A>c:

you would be returned to the WP subdirectory. Use of the $p option helps you to keep track of where you are at any point. You would be made instantly aware of your default directory by the prompt which would display the drive and directories that compose your current pathway. If you use this option, though, be ready for occasional prompts such as

C:\WP\COURSES\POLSCI\SMITH\PSC101>

TREE

An effective use of directories on large disk drives can lead to a huge number of files and directories. It may be that you have difficulty keeping track of what files are on the disk and which directories the files are located in. The TREE command is one of several DOS commands that can be of assistance. Simply entering TREE provides you with a listing of directories and subdirectories that looks like Figure 2-5.

```
Path:  \SS
Subdirectories:  NONE

Path:  \WP
Subdirectories:  WORKSHOPS
        OFFICE
        BOOK

Path:  \WP\WORKSHOPS
Subdirectories:  NONE
```

Figure 2-5. Sample Output from the TREE Command

Only the directory names are displayed. The TREE command can be issued with a /F option to display the names of files also. A sample display from the command, TREE /F, is shown in Figure 2-6.

```
Path:  \SS
Subdirectories:  NONE

Path:  \WP
Subdirectories:  WORKSHOPS
         OFFICE
         BOOK

Path:  \WP\WORKSHOPS
Subdirectories:  NONE

Files:  ANNOUNCE
        REGISTER.LST
        HANDOUT.01
        HANDOUT.02
```

Figure 2-6. Sample Output from the TREE /F Command

TWO SPECIAL FILES

When a computer running under MS-DOS is booted, the system looks to find out whether either or both of two files are present. These files, CONFIG.SYS and AUTOEXEC.BAT, contain instructions for the computer about how the system should be configured when control is turned over to the user. If these files exist, the commands they contain are executed. If the files do not exist default values are used. Both files are created by the user. Once created, the files are seldom altered, although the addition of new programs and peripherals to your system may require changes in both files.

CONFIG.SYS

CONFIG.SYS is the first file to be examined and executed by DOS. This file contains instructions that are used to adapt the operating system to the hardware. Some computers may have a mouse, two printers, a modem, or a digitizing tablet that make special demands on the operating system. CONFIG.SYS is read as the booting process is nearing completion in order for DOS to recognize and utilize the presence of these devices. A sample CONFIG.SYS file might contain the lines in Figure 2-7.

```
FILES=15
BUFFERS=24
DEVICE=MOUSE
DEVICE=ANSI.SYS
```

Figure 2-7. Sample CONFIG.SYS File

These lines are interpreted by DOS. Line 1 sets aside 15 locations in RAM, where information can be kept on up to 15 files that may be in use simultaneously. This may seem excessive but there are files that may not seem like files to you. The keyboard, or other standard input device, and the monitor, or other standard output device, are special files that are the origin of, and the destination of, characters being transmitted within the computer, in much the same fashion that a file on the disk is both the source and destination for characters.

The second line allocates RAM space for 24 locations where data can be kept as it is read from and written to files and various computer devices such as disk drives, the screen, and the memory. The third line adapts the system to a hand-moved mouse that is used with graphics programs. The last line enables the system to load another device driver that lets the screen and keyboard act like a standard communications terminal. Other device drivers may also be loaded in this file.

CONFIG.SYS may contain commands other than these, yet these commands may be entirely correct and necessary. Do not alter the CONFIG.SYS file unless you are certain of the effect of the changes.

AUTOEXEC.BAT

The second file whose command lines are executed, if the file exists, is the file AUTOEXEC.BAT. The AUTOEXEC.BAT file contains DOS commands that can, in many cases, be issued at the prompt line and be successfully executed. By placing the commands in this file, the user can have DOS set up the operating environment without the user having to enter the commands manually. Any file given the extension .BAT should be an executable file. That is, it should contain DOS commands and language statements that DOS can execute just as though they were executed by the user.

A sample AUTOEXEC.BAT file is shown in Figure 2-8.

```
ECHO OFF
DATE
TIME
PROMPT
PATH=C:\;C:\DOS\;C:\WP
```

Figure 2-8. Sample AUTOEXEC.BAT File

Line one causes DOS to execute the commands that follow as silently as possible to avoid extraneous information being sent to the screen. If an AUTOEXEC.BAT file exists, the system no longer automatically asks for the date and time. Hence, lines two and three prompt the user for the date and time. These lines may not be used if the system has a battery operated clock/calendar that keeps the date current. The fourth line changes the prompt to one which shows the complete pathway and the greater than sign. This line is executed before the user has seen a prompt.

Path

The final line is used to identify the directories for DOS to search when you enter a command at the DOS prompt. If this line was missing DOS would only search the current directory for the command file that contains the instructions on how the command is to be carried out. For instance, if you issued the FORMAT command DOS would need to know where this command was to be found on the disk. DOS would look for the command in the current directory. If the command file was found, the command would be executed. If the command file was not found, the search would stop if there was no PATH command in the AUTOEXEC.BAT file. If the command file was not found, but there was a PATH command in the AUTOEXEC.BAT file, DOS would use this information to continue searching.

The DIR and COPY commands are internal commands. Internal commands are loaded into RAM when the system is booted. These and other commands are found in the file COMMAND.COM, which must be located under the root directory. Internal commands are always found by DOS because they are always in memory. They do not have to be searched for.

A subdirectory named DOS is often used to provide a home for the numerous DOS commands that are available and are the external or transient command. External commands are not loaded into memory. External commands like FORMAT and DISKCOPY must be acquired from the disk. Rather than leaving all of these commands under root, where they are always seen when the DIR command is issued, a separate subdirectory places the commands (except COMMAND.COM, which must be in the root directory) into a location where they are accessible through the path command. If COMMAND.COM is not placed in the root directory, the system does not boot properly.

Whenever commands like FORMAT and DISKCOPY are issued, DOS searches for them on the disk. Unless the PATH command is given, DOS only looks for the command in the currently active directory and no further. The error message, "Bad command or file name" is displayed even though the command file exists in another directory. The PATH command forces DOS to look in all of the directories in which the command sought is likely to be found. The larger the number of directories that are included in the search path, the more likely it is that the command can be found. At the same time, if the command is incorrectly named, the longer it takes DOS to determine that the command file does not exist.

In the example shown in Figure 2-7, the PATH command tells DOS that in addition to searching the current directory, it should first search the root directory, then it should search the subdirectory DOS, and last it should search the subdirectory WP. No subdirectories are searched other than those listed and the current subdirectory. New subdirectories can be added when necessary.

Smart Files

There are three file extensions that identify files that can be executed: .COM, .EXE, and .BAT. The file AUTOEXEC.BAT is one of many files that can be given the .BAT extension. The .BAT files are the so-called smart files because they can be created and then executed by the user at any time by entering the filename. Smart files can be created with a word processor capable of creating text files and with EDLIN, the text editor provided with DOS (not discussed in this book). Short smart files can also be created with a variation of the COPY command. Many smart files are created to execute several DOS commands quickly in order to save the user time and to enable untrained computer users to use the computer effectively without having to understand DOS. One example of the creation of a smart file is described. You do not have to carry out these commands. If you do, make sure that the default directory is the root directory. One could create a smart file called WP.BAT by entering

```
copy con wp.bat
```

This COPY command copies the characters entered at the keyboard (the console) and places them in a file called WP.BAT. Upon the pressing of the Enter key, the cursor returns to the left margin and no prompt is displayed. The computer is awaiting characters from the console. You could enter the lines

```
cd wp
wp
cd \
```

and then close the file by pressing

F6   Function key 6
◄┘   Enter, to close the file and to receive the prompt, "1 File(s) copied."

Errors in the file can be corrected by recreating the file with the COPY command or by using another text editor. The file would be executed by entering

wp

When the smart file WP.BAT executes, the lines would be executed in sequence. They would be instructing DOS to change directories to the word processing subdirectory (line one) and then to issue the command wp with which to load the word processor (line two). You would then proceed to use the word processor. Whenever you exit the word processor and control returns to DOS, the third line that changes the directory back to the root is issued. Since there are no more lines in the file, the smart file completes its execution. The command wp could be executed many times.

.BAT files can be very complex. DOS provides a wide set of command structures similar to those found in programming languages like BASIC and Pascal. The lines of a .BAT file must be legal DOS commands.

COMMERCIALLY AVAILABLE DOS-RELATED PROGRAMS AND UTILITIES

DOS has its origins as the operating system for very small microcomputers. Many of the original machines that it was designed to operate had main memories (RAM) of only 64 K or 124 K. If DOS took up too much room in memory, then the corresponding sizes of programs and files that had to be held in memory were also reduced. Disk sizes were smaller also, so DOS had to fit on a single disk. As a consequence, DOS was designed to be as small as possible. As microcomputers increase their RAM, as their disk drives increase in capacity, and as they take on increasingly more sophisticated assignments such as multitasking (running several programs simultaneously), network connections, and windowing (being able to see several programs on the screen simultaneously), DOS has grown and diversified. This has led to the introduction of more commands and options.

As a consequence, understanding and managing DOS has become more difficult. At times there are commands that you would like to have that are not provided by DOS. A number of commercial programs have been introduced that can be purchased separately that can help users use DOS more effectively. Among these resources are:

1. *DOS managers.* These programs provide menus and screens that show you what commands are available, what files are present, and which directory you are in. They also introduce some commands that are not present in DOS, such as commands for renaming a directory or moving a file between directories. The visual interface to DOS lessens the need to memorize commands and options.

2. *Windowing software.* These programs allow you to run many programs simultaneously. Each program is visible in one of the windows on your monitor's screen. In one window you could be in DOS while in another you could be sorting a database. A third window might be running spreadsheet software. It should be noted that the extent to which your microcomputer can actually run these programs concurrently while they are doing compute-intensive or I/O (input/output) -intensive tasks depends on the speed and power of your computer's processor. Newer, faster computers can make effective use of this software.

3. *Disaster recovery software.* These programs help you to recover data that has been accidentally destroyed. Some programs allow you to unerase files that were deleted, retrieve data from files that have become corrupted, and unformat hard disks that were formatted. The extent to which these packages are successful depends upon the condition of the medium in question, and on not using the disk with other files and programs before the damage has been repaired. If you need help, get it immediately. Don't imagine the damage will heal itself.

EXERCISES

A.   Write out the DOS commands you would use to:

1. Create a subdirectory named BOOKFILE.

erase b:\Junk 2. With the prompt A> displayed, delete all of the files on disk drive B in a subdirectory JUNK.

3. Copy a file named HIDDEN.DOC on drive C and in a subdirectory named SECRETS, to drive A and name the duplicate file FOUND.BAK. Assume that the prompt is C:\>.

4. Copy a file named MYFILE.TXT on drive A and in a subdirectory named PAPERS to drive B and to a subdirectory BUSINESS, giving the duplicate file the same filename that it had on drive A. Assume that the prompt displays C:\>.

5. Assume that the prompt displays A\>. Display the names of files on disk drive C under the subdirectory WP, without displaying any other information about the files.

6. Assume that the prompt displays A\>. Display the names of files on disk drive C under the subdirectory WP that have the extension .TXT, pausing at each screenful of information.

7. Assume that the prompt displays C\>. Delete all of the files on disk drive C under the subdirectory WP that have the characters CH at the beginning of their filename.

8. Assume that the prompt displays C\>. a) Change directories to the subdirectory SS.
    b) Change to the subdirectory (of SS) WORK. c) What would the prompt display?

9. Assume that the prompt displays C:\WP\WORK\MEMOS>. a) What command would bring you to the directory WORK? b) With the same prompt described, what command would return you to the root directory? c) With the same prompt described above, if you entered the command CD, what pathname would be returned?

B.   With a blank diskette in drive A, execute the following commands. Use the DIR command to confirm that the commands you issue are executed correctly.

1. FORMAT the disk in drive A.
2. Change drives to obtain the prompt A\>.
3. Make three directories called DIR1, JUNK, and MISC.
4. Change directories to JUNK. Make a subdirectory FILES. Change directories to FILES.
5. Copy the file COMMAND.COM from the root directory of drive C to FILES.
6. Locate the file SORT.COM on drive C. It may be at the root or in a subdirectory DOS. Copy the file to the root of drive A.
7. Return to the root. Traverse the hierarchy of subdirectories with the CD command.
8. Use the command COPY CON THANKS.BAT to create a one-line file. The one line is ECHO YOU ARE WELCOME. Execute this file by entering THANKS.
9. Return to the root. Issue the TREE and the TREE /F commands.
10. Delete all files (not subdirectories) on the disk in drive A.
11. Remove all subdirectories from drive A.
12. With the type command, list the contents of the files AUTOEXEC.BAT and CONFIG.SYS that are found at the root directory of drive C.

C.   If you have access to the shareware diskette, Computer Tutorial (PC-SIG disk # 403), from Computer Knowledge, place this diskette in drive A and enter TUTOR to start the program. Work your way through modules 6 and 7 which have the titles, *Advanced IBM-PC DOS* and *DOS batch files*, respectively.

Appendix A

Summary of DOS Commands

This appendix summarizes the function of commands found in most versions of DOS 3.3. Readers are directed to the DOS manual for their microcomputer to obtain specific information about options available and about command syntax.

COMMAND	PURPOSE
APPEND	Defines a search path for all executable files (.EXE, .BAT, .COM).
ASSIGN	Reassigns drive names.
ATTRIB	Sets file attributes for reading and archiving.
BACKUP	Backs up files in a form readable by RESTORE.
BREAK	Enables/disables Ctrl-Break (Ctrl-C).
CHCP	Changes code page, i. e., toggles fonts.
CHDIR (CD)	Change directory.
CHKDSK	Checks disk and file status.
CLS	Clears the screen.
COMMAND	Starts a secondary command processor.
COMP	Compares two disks.
COPY	Replicates a file(s).
CTTY	Reassigns standard input, standard output, and standard error.
DATE	Sets the current system date.
DELETE (DEL)	Erases a file(s).
DIR	Displays a directory.
DISKCOMP	Compares two disks.
DISKCOPY	Replicates one disk on another.
ERASE	Same as DELETE.
EXE2BIN	Converts .EXE files to .COM files.
FASTOPEN	Retains memory of files already opened for quick reopening.
FDISK	Prepares a fixed disk for DOS.
FIND	Locates character strings in files.
FORMAT	Formats floppy, semirigid, and hard disks.
GRAFTABL	Installs a table of graphics characters for color graphics adapters (CGA).
GRAPHICS	Supports the printing of graphic displays with color graphic adapters (CGA).
JOIN	Logically "joins" a drive to a directory on another drive to create a single directory hierarchy.
KEYB	Selects between 17 different country keyboard codes.
LABEL	Sets the volume label for a storage unit.
MKDIR (MD)	Creates directories.
MODE	Sets printer, communications, and display characteristics.
MORE	Pauses standard output after 24 lines have been displayed.
PATH	Sets the drive and directories that should be searched to locate batch and command files.
PROMPT	Changes the prompt's characteristics.
RECOVER	Recovers damaged files.
RENAME (REN)	Changes filenames.
REPLACE	Replaces files that already exist on the target drive.
RESTORE	Restores files that were created with BACKUP.

RMDIR (RD)	Removes a directory.
SELECT	Makes bootable disks with predefined country characteristics.
SHARE	Enables or disables access to files by multiple people.
SORT	Sorts lines from standard input and passes the sorted lines to standard output.
SUBST	Substitutes a drive name for a directory pathway.
SYS	Transfers DOS to another disk.
TIME	Sets the system time.
TREE	Displays directories and trees in hierarchies.
TYPE	Displays the contents of a file.
VER	Displays the version of DOS in use.
VERIFY	Toggles checking to confirm the successful transfer of data to the disk.
VOL	Displays the volume label.
XCOPY	Extends copying of files especially in subdirectory hierarchies.

Glossary

. Symbolic representation for the current directory.

.. Symbolic representation of the parent directory of the current directory.

? The DOS wildcard for matching single characters in command line parameters.

* The DOS wildcard for matching multiple characters in command line parameters.

**** Symbolic representation for the root directory.

A

A> The DOS system prompt signifying drive A as the default drive.

Access The process of locating data stored in memory or on a disk.

Active directory See Current Directory.

Adapter cards A printed circuit card that controls a device, such as a display or a printer and makes it compatible with the computer's data bus.

Alphabetic keys The keys on the computer's keyboard that are arranged just as they are on a typewriter keyboard.

Alphanumeric characters Any combination of letters, numbers, symbols, and spaces.

Alternate key The key marked Alt and used to attach alternate meanings to other alphanumeric keys in WordPerfect, and for initiating macros in Lotus 1-2-3.

Application The product of a generalized application program such as a document from a word processor, a budget projection from a spreadsheet, or an inventory from a database manager.

Application program A program that allows users to produce specific applications of the computer to a particular area or need.

Arithmetic operators The arithmetic signs: /, *, +, -, ^.

ASCII American Standard Code for Information Interchange; the coding scheme whereby every character, number, or symbol is represented by an integer code between 0 and 255.

ASCII files (Text) Files saved in a format specified by the American Standard Code for Information Interchange. Files saved in this format often can be used by other programs or transmitted by modem because they have a standard format.

AUTOEXEC.BAT A batch file which, if it is present, is executed automatically whenever an MS-DOS-based computer is booted up.

Automatic repeat The characteristic of keys, if held down, to continue to enter the symbol they represent after the first entry of the character and a brief pause.

B

B> The DOS system prompt signifying drive B as the default drive.

Back copy A version of a file that is saved if extensive revisions or changes are going to be made. EDLIN and some other programs automatically create back copies.

Backup A process of making a second copy of a file to avoid loss of data. Backups may be created automatically by some applications programs.

Backup copy A duplicate of a file or disk that is saved in case the original file or disk is damaged.

Bad sector A disk sector that has been damaged and marked as unusable by DOS.

BAK An extension, automatically assigned by EDLIN and some other programs to the back copy of a file.

Batch file A text file containing DOS commands that are executed by entering the filename at the DOS prompt. Batch files must end with a .BAT extension.

Baud The rate at which data is transmitted. Baud is based on the number of bits transmitted per second.

Beep An audible sound, notifying a user of an error.

Binary Base-two numbering with the digits 0 and 1.

Binary file A file created with an applications program that contains non-ASCII codes specific to that program.

Bit Binary digit. The unit for constructing larger representational items such as bytes and words. Bits have two states, 0 and 1.

Boot To load and run the operating system. Derived from "pull yourself up by your own bootstraps."

Bootable disk A disk that contains hidden DOS files and COMMAND. COM and that is capable of booting the microcomputer. Also called a system disk.

Bootstrap See Boot.

Bug A program error.

Byte A unit of representation constructed from 8 bits. One byte represents a single character.

C **C>** The DOS system prompt signifying drive C, the hard drive, as the default drive.

Cancel To abort a program or command.

Carriage return (CR) A printer directive moving the print head down one line and back to the left margin. Issued by pressing Enter (Return) key on most programs.

Case The shape and size of a letter. Letters in a type style may be upper or lower case.

Case-sensitive A command that acts differently if characters are typed in lower or upper case.

Cathode ray tube (CRT) One type of computer screen. The screen similar to a television screen.

Character A symbol (numeric, alphabetic, punctuation, or mathematic) represented by one byte.

Character string See String.

Chip See Integrated Circuit.

Cold boot Starting the computer by turning it on.

Color display A monitor that displays color.

Color/Graphics Monitor Adapter The printed-circuit card for personal computers that provides low-level graphics and minimal colors.

Command An instruction to a computer that can be executed.

Command line The line on which a DOS command, its arguments and switches is entered.

Commercial software Software that has been copyrighted and licensed, is supported by the developer, and that must be paid for in advance of its usage.

Compiler A computer program that converts an entire source code program into machine executable form.

CON: Abbreviation for Console: refers to the keyboard and the monitor.

CONFIG.SYS A text file containing system configuration commands which is executed when a DOS system is booted.

Configuration The currently active default values for an operating system or for an application program. These values may be modifiable during operation.

Console The primary control device for a computer, generally the keyboard and monitor. See CON:.

Coprocessor A processing chip that carries out specialized operations for the processor such as graphics or mathematical data processing.

Copy protection Any of several techniques designed to prevent the copying of software.

Copyright Legal protection through registration with the Library of Congress.

CPI Characters per inch.

CPU Central processing unit. The unit that processes data and supports random access memory (RAM).

Current directory The default DOS directory. The directory that is employed first when DOS searches for files and executable commands unless otherwise directed.

Current drive The drive containing the disk on which DOS looks for a directory or file unless otherwise instructed.

Cursor The underscore character that indicates where characters will be entered or where commands will be carried out.

D

Data Alphanumeric and graphic input or output.

Data disk The disk used to store files.

Data file A file that contains the data used by an applications program.

Database An organized collection of related records containing data suitable for manipulation by a database program.

Debug To discover and correct syntactic and semantic errors in a program, function, macro, batch file, or subroutine.

Default configuration The initial defaults used to establish the operating characteristics of an operating system or applications program.

Default directory See Current Directory.

Default drive See Current Drive.

Default value The value used or the action taken when an acceptable alternative has not been specified.

Destination The target location for data or files transferred from a source location.

Directory A logical grouping of files and subdirectories on a disk. A directory's filenames, extensions, and subdirectory names are displayed together along with the file's size, creation time and date.

Directory hierarchy The tree-like, logical structure holding subdirectories. Subdirectories of root may have subdirectories created under them, and so on.

Disk drive The device that reads and writes files to disks.

Diskette A secondary storage medium for a computer. Diskettes come in floppy, rigid, and semirigid cases.

Display The monitor screen.

DOS Disk Operating System. The software that makes computer hardware useable.

Double density disk A disk with 360 Kb of storage.

Double sided A diskette with two surfaces on which to store files.

Drive name The two characters (a letter and a colon) that identify a disk drive. Examples include C: and A:.

Empty directory A directory which has no subdirectories or files beneath it.

Enter key Synonymous with Return key. Represented by broken arrow on some keyboards, the Enter key inserts a carriage return and a line feed.

Escape key The key used to back out of command sequences or from data entry in dBASE and 1-2-3, to cancel a command in DOS, and to indicate the number of times commands should be executed in WordPerfect.

Executable file A DOS file with the extension .BAT, .COM, or .EXE that can be executed by the DOS shell interpreter.

Expansion slot An electrical socket into which adapter boards are inserted to control communications with peripherals or to increase RAM.

Extension Up to three characters that are added to a filename to identify the contents of the file.

External commands (Transient commands) DOS commands that reside on the disk and are loaded into RAM when needed.

F

File A collection of data stored in a named and dedicated portion of a disk. Files can contain graphs, documents, databases, worksheets, programs, and other collections of data.

File specification The complete specification of a file including a drive letter, a pathway, a filename, and an extension. Also, abbreviated to filespec.

Filename The identifier that uniquely describes a file. Consists of from one to eight characters.

Floppy disk Diskettes which allow some physical flexibility, especially of the 3 1/2" and 5 1/4" size.

Formatting Initializing and preparing a disk so that it can record and store files produced by a particular computer system. Also, the appearance of text in a document or worksheet.

Function keys Keys marked F1 through F10 (or F12) that carry out specialized macro operations in DOS and in applications software.

H

Hard disk Secondary storage devices with a rigid disk(s).

Hidden file A program or DOS system file whose filename is not listed when the directory is displayed and which cannot be erased, copied, or otherwise affected by DOS until it is unhidden.

High density disk See Quad Density Disk.

I

I/O Abbreviation for input/output.

IBM compatible computer A computer capable of executing identically to an IBM computer. Also called a "clone."

Incompatible media Secondary storage media of different types; for example 3 1/2" and 5 1/4" floppy disks. This term is used in a DOS error message when a diskcopy is attempted.

Information Data to which meaning has been assigned.

Initialize To set up a diskette, a program or a device with default values and conditions.

Input The data that a program can process.

Input/output (I/O) A term referring to the processes of obtaining and transmitting data from the computer.

Insert mode A mode of data entry in which new text in inserted into existing text rather than overwriting it. Opposed to overwrite mode.

Install The program command that initiates the installation of a program on a computer.

Installation The process of tailoring the default values for an applications program to the hardware available and to the user's priorities for initial program parameters such as screen colors, margins, etc.

Installation program The program that installs the program, driver and text files needed to operate an applications program.

Integrated circuit Electronic devices that connect thousands of transistors on a silicon chip. Also referred to as an IC and as a chip.

Internal commands (Resident commands) DOS commands contained in the COMMAND.COM file that are always in RAM and available to the user when the DOS prompt is on the screen.

J   **Jacket** The outer covering on a floppy disk.

K   **Keyboard, extended** 101 keys.

Keyboard, standard 80 keys.

Keyword A word that is reserved by an application program for special meaning and that often cannot be used in an application.

Kill Terminate an executing program.

Kilo (K) A prefix approximately equal to one thousand (1,024).

M   **Mega** A prefix meaning approximately 1 million.

Megahertz (MHz) A frequency measurement. One megahertz equals 1 million cycles-per-second.

Menu A series of choices from which the user is to make selections.

Mode The state of an operation.

Modem Modulator/Demodulator. A device that permits the transmission of computer data over telephone lines and other media.

MS-DOS Abbreviation for Microsoft - Disk Operating System. The operating system used on IBM PC compatible computers.

N

Nonsystem disk A non-bootable diskette. A diskette that does not contain the hidden files and/or the COMMAND.COM file needed to successfully carry out a boot.

Num Lock key The key used to toggle the numeric key pad between lower and upper case.

Numeric keypad The block of ten keys holding numbers as upper case and cursor movement keys as lower case.

O

Object code A program that has been converted into a computer executable form.

Opening files To place a file into use so that it can be read and written.

Operating System A program that coordinates the operation of all parts of a computer system.

Output Data transferred to an output device.

Output device Any device receiving data from a computer. Common output devices are the monitors, printers, and plotters.

Overwrite mode The mode of data entry in which typed characters type over and replace existing text. Opposed to Insert mode.

P

Parent directory The directory above a subdirectory.

Path name A character string that describes the precise order of directories that DOS must traverse in order to locate a file or command. Part of the file specification.

PC Abbreviation for personal computer.

PC-DOS Abbreviation for Personal Computer - Disk Operating System. The operating system used on IBM personal computers. Comparable to MS-DOS.

Peripheral device Devices such as printers and modems connected to the system unit and communicating through an adapter card.

Plotter An output device that produces high-quality graphics, often by drawing the lines.

Port The electrical connector on a computer through which communication with other devices or other computers are maintained.

Printer An output device that produces characters, numbers and other symbols.

PRN Abbreviation for printer. The printer that DOS uses unless instructed otherwise. Can be LPT1, LPT2, or LPT3.

Program A sequence of instructions that a computer can execute to accomplish a task.

Program disk The disk that contains the main program for an application. Also called a System Disk.

D - 46   *Glossary*

Prompt The signal that control has been passed to the user and that the system is awaiting a command or data entry.

Public domain software Software that is not copyrighted or supported by the developer.

Q   **Quad density disk** A disk with 1.2 Mb storage.

Qwerty keys The standard arrangement of alphabetic and numeric keys. Derives from the letters on the top left row.

R   **Random Access Memory (RAM)** The portion of the computer's memory which stores the internal DOS commands, programs, and data. Also called main memory or primary memory.

Read-Only Memory (ROM) A computer component that can be read but not written (changed). One type of ROM chip contains the initial instructions for booting a computer.

Reboot See Warm Boot.

Return key See Enter Key.

Root directory The first directory on any disk. Root is created during formatting. All other directories are subdirectories of root.

Root See Root Directory.

S   **Save** To write a file to secondary storage.

Scrolling The line-by-line movement of data on the monitor.

Sector A 512-byte portion of a floppy or hard disk onto which data is written, or read from. Each track is divided into sectors to permit the location of data by a disk address. Also used to describe a single pie-shaped portion of a disk created by formatting.

Shareware Software that has been copyrighted but is distributed on a try-it-first basis. Then, if it is useful, contribute a recommended amount to the developer basis.

Shift-state keys The Alternate, Control and Shift keys: keys that change the state of the other keyboard characters.

Smart files See Batch Files.

Software Programs that are used with a computer system. In contrast to hardware.

Source code Original program code which is to be processed by a programming language compiler or interpreter.

Source disk The disk from which data is read or copied.

Source file The file from which data is read or copied.

Spindle hole The opening in the center of a floppy disk into which the disk drive spindle is inserted.

String One or more connected characters that are used as a unit for some computer operation.

Subdirectory A directory created beneath another directory.

Suspend Cause a program to pause in its execution.

System disk A disk containing the files needed for booting a booting system. Sometimes used to refer to the main program disk for an applications program.

System unit The component of a microcomputer system that contains the microprocessor, the data bus and expansion slots.

T

Text Readable characters including the alphanumeric characters, the numerals and punctuation marks. As opposed to non-visible, control codes. Also, the words in a message.

Timing hole A hole in a diskette that passes between timing holes in the diskette jacket and is used for determining the starting sector of a diskette.

Toggle The process of switching between two states. Also, any device, command, or command switch that has two states, on and off.

Typeover mode See Overwrite mode.

U

Unformatted disk An uninitialized disk. The condition of the disk when first shipped.

User A person who utilizes a computer system.

V

Volume label A name or character string of up to 11 characters, that can be assigned to any disk during formatting. Volume labels can be changed with the LABEL command.

W

Warm boot Restarting the computer by simultaneously pressing the Control, Alternate, and Delete keys instead of turning the computer off and then turning it back on.

Wildcards Characters used in DOS command parameters and in search operations to match one or more characters in the position of the wildcard in the string. Typically, a question mark matches one character, and an asterisk matches any number of characters.

Winchester disk See Hard Disk.

Write-protect notch A gap in a diskette jacket that when covered with a write-protect tab prevents the computer from writing to the disk.

Write protection A mechanism that prevents the alteration or deletion of files.

Write The process of copying data from RAM to a file.

INDEX

A>, D-39
Abort, Retry, Ignore, D-15-16
Access, D-39
Active directory. *See* Current directory
Adapter cards, D-39
Alphabetic keys, D-39
Alternate, D-4, D-39
Application, D-39
Application program, D-39
Arithmetic operators, D-39
Arrows, D-3, D-4
ASCII, D-39
ASCII files, D-39
Asterisk, D-4
AUTOEXEC.BAT, D-32, D-33-35, D-39
Automatic repeat, D-39

B>, D-39
Back copy, D-40
Backing up files, D-16
Backspace, D-4
BACKUP, D-29, D-40
Backup copy, D-40
Bad command or File name, D-15
Bad sector, D-40
BAK, D-40
.BAT, D-34
Batch file, D-40, D-46
Baud, D-40
Beep, D-40
Binary, D-40
Bit, D-40
Boot, D-40
Bootable disk, D-40
Booting, MS-DOS, D-8-9
Bootstrap. *See* Boot
Break, D-4

Bug, D-40
Byte, D-7, D-40

C>, D-40
Cancel, D-40
Caps lock, D-4
Carriage return (CR), D-40
Case, D-40
Case-sensitive, D-40
Cathode-ray tube (CRT), D-3, D-41
CD (Change Directory), D-25-26
Central processing unit (CPU), D-41
Character, D-41
Characters per inch (CPI), D-41
Character string. *See* String
Chip. *See* Integrated circuit
Cold boot, D-41
Color display, D-41
Color/graphics monitor adapter, D-41
.COM, D-34
Command line, D-41
Commands, D-41
    DOS, D-11-15, D-37-38
    external or transient, D-43
    hard disk-related and options,
        D-25-32
    internal or resident, D-44
Commercial software, D-35, D-41
Compiler, D-41
CON, D-41
CONFIG.SYS, D-32-33, D-41
Configuration, D-41
Console, D-41
Control, D-4
Coprocessor, D-41
COPY, D-13, D-14, D-28, D-29
Copy protection, D-16, D-41

Copyright, D-16, D-41
CPI. *See* Characters per inch (CPI)
CPU. *See* Central processing unit
    (CPU)
CR. *See* Carriage return (CR)
CRT. *See* Cathode-ray tube (CRT)
Current directory, D-41
Current drive, D-42
Cursor, D-3, D-42

Data, D-42
Database, D-42
Data disk, D-42
Data file, D-42
Date prompt, D-9
Debug, D-42
Default configuration, D-42
Default directory. *See* Current
    directory
Default drives, and prompts, D-10-11,
    D-30-31, D-42
Default path names, D-24-25
Default value, D-42
DELETE, D-4, D-13
Destination, D-42
DIR (Directory), D-11-12, D-27-28,
    D-42
    hierarchy of, D-20-25, D-42
    path names, D-24-25
    rationales, D-23
Disaster recovery software, D-35
DISCOPY, D-14
Disk drive, D-5, D-42
Diskette, D-5-8, D-42, D-43
    handling and storage, D-7-8
    structure, D-5-7
Disk operating system (DOS), D-42

Contents

Preface

This book has been written to teach its readers to use WordPerfect 5.1 software effectively. It offers practical, hands-on instruction in the use of a highly successful, commercial quality word processing program. This package is widely used in business and education. This software is fully functioned and capable of illustrating most of the major applications that one can develop with other commercial software packages of a similar nature.

Intended to meet several needs, *Beginning WordPerfect 5.1* can be useful in many settings. It can be used as a supplemental laboratory manual for courses that introduce students to computers and their applications, such as Introduction to Computing in Business, Computer Literacy, and Introduction to Microcomputer Software.

This book can also be used as a stand-alone text for short courses that focus on educating students in the main uses of microcomputers. The tutorial orientation of this book allows it to be used by a learner who wishes to work independently. The instructional approach utilized is entirely hands-on and step by step. Exercises are presented with detailed instructions on moving from the identification of a computing problem to its solution.

Each chapter concludes with a group of exercises that reinforce the techniques learned in that chapter. The exercises closely parallel the design of the document, worksheet, or database file presented in the chapter. In some cases, exercises are reused in subsequent chapters to enhance the student's product and to enable students to practice new techniques without unnecessary data entry.

A summary of the complete WordPerfect menu hierarchy is included for instructors who wish to cover material beyond the scope of this book. A glossary of WordPerfect terminology will also be helpful to students.

Much appreciation is due to the following persons who assisted in the development of this book:

Brent Bowman, University of Nevada, Reno

Sharon F. Harvey, Normandale Community College

Prasad Kilari, University of Nevada, Reno

Mark Simkin, University of Nevada, Reno

Their assistance and the special assistance given by Arthur Broten and Kerry Chase in the completion of this book is gratefully acknowledged.

Chapter 1

An Easy Entry into Word Processing

Chapter Outline

Introduction to WordPerfect
    Terminology
    WordPerfect Operations
Versions of WordPerfect
Printer Selection
Creating File Diskettes
Loading WordPerfect
A Business Memorandum
The Cancel Key
Entering Text
Changing the Default Directory
Saving Your File
Moving the Cursor
Editing
    Deleting Characters
    Deleting Words
    The Cancel/Undelete Key
    Inserting Text
    Typeover
    Entering Tabs
    Entering and Removing Blank Lines
Using Help Screens
Saving and Backing Up Your File
Printing Your File
Exiting WordPerfect
Confirming the Presence of the File
Exercises

WordPerfect is a powerful word processor that can be used to create documents as simple as a one-page letter or as complex as a textbook. It is easy to begin using WordPerfect and, as your requirements grow more complex, you will find that WordPerfect has capabilities to satisfy complicated formatting requirements. In this chapter you will create a very brief business memorandum with few special formatting requirements. In doing so you have the opportunity to

1.   Understand how word processors function;
2.   Obtain a WordPerfect working disk;
3.   Enter text into a document;
4.   Move the cursor in small and large steps;
5.   Edit and correct text with operations such as insert and delete;
6.   View the available Help screens;
7.   Print your document;
8.   Save and back up your file.

INTRODUCTION TO WORDPERFECT

Once you have used it, word processing is something you'll never want to do without. How many times have you had to make do with a poorly typed document because you didn't have the energy to retype it? Or have you wanted to redo a term paper because you found typographical errors, strikeovers, misspellings, or missing sentences--yet there wasn't time for another draft? Have you had to retype an entire page of a term paper to leave room for footnotes? Or have you wished that you had the luxury of moving some of the paragraphs and sentences to different places in your paper to give your paper better flow?

These and a hundred other wishes are answered with word processing software like WordPerfect. Word processors enable you to create documents that are stored as files on diskettes. Once created, these documents can be recalled, edited, and printed any number of times. To make changes and to review your revised documents without having to retype them is one of the most useful capabilities of your microcomputer. Among the features that you will appreciate having are:

1. Extensive **Help screens** that are called up quickly to help you if you forget how to complete a command;
2. **WYSIWYG** (What you see is what you get). The monitor screen in front of you can print a document almost exactly as you see it;
3. Extensive **cursor and screen movement capabilities** that allow you to move with speed and accuracy within documents you create;
4. **Function key commands** that are efficient to use;
5. **Editing commands** that allow alteration and revision of text material including moving and duplicating blocks of text, reformatting files, and recalling blocks of text that are deleted in error;
6. **Page and line formatting commands** that help you to design the appearance of printed output with control over the placement of such features as tabs, margins, footnotes, page numbers, headers, and footers;
7. Other **special features**, including global search and replace, the combining of files, the use of alternate font styles such as underlining and boldface, and file merging;
8. **Control over columns**, allowing you to shape text in correct, aesthetically pleasing patterns.

Not all of the diverse features of WordPerfect can be covered in this book, but by working through the exercises and by reading the explanations of how WordPerfect functions you will become proficient in its use. If you wish to go on to more advanced features you will have no difficulty. The WordPerfect Manual describes WordPerfect's advanced capabilities.

Terminology

Word processing is different from typing in the nicest ways. Although most of the new words and concepts are discussed as they are needed, perhaps a few terms introduced now will be helpful in obtaining a feeling for what word processing software can do that typewriters cannot.

Word wrap allows you to type the words of a paragraph without pressing the Enter key. On a typewriter you press the carriage return at the end of every line. In word processing, you simply type and the software determines how many words fit on a line. When the number of words exceeds the line length, the next word is automatically wrapped around to the next line. If you are a good typist, you can continue typing without looking at the screen to see where the margins are.

WordPerfect places **a soft return** at the end of a line when it is using word wrap. A soft return permits easy reformatting if the paragraph is given different margins, or if words are added and deleted, without your having to adjust words. Pressing the Enter key, however, enters a **hard return,** which cannot be reformatted by the word processor.

The **cursor** is the flashing underline that appears in the work area on your screen. The cursor identifies where text is placed if you start typing, or where commands for such actions as deletion or blocking take effect.

Keys automatically repeat when they are held down for more than a fraction of a second. WordPerfect is sufficiently fast that you rarely experience "type ahead," in which the remembered keystrokes exceed the typical limit of nineteen used by DOS. If you exceed the limit of remembered strokes, as when you hold down an arrow key too long, WordPerfect beeps at you. The beep does not affect your file. It is a gentle reminder that you are attempting to type characters that the computer cannot retain. When you hear the beep, slow down. Since the computer does not remember more than its limit of keystrokes, in some circumstances it may be necessary to retype some of the keystrokes.

If you reformat a paragraph, or an entire document, with new margins, WordPerfect automatically fills the lines with the greatest number of words possible. If the margins are widened, the number of words on each line is increased. The number is decreased if the margins are narrowed.

Keys are not restricted to typing only one character or carrying out a single function. **Alternate meanings** have been assigned to function keys. These alternate meanings are activated when the keys are pressed at the same time as either the Ctrl, Alt, or Shift keys.

WordPerfect, when it prints the document, produces a straight right-hand margin. This is because it automatically inserts blank spaces in front of some words to place the last printable character next to the right margin. This is called **full justification**. The type of justification can be changed so only the left margin is justified (ragged), so a line is centered, or so only the right margin is justified. WordPerfect can carry out the **automatic hyphenation** of words by breaking them into syllables.

WordPerfect Operations

There are five kinds of operations that you can conduct with WordPerfect:

1. **File operations** allow you to load, save, or read files on the disk.
2. **Data entry** allows you to enter text and embedded, or invisible, control commands into your document.
3. **Editing** commands change the text on the screen.
4. **Cursor and screen movement** commands change the location of the cursor or alter your view of the text but do not change the text in any way.
5. **Page and line format** changes affect such features as margins and tab stops.

WordPerfect permits operations on blocks of text. When you must work on large blocks of text, for instance, when you wish to move a paragraph from one location to another, you use a process called **blocking**. Pressing the Alt and F4 keys marks the beginning of the block. Moving the cursor to a new location causes the block to be **blocked**. Blocked text has a different appearance from the surrounding text; it appears in reverse video. After the text has been marked, the block operations can be executed. Block operations include moving a block from one location to another, copying (duplicating) the block to another location, saving part of a document into a new file, and deleting a block of text.

VERSIONS OF WORDPERFECT

WordPerfect is available in several versions. The most recent complete version is numbered 5.1. All of the commands given in this book are built around version 5.1. Most of the commands are similar to those in version 5.0.

PRINTER SELECTION

It is assumed in this text that you are using a copy of WordPerfect that has been preconfigured for the printer you are using. If you are working in a networked laboratory, WordPerfect should have been preconfigured for the printer you are to use.

In the event that your laboratory uses several printers, you will have to select a printer to print on. The printer selection section of the WordPerfect manual describes this procedure in detail. Review this information if it applies to your situation.

CREATING FILE DISKETTES

You need a diskette on which to save files. Check the diskettes with the DOS DIR command to be sure that they have been formatted, and that they do not contain any files that you need to save. When you have obtained a diskette that can be used, format it by placing the diskette in drive A. Make sure you are at the C> prompt and enter

format   a: The format command. You may choose to use FORMAT A: /V to assign a volume
                name to the disk as well
◄┘   Enter key
◄┘   Enter key, for no volume label

When the formatting process is complete, respond N to the prompt asking whether you wish to format another diskette, and place the second diskette in drive A when instructed to do so. Label the first diskette with your name, address, and telephone number, and the phrase *WP-Original Files.* Label the second diskette with the same information about yourself and the phrase *WP-Backup Files.*

LOADING WORDPERFECT

This text assumes that you are working with a hard disk drive microcomputer. This may not be the case. Consequently, your instructor must inform you about how to access WordPerfect and the other software used in this book if you are using a dual drive or networked floppy disk systems. If WordPerfect has been properly installed, the following procedure enables you to get started:

1. Place the formatted diskette labeled *Original Files* in drive A for saving document files (as opposed to the WordPerfect program).
2. Be sure that your printer and monitor are turned on. Sometimes this is done at the time the computer is turned on, but often they must be switched on separately.
3. The DOS C> prompt should be visible. Before proceeding, check to see what files exist on the diskette in the A drive by typing

    dir   a:

This command allows you to see what files may already exist (after you have been creating documents) so that you do not accidentally reuse a filename that is already present. You can also determine that you are using the correct diskette on which to save your files. Assuming that the DOS C> prompt is showing, enter

4.   cd   \:wp51

5. **wp**

6. You then see the blank work screen shown in Figure 1-1.

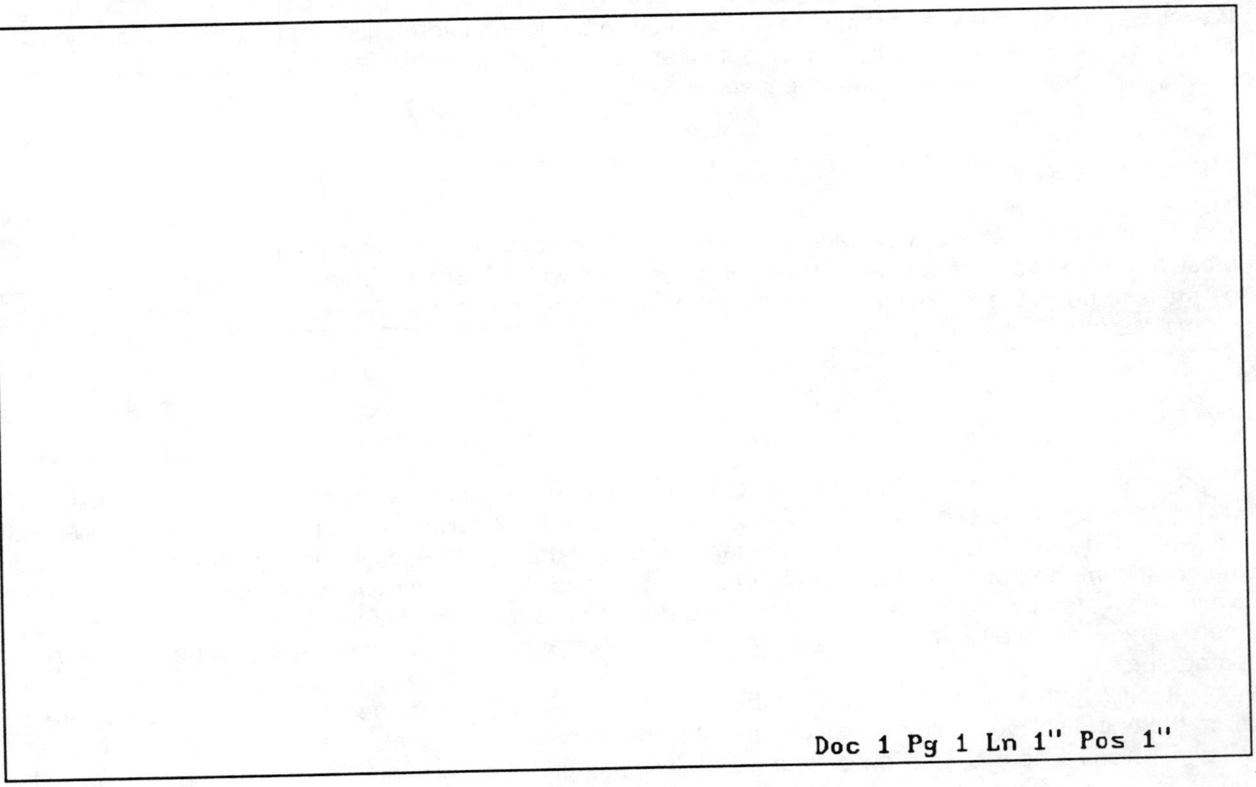

```



                                                     Doc 1 Pg 1 Ln 1'' Pos 1''
```

Figure 1-1. WordPerfect Screen

The blinking cursor is in the upper left corner of the screen and a status line will show:

1. The **document number.** WordPerfect allows you to work with two documents concurrently. Normally, you work with only one, so the document number should almost always be **1**. If you see **Doc 2,** return to document 1 by simultaneously pressing Shift and F3.

2. The **cursor location.** The location of the cursor in the file is shown by page (**Pg**), vertical position on the page (**Ln**), and by horizontal position on the page (**Pos**). The (Pos)ition of the cursor is generally at 8 inches or less, since most documents have right margins that must fit on paper 8 1/2 inches wide. It is possible to widen the right margin when wider paper is used. Then the Pos number may well be greater than 8 inches. Pos may be flashing on and off. This indicates that the Num Lock key is on. Remove the flashing by toggling the Num Lock once.

3. From time to time other messages may appear on the left side of the status line.

A BUSINESS MEMORANDUM

It may come as a surprise, but many important applications for computer usage do not involve mathematical manipulations. Word processing is, perhaps, the most readily identifiable use for a computer. Increasingly, businesses and organizations of all types are using word processing to improve their communications. Word processing is not solely the domain of secretaries. Many professionals spend considerable amounts of their time writing. The first application for which WordPerfect is used here is to create a business memorandum. A memorandum is a useful document to start with because it is not difficult to format. The memorandum in Figure 1-2, for instance, uses block paragraphs (the first line is not indented) and it does not have any underlining, bolding, or special columnar information. Learning to create this memorandum provides you with enough information about word processing to enable you to create many other documents that do not require special features, documents such as letters, class notes, and simple term papers.

THE CANCEL KEY

The function keys serve a wide variety of purposes, many of which are described in this text. If you press a function key and receive a menu or screen with which you are not familiar, or which should not be present, press the F1 key to cancel the command. Pressing F1, the Cancel key, returns you to the normal WordPerfect entry screen.

ENTERING TEXT

The cursor is placed at the start of the document. If you are revising a document that already exists, the cursor appears at the same location. The first portion of this exercise is to help you become familiar with text entry. Shown in Figure 1-2 is a memorandum that you are to type as it appears. When creating this memorandum, do not press Enter at the end of most lines. As you type you will notice how WordPerfect wraps the words from one line to the next. You do not have to hit the Enter key. You need only press the Enter key twice after the *Date:*, *To:*, *Fr:*, and *Re:* lines and twice after the last character of the first paragraph.

It is likely that the first line of your first paragraph may wrap to the second line at a point different from the text displayed below, in which case the line endings of your entire paragraph differ from those shown. This is a normal function of your particular system and is not a problem. WordPerfect adjusts the number of characters on a line to match the characteristics of the printer and default font selected for your system. Fonts conventionally chosen for standard text range from ten to fifteen characters per inch. Consequently, the number of characters and words that display on your screen may be different from that shown throughout this text. Simply continue to type in the text and allow the automatic wrap to control the form of your paragraph.

```
Date: September 15, 1991
    2 ENTER
To: Vice President T. L. White
    2 ENTER
Fr: Mr. F. Y. Black, Director, Marketing & Sales
    2 ENTER
Re: Departmental Computer Equipment
    2 ENTER
It has become increasingly clear that our department can save the
company money in a number of areas if it had immediate access to a
microprocessor.  I will cite three instances in which we could have
doe a better job and have been more productive.  J. Grey produced
a fifty page report for the XYZ Company that had to be retyped 3
times as it was revised and improved.  We needed to produce three
graphic displacys for a presentation to the ABC Corporation and
were told by the Graphics Department that they could not be made
abailable until two weaks after they were needed.  Finally, I had
to produce a projection of our expenditures for the next three year
planning period.  Without access to a spreadsheet accounting
program, this three hour task took a full day.
    2 ENTER
I believe that the Marketing and Sales Department should be allowed
to acquire a microcomputer with approopriate spreadsheet, graphics
and word processing software.  M. Brown in our department has taken
several computer courses and workshops.  She feels that she can
provide the training required for our staff.  With your approval
and budgetary support, we can help to maintain corporate
profitability.
```

Figure 1-2. Sample Memorandum

There are several words that are deliberately misspelled. These errors should be typed as they appear. They will be corrected later. If you make mistakes of your own, don't worry. If you catch a mistake right away, use the Backspace key to erase the character that is to the left and start typing again. If you miss some mistakes, correct them later.

Type in the text from Figure 1-2 and use the Enter key only as noted.

The memorandum's text is entered between a left margin which is indented 1 inch from the edge of the paper and a right margin which is indented 1 inch from the right edge of an 8 1/2 inch by 11 inch sheet of paper. These are the default margin settings. This means that a line of text would take up a maximum of 6 1/2 inches before wrapping to the next line. How many characters actually fit between these margins depends upon the size of the characters (font size) in use. Altering margins is covered in Chapter 5: Advanced WordPerfect Usage.

CHANGING THE DEFAULT DIRECTORY To Drive A:/B: (Floppy)

When you initially enter the WordPerfect work screen the default directory is C:. This can be changed so all listing, saving, and printing of files is done from a disk other than C:. To change the directory to A:, the one you want to work in, enter

F5	F5 key, to change the directory. Notice the prompt in the lower line indicating that an equal sign should be typed if you wish to change the default directory.
=	Equal sign to change the directory
a:	A prompt to indicate which directory to change to
◄┘	Enter key
F1	F1 key, to return to the work screen. F1 prevents the Directory A:\ screen from appearing. If you do see this screen, press the F7 key to return to the work screen. The default directory is A:.

SAVING YOUR FILE   *on Floppy Drive A: / B:*

It is a good idea to save your files frequently as you work on them. This protects you if there is a loss of power or if you commit a major error. Also, if you have to exit WordPerfect before you finish with the exercise you have to save your file and return to it later. Save the file by entering

F10	Function key F10, the Save Files key. The Save Files key saves the file but does not clear the document from the screen.
MEMO	The name of your file, which can be entered in upper or lowercase
◄┘	Enter key

If you plan to continue, do not execute the next six commands. If you must exit WordPerfect now, enter

F7	Function key F7, the Exit key
Y	Yes, to save the document
MEMO	The name of your file, which can be entered in upper or lowercase
◄┘	Enter key
Y	Yes, to save your file (appears only after the first time the file has been saved). Upper or lowercase letters may be typed to select options from all WordPerfect prompts and menus.
Y	Yes, to exit WordPerfect. Do not exit WordPerfect by turning off your computer. By exiting properly, WordPerfect removes certain files from your diskette that are no longer needed.

To retrieve your file, follow the procedure outlined in Chapter 2: Some Next Steps in Word Processing. Remember: using the F10 key to save a file retains the copy of the document in RAM so you can continue editing. Using the F7 key saves the file and clears the document from memory. Also, remember that a clear screen may be present in a document because a person may enter many hard returns (from pressing the Enter key). Thus, it is possible to retrieve a document into another document if you are not careful.

MOVING THE CURSOR

Excellent typists make typographical mistakes. Great writers rewrite their work. No matter how careful you are, documents you create need to be reworked. Before you can begin to edit your document, you must be able to move the cursor from one location to another. Do not use the Backspace key to move the cursor because this key erases all letters to the left of the cursor. You do not wish to have to retype large portions of your text simply to correct spelling errors.

WordPerfect provides a variety of commands that move your cursor to different locations without destroying any of the text that has been created. At this point you shall be introduced to seven groups of cursor movement commands. Practice them as they are described.

The arrow keys on the keypad move the cursor one character at a time in the direction that the arrow is pointing.

Pressing the Home key and then pressing the Left Arrow key moves the cursor to the left margin. The first printable character need not necessarily be in the first character position after the left margin since there may be spaces in front of this character.

The End key moves the cursor beyond the last character on a line. This character also may be a blank.

As your document becomes larger, it can no longer be seen on one screen and it is harder to move to specific locations. Several WordPerfect commands are especially helpful in moving between screens and in making bigger jumps from one place to another.

If the cursor is not on the first or last line, you can move the cursor to the top and bottom of the screen by pressing the grey minus and grey plus keys, respectively. If the cursor is on the first or last line of the screen, the pressing of the grey minus or plus sign advances you to the next screen (assuming that you are in a long document that has additional text above or below your current screen).

PgUp takes the cursor to the page before the current page, while PgDn takes the cursor to the following page. This is a short document, so the cursor cannot be moved beyond page 1.

The key sequence Home, Home, and Up Arrow returns the cursor to the top of the file. Home, Home, and Down Arrow moves the cursor to the bottom of the file.

Within a line, too, there are faster cursor movements than the arrow keys alone. Moving one character at a time with the arrow keys is slow. You can move rapidly by holding the Ctrl (Control) key and then pressing the Left Arrow or Right Arrow keys to jump forward and backward word by word. Hold the Control key down then press the selected arrow key. Finally, release the Control key.

Experiment with these movement keys. A summary of the cursor movement commands discussed so far is shown in Figure 1-3. When toggled on, the Num Lock key on the numeric keypad makes cursor movement keys unavailable.

KEY	ACTION
↑	Up one character
↓	Down one character
→	Right one character
←	Left one character
Home- ←	Left margin
End	End of line
Grey +	Bottom of screen or bottom of next screen
Grey -	Top of screen or top of previous screen
PgUp	Up one page
PgDn	Down one page
Home,Home, ↑	Top of file
Home,Home, ↓	Bottom of file
Control- →	Right one word
Control- ←	Left one word

Figure 1-3. Cursor Movement Commands

When you are moving your cursor, try to make your moves as quickly as possible. Much time is wasted by moving one character at a time with the arrow keys when another keystroke combination takes the cursor to its destination more quickly. You will be surprised at how quickly you memorize the keystrokes if you practice them.

The document in Figure 1-4 is short enough that you can see most of it on one screen. Many documents, of course, are not this short. Many of the cursor movement keys move the cursor into those portions of the document that are out of view but are still part of the document.

```
Date: September 15, 1991


To: ~~Vice President~~ T. L. White

Fr: ~~Mr.~~ F. Y. Black, Director, Marketing & Sales

Re: Departmental Computer Equipment

                                              could
It has become increasingly clear that our department ~~can~~ save the
                                                      ^
company money in a number of areas if it had immediate access to a
         computer                   3
micro~~processor~~.  I will cite ~~three~~ instances in which we could have
     n ^                could       ^
doe a better job and have been more productive.  J. Grey produced
  ^   50-                      ^
a ~~fifty~~ page report for the XYZ Company that had to be retyped 3
    ^                                                              3
times as it was revised and improved.  We needed to produce ~~three~~
                                                                  ^
graphic displaeys for a presentation to the ABC Corporation and
               ^
were told by the Graphics Department that they could not be made
     v       2   e
a~~b~~ailable until ~~two~~ weaks after they were needed.  Finally, I had
^                  ^      ^                                   3-
to produce a projection of our expenditures for the next ~~three~~ year
                                                              ^
planning period.  Without access to a spreadsheet accounting
                       3-
program, this ~~three~~ hour task took a full day.
                 ^


I believe that the Marketing and Sales Department should be allowed

to acquire a microcomputer with appro~~e~~priate spreadsheet, graphics
                                     ^
and word processing software.  M. Brown in our department has taken

several computer courses and workshops.  She feels that she can
                                      by
provide the training required ~~for~~ our staff.  With your approval
                                 ^
and budgetary support, we can ~~help to~~ maintain corporate

profitability.
```

Figure 1-4. Document with Editorial Notes

EDITING

The rewriting of a document involves many kinds of changes. The most obvious changes are the correction of spelling, grammatical, and typographical errors. Other changes may be more significant, including the movement or deletion of large blocks of text. Several editing commands are utilized here and others are introduced later. Assume that you had printed out the memorandum, corrected it by hand, and the changes you wished to make appear in Figure 1-4. What commands help you to make those corrections?

The following instructions guide you through some of the changes outlined in the edited copy. Others you can make on your own after you have been shown the correct technique.

Deleting Characters

The Del (Delete) key deletes the character immediately above the cursor. Place your cursor under the first o in the misspelled word *approopriate*. Press

Del	The Delete key. Notice that the *o* was removed and that the rest of the line was pulled left.

The Backspace key deletes the character to the left of the cursor. There is an unneeded *c* in the word *displacys*. Place your cursor under the *y* and press

Backspace	Backspace key. The letter *c* is erased and that portion of the line to the right of the cursor is pulled over.

Deleting Words

The words *help to* at the end of the second paragraph are superfluous and should be removed. With the cursor underneath any letter in a word, the simultaneous pressing of the Control and Backspace keys deletes the entire word. Move your cursor under the *h* in *help* and press

Ctrl-Backspace	Control and Backspace keys pressed simultaneously, to delete *help*. The space following a word is deleted along with the word. Place your cursor under either the *o* or the *t* in *to*.
Ctrl-Backspace	Control and Backspace, to delete the word *to*.

The Cancel/Undelete Key

Sometimes you can delete a word, or even a larger block of text, only to find that it really should not have been deleted. When WordPerfect deletes any block of characters, it places a copy of those characters in a portion of RAM where it can be retrieved. Undo the deletion by pressing

F1	Function key F1, the Cancel/Undelete key, *help to* is reinserted at the location of the cursor. The inserted text is highlighted. This key also cancels commands that are initiated, but not completed. Therefore, it does not reinsert deleted text in the middle of a command sequence, but cancels the command you began.
1	To restore the previously deleted characters. WordPerfect saves the three most recently deleted character strings. Pressing *2* instead of *1* shows you the previous deletion. You restored *help to,* return the cursor to the word *to* and delete it again with

Ctrl-Backspace   Control and Backspace, to delete the word

Inserting Text

To insert the word *could* between *and* and *have*, place your cursor under the space between the two words and press

Space   Space bar, to insert one space. Then type
could   The word to be inserted

With this insertion the characters on the line are pushed to the right. They may exceed the line length. As additional characters are entered the line is extended. WordPerfect takes care of the reformatting of the paragraph when you move your cursor to a new location and perhaps sooner if you enter many extra characters or if you move the cursor with an arrow key. Reformatting realigns the paragraph within the current margins.

Replace the spelled out numbers with the Arabic numerals. This requires you to delete the words with Control and Backspace keys. Insert the numbers by typing them in. Hyphens should be included in the words *50-page, 3-hour,* and *3-year.*

Typeover

The word *microprocessor* is to be replaced by the word *microcomputer.* You do not have to delete an entire word, only to have to retype part of it. There are many ways to approach this change. You can delete part of the word, letter by letter, with the Delete or Backspace keys. You can delete the entire word by pressing Control and Backspace. You can also place the cursor under the *p* and press the Space Bar to make *processor* a separate word and then press Control and Backspace to delete the *processor* portion of the word. Instead, place your cursor under the *p.* Now press

Ins   Insert key. Observe that the word *Typeover* appears on the status line. Typeover is a mode of typing in which the letters you type replace the letters previously on the line. Then type
computer   The word to be inserted. This leaves you with the word *microcomputerr*
Del   Delete key; delete the extra *r*
Ins   Insert key. The mode of character entry toggles between insertion and typeover each time the Insert key is pressed. The mode you leave WordPerfect in is a matter of choice, although most people prefer the insert mode.

Entering Tabs

The Tab key moves the cursor according to tab settings contained in a tab settings ruler. The default tab settings WordPerfect provides are 1/2 inch apart. Tab keys insert tabs into the document. If pressed many times, the Tab key moves to the last tab setting on a line and stops there. Pressing the Tab key again does not move the cursor to the next line. Indent the first paragraph by moving the cursor beneath the letter *I* in *It* and pressing

Tab   Tab key, to insert a tab. The line is pushed to the right. When the cursor is moved, the paragraph is rejustified.

If, when the Tab key is pressed, the cursor moves but a tab is not inserted, press the Insert key to change from typeover mode to insert mode.

Entering and Removing Blank Lines

If you have extra blank lines in your text, they can be removed in two ways. One way is to place your cursor behind the last letter of the previous line and to press the Delete key. This deletes the hard return at the end of the line, bringing the following line up if words from the line that follows fit. You can also put the cursor on the blank line and use the Backspace key. This also removes the invisible end of line marker to join the two lines. For instance, place your cursor on the blank line between the two paragraphs and enter

◄┘   Enter key, to add an extra line
Backspace   Backspace key, to remove the extra line

Lines of text can be broken by placing your cursor at the point where a break is to occur and pressing the Enter key.
The editing commands introduced thus far are summarized in Figure 1-5.

KEY	ACTION
Del(ete)	Delete character above cursor
Backspace	Delete character to left of cursor
Ctrl-Backspace	Delete word above cursor
F1	Reinsert a previous deletion
Ins	Toggle between insert and typeover

Figure 1-5. Selected Editing Keys

Finish editing the memorandum with these commands. When complete, the memorandum should look like Figure 1-6.

```
Date: September 15, 1991

To: T. L. White

Fr: F. Y. Black, Director, Marketing and Sales

Re: Departmental Computer Equipment

    It has become increasingly clear that our department could
save the company money in a number of areas if it had immediate
access to a microcomputer.  I will cite 3 instances in which we
could have done a better job and could have been more productive.
J. Grey produced a 50-page report for the XYZ Company that had to
be retyped 3 times as it was revised and improved.  We needed to
produce 3 graphic displays for a presentation to the ABC
Corporation and were told by the Graphics Department that they
could not be made available until 2 weeks after they were needed.
Finally, I had to produce a projection of our expenditures for the
next 3-year planning period.  Without access to a spreadsheet
accounting program, this 3-hour task took a full day.

    I believe that the Marketing and Sales Department should be
allowed to acquire a microcomputer with appropriate spreadsheet,
graphics, and word processing software.  M. Brown in our department
has taken several computer courses and workshops.  She feels that
she can provide the training required by our staff.  With your
approval and budgetary support, we can maintain corporate
profitability.
```

Figure 1-6. Completed Memorandum

USING HELP SCREENS

If you need assistance with some of the commands you may choose while creating, editing, and printing documents, there is a series of useful Help screens you can employ to remind you of the functions of the keys. The educational version of WordPerfect has only one Help screen. Call up Help by pressing

F3   The Help screen gives you two ways of reaching further Help screens

Pressing an alphabetic character presents a screen with commands that begin with that letter. Pressing a *U*, for example, tells you how to underline and undelete. Pressing the function key with or without pressing the Alt, Ctrl, or Shift keys displays information about the function of the key combination pressed. You are invited to press

◄⌐   Enter key, to exit Help

SAVING AND BACKING UP YOUR FILE

When your document has been completed, save your file by pressing

F10   Function key F10, the Save Files key for saving a document. Since the file was saved before, the name of the file, MEMO, appears automatically.

◄┘   Enter, to save your file

Y   Yes, to replace the old, uncorrected document with the new, revised version of MEMO

     Whenever you are asked to replace a previously existing file, if you answer *Y*, the new file (the one you have been working on) replaces or overwrites the old file. Once overwritten, the old file cannot be recovered. Respond with *N* if you wish to save the old file.

     Save your file again on your backup diskette by removing the files diskette from drive A and replacing it with your backup diskette. Save the file to the backup diskette with the same keystrokes.

PRINTING YOUR FILE

Now that the editing of the memorandum is finished and it has been saved, print out the document. In the next chapter you will revise and add text to the memorandum. To print out the file, check to see that the printer is turned on, displays either *on-line* or *select,* and has paper. Then press

Shift-F7   Shift and function key F7 pressed together, Print, to obtain the Print menu shown in Figure 1-7.

```
Print

     1 - Full Document
     2 - Page
     3 - Document on Disk
     4 - Control Printer
     5 - Multiple Pages
     6 - View Document
     7 - Initialize Printer



Options

     S - Select Printer              Epson LQ-500
     B - Binding Offset              0"
     N - Number of Copies            1
     U - Multiple Copies Generated by   WordPerfect
     G - Graphics Quality            Medium
     T - Text Quality                High






Selection: 0
```

Figure 1-7. Print Menu

1   Numeral *1* (or *F*) to print the full document

EXITING WORDPERFECT

Exit WordPerfect by pressing

F7   Function key F7, the Exit key. You see the prompt

                    Save Document? (Y/N) Yes (No)

N   No. Do not save your file again since it was saved just before printing. You see the prompt

                    Exit WP? (Y/N) No

Y   Yes, to exit WordPerfect. You could respond *N* to clear the screen and to begin typing another document

   In the sequence just described you saved your file first with the F10 key. The F10 key does not exit you from WordPerfect. Then you exited with the F7 key. When you wish to save your file, you may choose to press the F7 key first. Since this key asks you to save your file before exiting, you can avoid using the F10 at all.

CONFIRMING THE PRESENCE OF THE FILE

When the DOS prompt returns, you can confirm that the file was saved by entering

dir   a:

to see the response

        Volume in drive A has no label
        Directory of A:
        MEMO   1343 2-15-89 1:07a
        ** 1 File(s)   360448 bytes free**

You can go on with other computing activities at this point or you can turn the computer off.

EXERCISES

A.   Create the following letter, just as written, with the filename A:PLAINSMN. Bear in mind that the wrapped lines of your text may prove to be of different length than shown here.

May 19, 1990

Charles D. May
Editor, Daily Plainsman
Mountsville, IA 97673

Dear Mr. May:

I am a freshman at the state university this yaer. My major is journalizm. Professor Margaret Scotte who was a teacher of yours suggested that I contact you about the possibility of obtaing a summer job with your newspaper.

Thus far, I have taken two English composition courses and Jour. 200, Newspaper Writing. I especially ejnoy preparing human interest articles. Three of my class assignments have been published in our school newspaper. Dr. Scotte said that she would be happy to be a reference for me if you wished to contact her.

Iwill retrun to Mountsville for summer vacation on June 2nd. I will contact you then to see if any opening exist.

Sincerely,

Milton Morehoutte
Box 123,
Duffy Dormitory
State University
Anytown, IA 97621

After you have created the file, print it. Then make the following changes:

1. Insert
   --a blank space between *I* and *will* on the first line of the third paragraph,
   --*in* in the word *obtaing,*
   --the sentence, *I received an A in all three courses.* after sentence 1 of paragraph 2,
   --the sentence, *I will be available from June 2 to Sept. 3.* between the two sentences in paragraph 3,
   --the student's telephone number *(303-566-7899)* after his address,
   --an *s* after *opening,* in the last paragraph,
   --a comma before and after the phrase, *who was a teacher of yours.*
2. Replace
   --the lowercase *s* and *u* in *state university* with uppercase letters,
   --the *z* with an *s* in *journalizm,*
   --the words *your newspaper* in the last line of the first paragraph with *the Daily Plainsman,*
   --the word *happy* with *pleased.*
3. Separate the sentence beginning, *Dr. Scotte said . . .* into a separate paragraph by inserting a hard return.
4. Insert tabs at the beginning of each paragraph.
5. Fix any remaining errors in the document.

B.   Create the following letter with the filename A:JOHNSON as it is written:

February 19, 1991

Jack Johnson
Acme Campers and Trailers
270 East Market Street
Warbuck, CA 27779

Dear Mr. Warbuck:

This letter is to advice you that Ms. Marsha Dean who has been
your acount representative for the last four years hsa been
promoted to the position of Vice President for Design and
Production. In her new position, Ms. Dean will be able to apply
the knowledge about the recreational vehicle retail sales market
to the introduction of a new product line. The phaeton line of
camper tops to be announced shrotly will be trend setters for
sure.

Mr. Hugh Falkner will be assigned to service your account as of
June 21, 1987. Mr. Falkner has been with the company for six
years and has a through knowledge of the campout products line of
camper tops and trailers. He has owned his own camping supplies
company, so I am sure that he will be able to solve you problems.

Pleaselet us know if their is any way by which we can sevre you
better.

Sincerely,

Mary Muldowner,
Pressident,
Campout Products

        After you have created the file, print it. Then make the following changes:
1. Insert
        --a blank space between *Please* and *let* in the last sentence,
        --the second *c* in the word *acount*,
        --the sentence *Mr. Falkner can be reached at 205-566-7672.* after the single sentence in paragraph
        3,
        --the phrase, *I am pleased to announce that* as an introduction to the first sentence in paragraph 2,
        --an *o* in the word *through* to make it *thorough*,
        --an *r* after *you* in *you problems*,
        --the word *quickly* before the period, but after the word *problems*.

2. Replace
> --the lowercase *c* and *p* in *campout products* with uppercase letters,
> --the *c* with an *s* in *advice*,
> --the lowercase *p* in *phaeton* with an uppercase *P*,
> --*their* with *there* in the last sentence,
> --the word *sure* at the end of paragraph 1 with *certain*,
> --the spelling of the name *Falkner* with the spelling *Faulkner* throughout.

3. Delete
> --the extra *s* in *Pressident*,
> --the phrase *line of* in the second paragraph (and add an apostrophe to the end of *Products*).

4. Insert tab markers at the beginning of each paragraph.

5. Fix any remaining errors in the document.

C. Create another memorandum for Mr. Black in which progress in a new sales campaign is reported to the president of XYZ Corporation.

D. Write a letter home carefully explaining to your parents how the costs at college have risen dramatically and asking for money.

E. Begin writing your next term paper with WordPerfect.

F. Prepare a one-page biographical sketch of yourself.

Chapter 2

Some Next Steps in Word Processing

Chapter Outline

It is a rare document that can be created and printed without revision. The memorandum created in the last chapter was short and simple. It could have been written in one session by a person familiar with word processing. Often, however, a document is typed by one person and edited by another. Revisions made by the editor might be made in the file by still another person. This chapter extends your knowledge of WordPerfect by showing you how to:

1. Retrieve a previously created file;
2. Add text to that file;
3. Use the search and the search-and-replace commands;
4. Use boldfacing and underlining fonts;
5. Modify the margins and tabs for your document.

RETRIEVING A FILE

To retrieve your memorandum, boot your computer or, if it is already running, obtain the C> prompt. Place your files diskette in drive A. Then enter

cd wp	To change the default directory to the directory holding WordPerfect
wp	To load WordPerfect from the hard drive. Use the F7 (Exit key) to clear the screen if necessary. To bring your file MEMO into WordPerfect, make sure that the work screen is clear.
F5	Function key F5, the List Files key
=	Equal sign, to change the default directory
a:	To change the default directory to drive A
◄⤶	Enter key, to accept A:*.* as the default drive and directory from which to list files
◄⤶	Enter key, to see the names of the files on the default drive and directory
→,←,↑,↓	Arrow keys, as necessary, to highlight the filename MEMO and to see the List Files screen that looks similar to Figure 2-1.
1	To retrieve your file and place the cursor at the top of the document. The file should be identical to the file that you saved and printed out in Chapter 1: An Easy Entry into Word Processing. You are ready to alter the document.

```
03-03-90  01:54p              Directory A:\*.*
Document size:        0  Free:    320,512 Used:        1,618    Files:        1

.    Current    <Dir>                 |  ..    Parent    <Dir>
  WP2-4    .      1,618  03-03-90 01:38p















1 Retrieve; 2 Delete; 3 Move/Rename; 4 Print; 5 Short/Long Display;
6 Look; 7 Other Directory; 8 Copy; 9 Find; N Name Search: 6
```

Figure 2-1. The List Files Screen

This procedure is useful when you are not sure of the filename of a document that you wish to retrieve. Sometimes when you do know the filename, it is faster to press Shift and F10 simultaneously. You are prompted for the name of the file you wish to retrieve. If necessary, you can expand the filename by including a directory and pathname.

The List Files screen has many uses in addition to retrieving files. By highlighting a file's name you can:

1.   Delete a file from your disk,

2. Rename a file or move it to a different disk or directory if you are using directories,
3. Print a file from disk without accessing the Control Printer options,
4. Look inside a file without retrieving it in order to see whether its contents are what you expected,
5. Change directories if you are using directories,
6. Copy a file to another disk,
7. Reduce the listing of filenames to only those files that contain a target word,
8. Locate a file in the listing by typing its name letter by letter until WordPerfect highlights the filename you desire.

Mr. Black has decided to have his document edited to look as it does in Figure 2-2.

EDITING TEXT

The sentence added between paragraphs is to be entered now. Underlines will be added later. Using the cursor movement keys noted in the last chapter, move your cursor to the blank line currently separating the two paragraphs. Enter

◄⌐   Enter key, to enter another blank line above the cursor

Tab   Tab key, to indent the first word. Then type:

This is the only department that does not have a microcomputer for word and data processing operations.
◄⌐   Enter key, to introduce another blank line

Practice using the cursor movement commands listed in Figure 1-3. After a short while, believe it or not, the commands begin to come to you with no more thought than it takes to press alphabetic character keys.
Now move to the last character of the last paragraph.

Home,Home,↓ Home key pressed twice, followed by Down arrow, to move to the last sentence

Now press

◄⌐   Enter key twice, to end the paragraph and to insert a blank line between it and the
              paragraph being added

Tab   Tab key, to indent the next paragraph

An assessment of the needs of our department completed by M. Brown has determined that we need a system with these components:
◄⌐   Enter key. Do not put in the blank line now.

Date: September 15, 1991

To: T. L. White

Fr: F. Y. Black, Director, Marketing and Sales

Re: Departmental Computer Equipment

It has become increasingly clear that <u>our department could save the company money</u> in a number of areas if it had immediate access to a microcomputer. I will cite 3 instances in which we could have done a better job and could have been more productive. J. Grey produced a 50-page report for the XYZ Company that had to be retyped 3 times as it was revised and improved. We needed to produce 3 graphic displays for a presentation to the ABC Corporation and were told by the Graphics Department that they could not be made available until 2 weeks after they were needed. Finally, I had to produce a projection of our expenditures for the next 3-year planning period. Without access to a spreadsheet accounting program, this 3-hour task took a full day.

<u>This is the only department that does not have a microcomputer for word and data processing operations</u>.

I believe that the Marketing and Sales Department should be allowed to acquire a microcomputer with appropriate spreadsheet, graphics, and word processing software. M. Brown in our department has taken several computer courses and workshops. She feels that she can provide the training required by our staff. With your approval and budgetary support, we can maintain corporate profitability.

An assessment of the needs of our department completed by M. Brown has determined that we need a system with these components:

Personal computer, 640KB, hard drive	$2,000.00
Laser printer	1,500.00
Plotter	2,000.00
Software	1,500.00
Computer Furniture	675.00
Supplies, cables, power protector	950.00
TOTAL	$8,625.00

I shall set up an appointment with you for next week to discuss our request.

Figure 2-2.

TABS AND RULERS

You have already used the Tab key to indent paragraphs. WordPerfect has default tab settings (settings which it uses if you don't deliberately use different settings) which are currently hidden from view. To enter the list of equipment to be purchased and the prices for that equipment, it is awkward to have to keep tabbing. Setting a simpler tab settings ruler would be more efficient. It would also be helpful if the numbers being typed were automatically lined up on the decimal point. To see and to change the current settings in use, press

Shift-F8   Shift pressed simultaneously with function key F8, the Format key, to see the Format menu, which displays the options for setting Line, Page, Document, and Other formatting options shown in Figure 2-3.

```
Format

     1 - Line
               Hyphenation               Line Spacing
               Justification             Margins Left/Right
               Line Height               Tab Set
               Line Numbering            Widow/Orphan Protection

     2 - Page
               Center Page (top to bottom)   Page Numbering
               Force Odd/Even Page           Paper Size/Type
               Headers and Footers           Suppress
               Margins Top/Bottom

     3 - Document
               Display Pitch             Redline Method
               Initial Codes/Font        Summary

     4 - Other
               Advance                   Overstrike
               Conditional End of Page   Printer Functions
               Decimal Characters        Underline Spaces/Tabs
               Language

Selection: 0
```

Figure 2-3. Format Screen

1   Numeral *1* (or *L*) to see the Line Format menu shown in Figure 2-4

```
Format: Line

    1 - Hyphenation                    No

    2 - Hyphenation Zone - Left        10%
                         Right         4%

    3 - Justification                  Full

    4 - Line Height                    Auto

    5 - Line Numbering                 No

    6 - Line Spacing                   1

    7 - Margins - Left                 1"
                  Right                1"

    8 - Tab Set                        Rel: -1", every 0.5"

    9 - Widow/Orphan Protection        No



Selection: 0
```

Figure 2-4. Line Format Screen

8   To display the current tab settings. The ruler looks like that shown in Figure 2-5a.

```
L...L...L...L...L...L...L...L...L...L...L...L...L...L...L...
!    ^    !    ^    !    ^    !    ^    !    ^    !    ^    !    ^    !    ^
0"        +1"       +2"       +3"       +4"       +5"       +6"       +7"
Delete EOL (clear tabs); Enter Number (set tab); Del (clear tab);
Type: Left: Center: Right: Decimal: .= Dot Leader: Press Exit when done.
```

Figure 2-5a. Tab Setting Prompt

Tab markers are, by default, preset at every 1/2 inch and displayed as *L*s. On the second line vertical markers (|) indicate full inch increments and carets (^) designate half-inch increments. Numbers on the next line indicate the relative distance a point is from the current left margin. The numbering begins with 0 inch. If you press and hold down the Left arrow key, the positions from minus one inch to zero inch show also. Within a document, pressing the Tab key moves the cursor from tab setting to tab setting. If the cursor is at the last tab marker on a line, pressing the Tab key does not move the cursor.

There are seven types of tab settings. The *L* setting left-justifies text that is typed after the Tab key is struck. A *C* centers the text on either side of the tab. An *R* right-justifies, or inserts text to the left of the tab. Entering a *D* for a decimal tab justifies the numbers on the decimal point contained in the numbers typed. Typing the period option before typing the *R*, *L*, or *D* causes WordPerfect to insert dots up to the tabbed text, rather than blanks. Look at exercises C, D, and E at the end of this chapter to see how these tab settings function.

To remove a tab, move the cursor to that tab marker with the arrow keys and press the Delete key. All tabs from the location of the cursor to the right can be deleted by entering Control-End. Tabs can be added either by entering the position in tenths of an inch (for instance 1.4 for a tab marker at the fourth period after 1 inch) where the tab is to appear and pressing the Enter key, or by moving the cursor to the correct location and typing the tab letter. Using these adjustment commands, alter the settings to look like those shown in Figure 2-5b.

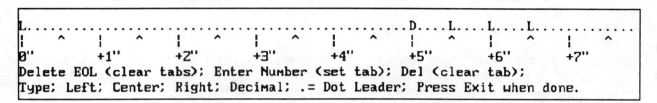

Figure 2-5b. Revised Tab Settings

Save the setting by pressing

F7	Function key F7, the Exit key, to exit the tab setting menu
◄┘	Enter key, to exit the Line Format menu
◄┘	Enter key, to exit the Format menu

When you press the Tab key, the cursor moves to the next L-marked tab setting and a tab code is inserted in the document. Any characters you type in after the Tab key appear after the tab marker.

The ruler you created affects the formatting of all the text inserted below the insertion of these settings into the document. It has no effect on those portions of the document which appear above the inserted tab ruler code. Similarly, any code entered is entered at the location of the cursor and affects all text from that point on. Sometimes a code does not appear to have an effect because another code is to the right or below that code, thereby canceling the effect of the first code. Press

◄┘	Enter key, to insert another blank line
Tab	Tab key, to insert a tab and to move the cursor to the tab marker
Personal computer, 640KB, hard drive	
	The item recommended for purchase
Tab	Tab key. Notice the prompt "Align char = ." that shows that the decimal point is used to align the numbers.
$2,000.00	The cost of the computer
◄┘	Enter key, to start a new line

Enter the remaining computer components and their prices as they appear in Figure 2-2 by pressing the Tab key, typing the item name, pressing Tab again, typing the cost for the item, and pressing the Enter key. Notice how the numbers align themselves when you press the period. Repeat this sequence until the list is finished.

Enter the final sentence.

USING SPECIAL FONTS

Underlining

Two sections of the text in the memorandum are to be underlined. WordPerfect enhances the impact of your writing with these styles of printer output called fonts. One method of including special fonts is to block the text to be underlined. Place the cursor under the *o* in *our* in paragraph 1 and press

Alt-F4	The Block key, to mark the beginning of the block. Notice the flashing prompt "Block on."
Ctrl→	Seven Control-Right Arrow key combinations, to highlight seven words and the trailing blank space
←	Left Arrow, to remove the blank space from the block
F8	The Underline key. The appearance of the letters on the screen change to reflect the use of the underline font and the block highlighting is removed.

Place your cursor under the *T* in *This* at the beginning of the second paragraph and type

Alt-F4	The Block key, to mark the beginning of the block
↓	Down Arrow, to highlight the entire first line
End	To highlight the entire second line
F8	The Underline key. After the blocked text is underlined, the blocking is removed.

Bolding

The F6 key is the Bold key. It can be employed in the same way as the Underline key. The F6 and F8 keys can be used together to both bold and underline text.

In the two examples used in the memorandum, underlining was introduced after the text was typed. The underlining was applied to a highlighted block. Underlining and bolding can be started during the entry of text. As you are typing, press the appropriate function key or keys (F6 or F8), and continue typing. When you wish to return to normal type, press the same function key(s) to return to normal type.

You can make the same font changes plus numerous others involving the size and appearance of text by using the Font key (Ctrl-F8). In the case of bolding and underlining as here, the effect is the same in one less keystroke by applying the techniques completed above. In a later chapter, however, the Font key is shown to be helpful for managing other kinds of font changes.

REVEAL CODES

You can usually tell when text has been bolded, underlined, centered, or otherwise altered in appearance by some code that has been inserted. What happens if you decide to change some of these codes? How do you find them? The Alt-F3 key is called the Reveal Codes key. By pressing this key combination you can open a window that lets you see the text and any codes that have been entered. Place your cursor under the first character of the third paragraph and press

Alt-F3	Alternate and function key F3 pressed simultaneously, the Reveal Codes key, to open a window that, in part, shows,

```
     I believe that the Marketing and Sales Department should be
C:\WP51\WPFIGS\WP3-2                            Doc 1 Pg 1 Ln 5" Pos 1.5"
{    ▲     ▲    ▲    ▲    ▲    ▲    ▲    ▲    ▲    ▲    ▲    }    ▲    ▲
[Tab][UND]This is the only department that does not have a microcomputer[SRt]
for word and data processing operations.[und][HRt]
[HRt]
[Tab]I believe that the Marketing and Sales Department should be[SRt]
```

Figure 2-6. Reveal Codes

The left brace shows where the left margin is located and the triangles show where the tabs are set for this block of text. **[UND]** is the code for begin underlining. **[und]** closes the underlining. **[Tab]** shows where the tab was inserted by pressing the Tab key. The cursor, located on the **[UND]** code, can be moved with the arrow keys and with any other keystrokes that normally move the cursor. **[SRt]** represents a soft return entered by WordPerfect and **[Hrt]** represents a hard return entered by pressing the Enter key. You can type characters and in fact use virtually all of WordPerfect's features in the Reveal Codes mode. The Delete and Backspace keys can be used to delete characters and codes at the cursor and to the left of the cursor, respectively. Delete any codes that are on your screen that do not appear in the sample shown above. To remove the Reveal Codes window, press

Alt-F3   The Reveal Codes key, to remove the window

SEARCHING

Forward Search

Often, changes to be made in a document are far apart. Visually searching for an incorrectly spelled word or for a phrase can be tedious. You can move directly to a specific word or string of characters with the WordPerfect search command.

Move to the top of the file with the Home, Home, Up Arrow key combination. Suppose that you wished to move to the word *clear* on the first line of the first paragraph. If you press F2 you receive the prompt,

-> Srch:

The arrow indicates that the search is to be started from the location of the cursor and proceeds to the end of the document. You do not have to be at the top of the document, but the search stops at the bottom of the document. Thus, a search may not find a character string you are looking for if it is located above the cursor. The cursor is requesting the entry of a string of (one or more) characters you wish to search for. Type

F2   The Search key
clear   The word to be searched for
F2   The Forward Search key, or the Escape key, to begin the search. Pressing this key advances you to the first occurrence of the word being searched for. The cursor stops at the last letter of the search string.

Press F2 twice more. WordPerfect uses *clear* as the default search string because it was the last string of characters searched for. Since this is the only occurrence of the word *clear,* you receive a message

* Not Found *

Repeat the search process with a different character string. Return the cursor to the top of the document and type

F2   The Forward Search key
the   The word to be searched for; *the* replaces *clear*
F2   To begin the search

Continue locating the string *the* by pressing pairs of F2 keys. After the fifth search, however, you find the character string *the*, but the entire word is actually *they*. WordPerfect located the character string *the*, not the word *the*. Because WordPerfect finds the precise string of characters you type, it could find *the* in *other*, *either*, or many other words. The shorter or more common the search string is, the more likely it is that WordPerfect will find many words in addition to the word you are actually seeking.

Reverse Search

You can use the simultaneous pressing of the Shift and F2 keys to reverse the direction of the search. The arrow in the prompt shows the direction of the search. Press

Shift-F2   The Reverse Search key
F2   To start the search

Press this key combination until there are no more occurrences of *the* to be found.

Finding Words

Return to the top of the document (Home, Home, Up Arrow), then press the F2 key to do a forward search. This time type a blank space with the space bar before and after the characters *the* so that the prompt line reads

-> Srch: the   The word *the* preceded and followed by spaces
        ^   ^

This defines the word more accurately. The space in front prevents WordPerfect from finding *the* in such words as *bathe* or *lathe* since a blank does not match any other character. The space behind prevents WordPerfect from finding the search string in words such as *they* or *these*. Press the F2 key until the last *the* is found to confirm that WordPerfect finds only *the* as a word.

Three helpful strategies for searching for a word without having to locate intermediate occurrences of the same search string are:

1.   Include the spaces on either side of the word to avoid finding the string being sought inside of other words.
2.   Don't search for a common word, but search for an uncommon word in the same line. For instance, if you wished to change *the aliens* to *those aliens* don't search for *the*, search for *aliens*.
3.   Search for more than one word. The search string can be *the XYZ*, which occurs much less frequently than the word *the* alone.

FILE COPIES VERSUS FILE ORIGINALS

When you retrieved a file, such as MEMO in this chapter, WordPerfect created a copy of the file on the diskette in RAM. As you make changes to the document you see on the screen, you are changing the copy, not the original. This has several important implications.

First, the good news. You may intentionally retrieve a file and not intend to save it. Suppose you submitted a magazine article for publication and you decided that the file could, with editing, make a chapter in a book you were starting. You don't want to change the original, but neither do you want to have to retype it just to have a different filename. You should retrieve the file as usual, make the changes, but save the file under a new name to protect the original file and to avoid extensive retyping.

More good news. You may execute a command that has widespread and deleterious results. It may be too time-consuming to undo the changes already made. For instance, you may have deleted the word *the* throughout a one hundred-page document. If you don't save the corrupted file, the original is still there. Discard the corrupted file and start over with the original.

Now the bad news. If your computer loses power or if you turn it off before you have saved your document, the changes are lost. Save files regularly! If you make a disastrous mistake, you can return to a relatively current original. If the file is not saved periodically, you may have to make the changes again.

SAVING UNDER A NEW FILENAME

Normally, when you edit a file you save the file under its original name. However, you may sometimes wish to save the file under a different name. By changing the name a new file is created, and the file with the filename used originally is left unchanged. The memorandum that has been edited and improved can, for instance, be saved as MEMO2, leaving the file MEMO unaltered. Do this by pressing

F10	The Save File key, to display the prompt
	Document to be saved: A:\MEMO
MEMO2	The new name for the file
◄┘	Enter key, to complete the renaming procedure

No confirmation command is requested since this is the first time that the file is being saved as MEMO2. Confirmation is only requested when the filename exists already and WordPerfect seeks to avoid the unnecessary altering of a file that should be left intact.

BACKING UP YOUR FILE

Back up the file by replacing the diskette in drive A with your backup files diskette and entering

F10	The key for saving a document
◄┘	Enter key. The remembered filename, MEMO2, is used again.

PRINTING

This file is complete. To print out the file, type _____ SHIFT - F7

Shift-F7   The Print key, to display the Print menu

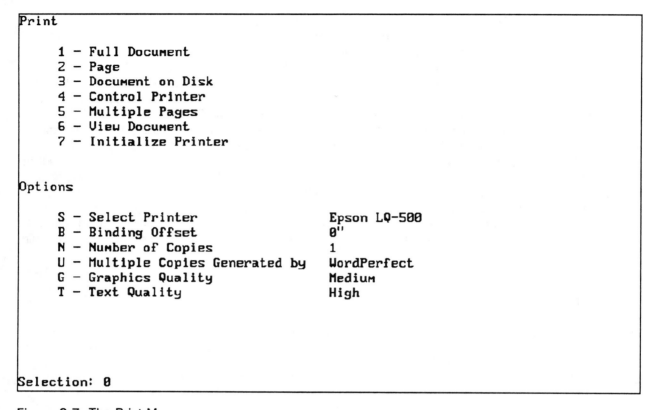

```
Print

     1 - Full Document
     2 - Page
     3 - Document on Disk
     4 - Control Printer
     5 - Multiple Pages
     6 - View Document
     7 - Initialize Printer


Options

     S - Select Printer            Epson LQ-500
     B - Binding Offset            0"
     N - Number of Copies          1
     U - Multiple Copies Generated by   WordPerfect
     G - Graphics Quality          Medium
     T - Text Quality              High




Selection: 0
```

Figure 2-7. The Print Menu

1   To print the document

SEARCHING AND REPLACING

The previously described search procedure is useful for changing one occurrence of a word. Frequently, there is a need to change many occurrences of a word or phrase. For example, it may not be until after a paper has been completed that it is found that key board should be keyboard or that back space should be backspace. The search-and-replace command makes the desired changes throughout the file where these corrections are to be made. There are two variations on the search-and-replace technique. Both variations begin with pressing the Alt and F2 keys.

　　You will be making many changes to the memorandum that you have created. The file will not be saved after the changes have been made. Do not worry, for the changes which you are making for illustrative purposes will not damage the properly constructed memorandum, MEMO2.

Replacement with Confirmation

There are three occurrences of the phrase *our department* in the memorandum. Suppose that Mr. Black decided that this phrase should be changed to read *the Marketing and Sales Department.* In a short memorandum like this, visually locating and exchanging the two phrases would not be difficult. It would be difficult if the file were twenty pages long and contained fifteen instances of the phrase.

Press the Home, Home, and Up Arrow keys to move to the top of the file. To have WordPerfect make the changes throughout the document, press

Alt-F2 The Search-and-Replace key. You receive the prompt

w/Confirm? No (Yes)

Y Yes, to indicate that you wish to see each string before the replacement operation is carried out

our department The new search string. WordPerfect remembers the previous search string which is replaced by *our department*.

F2 Function key F2, to enter the search string

the Marketing and Sales Department
The replacement string

F2 Function key F2, to enter the replacement string. WordPerfect finds the first occurrence of the string *our department*, and prompts you with

Confirm? No (Yes)

Y Yes, replace the string. WordPerfect makes the change and continues by locating the next occurrence of *our department*.

N No, do not replace the second occurrence of the string (to demonstrate that you have the option of making the change if you wish). The search continues.

Y Yes, replace the third occurrence of the string. Wait for the *** Please Wait *** message to disappear before proceeding.

Each time a *Y* or an *N* is pressed WordPerfect makes a change, if called for, and locates the next occurrence of the search string. If you do not wish the replacement to occur, press *N* and the phrase remains as it was.

Try the search-and-replace operation again. Press the Home, Home, Up Arrow key combination to go to the top of the file. Press

Alt-F2 The Search and Replace key, to start the search-and-replace operation
Y To request that each change be confirmed first
produc Search for the string, *produc*. The search string finds *produce, produced,* and *productive*
F2 Function key F2
creat The replacement string
F2 Function key F2
N No, do not make the replacement since the word would become *creattive.* (Do you see why?)

Continue the process of alternately replacing and not replacing the character strings until the last instance of *produc* has been located and changed.

Cancel Command

You can terminate the search-and-replace operation at any time by pressing the F1, or Cancel, key. The F1 key cancels nearly every operation that has been started in WordPerfect, not just the search-and-replace operation.

Replacement without Confirmation

The ability to see each location of the search string is useful, but you may wish to be able to effect all changes immediately and without individual prompts. There are four occurrences of *we.* Exchange the string *the Marketing and Sales Department* for *we* in one operation by pressing

Alt-F2   To search and replace. You receive the prompt

               w/Confirm? No (Yes)

N   No, or press Enter key, to indicate that you do not wish to see each string before the replacement operation is carried out

we   The new search string. Note the spaces on either side of the word, *we.*
^   ^   WordPerfect remembers the previous search string, *produc*
F2   Function key F2, to enter the search string

the Marketing and Sales Department
               The replacement string, with spaces on both sides of the replacement string

You must include the spaces in front of *the* and after *Department,* since the opening and closing were included in the search string. If you do not include the spaces here, the opening and closing words are united with the words on both sides of the search string.

F2   Function key F2, to enter the replacement string. WordPerfect finds all occurrences of the string we and makes changes wherever possible, including the *we* in *week* and *were* if you did not put spaces around *we.*

This process is often referred to as a global replacement. Figure 2-8 identifies the search and replace options.

KEY(S)	ACTION
F2	Search
Alt-F2	Search and Replace
Shift-F2	Reverse Search
F1	Cancel/Undelete

Figure 2-8. Search and Replace Options

QUITTING WITHOUT SAVING YOUR FILE

You have made several changes to your memorandum. It is not uncommon that global changes create more difficulties than they solve. If that happens, as is the case now, you should not save the corrupted file as MEMO2 because the altered document replaces the good version that was saved just before the printing operation. Press

F7	The Exit key
N	No, do not save the file
Y	Yes, exit WordPerfect

The prompt for DOS appears quickly, and the disk drive light does not go on. These are two indications that the corrupted file was not written to disk.

EXERCISES

A. Retrieve the letter, PLAINSMN, and
    --underline the name of the newspaper, *Daily Plainsman*,
    --search for every occurrence of the letters *ou*,
    Save the file and then,
    --replace every instance of *ti* with *xx*,
    --replace every other instance of *al* with *qq*,
    --quit without replacing the good version of PLAINSMN with this corrupted version.

B. Retrieve the letter, JOHNSON, and
    --use the F6 key to make bold the first appearances of the names, *Ms. Marsha Dean,* and *Mr. Hugh Faulkner,*
    --underline the phrase, *solve your problems quickly.*
    Save the file and then,
    --search for all instances of the word *the,*
    --search for all instances of the character string, *the,*
    --change all instances of *am* to *xx,*
    --change every other instance of *ou* to *in,*
    --quit without replacing the good version of JOHNSON with this corrupted version.

C. Create a tab settings ruler that uses Left (L), Right (R), and Decimal (D) tab markers to set up a table as follows:

Item	Number	Amount
Pencils	127	44.45
Pens	89	114.81
Banners	20	119.00
Pads	230	181.70
Note Books	75	446.25
Paper Packets	1250	2362.50
Total		3268.71

D. Create a tab settings ruler that uses Left (L), Center (C), and Decimal (D) tabs to set up a table as follows:

```
Company                     Sales Person        Amount

ABC Company                     Shaw             192.15
Real Thing Graphics             Wells           2683.20
Tinker & Tailor               Brownley          4780.00
Marjoram & Basil, Inc.          Wells             16.50
Pragmatic Exercise Inc.         Doe              165.78
Mallory & Mallory               Shaw             232.33
```

E. Create a tab settings ruler that uses Left (L) and Dotted Left (period, L) tabs to produce part of a table of contents as follows:

```
I.
INTRODUCTION TO COMPUTERS                               Pg
A Short History of Computers . . . . . . . . . . . . . . 1
Computers in Society . . . . . . . . . . . . . . . . . . 6
The Computer Market . . . . . . . . . . . . . . . . . . 10
You and the Computer  . . . . . . . . . . . . . . . . . 16

II.
WORD PROCESSING
What Is Word Processing?  . . . . . . . . . . . . . . . 17
Introductory Concepts . . . . . . . . . . . . . . . . . 20
```

WordPerfect has another, more flexible approach to creating tables of contents that is especially useful for long documents that change frequently. Check the WordPerfect Manual for information about this feature.

Chapter 3

Word Processing: A Résumé

The next document you create will be a résumé that requires the use of additional features of WordPerfect. In this chapter you will:

1.   Use stored format settings that help you to prepare résumés;
2.   Insert font changes as you enter text;
3.   Center individual lines and blocks of text between page margins;
4.   Move and delete blocks of text;
5.   Change uppercase letters to lowercase and vice versa.

Résumés are important documents for individuals since they are often a key component of the applicant screening process used by employers. Résumés are intended to provide up-to-date information about candidates. Consequently, résumés change each time the person's background changes, a condition that encourages the use of a word processor. The structure of a résumé is quite different from many other documents. This structure requires the use of different tab settings than you might use for a memorandum or a book. The résumé you create now will be modified significantly to illustrate how major changes can be made in a document.

Figure 3-1 is a résumé which a student believes will be helpful in applying for jobs after graduation.

HARRIET HARTLEY

22 Elm Street
West Washington, NV 89888
707-555-5665

PROFESSIONAL GOAL: To work within a challenging company and to interact with the public in a problem-solving environment.

EDUCATION: **WEST WASHINGTON HIGH SCHOOL**
2100 Parker Drive
West Washington, NV 89888
Academic Diploma, 1987

UNIVERSITY OF THE MOUNTAINS
Lake Hicauma, CA 12880
Bachelor of Science
Business Administration
1991

WORK EXPERIENCE: **SMITH & BAKER RETAILERS**
1 Black Oak Lane
West Washington, NV 89888
Assistant Buyer
Summer, 1988 - 1990

UNIVERSITY OF THE MOUNTAINS
Lake Hicauma, CA 12880
Student Activities Programming Assistant
Academic Year, 1989 - 1991

FLOWERS ARE FOREVER
Market Square
West Washington, NV 89888
Sales Clerk - Floral Arranger
Academic Year, 1987 - 1991

AWARDS AND
SCHOOL ACTIVITIES: Varsity Basketball, Omega Phi Beta, Outstanding Student Volunteer, President's Honor Roll, Crisis Call Volunteer.

SPECIAL SKILLS: Programming in BASIC and Pascal, Spanish (3 yrs.)

Figure 3-1. Résumé

In comparison with memoranda created in prior chapters, this document is considerably harder to construct. In developing the first draft of the résumé you will:

1. Create and use new tabs settings and new margins settings;
2. Enter boldfaced characters while you type;
3. Center text on a line.

FORMAT SETTINGS

People who work with word processors frequently find that many documents are similarly structured. In a university, a secretary may find that manuscripts in one discipline follow certain stylistic expectations (e.g., margins, line spacing, use of footnotes, etc.). A budget officer in a corporation may create project budgets with tables that use the same tab stops and margins. Students may find that term papers at their college are restricted to a particular style manual.

When there are recurring guidelines for the production of documents, it is often desirable to create a partial file with consistent line and page formatting commands that can be made a part of documents as soon as you begin to create them. You have seen that the Shift-F8 (Format) key can be used to modify tab settings, for example, once you have started a document. If tab settings change often within a document, modifying this ruler over and over takes unnecessary time, and your modifications may be inconsistent within documents and from one document to the next. You can create and save tab marker rulers and page format settings that are appropriate for the kinds of documents you work with. The resulting set of formatting values, called a WordPerfect Style (Alt-F8), can be retrieved at the start of each document that uses these settings.

Load WordPerfect

Follow the instructions given in earlier chapters for loading WordPerfect and for making drive A the default drive.

Defining the Style

First you must open a file that stores the codes used to facilitate the development of résumés. This set of codes is stored in a file called a style sheet. Press

Alt-F8   Alternate and F8 key, to display the first Styles menu. WordPerfect may display a list of predesigned styles.

```
Styles

   Name          Type        Description

   Bibliogrphy   Paired      Bibliography
   Doc Init      Paired      Initialize Document Style
   Document      Outline     Document Style
   Pleading      Open        Header for numbered pleading paper
   Right Par     Outline     Right-Aligned Paragraph Numbers
   Tech Init     Open        Initialize Technical Style
   Technical     Outline     Technical Document Style

















1 On; 2 Off; 3 Create; 4 Edit; 5 Delete; 6 Save; 7 Retrieve; 8 Update: 1
```

Figure 3-2. Styles Screen

3   To create a style. The Styles: Edit menu shown in Figure 3-3 appears.

```
Styles: Edit

     1 - Name

     2 - Type          Paired

     3 - Description

     4 - Codes

     5 - Enter         HRt
















Selection: 0
```

Figure 3-3. Edit Styles Screen

To define the characteristics of your formatting, press

1	To enter a name for the style
RESUME	The filename
◄┘	Enter key, to accept the filename
2	To declare a type. Paired, the default, refers to formatting of the sort that is always delimited, like boldface in which there is an opening and a closing code. Open refers to formatting codes like tabs and margins that do not require an ending code. The initial résumé settings would be open.
2	To define it as an open type
3	To enter a description of the style. You may use a maximum of fifty-four characters to describe the style. Type in *HARTLEY Resume 6/1/91* as the description.
◄┘	Enter key, to terminate the description
4	To prepare to place the desired formatting codes

At this point you view a split screen nearly identical to the Reveal Codes window, with the cursor positioned in the upper left-hand corner, ready for you to begin placing formatting codes. You accomplish this by entering the appropriate menus and setting the values desired.

Line Formatting

The Line Format key is used to control the appearance of characters on a single line. Line formatting codes will be entered first. Press

Shift-F8	The Format key, to see the Format menu (see Figure 2-3), which displays options for setting Line, Page, Document, and Other types of formatting codes
1	To see the Line Format menu

```
Format: Line

    1 - Hyphenation                        No

    2 - Hyphenation Zone - Left            10%
                          Right            4%

    3 - Justification                      Full

    4 - Line Height                        Auto

    5 - Line Numbering                     No

    6 - Line Spacing                       1

    7 - Margins - Left                     1"
                 Right                     1"

    8 - Tab Set                            Rel: -1", every 0.5"

    9 - Widow/Orphan Protection            No


Selection: 0
```

Figure 3-4. Line Format Screen

8   To receive the tab settings ruler. You are going to change the tab settings to suit the résumé to be constructed. Using the procedures described in the previous chapter, modify the ruler so that it looks like in Figure 3-5.

```
L.........L.............L...L...L...L...L...L...L...L...L...L...
|    ^    |    ^    |    ^    |    ^    |    ^    |    ^    |    ^
0"        +1"       +2"      +3"       +4"      +5"       +6"      +7"
Delete EOL (clear tabs); Enter Number (set tab); Del (clear tab);
Type; Left; Center; Right; Decimal; .= Dot Leader; Press Exit when done.
```

Figure 3-5. Revised Tab Settings

F7   The Exit key, to save the tab settings. You are returned to the Line Format menu.
◄┘   Enter key, to exit the Line Format screen and to return to the Format menu
◄┘   Enter key, to return to the Style version of the Reveal Codes window, to continue entering formatting codes. Notice your tab settings that now appear in the window.

Page Formatting

Whereas the Line Formatting menu gave you options for describing how a single line should be patterned, the Page Format menu options shown in Figure 3-6 allow you to describe how the page should appear.

Shift-F8	To again see the Format menu	
2	To see the Page Format menu shown in Figure 3-6	

```
Format: Page

    1 - Center Page (top to bottom)     No

    2 - Force Odd/Even Page

    3 - Headers

    4 - Footers

    5 - Margins - Top                   1"
                  Bottom                1"

    6 - Page Numbering

    7 - Paper Size                      8.5" x 11"
             Type                       Standard

    8 - Suppress (this page only)



Selection: 0
```

Figure 3-6. Page Format Screen

The settings to be used for the résumé file include only the choices 1, 6, and 8, which are covered shortly. Option 2 forces the number on the current page to be an odd or even number. This permits you, for example, to leave a gap in the numbering of pages to leave room to insert illustrations.

The headers (3) or footers (4) options place the same line of text at the top or bottom, respectively, of each page.

Option 5 is used to set the top and bottom margins in increments of one-hundredths of an inch. By default WordPerfect uses 1-inch margins.

Option 6 allows you to start numbering pages with a number other than 1. This allows you to create a large document, such as a book, in a group of files that can be printed separately and still have the pages numbered correctly. You can also reset a page number within a document. For instance, you may need to skip a page number to allow for a photograph to be inserted in the document.

With option 7 you identify the kind of form you are using for coordination with the form-handling capabilities of your printer.

To make the page format adjustments needed for the résumé file, type

6	To set the position of the page number. If a page number position is not set, page numbers will not be printed. Figure 3-7 shows the Format: Page Numbering menu.

```
Format: Page Numbering

    1 - New Page Number        1

    2 - Page Number Style      ^B

    3 - Insert Page Number

    4 - Page Number Position No page numbering
```
```
Selection: 0
```

Figure 3-7. Page Numbering Menu

4	To set the page number position
6	To place the page numbers at the bottom center of the page. You are returned to the Format: Page Numbering menu.
F1	Function key F1, to return to the Format: Page menu.
1	To center the page from top to bottom. The *No* on the screen changes to *Yes*. Since this format file may be used for very short résumés, this option places the résumé on the page with equally sized top and bottom margins. If the résumé exceeds one page, this code is ignored.
Y	Yes, center the page
8	To enter the Suppress Format menu shown in Figure 3-8

```
Format: Suppress (this page only)

     1 - Suppress All Page Numbering, Headers and Footers

     2 - Suppress Headers and Footers

     3 - Print Page Number at Bottom Center   No

     4 - Suppress Page Numbering              No

     5 - Suppress Header A                    No

     6 - Suppress Header B                    No

     7 - Suppress Footer A                    No

     8 - Suppress Footer B                    No




Selection: 0
```

Figure 3-8. Format Suppress Screen

1	To turn off the page numbering and headers and footers entirely. Since some résumés have only one page, it is unnecessary to include a page number. The No is changed to Yes for options 3-8.
◄┘	Enter key, to exit the Format: Suppress menu
◄┘	Enter key, to exit the Format: Page menu
◄┘	Enter key, to exit the Format menu and return to the Style Codes window. You now view the codes entered: [**Pg Numbering:Bottom Center**] which places the page number in position 6, the bottom center; [**Center Pg**] which centers the page if necessary; [**Suppress:PgNum,HA,HB,FA,FB**] which suppresses the page numbering and headers and footers, if any, on the first page.

Saving the Style

First exit the split screen mode for code/text entry by pressing

F7	To return to the Style: Edit menu
F7	To return to the primary Style menu, where you now see the résumé style listed by name. The highlighting cursor is positioned on the Résumé Style.
6	To save the new Style as the beginning of a Style library
STYLE.LIB	The filename of the Style library
◄┘	Enter key
1	To turn on, or activate the style

Alt-F3	To see that the codes entered have been discarded. You are now at the same point you would be if you had just booted WordPerfect, except that the file STYLE.LIB is now present on your files diskette. From the code [**Open Style:RESUME**] and from the tab settings, you see that the style has been retrieved.
Alt-F3	To remove the Reveal Codes window

Retrieving the Style

Assume that you had, in fact, just entered WordPerfect and that you wished to create a résumé. You would use this file (but don't since you already activated the style in the preceding steps) by typing

Alt-F8	The Style key, displaying the primary Style menu. Move the cursor to the style you want, or
7	To retrieve another Style library desired
STYLE.LIB	The filename of the Style library
◄─┘	Enter key, to display the Style library desired. Position the cursor on RESUME.
1	To turn on, or activate, the style highlighted by the cursor
Alt-F3	To see that the style has been retrieved. Notice the presence of the code [**Open Style:Resume**] and that the codes are in effect (notice the tab settings).
Alt-F3	To remove the Reveal Codes window

The Style feature becomes more powerful as additional styles are stored and grouped in libraries. It then provides substantial screen listings from which a variety of formats and text may be quickly selected for efficient document processing.

LINE AND BLOCK MANIPULATIONS

Centering and Changing the Font Attributes of a Line of Text

WordPerfect keeps track of the document's current margins and the font in effect. It can automatically compute the center point for the current margins and font, and insert text that is requested to be placed in the center. With the cursor at the beginning of the document, create and center the student's name by typing

Ctrl-F8	The Font key, to display the Font menu shown in Figure 3-9.

```
1 Size; 2 Appearance; 3 Normal; 4 Base Font; 5 Print Color: 0
```

Figure 3-9. The Font Menu

1	To display the Size Attribute menu shown in Figure 3-10.

```
1 Suprscpt; 2 Subscpt; 3 Fine; 4 Small; 5 Large; 6 Vry Large; 7 Ext Large: 0
```

Figure 3-10. The Size Attribute Menu

Superscripts and subscripts are included on this menu because these characters are made smaller than regular type. These choices are placed here for that characteristic rather than for the spatial relationship to the type on the Normal line.

5	To select Large font and return to the document
Ctrl-F8	The Font key, to again display the Font menu
2	To display the Appearance Attribute menu shown in Figure 3-11

```
1 Bold 2 Undln 3 Dbl Und 4 Italc 5 Outln 6 Shadw 7 Sm Cap 8 Redln 9 Stkout: 0
```

Figure 3-11. Font Appearance Attributes

1	To select Bold and to return to the document
Shift-F6	Center key, to move the cursor to the center of the line
Caps Lock	Turns entry to uppercase
HARRIET HARTLEY	The student's name
Ctrl-F8	The Font key, to display the Font menu
3	To return the font attributes to Normal (Shortcut: pressing the Right arrow key once at the end of the name also returns attributes to Normal)
◄┘	Enter key twice, to move to the next line of text to be entered
Caps Lock	Turns entry to lowercase

You have learned about several features having to do with the Font key: Ctrl-F8.

1. The primary menu enables you to change the size of the base font.
2. You can change the appearance of the base font.
3. You can return the attributes to Normal.
4. You can change the base font by selecting from the fonts available.
5. You can change to printing colors within a text.

Bolding and underlining, the most commonly used attributes, may be selected in two ways: either through the Font key or by means of the F6 and F8 keys. The effect of these attribute choices depends, of course, upon the capabilities of your printer. You may learn many of your particular printer's capabilities, including its handling of all font attributes, by printing the PRINTER.TST file located on the Conversion WordPerfect diskette.

Marking and Centering a Block of Text

The next three lines of the résumé are not in all uppercase, although individual words do begin with capital letters. You could enter and center these lines individually by pressing Shift-F6 and typing each line separately. This is perfectly acceptable. Another option, however, is to center a block of text.

There are several operations that WordPerfect allows on blocks of text, for instance, on these three lines, on two words, or on five characters. Among these operations are moving the block from one place in the file to another, deleting a block from the file, and copying the block to another location.

For illustrative purposes, type the three lines for the address at the left margin and hit the Enter key at the end of each line. Move the cursor to the left margin of the first of these lines (under the first 2 in 22). Then, type

Alt-F4	The Block marking key
↓	Down arrow twice

End	End key, to fully mark the three lines
Shift-F6	The Centering key
Y	Yes, to center all three lines

Making In-Line Font Changes

When you created documents in the preceding chapters, several lines and phrases were underlined after the text had been entered in the document. In the résumé, the first line, as well as many other lines of text, are bolded. There is no point in typing in text to be bolded, for example, only to have to return to each line later to insert the bolding codes. Boldfacing and all other font/attribute changes can be managed as you are typing, as they were when you typed Harriet Hartley's name, or they can be added to a block of text marked with the Alt-F4 key, as was done with the centering of Harriet Hartley's address.

As you enter lines that are to be bolded, you will generally find it easiest to press the F6 key first, type the text to be bolded next, and press the F6 key again to turn bolding off. If you forget to bold some text, use the blocking procedure to bold it.

If you wish to underline existing text, block the text and use the F8 key instead.

Entering Text

Enter the remainder of the sample résumé after you read the following information.

1. To embolden text, press the F6 key to begin the bolding, type the text, and press F6 to close the bolding. Text that is bolded can cover many lines.
2. Press Caps Lock on for appropriate lines.
3. Use the Tab key to place the cursor in the correct column for the *Education, Work Experience, Awards,* and *Special Skills* entry labels.
4. At the end of each entry line in *Education* and *Work Experience,* press the Enter key twice. The entries for *Professional Goal,* for *Awards and School Activities,* and for *Special Skills* should be broken with an Enter key since word wrap continues text at the left margin.
5. The underlining of text is accomplished in a fashion similar to bolding. Press F8 for underlining before you start typing the words to be underlined. Type the text. Then press F8 when you have typed the last letter to be underlined.

Enter the remainder of the résumé as shown in Figure 3-1. When it looks like the figure, go on to the next section.

SUGGESTIONS FOR MODIFICATION

Harriet Hartley took her résumé to a career planning center for a counselor to critique it. The counselor suggested several changes to the résumé to convey the most important facts about Harriet's background to potential employers more effectively. Among the counselor's suggested changes are:

1. The career goal is too vague. It should be specific to a particular vocation.
2. The work experience section emphasizes the agencies Harriet had worked for, not the positions that she had held.
3. The work experiences for the university and the retail store should be reversed since they are not in descending chronological order.

Deleting Blocks of Text

Harriet decided to change the Professional Goal to *A marketing position in a computer company*. To make this change, place your cursor under the *T* in *To* in the sentence explaining Harriet's professional goal. Delete the two-line entry with a block delete. Press

Alt-F4	The Block key, to begin the marking procedure
↓	Down arrow key twice
End	End key, to highlight the block defining the old sentence describing her career goal
Del	Delete key, to delete the block
Y	Yes, to confirm deletion

The block is deleted from the file, but the block is also stored in the computer's memory. Recall the block of text from the Hold Area by pressing

F1	Function key F1, Cancel/Undo, to highlight the last deleted text and undelete prompt
F1	Function key F1 a second time to cancel the retrieval

The retrieval of deleted text can be made more than once. If you pressed the F1 key again, here or elsewhere, additional copies of the remembered text would be entered into the file. As more text is deleted, any of the previous three deletions can be retrieved. Do not do this. Continue by entering

A marketing position in a computer	The replacement text
◄┘	Enter key
company	The second line of text
◄┘	Enter key, to separate this section from the next section

Moving Blocks of Text

The Alt-F4 combination used earlier to mark and center a block of text is also used to mark and move a block of text from one location to another. The employment date for Smith & Baker Retailers is chronologically earlier than the entry for the university. To place it correctly, it is not necessary to delete and retype the entry for Smith & Baker. Move it instead.

To move the text, place the cursor immediately under the *S* in *SMITH* and press

Alt-F4	The Block key to start marking
↓	Down arrow six times, to highlight the block of text, the blank line, and the empty space up to the cursor on the line containing *UNIVERSITY OF THE MOUNTAINS*
Ctrl-F4	To receive the prompt shown in Figure 3-12.

```
Move: 1 Block; 2 Tabular Column; 3 Rectangle: 0
```

Figure 3-12. The Move Menu

1	The selection to move the block and receive the prompt shown in Figure 3-13.

```
1 Move; 2 Copy; 3 Delete; 4 Append: 0
```

Figure 3-13.

1   To cut the block out of its present position and retrieve it elsewhere. You receive the prompt,

           Move cursor; press **Enter** to retrieve.

↓   Down arrow five times, to move the cursor under the first *F* in *FLOWERS ARE FOREVER*
◄┘   Enter key, to retrieve the block of text. The block is inserted between the university and florist shop entries.

It takes practice to get the block move procedure to work efficiently. After any move you may have to follow up with editing keys to place the text where you want it.

The counselor suggested moving the position titles to the top of each work experience entry to emphasize what Harriet had done, not whom she had worked for. The movement of titles also uses the Alt-F4 keys. Place your cursor under the *S* in *Student Activities Programming Assistant,* and press

Alt-F4	To begin marking the block
↓	Down arrow
Ctrl-F4	The Move key
1	To choose to move the block
1	To cut the text from the document
↑	Up arrow, to move the cursor under *U* in *UNIVERSITY*
◄┘	Enter key, to reinsert the block of text. The position title on your display is likely shown in a different color or intensity because WordPerfect is treating it as being bolded and underlined.
Alt-F3	The Reveal Codes key, to see the codes embedded in the text. Notice that the line begins with a [Bold] that is not closed until [bold] appears after *MOUNTAINS.* The code [UND] is highlighted by the cursor.
Home,←	Home and Left arrow, to highlight *W*
←	Left arrow to highlight [BOLD]
Del	Delete key, to delete the opening and closing bolding codes. The position title now appears underlined, but the section title and the name of the university are no longer bolded. Block and make bold the job title using the instructions given earlier in the chapter. Do not rebold the name of the university.
Alt-F3	To remove the Reveal Codes window

Because of the complexity of moving tabs and hard returns, text often does not line up neatly. When this occurs you have to edit with the Delete key and insert additional tabs.

Repeat the shifting of the position titles for the other jobs as well.

Removing Bolding and Underlining Codes

The bolding and underlining should be changed to incorporate the suggestion of the counselor to emphasize positions and not the employers. Only the job titles should be bolded. Nothing should be underlined. In order to eliminate the codes that turn these fonts on and off, you must be able to see them. Type **Alt-F3** to open the Reveal Codes window and to see the embedded codes.

Use the arrow and other cursor movement keys to move the cursor to the location of the codes for bolding, **[BOLD]** and **[bold]**, and for underlining, **[UND]** and **[und]**. Delete the codes surrounding the employing organization and the position title with the Delete key or the Backspace key. To use the Delete key, the cursor must be positioned on the code to be deleted. To use the Backspace key, the cursor should be to the right of the code being removed. Deleting one of the codes in a pair also deletes the matching code. Type Alt-F3 to close the Reveal Codes window.

Block Bolding and Changing Case

It was recommended that the position held should be bolded and that it should be uppercased. To illustrate, place the cursor under the *S* in *Student Activities Programming Assistant,* and type

Alt-F4	To begin marking the block
End	End key, to mark the line
Shift-F3	The (case) Switch key which gives you the opportunity to change all of the blocked letters to upper or lowercase
1	To convert the line to uppercase. The cursor moves to the end of the line and the blocking disappears.
Alt-F4	To begin marking the block
Ctrl- ←	Control and Left arrow three times to place the cursor under the *S* in *Student,* thereby highlighting the position title a second time
F6	The Bold key, which emboldens the line and cancels the blocking command

Make these changes with the other position titles.

SMITH & BAKER RETAILERS should also be converted, but it should be altered so that each word has an initial capital letter and the rest of each word is lowercase. This is accomplished, for example, by placing the cursor under the *M* in *SMITH* and typing

Alt-F4	To begin marking the block
End	End key, to mark the line
←	Left arrow, to remove block from address
Shift-F3	The (case) Switch key
2	To convert the line to lowercase and cancel blocking

There is no way to quickly capitalize all of the first letters. It is possible to block each letter and convert it to uppercase, but this takes more keystrokes than simply deleting and replacing the letters. You can either delete each such letter and insert a capital or you can toggle the Insert key to typeover and replace the appropriate characters.

Effect this change with the other employers. The résumé should now look as it does in Figure 3-14.

HARRIET HARTLEY

22 Elm Street
West Washington, NV 89888
707-555-5665

PROFESSIONAL GOAL: A marketing position with a computer company.

EDUCATION: **WEST WASHINGTON HIGH SCHOOL**
2100 Parker Drive
West Washington, NV 89888
Academic Diploma, 1987

UNIVERSITY OF THE MOUNTAINS
Lake Hicauma, CA 12880
Bachelor of Science
Business Administration
1991

WORK EXPERIENCE: **STUDENT ACTIVITIES PROGRAMMING ASSISTANT**
University of the Mountains
Lake Hicauma, CA 12880
Academic Year, 1989 - 1991

ASSISTANT BUYER
Smith & Baker Retailers
1 Black Oak Lane
West Washington, NV 89888
Summer, 1988 - 1990

SALES CLERK - FLORAL ARRANGER
Flowers Are Forever
Market Square
West Washington, NV 89888
Academic Year, 1987 - 1991

**AWARDS AND
SCHOOL ACTIVITIES:**   Varsity Basketball, Omega Phi Beta,
Outstanding Student Volunteer, President's
Honor Roll, Crisis Call Volunteer.

SPECIAL SKILLS: Programming in BASIC and Pascal,
Spanish (3 yrs.)

Figure 3-14. Completed Résumé.

SAVING AND BACKING UP YOUR FILE

When your document has been completed, save your file by typing

F10	The Save File key, for saving a document
HARTLEY.RES	The filename
◄⎤	Enter key, to save your file

Save your file again to your backup diskette by removing the diskette from drive A and replacing it with your backup diskette. The keystrokes this time are slightly different, since you have already specified the filename to the system.

F10	The Save File key
◄⎤	Enter key, to accept HARTLEY.RES as your filename and to save your file

PRINTING YOUR FILE

Now that the editing of the memorandum is finished and it has been saved, print out the document. In the next chapter you will revise and add text to the memorandum. To print out the file, type

Shift-F7	To bring up the primary Print menu
1	To print the document

EXITING WORDPERFECT

Exit WordPerfect and return to DOS by pressing

F7	The Exit key
N	To avoid saving your file again. If you wish you can combine saving a file and exiting WordPerfect by saving after pressing the F7 key.
Y	Yes, to exit WordPerfect. You can also respond *N* and when the screen is cleared, you can begin typing another document or you can exit as suggested.

You will receive the DOS prompt at this point. You can turn the computer off if you wish.

EXERCISES

A.　Modify Harriet Hartley's résumé so that the two entries for education are reversed.

B.　Create the following résumé using STYLE.LIB style named RESUME.

DIXON MARS

557 Waterbrook Farm Rd.
Covington Cove, NH 12111
323-718-9812

PROFESSIONAL GOAL: To employ my educational skills in the context of an exciting, upper-level, management position within an international corporation.

EMPLOYMENT: **WEEKLY GAZETTE**
Newspaper Delivery Boy
High Falls, MA 37456
BURGER HEAVEN
Short Order Cook
High Falls, MA 37456

EDUCATION: **JOHNSON COUNTY JUNIOR COLLEGE**
A.S. in Business Administration
1987

WILSON STATE UNIVERSITY
B.A. in Public Administration
1989

**AWARDS AND
SCHOOL ACTIVITIES:**   Varsity Track (3 yrs.), Spanish Club (President), Alumni Solicitation Drive Volunteer, Ecology Club, Student Council (2 yrs.), Data Processing Management Association

LANGUAGES SPOKEN: Spanish, Russian, German

Modify the résumé to make it stronger by making the following changes:
--Change the professional goal to, *To work in the overseas division of an international hotel chain.*
--Delete the entire, weak employment history and replace it with a functional description of Mr. Mars' skills as follows:

FUNCTIONAL SKILLS:
PLANNING: Developed an organized approach to the distribution of student government funds to approved organizations, reviewed all student organizational plans and projects, served as parliamentarian

DIRECTING: Started the Ecology Club, created the aluminum can recycling effort, managed a trip to Mexico City during Spring break, served as a student coordinator for statewide telephone marathons

TRAVEL: Lived in Madrid, Spain for 6 months, toured
                             Japan for 2 weeks with family, attended the
                             Study Abroad Program in Bonn, West Germany,
                             organized trip to Mexico City, biked the
                             Appalachian Trail

--Reverse the entries under education.

--Insert the section *INTERNATIONAL STUDIES COURSES:* and list the following courses:

ECON. 242 International Economics
MGRS. 342 International Business
PADM. 313 Independent Study: Trade Barriers in the
Japanese Trade Market
LANG. 433 Russian Literature in Translation
PADM. 412 Comparative Study of Bureaucracies
Russian-4 language courses
German-6 language courses
Spanish-4 language courses

C.   Use the Style RESUME to create your own résumé for use in job seeking.

Chapter 4

Using the Outline Feature

Chapter Outline

Date/Outline Key
Editing the Outline
      Deleting Paragraph Markers
      Moving Sections of the Outline
      Adding Additional Entries
      Deletion to End-of-Line
      Changing the Tab Settings
      Changing the Numbering Style
Saving and Backing Up the File
Printing the File
Exiting WordPerfect
Exercises

Writers in all fields find themselves outlining the text of documents they must prepare. Authors outline the chapters that compose the books they write; professionals in many fields prepare reports and proposals that are highly stylized in form and find that outlining the points to be made in each section is helpful; and students are often required to submit outlines of term papers before the papers themselves are submitted. This chapter is designed to show you how to effectively use the outlining capabilities of WordPerfect. This chapter is preparatory to the following chapter in which you type a short academic paper that is based on this chapter's outline. In this chapter you will:

1. Use the Date/Outline key to create an outline for a term paper;
2. Add and delete subsections of the outline;
3. Use the [**Par Num:Auto**] code to automatically number and letter different levels of an outline;
4. Move sections of an outline to new locations in the outline to see how WordPerfect automatically renumbers sections and subsections of an outline;
5. Use the Delete-to-end-of-line key;
6. Reset the tab settings to change the appearance of the outline;
7. Reset the outline's numbering style to meet your requirements.

The outline you will work with has been developed as the basis for a term paper by a student in a class on computers in business. The outline is incomplete since the student is still gathering research information to use in the paper. The outline currently looks like Figure 4-1.

```
┌─────────────────────────────────────────────────────────────────────┐
│THE PROS AND CONS OF WORD PROCESSING                                   │
│                                                                       │
│I.    INTRODUCTION TO WORD PROCESSING                                  │
│                                                                       │
│II.   DISADUANTAGES OF WORD PROCESSING                                 │
│      A.    Cost                                                       │
│      B.    Professional Time Lost                                     │
│      C.    Word Processing Inadequacies                               │
│      D.    Investments in Manual Typewriters                          │
│                                                                       │
│III.  ADUANTAGES OF WORD PROCESSING                                    │
│      A.    Reduced Costs                                              │
│      B.    Reduced Production Time                                    │
│      C.    Higher Quality Output                                      │
│                                                                       │
│IV.   CONCLUSION                                                       │
│                                                                       │
│                                                                       │
│                                                                       │
│                                                                       │
│                                                                       │
│                                                                       │
│                                                                       │
│Outline                                      Doc 1 Pg 1 Ln 3.33" Pos 1"│
└─────────────────────────────────────────────────────────────────────┘
```

Figure 4-1. The Outline

DATE/OUTLINE KEY

Begin to create the outline by entering the title. Enter

Caps Lock   To set the keys to uppercase
THE PROS AND CONS OF WORD PROCESSING
                          The outline title, which is not numbered. Do not press the Enter key. If you did,
                          press the Backspace key to return the cursor to the column immediately after
                          the word *PROCESSING.*

     One function of the Date/Outline key is the ability to turn the outlining feature off and on. Examine
the Date/Outline menu by pressing

Shift-F5   The Date/Outline key, to see the menu

```
┌─────────────────────────────────────────────────────────────────────┐
│ 1 Date Text; 2 Date Code; 3 Date Format; 4 Outline; 5 Para Num; 6 Define: 0│
└─────────────────────────────────────────────────────────────────────┘
```

Figure 4-2. Date/Outline Menu

     The only option to be used here is the fourth choice: Outline

4   Presents the Outline menu

```
Outline: 1 On; 2 Off; 3 Move Family; 4 Copy Family; 5 Delete Family: 0
```

Figure 4-3. Outline Menu

1   Set Outline on

There is no obvious change on the screen except for the word Outline at the bottom left corner. Were you to look at the work area of the screen with the Reveal Codes key, Alt-F3, you would not see any different control codes either. From now on, however, every time you press the Enter key, WordPerfect automatically inserts a code that looks like **[Par Num:Auto]**. WordPerfect keeps track of these codes in such a way that it automatically letters or numbers each code according to the sequence in which it appears and according to the number of tabs that precede it. The number of tabs preceding the paragraph marking code determines the level of the item being numbered (Roman numeral, capital letter, Arabic numeral, etc.), whereas striking the function key F4 enables text entry at the particular level.

Begin to create the outline by pressing

◄┘	Enter key once, to see the Roman numeral **I.** appear. The numeral appears on the line immediately underneath the title. A blank line should separate the title from the outline.
◄┘	Enter key, to insert a hard return in front of the command code
F4	The Indent key, to anchor the paragraph marker
Alt-F3	The Reveal Codes key, to see the codes **[Par Num:Auto][->Indent]** which denote the paragraph marker and the indented line key. The paragraph marker produces the **I.** and the indent key anchors the marker so it does not continue to move down the page with each pressing of the Enter key.
Alt-F3	Alternate key and function key F3, to remove the Reveal Codes window

INTRODUCTION TO WORD PROCESSING

	The first main section heading
◄┘	Enter key, to terminate the line and to insert a second paragraph marker that displays **II.**
◄┘	Enter key, to insert a blank line between major sections
F4	The Indent key, to anchor the second heading

DISADVANTAGES OF WORD PROCESSING

	The second heading
◄┘	Enter key, to terminate the line and to insert a third paragraph marker that displays **III.** The next entry, however, is to be a subsection of section **II.**
Tab	Tab key. The paragraph marker moves to the next level in and begins the subsection identification with an **A.**
F4	The Indent key, to anchor the marker
Caps Lock	To toggle caps off
Cost	The first subsection
◄┘	Enter key, to display **B.** with the cursor at the second level heading
F4	The Indent key

Professional Time Lost

	The next subsection
◄┘	Enter key, to display **C.**

Tab	Tab key, to intentionally put an extra and unnecessary tab into the text. The marker now shows **1**.
Alt-F3	The Reveal Codes key, to see the codes **[Tab][Tab][Par Num:Auto]**. You can see the extra tab and paragraph markers. Were you to try to delete the paragraph marker you would find it awkward to reinsert it without leaving an extra blank line.
Shift-Tab	Shift and Tab keys, to remove one tab marker. The paragraph marker displays **C**. Shift-Tab reduces the level for headings that have not been anchored with F4.
Alt-F3	Alternate key and function key F3, to remove the Reveal Codes window
F4	The Indent key

Word Processing Inadequacies
> The next subsection heading

Arrow Keys Versus the Enter Key

When outlining has been turned on, you can move freely with the arrow keys without inserting new paragraph markers. If you press the Enter key, however, a paragraph marker is inserted. If you make a mistake, you can backspace or delete extra paragraph markers easily. This is described below.
> Continue entering and editing the outline until it appears as it is displayed in Figure 4-1.

EDITING THE OUTLINE

Deleting Paragraph Markers

Codes produce the Roman and Arabic numerals as well as the letters that identify each section and subsection. If you need to delete a marker, you should use the Reveal Codes key to place the cursor on the paragraph marker. It is highlighted. Then delete the code with the Delete key. You may also delete the marker with the Backspace key if the marker is to the left of the cursor. You need only to delete the marker once even though the marker produces a multi-character display such as **III**. You may need to delete other codes and text on a line to modify the outline.

Moving Sections of the Outline

After reviewing the outline, the student decides that the paper will probably end up with a positive conclusion about the future of word processing. The placement of the disadvantages of word processing at the beginning of the paper is undesirable from this point of view. The advantages should be listed first. Text in an outline can be physically moved around and WordPerfect automatically redetermines the correct section and subsection numbers. Reverse the order of the two sections by placing the cursor on the blank line between sections **II.** and **III.** and entering

Alt-F4	The Block key
↓	Down arrow five times, to highlight four lines with text and the cursor appears on the blank line between sections **III.** and **IV.**
Ctrl-F4	The Move key, to see the prompt line shown in Figure 4-4.

```
Move: 1 Block; 2 Tabular Column; 3 Rectangle: 0
```

Figure 4-4.

1   Move the highlighted block. The prompt shown in Figure 4-5 appears.

```
1 Move; 2 Copy; 3 Delete; 4 Append: 0
```
Figure 4-5.

1   Move the block. The block of text is temporarily removed from the screen. The prompt line changes again to

                               Move cursor; press **Enter** to retrieve.

↑   Up arrow six times, to place the cursor on the blank line between sections I. and II.

◄┘   Enter key, to reinsert the previously cut text. Notice that all of the numbering markers for the sections and the subsections are correct.

The movement and copying capabilities of the Control-F4 keys can be used in any document, not just in outlines.

Adding Entries

As the student continues reading about word processing, several additional subsections are found to be needed. A subsection is to be inserted after subsection II.C. The arrow keys enable you to move around without inserting new paragraph markers even though outline is toggled on. Move the cursor after the word *Output* and press

◄┘   Enter key, to insert a hard return and to insert another subheading marker which displays **D**.
F4   The Indent key

Improved Morale   The new subsection

Another subsection is missing which should occur after subsection III.A. Place your cursor after *Cost* and enter

◄┘   Enter key, to insert a new subheading marker. Notice how the letters resequence automatically.
F4   The Indent key, to anchor the marker

Vendor Dependence   The heading to be inserted

Deletion to End of Line

The student completing the outline has not been able to locate any references to support his assertion that the use of word processing improves morale. Since he cannot document this belief he will eliminate this topic from his paper. You have already deleted text one character and one word at a time. To delete an entire line one letter, or even one word, at a time is time-consuming. When the line contains embedded codes and the user is not careful in responding to prompts, default protections may allow some of the codes to remain on the line where they can cause difficulties later. WordPerfect allows you to delete all of the characters and codes on a line. Put the cursor on the line with the heading *Improved Morale* and type

Home, ←	Home followed by Left arrow, to place the cursor at the beginning of the line
Ctrl-End	Delete-to-End-of-Line key, to remove all characters except the hard return code which keeps the blank line
Del	Delete key, to remove the hard return code

The Delete-to-end-of-Line key can be used in all documents, not just in outlines. It deletes all characters and codes from the location of the cursor on the line. If it is in the middle of the line, text to the right of the cursor is deleted while the text to the left is left intact.

The entry in section III., **E. Investments in Manual Typewriters,** is another subsection that must be deleted because of a lack of documentation. Delete it in the same manner described above.

Changing the Tab Settings

By utilizing the default tab settings, the section and subsection headings are farther apart than the student would like them to be. Since a topic outline has to be turned in before writing the paper, the student would like to use different tab settings. Press

Home,Home, ↑	Home key twice followed by Up arrow, to move the cursor to the top line
Shift-F8	The Format key
L	Line formatting
T	Tab set, to change the Tab settings

Review the tabs and rulers section of Chapter 2: Some Next Steps in Word Processing, to review how tab settings are altered. Change the tab ruler so that L tab settings are located at every fourth marker location up to +1.5 inches. The outline changes its spacing as you enter the L's. When you have inserted and deleted the L's required, press

F7	The Exit key, to insert the tab settings in the document. Immediately, the spaces between the titles and paragraph marker displays are reduced, as are the indented distances for each level.
◄┘	Enter key, to exit the Format: Line screen
◄┘	Enter key, to exit the Format screen

Your outline should now appear as it does in Figure 4-6. Print the outline.

```
THE PROS AND CONS OF WORD PROCESSING

I.    INTRODUCTION TO WORD PROCESSING

II.   ADVANTAGES OF WORD PROCESSING
      A.    Reduced Costs
      B.    Reduced Production Time
      C.    Higher Quality Output

III. DISADVANTAGES OF WORD PROCESSING
      A.    Cost
      B.    Vendor Dependence
      C.    Professional Time Lost
      D.    Word Processing Inadequacies

IV.   CONCLUSION
```

Figure 4-6.

Changing the Numbering Style

Thus far, you have used the default numbering pattern for outlines. This pattern follows the order:

I. Roman numeral for sections;
    A. Capital letter for subsections;
        1. Arabic numeral for sub-subsections;
            a. Lowercase letter for sub-sub-subsections;
                (1) Enclosed Arabic for sub-sub-subsections;
                    (a) Enclosed lowercase letters . .;
                        i) Lowercase Roman numerals with right parenthesis ...;
                          a) Lowercase letters with right parenthesis ...

If you wish, you can alter the pattern by placing the cursor on the blank line above section I. and typing

Shift-F5   The Date/Outline key
6   Define other options, to see Figure 4-7

```
Paragraph Number Definition

   1 - Starting Paragraph Number              1
         (in legal style)
                                              Levels
                        ▋1▐  ▋2▐  ▋3▐  ▋4▐  ▋5▐  ▋6▐  ▋7▐  ▋8▐
   2 - Paragraph         1.   a.   i.  (1)  (a)  (i)   1)   a)
   3 - Outline           I.   A.   1.   a.  (1)  (a)   i)   a)
   4 - Legal (1.1.1)     1   .1   .1   .1   .1   .1   .1   .1
   5 - Bullets           •    o    -    ■    ✶    +    •    x
   6 - User-defined

   Current Definition    I.   A.   1.   a.  (1)  (a)   i)   a)
   Attach Previous Level      No   No   No   No   No   No   No

   7 - Enter Inserts Paragraph Number         Yes

   8 - Automatically Adjust to Current Level   Yes

   9 - Outline Style Name




Selection: 0
```

Figure 4-7. Paragraph Definition Screen

At this point you have four choices open to you. Choice 2, Paragraph, exhibits the Arabic numerals first, the lowercase alphabetic characters second, and so on. Choice 3 is the outline numbering that you have been using. Choice 5 switches the level marking symbols to those displayed on the screen. Choice 6, User-defined, allows you to design the display style you would like to use. You will convert the outline to the legal style, choice 4, by entering

4	To select legal numbering
◄⌐	Enter key, to exit the Paragraph Number Definition screen
◄⌐	Enter key, to exit the Date/Outline screen
+	Grey plus key, to move to the bottom of the page. This immediately converts the displays to the legal style even though the paragraph marker codes embedded in the text have not been altered.

The outline appears as shown in Figure 4-8.

```
┌──────────────────────────────────────────────────────────────────────┐
│THE PROS AND CONS OF WORD PROCESSING                                    │
│                                                                        │
│1    INTRODUCTION TO WORD PROCESSING                                    │
│                                                                        │
│2    ADVANTAGES OF WORD PROCESSING                                      │
│     2.1 Reduced Costs                                                  │
│     2.2 Reduced Production Time                                        │
│     2.3 Higher Quality Output                                          │
│                                                                        │
│3    DISADVANTAGES OF WORD PROCESSING                                   │
│     3.1 Cost                                                           │
│     3.2 Vendor Dependence                                             │
│     3.3 Professional Time Lost                                         │
│     3.4 Word Processing Inadequacies                                   │
│                                                                        │
│4    CONCLUSION                                                         │
│                                                                        │
│                                                                        │
│                                                                        │
│                                                                        │
│                                                                        │
│                                                                        │
│Outline                                  Doc 1 Pg 1 Ln 1" Pos 1"        │
└──────────────────────────────────────────────────────────────────────┘
```

Figure 4-8. Legal Style Outline

SAVING AND BACKING UP THE FILE

Save your file by typing

F10	The Save key
OUTLINE	The filename
◄┘	Enter key, to accept *OUTLINE* as the filename

Save your file again to your backup diskette by removing the diskette from drive A and replacing it with your backup diskette. Save the file to the backup diskette with the same keystrokes, except that the filename is supplied by the system this time.

PRINTING THE FILE

Now that the editing of the outline is finished and it has been saved, print the document. To print the file, type

Shift-F7	To obtain the prompt
1	To print the document

EXITING WORDPERFECT

Exit WordPerfect by pressing

F7	The Exit key
N	To avoid saving your file again
Y	Yes, to exit WordPerfect or type *N* and begin typing another document

EXERCISES

A. Outline this chapter of this book by hand. Then create the outline using the outline feature. Convert the outline to a legal style of numbering.

B. Create the following outline for a student term paper on computer data storage:

```
COMPUTER MEMORIES

    I.   Random Access Memory
         A.   Also called RAM, Main, Core storage
         B.   Very fast
         C.   Volatile
              1.   Lost when power is turned off
              2.   Recoverable only in certain computers
    II.  Cache Memory
         A.   High-speed storage
         B.   Found close to RAM
         C.   Stores data that are expected to be used shortly
         D.   Avoids long search times
    III. Secondary Storage
         A.   Disk drives
         B.   Cassettes and tapes
         C.   Older technologies
              1.   Cards
              2.   Drums
              3.   Paper tapes
```

C. Create the following outline. After you have entered the outline, use the Other Options choice of the Outline key to set the level designator numbers and letters as they are displayed. Reset the tab markers so that an *L* appears at columns 10, 12, 14, 16, and 18 so the outline is spaced as shown.

FLOPPY DISK DRIVES

A.   General Points
          I.   Somewhat flexible
          II.   Ruined by heat, contaminants, and magnetism
          III. Removable
B.   Density
          I.   Normal (out-of-date) for single-sided disks
          II.   Double Density
                    i.   Introduced with double-sided disks
                    ii.   Stores 360 Kb of data
          III. Quad Density
                    i.   Found on 80286 microcomputers
                    ii.   Stores 1.2 Mb of data
                    iii.   Cannot be read by double density drives
                    iv.   Can read double density disks

Chapter 5

Advanced WordPerfect Usage

Chapter Outline

The documents created thus far have demonstrated many WordPerfect features. You are now able to produce many types of documents. Still, there are many other features that you can use to give your documents a professional look. While not all of the features can be dealt with here, you will be able to experiment with the remaining features on your own if you wish to do so. In this chapter you will:

1. Use hanging paragraphs in which a number can appear inside of the temporarily widened left margin;
2. Center individual lines and blocks of lines;
3. Use automatic hyphenation;
4. Insert hard page breaks;
5. Insert commands that alter the appearance of a page. The commands can be used for footnoting, for changing margins, for using header and footer lines, and for changing line spacing.

The document in this chapter is a short paper. On the surface it appears easy. It uses some features that you have used before, such as font changes and line centering. The indented paragraphs (lettered subsections) are different and, after the initial text has been entered, you will be adding features such as footnotes, headers, and page numbers. These features are available in any sophisticated word processing software.

     Figure 5-1 is a short paper produced by a student in an introductory computing class. Initially, this paper will be created with WordPerfect's default tab ruler.

THE PROS AND CONS OF WORD PROCESSING
<Your Name>

I. <u>INTRODUCTION TO WORD PROCESSING</u>

There are many ways in which computers can operate on textual information. Text editors are normally used to create programs or data to be processed by programs. Text editors are not adapted to preparing letters, term papers and other documents. They have little capability for formatting the text in a variety of styles. Some programming languages, most notably Snobol, are adept at analyzing text files, but they are almost useless for preparing normal business and personal communications.

Word processors and text formatters, software designed to produce written documents, are improving steadily. Word processors are generally categorized as displaying a document on the computer monitor in much the same appearance as that of the printed document. Text formatters, on the other hand, produce files in which there are large numbers of "dot" commands that will be used by the formatter to guide printing. The file looks substantially different from the eventual printed document since word filling, footnotes, margin settings and type faces are not arranged by the formatter until the document is printed.

II. <u>ADVANTAGES OF WORD PROCESSING</u>

Word processing software capabilities have been developing rapidly. The number of word processing packages is large and the number of persons who use word processors in their work and for personal usage is also substantial. Many people do not begin to utilize all of the capabilities their word processors possess, but they are likely to realize at least some of the advantages noted by some of the writers who have studied the use of word processing in industry. Among the advantages of word processors and text formatters are the following:

A. <u>Reduced Cost</u>. Errors can be corrected rapidly, greatly
    reducing the time involved in producing a document. Of
    greater importance, revisions to documents are significantly
    less costly than are complete retypings of documents.

B. <u>Reduced Production Time</u>. When documents are revised, the
    editor need only proofread the altered text for accuracy.
    Previously acceptable text will not have changed. This is
    different from typed text in which an entire document must be
    reread to be certain that new errors have not slipped in.

C. <u>Efficient Staff Usage</u>. Documents can be entered by relatively
    untrained, lower-cost typists. Corrections and complex
    formatting can be turned over to more skilled word processing
    operators in later revisions.

D. <u>Higher Quality Output</u>. Because revisions are easy to make,
    managers and other writers are less hesitant to revise and
    reprint documents until they are precisely correct.

III. <u>DISADVANTAGES OF WORD PROCESSING</u>

Even though there is almost universal agreement that word processing is an essential element in the modern business environment, there are drawbacks to its usage. These disadvantages include:

A. <u>Cost</u>. Word processors are significantly more expensive to buy and maintain than are standard typewriters. Personnel must be trained to use the word processors.

B. <u>Vendor Dependence</u>. Each word processing software package is unique. Document files cannot be easily shared, if at all, between different word processors or word processing software packages. Once a company has committed itself to one approach, change is costly.

C. <u>Professional Time Lost</u>. Many people who used to dictate or write out documents by hand find that they prefer to type their own drafts of documents. They may then find that they prefer to do the editing themselves because it is faster than writing notes about changes to be made and then having to explain the notes to a secretary. To be certain the document is correct, they print it out. Before you know it a professional being paid $40,000 a year is doing the job of a $15,000 a year secretary.

D. <u>Word Processing Inadequacies</u>. There are many differences among word processors. Even with the best word processors there will be special capabilities like equation formatting, table production and interfaces with type setting equipment that are not available. The production of some documents may be difficult and the organization may find that several different word processors will be needed to meet all of the

Figure 5-1.

TEXT MANIPULATIONS

Centering and Boldfacing

The first line is bolded and centered. Do this by pressing

Shift-F6	The Center key combination
F6	The Bold key, to turn bolding on. Notice the change in color or intensity of the Pos number.
Caps Lock	To turn letters to uppercase. Then type

THE PROS AND CONS OF WORD PROCESSING

	The paper's title
F6	To turn bolding off
◄┘	Enter key, to complete the centering of the line

Enter and center your name (without bolding) in the same manner. Press the Enter key twice to move the cursor down two lines.

Underlining

The text on the line beginning with the Roman numeral *I.* is to be underlined. To enter this line place your cursor at the left margin and type

I.	The section designator
Space,Space	Space bar twice, to insert two spaces between the section number and the heading
F8	The Underline key, to turn underlining on. Notice the change in appearance of the Pos number. Then type

INTRODUCTION TO WORD PROCESSING	
	The subsection heading
F8	To turn underlining off
◄⌐	Enter key

Use the same technique for underlining the two additional lines with Roman numerals as they occur in the text. Enter the first three paragraphs and stop when you reach the end of the paragraph immediately before the first subsection, A.

SAVING YOUR FILE

Before proceeding further, save your file by entering

F10	The Save key
paper	The filename
◄⌐	Enter

As you work through the following instructions for modifying the paper, save the file whenever you reach a point of completion. Then, if you make a mistake, you can remove the degraded version of the file that you see on your screen by exiting with the F7 key and not saving the file. Respond *N* to the prompt asking whether you wish to exit WordPerfect, and after a blank work screen appears, retrieve the preserved version of PAPER with the Shift-F10 key combination.

HANGING PARAGRAPHS

The paragraphs marked A, B, C, etc., are called hanging paragraphs. This is because the label is hanging in the left margin that has been temporarily widened. The typing of the hanging paragraphs will be difficult if you use the Tab key for indentation. Using the Tab key after each word wrap, you would have to move the cursor to the left margin to enter additional tabs to place the text at the correct location. In addition, if you start editing the text by inserting and deleting words, you will find that the tab markers will have to be adjusted constantly.

To employ a hanging paragraph, the F4 key is used to create a temporary indentation that will remain in effect until the Enter key is pressed. Skip a line between paragraphs and create the first such paragraph by typing

A.	The subsection label
F4	The Indent key
F8	The Underline key, to turn underlining on
Reduced Costs	The subsection heading to be underlined
F8	The Underline key, to turn underlining off
	A period that is not underlined
Space, Space	Space bar twice

Errors can be corrected rapidly . . . .

	The text for the hanging paragraph
◄┘	Enter, pressed once at the end of the paragraph. The cursor returns to the default left margin.

Enter the remaining hanging paragraphs in the same fashion. When the paper is complete, save it with the Save Files key, F10.

PRINTING THE FILE

When the paper is complete, print it by pressing

Shift-F7	The Print Document key
1	To print the full text

LINE FORMATTING COMMANDS

WordPerfect is almost entirely a "What-you-see-is-what-you-get" word processor. So far, the documents you have created have printed out as they appeared on the screen. The current document is lacking in some features that you have probably begun to sense are needed. There are additional controls you can use over the final appearance.

You have already used some page formatting controls when you added page numbers, suppressed the printing of page numbers on the first page, and centered résumés on a page. Now you will use some added features.

Margin Changes

WordPerfect uses default margins of 1 inch from the left edge of the paper and 1 inch from the right edge of the paper. You may wish to alter the margin for several reasons. If you use paper that is not 8 1/2 by 11 inches there is more or less space on a line than can be filled. If you change the character size to compressed type, or if you use proportional type, you can get more characters on a line and the left margin is closer to the left edge of the paper. Margins are easily changed. To change the margin for this paper, move the cursor to the top of the document and enter

Shift-F8	The Format key, to display the Formatting Prompt screen
1	Line formatting (or press *L*)
7	Margins change (or press *M*)
1.5	To increase the left margin, thereby decreasing the size of the printed line
◄┘	Enter key
1.5	To increase the right margin, again decreasing the size of the printed line
F7	The Exit key, to return to the document.

+   Grey plus sign, to reformat the visible and the nonvisible portions of the document.

Line Spacing

It is desirable to print all of your drafts of a large document in single space to conserve paper and printing time. Once you have finalized the paper size, however, you may wish to shift to double spacing. Do this by returning your cursor to the top of the document, then enter

Shift-F8	The Format key
1	Line, to alter the line formatting
6	Line spacing
2	To set double spacing on from the top
◄┘	Enter key
F7	Exit key. The change in line spacing is immediately visible.

Notice that extra lines, between paragraphs for instance, cause WordPerfect to show three blank lines. These lines are not needed in a double spaced document. **Locate the extra lines throughout the document and delete them.**

Hyphenation

By default WordPerfect does not automatically hyphenate any words. When hyphenation is turned off, the default condition, complete words are wrapped to the next line if they do not fit on the previous line. This does not always produce a satisfactory document. If hyphenation is off, a line with very few words will have larger than desirable spaces between the words. In some cases, depending upon your printer's capabilities, these spaces can be fine-tuned by resetting kerning and right-justification values from the Format menus. A kern is an extension to the body of a letter and kerning is the ability of WordPerfect to overlap the kerns of letters into the spaces of other letters. In all cases, however, when hyphenation is on, words will be hyphenated and fewer large spaces will appear between words.

Turning hyphenation on enables WordPerfect to suggest where words should be broken. Hyphens inserted in a word are soft hyphens because WordPerfect will change them if a paragraph is reformatted or if the margins of a document change and the complete word is able to be printed on a single line. There are two limits that define the full hyphenation zone. The zone looks like that pictured in Figure 5-2.

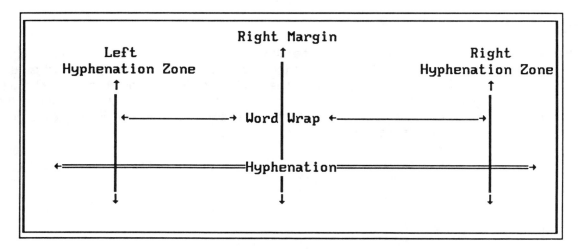

Figure 5-2. Hyphenation Zones

When hyphenation is turned on, WordPerfect follows these rules.

1. A word that ends before the right margin will not be hyphenated.
2. A word that begins after the right margin is word wrapped.
3. A word that begins after the left hyphenation zone and extends beyond the right margin will be wrapped to the next line.
4. A word that begins at or before the left hyphenation zone and extends beyond the right margin will be hyphenated.
5. Hyphenation will be suggested in syllables, falling between the left and right hyphenation zones.

By reducing the size of the hyphenation zone, more words will be forced by WordPerfect to be hyphenated.

Make sure that your cursor is at the top of the document and enter

Shift-F8	The Format key
1	Line Format. Hyphenation is shown to be off. The hyphenation zone, also called the H-Zone, is shown to be 10% and 4%.
1	Hyphenation.
Y	Yes, turn hyphenation on
2	Hyphenation Zone, to change the default H-Zone of 10% and 4%
6	The new left hyphenation zone that will be a smaller percentage of the print line's width
◄┘	Enter key
◄┘	Enter key. The right hyphenation zone will not be changed
◄┘	Enter key, to exit the Line Format screen
F7	Exit key, to exit the Format screen
+	Grey plus sign as necessary, to move through the document. Although WordPerfect may select a different word for different documents and WordPerfect setups, you will be prompted to position the hyphen for some words. The prompt may appear as

Position hyphen; Press ESC stead-̲ily

The prompt is allowing you to choose whether the flashing underscore is where you would like to place the hyphen. Your options at this point are to press:
1. the Left Arrow key to move to a more appropriate breaking point;
2. ESC to insert the hyphen;
3. F1, the Cancel key, to prevent hyphenation.
If you use the arrow key to move the cursor to a new hyphenation location, you press Escape when you have found that location. If you press Cancel, a Slash (/) will be placed in front of the word when you look at it on the Reveal Codes window (Alt-F3), but the Slash will not be seen in the normal work area, nor will the Slash print out. The Slash simply indicates that the word has been explicitly prevented from being hyphenated. Press

Esc	To hyphenate the word as suggested by WordPerfect. The document returns to the screen and the word is shown hyphenated.
Grey +	Grey plus key several times. WordPerfect will identify other words that need to be hyphenated. As you are prompted to do so, select locations in which to hyphenate these words.

Continue pressing the grey plus key and as you progress through the document hyphenate the remaining words. Because the hyphenation zone has been set somewhat arbitrarily, some words will be forced to break that you might prefer to have left un-hyphenated. This is acceptable since this is only an exercise.

PAGE FORMATTING COMMANDS

Headers and Footers

It is often desirable on long documents to have common identification lines at the top and/or bottom of each page. Identification lines at the top of the page are called headers, and those at the bottom are called footers. You might want to identify the pages with one or more identifiers such as the date, the words "Draft" or "Top Secret," or the title of the document. You have already used the Format key (Shift-F8) that allows the entry of a footer, and you have seen the Format Screen that appears after pressing the Format key. Place the cursor at the top of the document and press

Shift-F8	To call up the Format screen
2	Page formatting
4	Footers, or press *F,* to enter the first part of a footer line
1	To enter the left footer (Footer A)
2	To have the footer appear on every page

Word Processing J. Knowsit

	The footer to be printed. Use appropriate function and cursor movement keys to center, bold, underline or otherwise format the footer. To print the page number as part of the footer or header, press Ctrl-B at the correct location.
F7	Exit key; exit footer entry. The Page Format screen returns the message "FA Every Page." A position A footer will be printed on every page of the document.
8	To suppress the printing of the footer on the first page since the title and name are already on the page
3	To print only the page number at the bottom center of first page. The footer is not printed.
Y	Yes, accept this option
◄┘	Enter, to exit the Suppress screen

Page Numbers

Most documents should include page numbers to facilitate the reader's task of locating important sections, to make notes about points raised and so forth. Page numbers are requested from the Page Format screen.

6	Page numbering (or press 7)
4	To set the page number position
3	To select the upper right corner of the page. Other options are available. Page numbering will begin at the position of the page location code, consequently it is important that this code is inserted at the top of the document and before any text that is to be printed.
F7	Exit key, to return to the document

Footnotes

In typing, the placement of footnotes is always a challenge. You must keep track of the number of lines you have typed and leave enough space to put the footnote(s) at the bottom of the page. If you are using footers, correct placement of the footnote is a big chore. Small miscalculations may force you to retype an entire page. WordPerfect takes care of these calculations for you.

Assume that you wished to include a footnote citation to document a conclusion in the first paragraph in Figure 5-1. Do this by placing your cursor immediately behind the period following the word *communications* at the end of the first paragraph. Press

Ctrl-F7	The Footnote key
1	Footnote, to begin to create a footnote that appears at the bottom of the current page, the first page in this case. Note: do not confuse a footnote with an endnote. The footnote appears at the bottom of the current page while the endnote appears at the end of the document.
1	Create, to start a new footnote. Do not erase the *1* that appears next. This is the footnote number created by WordPerfect.
F4	Function key F4 to indent the footnote's text

Wells, M. T. "Approaches to Word Processing," <u>Journal of Spurious Results</u>, Vol. 10, Number 13, May 1989, pp. 2224.

	The text for the footnote. Some of the text in the footnote is underlined with the F8 key, and you may be prompted for a hyphen for the word *Processing.*
F7	The Exit key, to close the footnote. A footnote number, 1, appears at the location of the cursor. This number will be superscripted automatically if your printer is capable of superscripting.
Alt-F3	The Reveal Codes key
←	Left arrow, to see the code

[Footnote:1;[Note Num][->Indent] Wells, M. T. "Approaches ...]

	that creates a footnote and note number that produces the number 1. The beginning of the footnote can also be seen in the window but nowhere in the document until it is printed.
Alt-F3	Alternate key and function key F3 pressed simultaneously, to close the Reveal Codes window. Additional footnotes could be added in the same fashion throughout the document.

HARD PAGE BREAKS

As you look at your document you may see that at the top of page 2, one line containing part of a sentence appears. A document looks better if at least two lines of the text follow immediately after the heading introducing that section and if at least two lines of a paragraph carry over to the following page. It is desirable to force the printer to move to the next page before the previous line is printed. The command for forcing the printer to eject to the next page is called a hard page break. A soft page break, seen on your screen as a row of dotted lines, is the page break which is entered by WordPerfect when it determines that it has printed the maximum number of lines on a page as specified by the page formatting commands. Put a hard page break in your document by placing your cursor after the third line from the bottom of page 2 and pressing

Ctrl-◂⌐	The Hard Page Break key. A row of equal signs appears that represents a hard page break.
Alt-F3	The Reveal Codes key, to see the code [HPg] noting that the writer caused the page to break at this point
Del	Delete key, to delete the now unneeded blank line created with [HRt]
Alt-F3	The Alternate and F3 keys pressed simultaneously, to remove the Reveal Codes window

A hard page break will not be affected by the reformatting of the document. If a hard break is inserted and reformatting caused the break to appear two lines from the top of a page, a break would still occur. Sometimes this is acceptable since you may wish to ensure that the next item, a table perhaps, begins at the top of the page regardless of the amount of white space left on the previous page.

SAVING AND BACKING UP THE FILE

Save your file by typing

F10	The key for saving a document
PAPER2	Your filename
◂⌐	Enter, to enter PAPER2 as the filename

Save your file again to your backup diskette by removing the diskette from drive A and replacing it with your backup diskette. Save the file to the backup diskette with the same keystrokes, except that this time the system prompts you with the filename.

THE PRINT CONTROL SCREEN

In all of the preceding chapters, the printing of a document was completed by selecting the first choice on the following menu that was displayed when you pressed the Shift and F7 keys. The selection of **1** printed the entire document as it currently appeared on the screen. In this section you will learn how to print one document while working on another document.

F10	The Save key
ERASEME	A new filename, cleverly selected so you avoid replacing PAPER2; the filename will suggest erasing the file at a later date
◂⌐	Enter

Call up the Print Control screen by pressing

Shift-F7	The Print key, to see the menu shown in Figure 5-3.

```
Print

      1 - Full Document
      2 - Page
      3 - Document on Disk
      4 - Control Printer
      5 - Multiple Pages
      6 - View Document
      7 - Initialize Printer


Options

      S - Select Printer              Epson LQ-500
      B - Binding Offset              0"
      N - Number of Copies            1
      U - Multiple Copies Generated by  WordPerfect
      G - Graphics Quality            Medium
      T - Text Quality                High




Selection: 0
```

Figure 5-3. Print Control Screen

The Print Control screen offers such a wide variety of ways in which to alter the basic print command that all of the options cannot be described in this book. In summary, the Print Control section has choices numbered 1 through 7, S, B, N, U, G, and T. Some of the primary choices are described in Figure 5-4.

CHOICE	FUNCTION
P	Prints the page the cursor is currently on.
D	Prints the document that is on your diskette, not the one which is currently on your screen and in RAM. After pressing *D* you would be prompted for the filename, including the drive and directory if these are different from the current defaults.
C	Controls the printer to cancel one or all printing commands that have been queued up.
V	Views the document the way WordPerfect will print it. This will enable you to see the pages with page numbers, footers, etc. before you waste paper and the time in printing a document that is incorrect.
S	Selects from among the printers that have drivers installed on your copy of WordPerfect.
N	Alters the number of copies of the document that can be printed with one command.

Figure 5-4. Selected Print Control Options

The Current Job and Job List sections of the screen provide you with information about the last print job submitted, as well as about the queue of print jobs that have been submitted in previous print commands. Continue to print the file ERASEME with

D   Print a document on the disk command, which then prompts you with

                              Document Name:_

A:ERASEME   The file to be printed which is currently found on drive A. The drive letter need not be typed if the default drive is B.

◄┘   Enter key

◄┘   Enter key, to print all of the pages in the document. If you did not wish to print the entire document, you can print individual pages. If you entered *5*, you would print only page 5. If you entered *5-10*, you would print pages 5 through 10. If you entered *5-*, you would print the document from page 5 to the end. If you entered *5-10,15* you would print pages 5 through 10 and 15.

When the default entry of 0 returns as the Selection on the Print Control, press

◄┘   Enter, to return to the WordPerfect work screen

NONJUSTIFIED RIGHT MARGINS

The paper you have just printed has, by default, a justified right margin. Spaces are inserted between words and punctuation to evenly space them across the line. Look carefully at the words in the first paragraph and you may detect extra space that has been inserted throughout the lines in order to force the last printed character to the last column. Many people prefer, especially when narrow margins are in use, to use a ragged right margin in which no blanks are inserted and in which the line stops as soon as the last character is printed. See what this looks like by returning the cursor to the top of the document and pressing

Shift-F8	The Format key
1	Line
3	Justification
1	Left, to justify the left margin, but not the right margin
F7	The Exit key, to exit the Line Format screen

Print the document again to see the difference the removal of the justification option makes.

VIEWING THE DOCUMENT

WordPerfect is not exactly a "What-you-see-is-what-you-get" word processor. You normally do not see page numbers, footers, or footnotes, for example, even though these will appear in the final document. You may wish to check these and other features before you print the document. Spotting an error before printing the document will save you the time and expense of unnecessary printing. To see what the document looks like without printing it, move the cursor to the beginning of the document and enter

Shift-F7	The Print key
6	View, to see the full first page of the document
PgDn	The Page Down key, to see the next page. You may use the PgUp and PgDn keys to look at the entire document. When you have finished viewing the document as it will eventually appear, press
F7	The Exit key, to return to the WordPerfect editing screen

EXITING WORDPERFECT

Exit WordPerfect by typing

F7	The Exit key
Y	Yes, save the file
PAPER3	The filename
◄┘	Enter. You may receive requests to adjust the hyphens in some of the words before the document is saved. Do so with the Escape and Left Arrow keys.
Y	Yes, to exit WordPerfect, or type *N* and begin the exercises

EXERCISES

A.   Use WordPerfect to produce your next term paper or class assignment.

B.   Choose sections of this or some other book that uses underlining, bolding, indented paragraphs, columns, or other special formatting features, and try to reproduce them with WordPerfect.

C.   Using the paper, "The Pros and Cons of Word Processing," produced in this chapter, indent four entries under the paragraph entitled, *A. Reduced Costs.* Revise the paragraph to include the following subentries. Press the Tab key before the subsection number and the Indent key after the subsection number.

A.   <u>Reduced Costs</u>. Errors can be corrected rapidly, greatly reducing the time involved in producing a document. Of greater importance, a revision of a document is significantly less costly than is a complete retyping of the document.
1.   Cheap printers can produce draft work quickly and inexpensively,
2.   Expensive laser printers can be used to produce final documents,
3.   Proofreaders do not have to reread entire documents,
4.   Document files can be accessed by some typesetting machines. Therefore, documents do not have to be keyed in again.

Then use the same ruler to add entries beneath the paragraph entitled, *C. Higher Quality Output,* so that it appears as:

C.   <u>Higher Quality Output</u>. Because revisions are easy to make, managers and other writers are less hesitant to revise and reprint documents until they are precisely correct.
1.   Laser printers can be acquired to produce cleaner, neater output,
2.   Spelling checkers, style checkers, and thesauruses can be used to assure correct output,
3.   Documents can be merged and reused, thereby reducing the chance for the introduction of errors,
4.   Data from worksheets and databases can be added without retyping.

Find and delete the margin change, [L/R Mar:1.5",6.5"], the line spacing code [LnSpacing:2], and the hard page break, [HPg]. Save the revised document as PAPER4. Print the document.

Chapter 6

Advanced Editing Aids:
The Spelling Checker and the Thesaurus

Chapter Outline

Word processing software programs like WordPerfect are unable, at this point in their development, to have a substantial impact on the qualitative aspects of writing. Other types of software might provide help in arranging paragraphs to be sure that they are in correct order. They cannot determine whether you have incorrectly selected *their* when *there* was the homonym of choice. Was the theme of your paper strongly presented? Did you exercise forceful usage of adjectives and adverbs? Were the best arguments brought to bear on your point? Is the punctuation placed in the right location? On these and many other important aspects of writing, WordPerfect is silent.

WordPerfect does not have these features, but it does have two other capabilities that you will appreciate having to enhance the quality of your writing: a spelling checker and a thesaurus. In this chapter you will:

1. Use the built-in thesaurus to suggest words that can replace words already in a document;
2. Use the thesaurus to suggest words that can replace a word that you are thinking about, but have not yet entered into the document;
3. Use the spelling checker to correct improperly typed words in a document.

THE THESAURUS

Writing an effective document depends on many things, not the least of which is the use of appropriate words to achieve the intended effects on the reader. Words must be selected carefully. Though a word may seem to be adequate when first used in a sentence, you may later wish to replace it with a word that has a stronger, more precise meaning.

Without WordPerfect you would probably look up a word in a printed thesaurus to find a list of synonyms which have approximately the same meaning as the word you started with and antonyms which mean the opposite. The entry for the word *approximately* in the thesaurus, for example, proposes words like *about, almost,* and *roughly* as possible substitutes. If one of the suggested words sounds better in the context of your writing, you would replace *approximately* with that word.

WordPerfect allows you to do this manual search-and-replace sequence rapidly and conveniently. The procedure to use the thesaurus is so smooth that you use it often.

Replacing an Existing Word

Load WordPerfect and retrieve the file *PAPER* that was written in the last chapter. Place the cursor under any letter in the word *ways* on the first line. Assume that you would like to see if you can find a word that is somewhat more distinctive. Type

Alt-F1   The Thesaurus key. As shown in Figure 6-1, the lower three-fourths of the
                                    screen is replaced by a three-column window that displays synonyms of the
                                    word above the cursor.

```
  I.  INTRODUCTION TO WORD PROCESSING

       There are many ways in which computers can operate
   on textual information.  Text editors are normally used
   to create programs or data to be processed by programs.
┌─way=(n)════════════════════════════════════════════════════════════
  1 A •custom
    B •habit
    C •manner
    D •practice

  2 E •means
    F •method
    G •procedure
    H •process
    I •technique

  3 J •avenue
    K •course
    L •direction
    M •route
    ─────────────────────
1 Replace Word; 2 View Doc; 3 Look Up Word; 4 Clear Column: 0
```

Figure 6-1. Sample Thesaurus Screen

The word itself is repeated in a label, **way (n)**, where the (n) indicates that the words displayed are synonymous with the noun form. Other words may display (n), (ant) for antonym, or (v) for verb. The thesaurus menu that appears is shown in Figure 6-2.

```
  1 Replace Word; 2 View Doc; 3 Look Up Word; 4 Clear Column: 0
```

Figure 6-2. Thesaurus Menu

Thirteen possible synonyms are suggested for *ways.* Each synonym is preceded by a letter. Substitute the word *method* for *ways* by typing

1	To select the menu choice Replace Word
◄┘	Enter key, to select the word *method.* Either an upper or lowercase letter can be typed. The Thesaurus window disappears and the substitution is made in the document.
s	To make *method* plural

Move the cursor to place it beneath the word *Reduced* in subsection B of section II. It is generally held that repetitions of a word in close proximity detract from the word's usefulness. Find a substitute by pressing

Alt-F1	The Thesaurus key, to recall the Thesaurus screen. The synonyms for the verb form of reduced are under the **reduced(v)** label and the antonyms of reduced are under **reduced(ant)**
1	To replace the word *Reduced*
a	To select *decrease* as the substitute. Notice that the first letter of *Decrease* is capitalized just as was the first letter in *Reduced.*
d	To make the word past tense

Expanding the Search

The word *complex* appears in subsection C of section II. Again, assume that you wish to find a synonym for this word. Place your cursor under *complex* and type

Alt-F1	The Thesaurus key. Perhaps seeing the list does not suggest an adequate replacement.
3	To begin to look up a synonym of *intricate.* Words on the screen that are preceded by dots have synonyms that can be looked up. Words without dots in front of them cannot be searched for any further.
C	The letter preceding *intricate.* A complete word could be typed here and that word would be looked up.
◄┘	Enter key. A list of synonyms for *intricate* appears in the second column and each is preceded by a letter. The letters no longer appear in the first column.
←	Left arrow, to move the letters to the first column. This is to show that you can still choose a replacement from the original list.
→	Right arrow, to see the second list
1	To start the replace operation
F	To replace the word *complex* with *involved*

Viewing the Document

Sometimes the Thesaurus window does not reveal enough of a word's context for you to determine which of several synonyms would be suitable. You may wish to see more of the document. Place your cursor under the word *skilled* in the same sentence and type

Alt-F1	The Thesaurus key. The list of possible substitutions appears.
2	To open the view document option. Observe that the cursor appears on the line.
↑	Up arrow five times, to see additional lines above the line containing *typists*
↓	Down arrow as necessary to expose more lines below

F7	The Exit key, to return to the substitutions list where *skilled* is still highlighted
1	To start the replacement operation
J	To substitute *talent* for *skill*
ed	To change to past tense
←	Left arrow, to put the cursor under the *o* in *over*
Ctrl-Backspace	To delete *over*

When you move the cursor vertically, the line is reformatted.

Looking Up a Word

So far, each of the examples used began with a word that has already been typed into the document. If you have a need as you are typing to find an alternative for a word you feel is weak, you may wish to look it up immediately, rather than typing in the questionable word first. Place your cursor behind the period of the last sentence of the document and type

Space,Space	Space bar twice, to separate the previous sentence from the next one to be typed

In addition to increased sales, it is likely that the word processing industry will introduce

	The beginning of a new sentence with a space following introduce
Alt-F1	The Thesaurus key
significant	The word to be looked up
◄⌐	Enter key
1	To replace, even though *significant* has not been typed into the document
A	To enter *important*

improvements in desktop publishing that will sustain the momentum already present.

	To end the sentence

THE SPELLING CHECKER

Proofreading is a crucial skill. Even excellent spellers make typographical errors or come across words whose spelling they cannot recall. For poor spellers, proofreading is even more critical. But good proofreading assumes that you recognize an incorrectly spelled word when you see it. It also assumes that you look carefully at each and every word and not become distracted from time to time. Of course, few of us, when proofreading a very long paper, can meet both of these conditions. WordPerfect has the answer to this problem: a spelling checker that checks each and every word in your document to see if it recognizes it. If it does not, it offers you opportunities: to change it, if it is, indeed, spelled incorrectly; to ignore the unrecognized spelling; or, if the word is spelled correctly, to add the word to WordPerfect's list of words it recognizes so that the word is not flagged as incorrect in the future.

Introducing Some Intentional Errors

For illustrative purposes, enter the following words and character strings in the text of the term paper. These errors will be corrected with the spelling checker afterwards. Enter

1.   *tany* instead of many in paragraph 1;
2.   *XYZ* after *which* in front of *Text,* and after *letters*, all in paragraph 1;

3. *Chemo-therapy* after *steadily.* at the end of sentence 1 of the second paragraph;
4. *Are* behind the word *are* and in front of the word *generally* in paragraph 2;
5. Change *capabilities* to *capaibilities* in paragraph 3, and *noted* to *nted,* which is also in paragraph 3.

Press

Home,Home, ↑   To return the cursor to the top of the document

Spell Check by Word

At times you may enter a word, look at it, and question whether it is properly spelled. If there is any doubt in your mind you can check the spelling for this one word immediately. You do not have to check the spelling of all words in your document. Before proceeding, place your cursor under the *t* in *operate* in the beginning sentence of the first paragraph. Then press

Del   The Delete key, to delete the *t.* The word is obviously spelled incorrectly. Leave the cursor under the final *e.*
Ctrl-F2   The Spell key. You receive the prompt

Check: 1 Word: 2 Page: 3 Document: 4 New Sup. Dictionary: 5 Look Up: 6 Count: 0

Figure 6-3. Spell Screen Menu

1   To check the spelling of the word above the cursor. A Spell Screen is shown in Figure 6-4. A list of words preceded by letters appears on the screen and *operae* is put into reverse video to indicate that the word is incorrectly spelled. The words that are suggested as possible substitutes are similar in spelling to *operae.* That is, by adding, transposing, or changing one or two letters in the original word, the suggested word could be constructed. Since the word is misspelled, various alternatives that are given may be very different from the desired spelling. A new prompt appears with the choices that are shown in Figure 6-3. Not all of these choices will be demonstrated.

```
                         <Your Name>

    I.  INTRODUCTION TO WORD PROCESSING

        There are mny methods in which XYZ computers can
    operae on textual information.  Editors are normally
    used to create programs or data to be processed by
    programs.  XYZ Text editors are not adapted to prepar-
    ing letters XYZ, term papers and other documents.  They
    have little capability for formatting the text in a
    variety of styles.  Some programming languages, most
                                        Doc 1 Pg 1 Ln 2" Pos 1.5"

    ▲   {   ▲    ▲    ▲    ▲    ▲    ▲    ▲    ▲    ▲    ▲  }   ▲    ▲    ▲

    A. opera           B. operas          C. operate
    D. opere           E. apiary          F. aporia
    G. aporiae         H. appear          I. upper
    J. yapper          K. yauper




Not Found: 1 Skip Once; 2 Skip; 3 Add; 4 Edit; 5 Look Up; 6 Ignore Numbers: 0
```

Figure 6-4. Sample Spell Screen

The options that are available through the spell screen are described in Figure 6-5.

OPTION	MEANING
Skip Once	Do not change this word, but go on to the next misspelled word. If this word appears again, pause to see if it should be changed at that location.
Skip	Do not change this word. Store its spelling and if this word appears again, ignore it.
Add	Keep in a dictionary that is in addition to the built-in dictionary of about 100,000 words. The second dictionary can contain technical terms and proper names that you may use, but that many other people would not.
Edit	Change the word that is highlighted.
Look Up	Identify similarly spelled words using the "wild card" characters * and ? (as in DOS) to display the correct spelling; also identify words that sound like the currently highlighted word.
Ignore Numbers	Pass over values in the spelling check.

Figure 6-5. Spell Screen Choices

C	To replace the incorrectly spelled word with choice C in the suggested word list
F1	The Cancel key, to notify WordPerfect to discontinue the search for other misspelled words

Add Word

You will now utilize several additional commands with the Spell menu. With the cursor at the top of the document, enter

Ctrl-F2	The Spell key
3	To check spelling throughout the term paper. If you have introduced other spelling errors than those specifically included, you may have to read ahead to see how to fix an incorrect spelling.

The spelling checker may stop at your name and place it in reverse video. Not surprisingly, this word is not contained in the 100,000-word dictionary provided by WordPerfect because your first and last names are proper nouns. The spelling dictionary has very few names. The student plans to continue to use WordPerfect for many years and decides that it would be a waste of time to have the spelling checker find his name each and every time it appears in one of his writings. WordPerfect keeps a second dictionary containing words that this user feels are sufficiently repetitive to store them. This second dictionary can house proper names and technical terms that many other people do not use frequently. To illustrate how to add a word, press

3	The add-a-word choice. The word is added to the previously empty supplementary dictionary.

When the words *Snobol, desktop*, and *Chemo-* appear, repeat this command.

Edit Word

The spelling checker moves on to the next word that it does not recognize, *tany.* This word is certainly spelled incorrectly. Choose

4	To edit the word. The cursor appears under the *t* and the highlighting disappears.
Del	Delete key, to remove the *t*
m	The letter *m,* to correct the spelling
F7	The Exit key, to note that the word has been corrected. WordPerfect will not accept another incorrect spelling, but returns the prompt that includes the edit option to allow you to try to fix it again.

As they appear, correct the spelling of *capaibilities* and *nted* with this option.

Skip Word

The next word highlighted by WordPerfect is *XYZ.* Assume that this is another technical term, the name of a company, that is spelled correctly. Since this word may not appear in future papers it is desirable to skip it rather than to add it to the dictionary. There are two ways to do this: to skip it once but flag future occurrences of XYZ, and to skip it throughout the remainder of the document. To skip it once, enter

| 1 | To skip XYZ once. The second occurrence is highlighted. |
| 2 | To skip all future occurrences of XYZ. The third occurrence is not flagged as unrecognizable by WordPerfect. |

Double Word

It is common to type double words both by accident and by design. It is not always clearly wrong to have double words. For instance, *That that was wrong is clear!* is a correctly written sentence, while the highlighted instance of *are are* is certainly an error. WordPerfect finds double words. If you feel the word pair is apt, skip the occurrence by typing either a *1* or a *2*. Delete one of the words, the second, by pressing

| 3 | To delete the undesired second word |

Choice 4 allows you to change one of the words by editing it. This choice would enable you to change *tip tip* to *tip top* without retyping two of the letters. You can prevent further double word checking with choice 5.

Word Count

At the end of its search, WordPerfect reports how many words are in the document, or on a page if the search is restricted to one page. If only a word count is desired, you can choose Count from the spelling checker's original prompt.

There is no reason to save this file. If you wish to save the file, however, follow the instructions contained in earlier chapters.

PRINTING THE FILE

Now that the editing of the term paper is finished and it has been saved, print out the document by typing

| Shift-F7 | To obtain the Print prompt |
| 1 | To print the document |

EXITING WORDPERFECT

Exit WordPerfect by typing

F7	The Exit key
N	**N**o, do not save the file
Y	**Y**es, to exit WordPerfect, or type *N* to begin the exercises

EXERCISES

A.   Make a copy of the term paper produced in Chapter 5: Advanced WordPerfect Usage, and name it TEST1.
1. Change the spelling of twenty words scattered throughout the paper to make them incorrect.
2. Introduce three double words.

3. Use global search-and-replace to change the spelling of *the* to %w&.
4. Use the spelling checker to correct all of the changes made except for %w&, which should be skipped as the spelling checker works through the text.

B.   Make a copy of the term paper produced in Chapter 5: Advanced WordPerfect Usage, and name it TEST2. Exchange the following words with one suggested by the thesaurus:

create	capability	adept
different	possess	accuracy
vendor	certain	expensive

C.   Use the spelling checker to examine and correct one of the documents you prepared in earlier chapters. Change ten words you used with words suggested by the thesaurus.

D.   Create a paragraph with the intention of using the text that follows. Before you type the boldfaced words, however, use the thesaurus to look up the bolded word and use one of the alternatives proposed, if there is one. Sometimes a root word can be found when a word with modified endings can be located.

The **wildly angry** man **whirled** a chain **around** his head **menacingly**. As the **crowd** scattered, the sheriff **drew** his **revolver**. "Stop," he said, **pointing** his **weapon** at the man. The man **meekly** put down the **chain** and **cried**.

Merging

F9, Shift F9, Ctrol F9

Chapter 7

Merging Files: The Form Letter

Chapter Outline

The ability to merge files and create a personalized form letter is a primary advantage of word processing. The creation of merged files saves considerable time. In little more than the time it takes to create one letter, you can create hundreds, all identically correct and perfectly formatted. In addition, once the proper files have been set up, they can quickly be modified for later applications. Merged files can be used to create mass mailings and multiple letters of application for jobs, and to fill out forms.

    This chapter will extend your knowledge of WordPerfect by showing you how to:

1. Create a primary file consisting of the form letter and merge codes which direct the merge;
2. Create a secondary file containing the records for the merge;
3. Use the Merge Codes menu to begin the merge;
4. Use keyboard entry in a merge;
5. Manage blank field names in a merge.

THE FORM LETTER

You have, no doubt, received form letters. A form letter is personalized with your name and address, although the body of the letter is identical to that sent to many others. The form letter consists of variable, personalized text and unchanging text, which remains identical from one letter to the next. Each kind of information is stored in a separate file. The variable information, often consisting of names and addresses, is stored in the secondary file, also called a data file, containing the data that will be used to fill in the blanks of the form letter. Unchanging information, consisting of the body of the letter and other elements, is stored in the primary, or main, file. Merging combines these two files into a third file which consists of the product of the merge: all of the finished letters.

THE PRIMARY FILE

Previously you created Harriet Hartley's résumé. Imagine that Ms. Hartley wishes to send her résumé to many firms to secure a position. With merging, she can save time and effort. Figure 7-1 shows the primary file that must be created. This file contains the text of her letter and the merge codes which control placement of the variable information. Merge field codes are entered through a Merge Codes menu found on function key Shift-F9. Although codes like {FIELD}1~ appear on the screen, these codes cannot be typed on the work screen; they must be entered through the Merge Codes menu.

```
{DATE}          shift F9, 6, Date

{FIELD}1~
{FIELD}2~
{FIELD}3~
{FIELD}4~

Dear {FIELD}6~:

I am writing in the hope that I might be considered for an entry
level marketing position with your company.

Having just graduated from the University of the Mountains with a
B. S. in Business Administration, I am eager to begin my
professional career.  Based upon my experience and qualifications,
summarized in the attached resume, I believe I could make a
valuable contribution to your firm.

I can be reached by telephone at 707-555-5665 during working hours.
I would welcome the chance to discuss employment possibilities with
you and would be happy to appear in person for an interview you
might schedule at your convenience.

I look forward to talking with you.

Sincerely,



Harriet Hartley
22 Elm Street
West Washington, NU 89888

Enclosure: Resume
```

Figure 7-1.

Overview: Field Numbers and Text

Notice that the primary file begins with a number of merge codes: {FIELD}1~, {FIELD}2~, and so forth. The merge codes indicate to WordPerfect which field values are to be merged and where they are to be merged. In this case, field values 1, 2, and 3 are to merge at the beginning of the letter, and field value 6 is to appear in the salutation line, after the word *Dear*. After that point the primary file is all standard text.

Creating the Primary File

With the cursor positioned at the top left corner of the opening WordPerfect screen, press

Shift-F9	The Merge Codes key, to display the Merge Codes menu. You should now see this menu at the bottom of your screen, with the cursor blinking in the position after the colon.

```
1 Field; 2 End Record; 3 Input; 4 Page Off; 5 Next Record; 6 More: 0
```

Figure 7-2. Merge Codes Menu

1	To select the F or Field code. You are prompted for the field number to be inserted.
1	To select Field Number 1, the first field to be put into the secondary file which is yet to be created. The first field will contain the full name of the individual receiving the letter.
◄┘	Enter key, to execute the selection. {FIELD}1~ appears on the screen
◄┘	Enter key, to move the cursor to the next line
Shift-F9	The Merge Codes key, to display the Merge Codes menu
1	To select the Field Code
2	To select Field Number 2. This field in the secondary file will contain the individual's title.
◄┘	Enter key, to execute the selection
◄┘	Enter key, to move the cursor to the next line
Shift-F9	The Merge Codes key, to display the Merge Codes menu
F	To select the Field Code
3	To select Field Number 3. This field in the secondary file will contain the name of the organization of the person being written to.
◄┘	Enter key, to execute the selection
◄┘	Enter key twice, to create a blank line
Dear	As the beginning of the salutation
Space	To separate words
Shift-F9	The Merge Codes key, to display the Merge Codes menu
1	To select the Field Code
6	To select Field Number 6
◄┘	Enter key, to execute the selection. {FIELD}6~ will appear on the screen. This field contains the name to be used in the salutation of the letter.
:	To put in the colon ending the salutation
◄┘	Enter key twice, to create a blank line before the beginning of the body of the letter

Now type in the rest of the letter as standard text. Save the file as **LETTER.PF**. Exit the document but not WordPerfect, leaving the blank beginning WordPerfect screen.

THE SECONDARY FILE

Shown below as Figure 7-3 is the secondary or data file.

```
Dr. Everett Murchison{END FIELD}
Director of Marketing{END FIELD}
Collegiate Computing Systems{END FIELD}
1028 Westport Boulevard
Islandview, California 98765{END FIELD}
707 441-6652{END FIELD}
Dr. Murchison{END FIELD}
{END RECORD}
===============================================================
Mr. G.N. Dayton{END FIELD}
Chief Executive Officer{END FIELD}
National Information Systems{END FIELD}
555 Industrial Parkway
Census, Ohio 29534{END FIELD}
299 600-0000{END FIELD}
Mr. Dayton{END FIELD}
{END RECORD}
===============================================================
Mr. Edson Baker{END FIELD}
President{END FIELD}
Smith & Baker Retailers{END FIELD}
1 Black Oak Lane
West Washington, Nevada 89888{END FIELD}
{END FIELD}
Edson{END FIELD}
{END RECORD}
===============================================================
```

Figure 7-3. Secondary File

Overview: Records, Field Numbers, and Field Values

The secondary file consists of a number of records, each containing specific information of different kinds. In the example above, the records consist of the following fields: (1) name, (2) title, (3) company, (4) street address/city/state/ZIP code, (5) phone number, and (6) the name (two with courtesy titles). Notice that each field is terminated with the merge code **{END FIELD}** and that each record is terminated with **{END RECORD}** followed by a hard page break. Also notice that the address field is entered on several lines before the **{END FIELD}** is found. A field's value is considered to be everything between the previous field's **{END FIELD}** and the field's own **{END FIELD}**, regardless of the number of lines separating the two codes. If you omit an **{END FIELD}** code, the contents of two fields would be combined into one field.

Although the field numbers are not displayed, the fields are designated by number according to their order. That is, WordPerfect counts the fields in each record beginning with the number 1. Field value number 1, therefore, is whatever text precedes the first merge code **{END FIELD}** in the record. If you forget to include a field **{END FIELD}** code even when the field is empty of information, WordPerfect will assume that the data from the next field should be used. Consequently, if the data for a field were not available, say a person's title, an {END FIELD} should be entered on a line by itself to indicate that there was no value to be included in this location. The information that is entered for each field is called the field's value. Mr. Edson Baker is the value of field 1 for record number 3.

Creating the Secondary File

With the cursor positioned at the top left-most column of the opening WordPerfect screen, type

Dr. Everett Murchison

	As the first field value of the first record
F9	The Merge R key, to insert the first {END FIELD} code, indicating the end of the first field value. Notice that the cursor automatically wraps, by inserting a hard return, to the next line. It is important that an extra hard return is not placed at the end of the field, since that would interfere with the proper functioning of the merge.

Director of Marketing

	As the second field value of the first record
F9	The Merge R key, to terminate the field and to insert the second {END FIELD} code. Again, the cursor wraps to the next line.

Collegiate Computing Systems

	As the third field value
F9	The Merge R key, to insert the third {END FIELD} code

1028 Westport Boulevard

	As the first line of the fourth field value
◄┘	Enter key, to move the cursor to the next line. Notice in this case that we wish to create a two-line field value. We are combining the street address and city/state/ZIP as one field value, separated by a hard return. In this case we want the hard return to become a permanent part of the field value: whenever we wish to merge field value 3, we are assuming we will want it to appear on two separate lines with a hard return following the street address.

Islandview, California 98765

	As the second line of the fourth field value
F9	The Merge R key, to insert the fourth {END FIELD} code
707 441-6652	As the fifth field value. This field will not be used in this letter.
F9	The Merge R key, to insert the fifth {END FIELD} code
Dr. Murchison	As the sixth field value, the salutation
F9	The Merge R key, to insert the sixth {END FIELD} code. Now you must terminate the record with the {END RECORD} code.
Shift-F9	The Merge Codes key
2	Notice that when the code is inserted, a hard page break is also inserted and the cursor automatically wraps to the beginning of the next line. You are now ready to type in the second record.

Type the second and third records in precisely the same way, with one exception. Notice that the phone number field value (number five) in the third record is blank. In cases where there is no value to enter, the Merge code ({END FIELD}) is still entered on the line by itself. This allows WordPerfect to keep track of correct field numbers throughout a record. All records must have the same number of fields, even if some are blank. If you accidentally omit a field, correct your omission by placing the cursor to the left of the {END FIELD} on the previous line. Then press F9. This will insert a new merge code symbol at the end of that line and will move the cursor to the next line. Add the field's missing value.

EXITING THE DOCUMENT

Once you have entered all three records and have insured that they are identical to those shown in Figure 7-3, enter

F7	The Exit key
Y	Yes, save the file
RECORDS.SF	The name of the file
◄┘	Enter key
N	No, do not exit WordPerfect, and leave the WordPerfect screen displayed

MERGING THE FILES

If the screen has not been cleared, repeat the instructions for exiting shown above. You should not begin the merge if text remains on the WordPerfect editing screen. You are now ready to merge the two files. Press

Ctrl-F9	The Merge/Sort key, to display the Merge/Sort menu. You should see this display at the bottom of the screen:

```
1 Merge; 2 Sort; 3 Convert Old Merge Codes: 0
```

Figure 7-4. Merge/Sort Menu

1	To select Merge and to display the prompt for primary file
LETTER.PF	The name of the primary file
◄┘	To start the merge process and to receive the prompt for secondary file
RECORDS.SF	The name of the secondary file
◄┘	To execute the merge process

WordPerfect now merges the information from the RECORDS.SF file with the text and codes in the LETTER.PF file, producing a third file on the screen (which has not been written to disk) consisting of three letters separated by hard page breaks.

If you managed the entire merge correctly, the address and salutation lines of the letters should look like Figure 7-5.

```
February 15, 1991

Dr. Everett Murchison
Director of Marketing
Collegiate Computing Systems
1028 Westport Boulevard
Islandview, California 98765

Dear Dr. Murchison:
    :
    :
    :
==========================================
February 15, 1991

Mr. G.N. Dayton
Chief Executive Officer
National Information Systems
555 Industrial Parkway
Census, Ohio 29534

Dear Mr. Dayton:
    :
    :
    :
==========================================
February 15, 1991

Mr. Edson Baker
President
Smith & Baker Retailers
1 Black Oak Lane
West Washington, Nevada 89888

Dear Edson:
    :
    :
    :
```

Figure 7-5.

Notice that in the third record, WordPerfect correctly counted past the blank, fifth field value to use Edson in the salutation. You have mastered one of the techniques for handling blank field values in the secondary file. You will learn the other one, how to apply this to the primary file, in the next section.

PRINTING THE LETTERS

The merged letters are printed with the Shift and F7 keys in the same way any other document is printed. Print the letters.

Since you can always reproduce these letters by merging the primary and secondary files again, there is no reason to save the merged letters. Use the F7 key to exit from the document without saving it, but return to the opening WordPerfect screen.

FURTHER HELPFUL MERGE OPERATIONS

In this section you will learn three more merge codes, which allow you to insert the current date automatically, to pause for keyboard entry, and to display a message. We will modify Harriet Hartley's cover letter so that it looks like Figure 7-6.

```
{DATE}

{FIELD}1~
{FIELD}2~
{FIELD}3~
{FIELD}4~

Dear {FIELD}6~:

In response to your recent advertisement in {INPUT}Cite ad source~, I am
writing in the hope that I might be considered for an entry level
marketing position with your company.

Having just graduated from the University of the Mountains with a
B. S. in Business Administration, I am eager to begin my
professional career.  Based upon my experience and qualifications,
summarized in the attached resume, I believe I could make a
valuable contribution to {FIELD}3~.

I can be reached by telephone at 707-555-5665 during working hours.
I would welcome the chance to discuss employment possibilities with
you and would be happy to appear in person for an interview you
might schedule at your convenience.

I look forward to talking with you.

Sincerely,


Harriet Hartley
22 Elm Street
West Washington, NV 89888

Enclosure: Resume
```

Figure 7-6.

Insert another field so the address prints on the letter. Place the cursor at the blank line following {FIELD}3~ and enter

Shift-F9	The Merge Codes key, to display the Merge Codes menu
1	To select the field code
4	To select field number 4

◄┘   Enter key, to execute the selection
◄┘   Enter key, to place a blank line after the {FIELD}4~ line

Retrieving a File

Beginning from the opening WordPerfect screen, retrieve the form letter file by entering,

Shift-F10   The Retrieve files key. This key can retrieve files more quickly than function key
                     F5.
LETTER.PF   The filename of the file to be retrieved
◄┘   Enter key

Inserting the Current Date in a Merge

WordPerfect will insert the computer system's date in a document every time the merge process is used.
Rather than typing in a date which has to be continually edited, let WordPerfect insert the date you enter
in response to the MS-DOS date prompt.
     With the cursor positioned under the first brace in the {FIELD}1~ code, press

Shift-F9   The Merge Codes key, to display the Merge Codes menu
6   Select from additional codes
D   To insert a {DATE} (^D) code, or alternatively, use the Down arrow to highlight
                     this choice
◄┘   Enter key, to select the date code
◄┘   Enter key, to insert a blank line between the date code and the Field 1 code

     Simple codes such as the {DATE} may also be entered by pressing Control and the code
character (e.g., D) simultaneously. This saves one keystroke over entering the Merge Codes menu.
However, field codes (e.g., {FIELD}2~) cannot be entered in this way, and {END RECORD} and {END
FIELD} are more efficiently entered from Shift-F9 since they are always followed by another code, [HPg]
and [HRt] respectively. Overall it may be simpler to use Shift-F9 for all merge codes.
     The Date Code will merge the current date into this position in the document. Current date
assumes that the computing system running WordPerfect has been booted up properly so that the
current date is known to the system.

Inserting a Message and a Pause for Keyboard Entry

WordPerfect can combine information from three sources into a document: the primary file, the
secondary file, and the keyboard. Input from the keyboard is entered during the merge process.
     Position the cursor under the *I* at the beginning of the first paragraph of the letter, *I am writing . . .
. .* Type

In response to your recent advertisement in
                     As a new beginning to the sentence
Space   Space bar, to prepare for the text to follow
Shift-F9   The Merge Codes key, to display the Merge Codes menu
6   Select *More*
I   Select *{INPUT}message~*
◄┘   Enter key

Cite ad source	As the message to be displayed at this point in the text
◄┘	Enter key, to insert the date code after the message code. Now the merge will pause at this position and the message *Cite ad source* will be displayed at the bottom of the screen as a prompt.
,	To place a comma after the name of the source of the advertisement
Space	Space bar, to leave a space after the comma

Further Personalizing the Body of the Letter

Since it never hurts to mention the firm to which one is applying in the body of the letter, press the Down Arrow as necessary, to move down to the last line of the second paragraph of the body of the letter.

Backspace	Ten times to delete the period and words *your firm*
Shift-F9	The Merge Codes key, to display the Merge Codes menu
1	To choose the Field code. You are prompted for the Field number.
3	To select the third field, the company name
◄┘	Enter key. {FIELD}3~ is inserted at that point.
.	To end the sentence

     Replace the old version of **LETTER.PF** and exit the document with the F7 key. Do not exit WordPerfect.

Managing Keyboard Entry During Merge

From a blank WordPerfect screen you are now ready to again merge the two files. Press

Ctrl-F9	To display the Merge/Sort menu
1	To display the prompt for the primary file
LETTER.PF	The name of the primary file
◄┘	Enter key, to receive the prompt for secondary file
RECORDS.SF	The name of the secondary file
◄┘	Enter key, to execute the merge

     The merge pauses after the word *in*. Notice that today's date has been placed at the top of the letter (assuming your system was booted up with the correct date). Also notice that the phrase *Cite ad source,* the prompt you inserted at this point in the primary file, appears at the bottom of your screen. Now type

Career Chronicle	
	As the fictitious name of the publication where the advertisement is said to have appeared
F9	The Merge key, to continue the merge after the insertion. Note that at pauses for keyboard entry, the Merge key continues the merge, whereas the Merge/Sort key (Ctrl-F9) can be used to halt the merge at any point. The merge continues in this case, automatically inserting the firm name at the end of the second paragraph, through the end of the first letter and into the second, pausing again for keyboard entry. Type

Headhunter's Digest
  As the advertisement source for the second letter

F9
  To continue the merge. The same pause occurs in the third letter.

West Washington Weekly
  As the advertisement source for the third letter

F9
  To continue the merge, which terminates automatically at the end of the third letter

Home, Home, ↑
  Return to the top of the document

Grey +
  Scroll through the three letters to ensure that all elements of your merge worked successfully. Except for your current date appearing instead of [today's date], the three should look like the portion of the Figure 7-7 shown below:

```
February 15, 1991

Dr. Everett Murchison
Director of Marketing
Collegiate Computing Services
1028 Westport Boulevard
Islandview, California 98765

Dear Dr. Murchison:

In response to your recent advertisement in Career Chronicle, I am
writing in the hope that I might be considered for an entry level
marketing position with your company.

Having just graduated form the University of the Mountains with a
B. S. in Business Administration, I am eager to begin my
professional career.  Based upon my experience and qualifications,
summarized in the attached resume, I believe I could make a
valuable contribution to Collegiate Computing Systems.

I can be reached ...
```

Figure 7-7. Portion of Merged Letter

Once you have inspected the three letters and found them correct, print them. You may exit the document without saving it. Return to the beginning WordPerfect screen if you wish to continue. The document could, of course, be saved like any other document, if you wish.

FURTHER MODIFICATIONS TO THE LETTERS

After the merge has been completed you are free to edit the letters in the file. If you wished to add a paragraph or additional sentences for some letters, you can simply type them in before the file is printed. Similarly, if some sentences need to be modified or deleted, that can be done also.

OTHER USES OF MERGE

This chapter has introduced you to the merging process. In addition to producing personalized letters, merging can be used for other documents. Merging is used to produce mailing labels, to print addresses on envelopes, telephone lists from secondary files, memorandums, and legal documents in which the text is unchanging but a client's name and other information changes.

EXERCISES

A.   Create a primary file called MEMOHDR.PF which consists of the following text and merge codes:

```
To: {INPUT}Memo to whom? ... Then press F9~

Fr: {INPUT}Memo from whom? ... Then press F9~

Re: {INPUT}Enter the topic/reference ... Then press F9~

Date: {DATE}

{INPUT}Input the memorandum.  Press F9 at the end~
```

Speculate on what purpose for what sort of user this primary file is intended to serve. Next, run a merge with this file; note that no secondary file is needed, since only keyboard entry is required. Finally, critique this primary file's design: what might be done differently?

B.   With reference to **RECORDS.SF** as the secondary file, create a primary file called **DAYLIST.PF** which displays the fields of name, title, company, and phone number across the page on a single line. The heading for this list should read like this:

Resumes sent on {DATE} to the following executives:

Follow this with a blank line and headings (the fields noted above would serve) for the listing to appear beneath them in tabular form. Put in a {NEXT RECORD} code at the end of each line to force the merge to read the next record without putting in an automatic hard page end. Merge the files to test your design, and make whatever adjustments are necessary.

Chapter 8

Use of the Mouse

Chapter Outline

THE PURPOSE OF THIS CHAPTER

This text has been written with the assumption that the persons using it are not using a microcomputer with a mouse attached. Some users do have mouse devices, however. This chapter is intended to provide you with an overview of how the mouse is used so you can make the transition from keyboard-oriented commands to mouse-oriented commands.

WHAT IS A MOUSE?

A mouse is a handheld device that allows a computer user to speed up word processing operations such as:
1. identifying blocks of text that are to be moved or copied,
2. selecting choices from a mouse-oriented series of pop-up menus,
3. moving and scrolling the cursor.

Mouse devices are also used heavily for graphics operations in other types of programs. There are two types of mouse devices available: two button and three button. These are pictured in Figure 8-1a and Figure 8-1b. One type of mouse senses its movement by a roller that moves over any flat surface. Other mouse devices generate light that reflects off of a special tablet with grid markings. The detection of the grid markings indicates the direction and amount of movement of the mouse. The mouse moves easily on an appropriate surface so avoid applying excessive pressure. The mouse can be lifted off of the surface if necessary and brought back down to a new location without moving the cursor arrow.

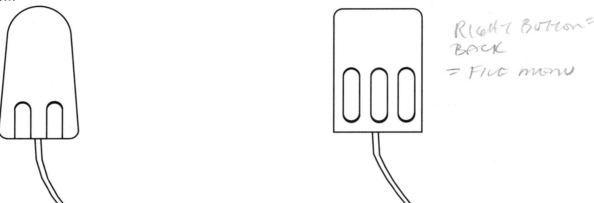

RIGHT BUTTON =
BACK
= FILE menu

Figure 8-1a. A Two-Button Mouse   **Figure 8-1b**. A Three-Button Mouse

MOUSE OPERATIONS IN WORDPERFECT

Both types of mouse devices can be used with WordPerfect. The mouse creates a block (▌) called a pointer. The pointer does not replace the cursor. The cursor is still visible. The pointer appears when the mouse is activated and disappears when the keyboard is in use. If you move the mouse and the pointer is not visible, continue moving the mouse around until it becomes visible.

Pointing	The movement of the mouse so that the pointer block (▌) is moved to a new location.
Clicking	The rapid pressing and releasing of the left button (Enter key).
Canceling	Pressing the middle button on a three-button mouse; clicking the right button to obtain the menu bar and clicking the right button a second time; pressing the F1 (Cancel) key.
Dragging	Holding a button down while moving the mouse pointer.
Exiting	Pressing the right button, when a menu or some prompts are in view, is equivalent to pressing the Exit key (F7).
< choice >	A notation used in this chapter to request that the pointer block be placed on a menu selection or object before activating a command.

For either type of mouse, pressing the left button acts the same as the Enter key. The button on the right is the same as the Escape key. For any operation that requires Enter or Escape, one can press the mouse buttons or the keys on the keyboard.

SAMPLE OPERATIONS

The Menu Bar

The menu shown in Figure 8-2 can be brought to the top of the work screen by pressing the right button. The pointer can be moved from the document into the menu bar. A pop-up menu for a highlighted menu choice can be brought into view by moving the pointer to the desired choice and pressing the left button (Click(L)). A choice from the pop-up menu can be made by moving the pointer up and down, to select the needed choice. Then click the left button (Click(L)) on the choice. The menu bar can be removed from view at any time by pressing the right button.

File **Edit Search Layout Mark Tools Font Graphics Help**

Figure 8-2. The Menu Bar

See the menu bar by pressing

Click(R)   Click the right button, to see the menu bar as shown in Figure 8-2
Click(R)   Click the right button a second time, to remove the menu bar

You will see shortly how you can make selections from the menu bar.

Scrolling

The pointer can be moved around inside of the document window. Normally, the pointer cannot be moved out of the current window. The right button when depressed, however, allows you to move the cursor beyond to the bottom or top of the screen. Continued depression of this button and "pushing" up against the edge scrolls the text in the document into view.

The mouse does not scroll left or right of the margins, above or below the top or bottom of the document. Although the mouse may place the pointer in an area of the document where there are no characters or embedded codes, when text is blocked, the pointer moves to the closest text.

Responding to Prompts

Prompts such as "Save file?: Yes (No)" permit use of the mouse to place the pointer on the desired choice and to select the choice by pressing the left button (Click).

Using the Keyboard

Keyboard commands can be interspersed with mouse-originated commands.

Blocking

The primary use for a mouse in edit mode is to block text and then to move, delete, or copy that text. The mouse replaces the use of the arrow keys. The arrow keys may take considerably more time to use than the mouse does. Using keyboard commands, retrieve a document of your choice for practice in this lesson. When the document is in view, move the mouse to obtain the pointer. Place the pointer at the beginning of a paragraph and enter

Drag(L)	Press the left button and hold it down to set blocking on. A prompt to this effect appears in the lower left of the screen.
Move	Move the pointer with the mouse to place the pointer at the right-most character in the last line of the text to be moved, highlighting the text as the pointer is moved
Release	Release the left button, to stop blocking
Click(L)	Click the left button, to remove blocking

Blocking is used later in this lesson.

Moving the Cursor

The cursor and the mouse pointer block are different. The pointer block can be used to move the cursor to a new location, however. Move the pointer with the mouse to any location other than one at which the cursor is located.

| Click(L) | Click the left button a second time. The cursor moves to the location of the pointer block. |

Blocking Operations

Blocking can be used to move, copy, and delete text. Try moving some text by placing the pointer at the beginning of a paragraph and entering

Drag(L)	Click the left button and hold it down to set blocking on. A prompt to this effect appears in the lower left of the screen.
Move	Move the pointer with the mouse, to place the pointer at the right-most character in the last line of the text to be moved.
Release	Release the left button, to stop blocking
Click(R)	Click the right button, to call up the menu bar
<Edit>	Move the pointer onto Edit
Click(L)	Click the left button, to bring the pop-up menu for Edit into view
<Delete>	Move the pointer down with the mouse, to highlight Delete
Click(L)	Click the left button, to activate Delete. A prompt, "Delete Block? No (Yes)" appears.
<Yes>	Move the pointer block onto "Yes"
Click(L)	Select "Yes." The text is deleted.

This technique is equally applicable to moving and copying text. Moving is shown next. Practice copying on your own.

Moving

Moving text is another block operation that illustrates how the mouse can be used to replicate keyboard operations.

Drag(L)	Depress the left button. Blocking is toggled on. Move the mouse, continuing to hold down the left button, to the last character in the paragraph.
Release	Free the left button. The text remains blocked.
Click(R)	Click the right button, to call up the menu bar
<Edit>	Select Edit

Click(L)	Click the left button, to call up the pop-up menu
<Move>	Select the Move option
Click(L)	The blocked text is cut from the document. The prompt "Move the cursor; **Press Enter** to retrieve" appears.
Move ↑↓	Move the pointer block to a new location
↵	Enter key, to bring the text back to a new location

File

Other menus can be recalled and activated in a manner similar to that shown for deletion. Examine one of the pop-up menus more closely. Continue by entering

Click(R)	Click the right button, to toggle the menu bar on
<Edit>	Move the pointer to highlight Edit on the menu bar
Drag(L)	Depress the left button
Move → ←	Roll the mouse left and right, keeping the pointer inside of the menu bar, to see the pop-up menus associated with each menu choice
<File>	Stop the pointer on File
Click(L)	Click the left button, to select File and to view the pop-up menu shown in Figure 8-3

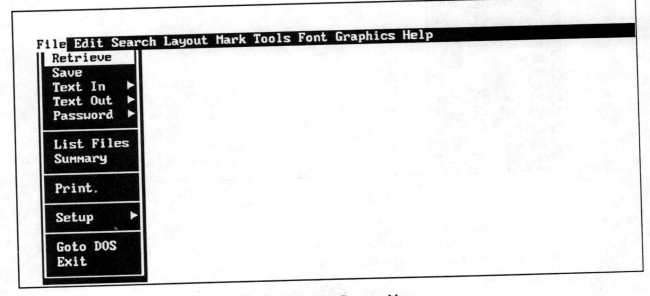

Figure 8-3. File Pop-up Menu

Move ↓↑	Roll the mouse up and down to highlight the choices on the pop-up menu
<List Files>	Highlight the choice List Files
Click(L)	Click the left button, to select List Files. The prompt for showing a directory listing appears. Change this directory if necessary.
Click(R)	Click the right button, to see the files available to choose from in the current directory
Drag(L)	Depress the left button, to highlight filenames. By moving the pointer to different filenames, they can be selected for menu choice activities.
<filename>	Highlight any filename of your choice

Move ↓↑	Move the pointer block out of the highlighted filename down to the menu area
<6 Look>	Select the Look option
Click(L)	Click the left button, to view the first page of the document
Click(R)	Click the right button, to stop looking at the document
Click(R)	Click the right button, to exit

Edit

The Edit pop-up menu is shown in Figure 8-4. The choices are many of the same as available with the F3 and F4 key operations.

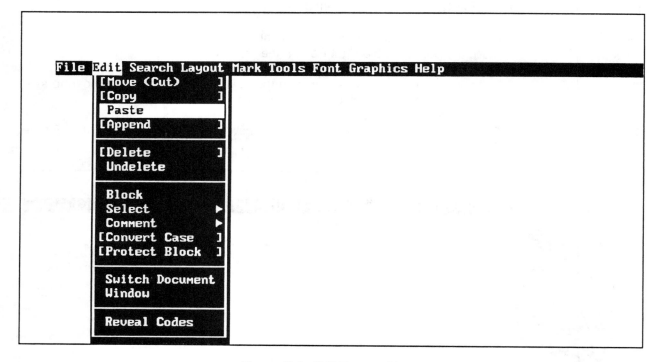

Figure 8-4. Edit Pop-up Menu

Click(R)	Call up the menu bar
<Edit>	Highlight Edit with the mouse pointer
Click(L)	Click the left button to select Edit
Drag(L)	
Move ↓↑	Roll the mouse up and down to highlight the choices
<Window>	Highlight the choice Window
Click(L)	Click the left button to select Window
12	Type *12* to select the window size
Click(R)	Click the right button, to complete the operation. Now you are able to view documents 1 and 2 concurrently.

Follow the same steps to reset the window to twenty-four lines.

Search

The Search pop-up menu is shown in Figure 8-5. The choices are the same as those that are available with the Search key (F2).

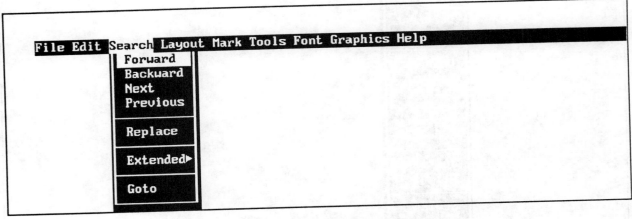

Figure 8-5. Search Pop-up Menu

Click(R)	Click the right button to call up the menu bar
<Search>	Highlight the Search option
Click(L)	Click the left button, to select the Search option and view the Search menu
Move ↓↑	Roll the mouse to the choice *Forward*
Click(L)	Click the left button to select *Forward*. You are prompted to enter a word at the "-> Srch:" prompt
the	With spaces on both sides, enter the word *the* or any word that is contained in your document
Click(R)	Click the right button to complete the operation and to have the cursor moved to the first instance of the word in your document

Other types of searches can be carried out in a very similar fashion.

Layout

The Layout pop-up menu is shown in Figure 8-6. The choices are many of the same as those available with the F7 and F8 key operations. Enter the following:

Click(R)	Click the right button to obtain the menu bar
<Layout>	Highlight the Layout option
Click(L)	Click the left button to select the layout option
Move ↓↑	Roll the mouse pointer
<Align>	Select *Align*
Click(L)	Click the left button, to call another pop-up menu associated with Align
Move ↓↑	Roll mouse cursor
<Hard Page>	Select *Hard Page,* to enter a hard page code
Click(L)	Click the left mouse key, to enter the code

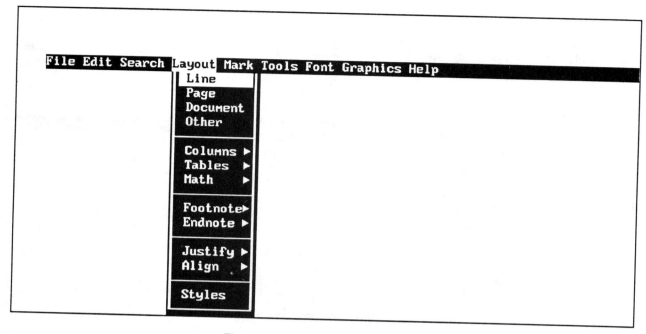

Figure 8-6. Layout Pop-up Menu

Mark

The Mark pop-up menu is shown in Figure 8-7. The choices are the same as those that are available with the F5 key options.

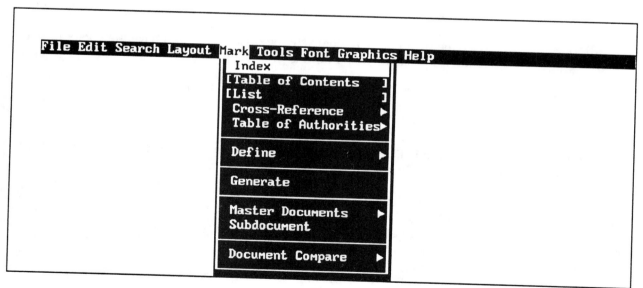

Figure 8-7. Mark Pop-up Menu

Tools

The Tools pop-up menu is shown in Figure 8-8. The choices are many of the same as available with the Alt-F1 (Thesaurus), Ctrl-F2 (Spell), Ctrl-F3 (Line Draw), F9 (Merge/Sort, Merge codes) Alt-F10 (Macro) keys.

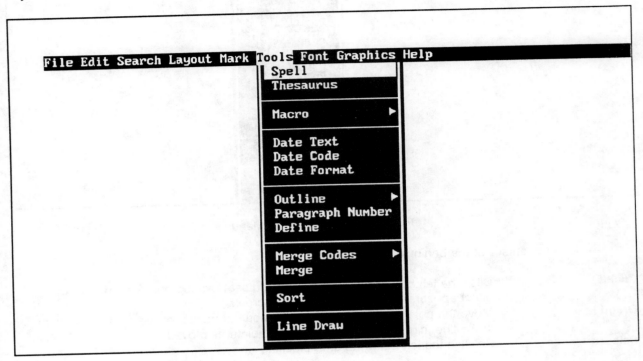

Figure 8-8. Tools Pop-up Menu

Click(R)	Click the right button, to obtain the menu bar
<Tools>	Highlight Tools
Click(L)	Click the left button, to select Tools
Move ↓↑	Move pointer to the selection Spell
Click(L)	Click left mouse button to select the Spell option
Move ↓↑	Move mouse pointer to the bottom of the screen and highlight **2 P**age, to have spelling checker review the page for spelling errors
Click(L)	Click the left button, to select and initiate the Page spell check. If any words are highlighted by the spelling checker, use the mouse to make selections from the Spell menu by clicking the left button or pressing function key F1 to cancel.

Font

The Font pop-up menu is shown in Figure 8-9. The choices are the same as those that are available with the F3 and the F8 keys.

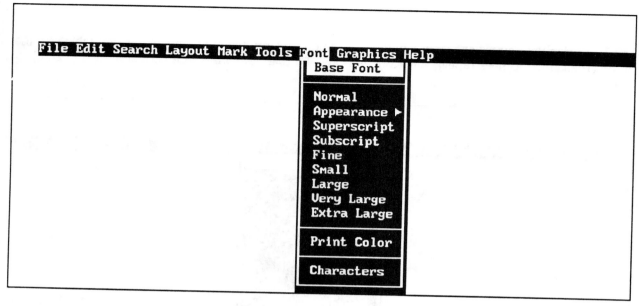

Figure 8-9. Font Pop-up Menu

Place the cursor at the beginning of a line and enter

Click(L)	Click the left button and hold it down, to set blocking on. A prompt to this effect appears in the lower left of the screen.
Drag(L)	Move the pointer with the mouse to place the pointer at the right-most character in the line, highlighting the text as the pointer is moved
Release	Release the left button to stop blocking

Underline the blocked text by entering

Click(R)	Click the right button to obtain the menu bar
<Font>	Highlight the option Font
Click(L)	Click the left button, to select Font
Move ↓↑	Roll the mouse pointer
<Appearance>	Highlight Appearance to alter the appearance of the text you will type shortly
Click(L)	Click the left button, to select Appearance
<Underline>	Highlight Underline
Click(L)	Click the left button, to select the underlining option. The text is underlined and shows a different background color.

Graphics

The Graphics pop-up menu is shown in Figure 8-10. The choices are the same as those that are available with the Alt-F9 key (Graphics).

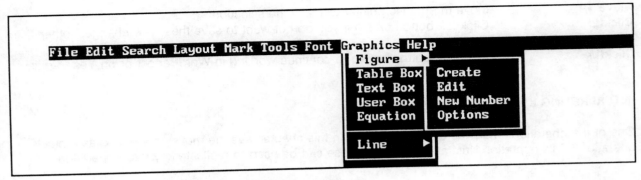

Figure 8-10. Graphics Pop-up Menu

Help

The Help pop-up menu is shown in Figure 8-11. The choices are the same as those that are available with the F3 key (Help).

Figure 8-11. Help Pop-up Menu

Click(R)	Click right button to obtain the menu bar
<help>	Highlight Help selection
Click(L)	Click the left button, to select Help
Move ↓↑	Roll pointer to Template
Click(L)	Click the left button to select Template, to view the Help template that would ordinarily go over the function keys on the keyboard
Click(R)	Click the right button, to cancel the Help template and return to document

Windowing

Control-F3 can be used to split the screen so you can see two documents. When the screen is split, the mouse can move the pointer from one window to the other.

EXITING

Documents can be exited using a mouse, also. To exit the document you are in, press

Click(R)	Click the right button to obtain the menu bar
<File>	Highlight the file option
Click(L)	Click the left button to call up the File pop-up menu
Move ↓↑	Move the pointer to the selection Exit
Click(L)	Click the left button, to select the exit option. The R.S.V.P prompt asking whether you wish to save the document appears.

Move ↓ ↑	Move the mouse pointer to make the selection
Click(L)	Click left button on **No** if you do not want to save these few changes, otherwise click on **Yes**
Click(L)	Press left button on **No** to continue working in WordPerfect or on **Yes** to quit.

INTERPRETING KEYBOARD COMMANDS

One of the operations that was discussed earlier in this chapter was the movement of text as a block operation. This operation illustrates how the mouse can be used to replicate keyboard operations.

MOUSE COMMAND	ACTION	KEYBOARD COMMAND
Drag(L)	Start blocking the text to be moved	Alt-F4
Move	Move the cursor (pointer) to the end of the block	Arrow keys
Release	Stop blocking	
Click(R)	Call up the menu bar	Ctrl-F4
<Edit>	Select Edit	**Move: 1 Block**
Click(L)	Activate Edit	
<Move>	Select Move	**1 Move;**
Click(L)	Cut text	
Move	Move the cursor to the "move to" location	Arrow keys
◄⌐	Enter the text at the location of the cursor	◄⌐

SUMMARY

Many software programs are being designed to take advantage of mouse capabilities. Initially, it takes time to practice using the mouse enough to gain a comfortable familiarity with mouse-oriented commands. After this initial period of adjustment, you will find that using a mouse can make many operations seem more natural and efficient. The effort involved is worth your time.

Appendix

Function Key/Menu/Screen Summary

F1 Cancel/Undo
  Restore
  Previous Deletion
F2 Forward Search
F3 Help
F4 Indent
F5 List Files
  Retrieve
  Delete
  Move/Rename
  Print
  Short/Long Display
  Look
  Other Directory
  Copy
  Find
    Name
    Document Summary
    First Page
    Entire Document
    Conditions
    Undo
  Name Search
F6 Bold
F7 Exit
F8 Underline
F9 End Field
F10 Save
F11 Reveal Codes
F12 Block
Shift-F1 Setup
  Mouse
    Type
    Port
    Double Click Interval
    Submenu Delay Time
    Accelerator Factor
    Left-handed Mouse
    Assisted Mouse Pointer
  Display
    Colors/Fonts/Attributes
    Graphics Screen Type
    Text Screen Type
    Menu Options
    View-Document Options
    Edit-Screen Options

  Environment
    Backup Options
    Beep Options
    Cursor Speed
    Document Management/Summary
    Fast Save
    Hyphenation
    Prompt for Hyphenation
    Units of Measure
  Initial Settings
    Merge
    Date Format
    Equations
    Format Retrieved Documents for Default
  Printer
    Initial Codes
    Repeat Value
    Table of Authorities
    Print Options
  Keyboard Layout
    ALTRNAT
    ENHANCED
    EQUATION
    MACROS
    SHORTCUT
  Location of Files
    Backup Files
    Keyboard/Macro Files
    Thesaurus/Spell/Hyphenation
      Main
      Supplementary
    Printer Files
    Style Files
      Library Filename
    Graphic Files
    Documents
Shift-F2 Reverse Search
Shift-F3 Switch
Shift-F4 Indent Left/Right

Shift-F5   Date/Outline
  Date Text
  Date Code
  Date Format
  Outline
    On
    Off
    Move Family
    Copy Family
    Delete Family
  Para Num
  Define
    Starting Paragraph Number
    Paragraph
    Outline
    Legal
    Bullets
    User-Defined
    Enter Inserts Paragraph Number
    Automatically Adjust to Current Level
    Outline Style Name
Shift-F6   Center
Shift-F7   Print
  Print
    Full Document
    Page
    Document on Disk
    Control Printer
    Multiple Pages
    View Document
    Initialize Printer
  Options
    Select Printer
    Binding Offset
    Number of Copies
    Multiple Copies Generated By
    Graphics Quality
    Text Quality
Shift-F8   Format
  Line
    Hyphenation
    Hyphenation Zone
    Justification
    Line Height
    Line Numbering
    Line Spacing
    Margins (Left/Right)
    Tab Set
    Widow/Orphan Protection

  Page
    Center Page
    Force Odd/Even Pages
    Headers
    Footers
    Margins (Top/Bottom)
    Page Numbering
    Paper (Size/Type)
    Suppress
  Document
    Display Pitch
    Initial Codes
    Initial Base Font
    Redline Method
    Summary
  Other
    Advance
    Conditional End of Page
    Decimal/Align Character
    Thousands' Separator
    Language
    Overstrike
    Printer Functions
    Underline (Spaces/Tabs)
    Border Options
Shift-F9   Merge Codes
  Field
  End Record
  Input
  Page Off
  Next Record
  More
Shift-F10   Retrieve
Alt-F1   Thesaurus
  Replace Word
  View Document
  Look Up Word
  Clear Column
Alt-F2   Search and Replace
Alt-F3   Reveal Codes
Alt-F4   Block
Alt-F5   Mark Text
  Cross-Ref
  Subdoc
  Index
  ToA Short Form
  Define
  Generate

Alt-F6   Flush Right
Alt-F7   Columns/Table
  Columns
    On
    Off
    Define
  Tables
    Create
    Edit
  Math
    On
    Off
    Define
    Calculate
Alt-F8   Style
  On
  Off
  Create
  Edit
  Delete
  Save
  Retrieve
  Update
Alt-F9   Graphics
  Figure
  Table Box
  Text Box
  User Box
  Line
  Equation
Alt-F10   Macro
Ctrl-F1   DOS Shell
  Go to DOS
  DOS Command
Ctrl-F2   Spell
  Word
  Page
  Document
  New Supplementary Dictionary
  Look Up
  Count
Ctrl-F3   Screen
  Window
  Line Draw
  Rewrite

Ctrl-F4   Move/Copy
  (Blocking Off)
    Sentence
    Paragraph
    Page
    Retrieve
  (Blocking On)
    Block
    Tabular Column
    Rectangle
Ctrl-F5   Text In/Out
  DOS Text
  Password
  Save As
  Comment
  Spreadsheet
Ctrl-F6   Tab Align
Ctrl-F7   Footnote
  Footnote
  Endnote
  Endnote Placement
Ctrl-F8   Font
  Size
    Superscript
    Subscript
    Fine
    Small
    Large
    Very Large
    Extra Large
  Appearance
    Bold
    Underline
    Double Underline
    Italic
    Outline
    Shadow
    Small Cap
    Redline
    Strikeout
  Normal
  Base Font
    Select
    Name Search
  Print Color
Ctrl-F9   Merge/Sort
  Merge
  Sort
  Convert Old Merge Codes
Ctrl-F10   Macro Definition

Glossary

. Symbolic representation for the current directory.

.. Symbolic representation of the parent directory of the current directory.

* The DOS and WordPerfect wild card for matching multiple characters in command line parameters.

**** Symbolic representation for the root directory.

A   **A>** The DOS system prompt signifying drive A as the default drive.

Active document The document, 1 or 2, in which the cursor is currently positioned.

Alignment The placement of text on a line.

Alphabetic keys The keys on the computer's keyboard that are arranged just as they are on a typewriter keyboard.

Alphanumeric characters Any combination of letters, numbers, symbols, and spaces.

Alternate key The key marked Alt and used to attach alternate meanings to other alphanumeric keys in WordPerfect.

Application The product of a generalized application program such as a document from a word processor, a budget projection from a spreadsheet, or an inventory from a database manager.

Application program A program that allows users to produce specific applications of the computer to a particular area or need.

ASCII American Standard Code for Information Interchange; the coding scheme whereby every character, number, or symbol is represented by an integer code between 0 and 255.

ASCII files Text files saved in a format specified by the American Standard Code for Information Interchange. Files saved in this format often can be used by other programs, or transmitted by modem because they have a standard format.

Automatic repeat The characteristic of keys, if held down, to continue to enter the symbol they represent after the first entry of the character and a brief pause.

Auxiliary files Files that an application program uses to supplement the main program files.

B   **B>** The DOS system prompt signifying drive B as the default drive.

Back up A process of making a second copy of a file to avoid loss of data. Backups may be created automatically by some applications programs.

Backup copy A duplicate of a file or disk that is saved in case the original file or disk is damaged.

Bad sector A disk sector that has been damaged and marked as unusable by DOS.

Beep An audible sound notifying a user of an error.

Binding width The addition of extra space in the left margin for odd-numbered pages and in the right margin for even-numbered pages to allow space for a binding mechanism.

Block In WordPerfect, a highlighted block of text that is to be copied, moved, or otherwise manipulated. Also, a contiguous character string.

Block protect In WordPerfect, a pair of codes that prevents the intervening text from being divided by a soft page break.

Block text In WordPerfect, the process of highlighting text with the Move key (Ctrl-F4).

Bold text Text that is darker or "brighter" than normal text.

Boot To load and run the operating system. Derived from "pull yourself up by your own bootstraps."

Byte A unit of representation constructed from eight bits. A byte represents a single character.

C   **C >** The DOS system prompt signifying drive C, the hard drive, as the default drive.

Cancel To abort a program or command.

Carriage return (CR) A printer directive moving the print head down one line and back to the left margin. Issued by pressing the Enter (Return) key on most programs.

Case The shape and size of a letter. Letters in a type style may be uppercase or lowercase.

Case sensitive A command that acts differently if characters are typed in lowercase or uppercase.

Center In WordPerfect, the use of the Center key (Shift-F6) to position a word or phrase between the current margins.

Center indent A WordPerfect code (Shift-F4) that temporarily indents text equally from the right and left margins.

Center page A WordPerfect code that places text on a page with equal top and bottom margins.

Character A symbol (numeric, alphabetic, punctuation, or mathematic) represented by one byte.

Character string See String.

Code A symbol embedded in the text of a document that affects the formatting or printing of the text.

Cold boot Starting the computer by turning it on.

Color display A monitor that displays color.

Color/Graphics Monitor Adapter The printed-circuit card for personal computers that provides low-level graphics and minimal colors.

Command An instruction to a computer that can be executed.

Commercial software Software that has been copyrighted and licensed, is supported by the developer, and that must be paid for in advance of its usage.

Compressed type Small type size. For example, a type size of 17.5 cpi. A typical size is 10 or 12 cpi.

Condensed type See Compressed type.

Configuration The currently active default values for an operating system or for an applications program. These values may be modifiable during operation.

Control code A code entered by pressing the Control key and another key at the same time. The caret, ^, often symbolizes the Control key. Control keys permit the issuance of DOS commands for disparate activities such as rebooting, aborting a program, and suspending program execution. In WordPerfect, Control codes insert formatting codes.

cpi Characters per inch.

CPU Central processing unit. The unit that processes data and supports random access memory (RAM).

Current directory The default DOS directory. The directory that is employed first when DOS searches for files and executable commands unless otherwise directed.

Current drive The drive containing the disk on which DOS looks for a directory or file unless otherwise instructed.

Cursor The underscore character that indicates where characters will be entered or where commands will be carried out.

D **Data disk** The disk used to store files.

Database An organized collection of related records containing data suitable for manipulation by a database program.

Database field One element in a database structure that is defined by a field name, a length, and a type.

Database record The fields that compose an entry in a database.

Debug To discover and correct syntactic and semantic errors in a program, function, macro, batch file, or subroutine.

Decimal tab A tab marker for which numbers are centered on a period.

Default directory See Current directory.

Default drive See Current drive.

Default value The value used or the action taken when an acceptable alternative has not been specified.

Desktop Publishing A software package that integrates graph and text materials suitable for high quality publications.

Destination The target location for data or files transferred from a source location.

Dir In DOS, the command for listing the names of files and directories.

Directory A logical grouping of files and subdirectories on a disk. A directory's filenames, extensions, and subdirectory names are displayed together along with the file's size, creation time, and date.

Directory hierarchy The treelike, logical structure holding subdirectories. Subdirectories of root have subdirectories created under them, and so on.

Disk drive The device that reads and writes files to disks.

Diskette A secondary storage medium for a computer. Diskettes come in floppy, rigid, and semirigid cases.

Display The monitor screen. Also, in dBASE, a command for listing the contents of records.

Doc number In WordPerfect, the number of the document the cursor is located in. Two documents may be in use simultaneously.

DOS Disk Operating System. The software that makes computer hardware usable.

Dot leader tab A tab marker that fills the space up to tabbed text with dots rather than blank space.

Double-density disk A disk with 360 Kb of storage.

Double sided A diskette with two surfaces on which to store files.

Drive name The characters (a letter and a colon) that identify a disk drive. Examples include *C:* and *A:*.

E   **Edit** To check or modify documents, worksheets, data, or program codes.

Embedded code A word processing code that affects the formatting but not the contents of the document.

Empty directory A directory that has no subdirectories or files beneath it.

Endnote A reference or citation that appears at the end of a document.

Enter key Synonymous with Return key. Represented by a broken arrow on some keyboards. The Enter key inserts a carriage return and a line feed.

Error message A warning that a command cannot be performed as requested.

Escape key The key used to back out of some command sequences in WordPerfect, to cancel a command in DOS, and to indicate the number of times commands should be executed in WordPerfect.

Extension Up to three characters that are added to a filename to identify the contents of the file.

F   **File**   A collection of data stored in a named and dedicated portion of a disk.   Files can contain graphs, documents, databases, worksheets, programs, and other collections of data.

File specification   The complete specification of a file including a drive letter, a pathway, a filename, and an extension.   Also, abbreviated to filespec.

Filename   The identifier that uniquely describes a file.   Consists of from one to eight characters.

Floppy disk   Diskettes that allow some physical flexibility, especially of the 3 1/2" and 5 1/4" size.

Flush right   In WordPerfect, to force text to align with the right margin.

Font   A typeface such as elite, Gothic Roman, or italics.

Footnote   A reference or citation that appears at the bottom of a page.

Form feed (FF)   A printer control character that advances the paper to the next sheet.

Formatting   Initializing and preparing a disk so that it can record and store files produced by a particular computer system.   Also, the appearance of text in a document or worksheet.

Formatting code   See Embedded code.

Function keys   Keys marked F1 through F10 (or F12) that carry out specialized macro operations in DOS and in applications software.

G   **Global search-and-replace**   The ability to locate and modify all instances of a character string or value found in a worksheet, document, database, or other file.

Graphics   The use of images in an applications program.

H   **Hanging indent**   In WordPerfect, the temporary indentation (movement of the left margin) of a paragraph with the Indent (F4) key.   The indentation terminates with the first hard return.

Hard disk   Secondary storage device with a rigid disk.

Hard font   A font built into a printer or provided on a font cartridge that is inserted into a printer.

Hard hyphen   A hyphen inserted in a WordPerfect document when you press the hyphen key.

Hard page break   In WordPerfect, a code inserted with Ctrl-Enter to force the printer to move to the next sheet.   Hard page breaks are not adjusted if text that is added or deleted expands or reduces the number of lines on the page.

Hard return   In WordPerfect, a code inserted when the Enter (Return) key is pressed.   Indicates that the line should be broken at that point and that words should not be filled from below if text above the code is deleted.

Hard space   In WordPerfect, a space entered with Home-Space Bar to keep two words together on a line.

Help An on-line program for providing assistance.

Help key The key that recalls Help screens (F3 in WordPerfect).

High density disk See Quad-density disk.

Home key The key that, in association with directional arrows, moves the cursor in WordPerfect.

Hot zone An adjustable area to the left of the right margin in a document. Words beginning to the left of the hot zone and extending beyond the margin are hyphenated.

Hyphenation The division of words that extend across the hot zone into two parts, one part on each of two lines, divided by a hyphen. Hyphenation can be toggled on and off.

I **IBM-compatible computer** A computer capable of executing identically to an IBM computer. Also called a clone.

Indent Use of the Tab key to insert a tab code in a WordPerfect document.

Initialize To set up a diskette, a program, or a device with default values and conditions.

Insert mode A mode of data entry in which new text is inserted into existing text rather than overwriting it. Opposite of overwrite mode.

Installation The process of tailoring the default values for an applications program to the hardware available and to the user's priorities for initial program parameters such as screen colors, margins, and so on.

J **Justification** See Alignment.

K **Kerning** A way of spacing printed characters so that they are closer together.

Key field A field in a secondary file used for sorting.

Keyboard, extended 101 keys.

Keyboard, standard 80 keys.

L **Line draw** Use of the Screen key (Ctrl-F3) in WordPerfect to draw single- and double-line boxes in documents.

Line feed (LF) A control code that advances the printer head to the next line.

Line format That portion of the Format menu that adjusts the default characteristics of a line such as the margins, height, tab ruler, and line spacing.

List files The key (F5) in WordPerfect that displays filenames in the default directory and permits their manipulation.

List of Styles A group of predefined sets of formatting codes created as a part of a document, or saved as a separate file to be used by all documents of the same type.

Ln In WordPerfect, the line the cursor is located on.

Look A List Files option that enables the user to see the contents of documents before the document is retrieved.

M **Margin** The blank space borders at the top, bottom, left, and right of a printed document, worksheet, or database report.

Margin release The process of moving the cursor one tab stop to the left of the left margin. Executed with Shift-Tab in WordPerfect.

Margin setting A WordPerfect code that specifies the amount of blank space above, below, to the left, and to the right of text.

Mark Text The key in WordPerfect used to block text so that it can be moved, copied, indexed, referenced, or otherwise used to insert formatting commands.

Menu A series of choices from which the user is to make selections.

Merge Codes key In WordPerfect, Shift-F9, used to select and insert a merge code into a document.

Merge/Sort key In WordPerfect, Ctrl-F9, used to initiate a merge or sort operation involving a primary and a secondary file.

Merging The operation by which data from a data or secondary file are merged with a primary file (a document) to produce a series of unique documents.

Mixed case Text containing both uppercase and lowercase characters.

MS-DOS Abbreviation for Microsoft-Disk Operating System. The operating system used on IBM PC compatible computers.

N **Nonproportional spacing** Requires each printed character to occupy the same amount of space.

Nonsystem disk A nonbootable diskette. A diskette that does not contain the hidden files and/or the COMMAND.COM file needed to successfully carry out a boot.

Num Lock key The key used to toggle the numeric keypad between lowercase and uppercase.

Numeric keypad The block of ten keys holding numbers as uppercase and cursor movement keys as lowercase.

O **Operating System** A program that coordinates the operation of all parts of a computer system.

Outline A WordPerfect feature that inserts outlining codes that automatically designate the number and/or letter to identify each level of entry in an outlined list.

Output device Any device receiving data from a computer. Common output devices are the monitors, printers, and plotters.

Overstrike The printing of one letter in the same space occupied by another letter to produce the new letter.

Overwrite mode The mode of data entry in which typed characters type over and replace existing text. Opposite of Insert mode.

P   **Page break** The point at which paper in the printer will be ejected.

Page format That portion of the Format key (Shift-F8) in WordPerfect used, for example, to center text on a page, set binding widths, set page numbering, change top and bottom margins, add headers and footers, and change paper size.

Parent directory The directory above a subdirectory.

Path name A character string that describes the precise order of directories that DOS must traverse in order to locate a file or command. Part of the file specification.

PC Abbreviation for personal computer.

PC-DOS Abbreviation for Personal Computer - Disk Operating System. The operating system used on IBM personal computers. Comparable to MS-DOS.

Peripheral device Devices such as printers and modems connected to the system unit and that communicate through an adapter card.

Pg In WordPerfect, the page the cursor is located on.

Pitch The number of characters printed per inch. The most frequently used pitches are 10 pitch (pica) and 12 pitch (elite).

Pos In WordPerfect, the column in which the cursor is located.

Primary document In merge printing, the document that contains the text to be repeated in all copies, as well as the codes that direct the insertion of data from the secondary, or data file.

Printer control The WordPerfect command (Shift-F7, C) used to manage the printing of documents. This includes canceling a job, stopping and restarting the printer, and changing a job's priority.

Printer control codes Codes that control the operation of the printer. Control codes may change type sizes and styles, send line feeds and page feeds. Printer command codes are often particular to specific printers. Application programs include driver sets that convert user-entered control code symbols to printer control codes designed for a specific printer.

Program A sequence of instructions that a computer can execute to accomplish a task.

Program disk The disk that contains the main program for an application. Also called a System Disk.

Prompt The signal that control has been passed to the user and that the system is awaiting a command or data entry.

Proportional spacing The technique of adjusting the space given to characters on a print line to match their width. A *W* is given more space than an *i*.

Public-domain software Software that is not copyrighted or supported by the developer.

Q   **Quad-density disk** A disk with 1.2 Mb storage.

Qwerty keys The standard arrangement of alphabetic and numeric keys. Derives from the letters on the top left row.

R   **Random Access Memory (RAM)** The portion of the computer's memory that stores the internal DOS commands, programs, and data. Also called main memory or primary memory.

Read The process of copying data from a file into RAM.

Reboot See Warm boot.

Record A single entry in a database. Also the collection of related fields that compose a record structure.

Reformatting Re-adjusting text in a document after changes have been made. Also, formatting a disk a second time.

Retrieve Load a worksheet into RAM.

Return key See Enter key.

Right-justified tab A tab marker that places text to the left of the tab.

Root directory The first directory on any disk. Root is created during formatting. All other directories are user-created subdirectories of root.

R.S.V.P. A WordPerfect request for a yes-or-no response.

Ruler A WordPerfect code that specifies the left and right margins.

S   **Save** To write a file to secondary storage.

Scrolling The line-by-line movement of data on the monitor.

Search The automatic location of a user-entered character string.

Search-and-replace The automatic location and replacement of a user-entered character string with another user-entered character string.

Search string The user-entered character string which is to be located through a search command.

Second document The document seen in the second WordPerfect window.

Secondary file A file that stores variable information to be merged into the primary document during a merge printing operation. Also known as a data file.

Sector A 512-byte portion of a floppy or hard disk onto which data are written, or read from. Each track is divided into sectors to permit the location of data by a disk address. Also used to describe a single pie-shaped portion of a disk created by formatting.

Setup The initial configuration of a program or hardware device.

Shareware Software that has been copyrighted but is distributed on a try-it-first basis. Then, if it is useful, the user contributes a recommended amount to the developer.

Shift-state keys The Alternate, Control, and Shift keys: keys that change the state of the other keyboard characters.

Soft font A font supplied on a floppy disk that can be downloaded to a printer.

Soft hyphen A hyphen inserted by WordPerfect through automatic hyphenation.

Soft page break In WordPerfect, a code automatically inserted to eject the paper to the next page when the maximum number of lines on a page has been printed. Soft page breaks are adjusted if text that is added or deleted expands or reduces the number of lines on the page.

Soft return The code inserted by WordPerfect at the end of a line that is word wrapped. A soft return can be automatically reformatted. Opposite of a hard return.

Soft space A normal space entered with the space bar. In WordPerfect, a soft space can be used to break words.

Software Programs that are used with a computer system. (In contrast to hardware.)

Source disk The disk from which data are read or copied.

Source file The file from which data are being read or copied.

Status line The bottom line of WordPerfect documents.

String One or more connected characters that are used as a unit for some computer operation.

Styles Previously defined formats that can be quickly incorporated in documents.

Styles library The default list of styles. The Styles Library is designated with the Setup key to serve the most commonly used documents.

Subdirectory A directory created beneath another directory.

Subdocument In WordPerfect, a document that is used as part of a master document.

Subscript A half-sized number or letter placed one-half line beneath the current line.

Superscript A half-sized number or letter placed one-half line above the current line.

Switch The movement of the cursor between documents.

System disk A disk containing the files needed for booting a booting system. Sometimes used to refer to the main program disk for an applications program.

T **Tab indent** See Indent.

Tab-Left indent A tab marker that anchors text on the left with text expanding to the right.

Tab-Right indent A tab marker that anchors text on the right with text expanding to the left.

Tab setting A marker indicating the location to which a Tab code will move the cursor or place text that has been tabbed.

Text Readable characters including the alphanumeric characters, the numerals, and punctuation marks (Opposed to nonvisible control codes). Also, the words in a message.

Toggle The process of switching between two states. Also, any device, command, or command switch that has two states, on and off.

Typeface See Font.

Type size The (point) size of a printed character.

Typeover mode See Overwrite mode.

U **Underlining** Paired codes that place a line beneath enclosed text.

Unformatted disk An uninitialized disk. The condition of the disk when first shipped.

Unit of measurement The scale by which characters are displayed and printed. The scale can be in inches, centimeters, point size, WordPerfect 4.2 column size, and other sizes.

User interface The manner in which a computer user accesses a software package's commands and files.

W **Warm boot** Restarting the computer by pressing the Control, Alternate, and Delete keys instead of turning the computer off and then turning it back on.

Wild cards Characters used in DOS and WordPerfect commands and in search operations to match one or more characters in the position of the wild card in the string. A question mark matches one character, and an asterisk matches any number of characters.

Window A partial view of a larger document, worksheet, or database.

Word wrap The placement of a soft return code at the end of a line and the movement of a word outside of the hyphenation zone to the next line.

WYSIWYG (What you see is what you get) A word processor prints a document in a form identical to that seen on the monitor screen.

INDEX

Contents

4 Lotus Graphing

5   Using Built-In Functions and Formulas: A Project Costing Model

6   What If . . . ?

Preface

This book has been written to teach its readers to use *Lotus 1-2-3, Release 2.2* software effectively. It offers practical, hands on instruction in the use of a highly successful, commercial-quality worksheet program. This package is widely used in business and education. This software is fully functioned and capable of illustrating most of the major applications that one can develop with other commercial software packages of a similar nature.

Intended to meet several needs, *Beginning Lotus 1-2-3, Release 2.2* can be useful in many settings. It can be used as a supplemental laboratory manual for courses that introduce students to computers and their applications, such as Introduction to Computing in Business, Computer Literacy, and Introduction to Microcomputer Software.

This book can also be used as a stand-alone text for short courses that focus on educating students in the main uses of microcomputers. The tutorial orientation of this book allows it to be used by a learner who wishes to work independently. The instructional approach utilized is entirely hands-on and step by step. Exercises are presented with detailed instructions on moving from the identification of a computing problem to its solution.

Each chapter concludes with a group of exercises that reinforce the techniques learned in that chapter. The exercises closely parallel the design of the document, worksheet, or database file presented in the chapter. In some cases, exercises are reused in subsequent chapters to enhance the student's product and to enable students to practice new techniques without unnecessary data entry.

Summaries of the Lotus command hierarchy, functions, and macro commands are included for instructors who wish to cover material beyond the scope of this book. A glossary of Lotus terminology will also be helpful to students.

Much appreciation is due to the following persons who assisted in the development of this book:

Thomas Ashby, Oklahoma City College
Robert Benjamin, Taylor University
Richard Bernardin, Cape Cod Community College
Brent Bowman, University of Nevada, Reno
Louis Gioia, Nassau Community College
Patricia Green, Temple Junior College
Monica Johnson, Governor's State College
Prasad Kilari, University of Nevada, Reno
Ronald Maestas, New Mexico Highlands University
Robert Marshburn, West Virginia Institute of Technology
Mark Simkin, University of Nevada, Reno
Janet Spears, Blackhawk College

Their assistance is gratefully acknowledged. The special assistance of Kerry Chase in the preparation of this book is also gratefully acknowledged.

Fritz H. Grupe

Chapter 1

The Basics of Lotus 1-2-3

Chapter Outline

AN ORIENTATION

This chapter is intended to be a brief introduction to the nature of worksheets and to the techniques of working with Lotus 1-2-3, Release 2.2. It has been designed as a tutorial guide you should work through on the computer as you read. If you find that you have to exit before this chapter is completed, skip to the section, Quitting Lotus 1-2-3, at the end of the chapter.

    Additional information is given to you about the intricacies of 1-2-3 as you work through future chapters. This chapter is provided in order to give you a preliminary feeling for the layout of the microcomputer keyboard as it relates to 1-2-3 and to introduce terms and concepts you need to know before you start to construct worksheets in the chapters that follow. For more details of this nature, consult the 1-2-3 manual or other texts about 1-2-3.

LOADING LOTUS 1-2-3

If your copy of 1-2-3 has been properly installed on a hard disk microcomputer, the entry into 1-2-3 should be easy. Consult your manual for instructions on the correct method of installation if this process has not been completed. Boot your computer if necessary, and obtain the C> prompt. Enter

cd lotus   Move to the directory LOTUS

If you have a dual-drive system, boot your computer and obtain the A> prompt. Place the 1-2-3 system diskette in disk drive A and place a formatted diskette with available space for saving your 1-2-3 worksheet files in disk drive B. Type

lotus   The command for loading Lotus 1-2-3. Shortly, you see the access menu screen as shown in Figure 1-1. The cursor highlights the characters 1-2-3, an indication that if you press the Enter key, the loading of 1-2-3 is initiated. Normally, this is the choice you need. There are four other options: PrintGraph, Translate, Install, and Exit.

```
┌─────────────────────────────────────────────────────────────────┐
│ 1-2-3  PrintGraph  Translate  Install  Exit                       │
│ Use 1-2-3                                                         │
├─────────────────────────────────────────────────────────────────┤
│                     1-2-3 Access System                           │
│                   Copyright  1986, 1989                           │
│               Lotus Development Corporation                       │
│                   All Rights Reserved                             │
│                     Release 2.2                                   │
│                                                                   │
│ The Access system lets you choose 1-2-3, PrintGraph, the Translate utility,│
│ and the Install program, from the menu at the top of this screen.  If     │
│ you're using a two-diskette system, the Access system may prompt you to   │
│ change disks.  Follow the instructions below to start a program.          │
│                                                                   │
│ o  Use → or ← to move the menu pointer (the highlighted rectangle │
│    at the top of the screen) to the program you want to use.      │
│                                                                   │
│ o  Press ENTER to start the program.                              │
│                                                                   │
│ You can also start a program by typing the first character of its name.│
│                                                                   │
│ Press HELP (F1) for more information.                             │
│                                         Press NUM LOCK            │
└─────────────────────────────────────────────────────────────────┘
```

Figure 1-1. Access Menu Screen

These menu choices can be chosen by either typing the first letter of the selected word or by moving the cursor with the left and right arrow keys, highlighting the desired word, and pressing Enter.

These two approaches, highlighting and entering or typing the first letter of the command, can be used in all 1-2-3 menus since the choices in any menu always begin with unique characters.

◄┘   Enter key, to choose entry into 1-2-3. While 1-2-3 is loading, you see a screen indicating that Lotus 1-2-3 is a copyrighted program of Lotus Development Corporation. Finally, you see the 1-2-3 worksheet screen as shown in Figure 1-2. Upon entry into 1-2-3, a new, blank worksheet is always provided.

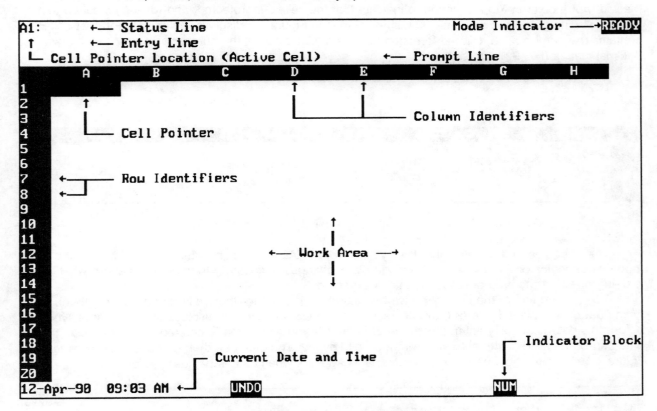

Figure 1-2. Lotus 1-2-3 Screen

THE LOTUS 1-2-3 WORKSHEET SCREEN

A 1-2-3 screen consists of two sections: (1) a work area, or window that is bounded by a highlighted (reverse video) column of numbers, beginning with the number 1, which identify each of the 8,192 rows, and (2) a highlighted row of letters, beginning with A, which identify the 256 columns into which a worksheet can be divided. A cell is the location in the grid of a row and a column. For instance, the cell address C13 uniquely identifies the cell found at the intersection of column C and row 13. The portion of a 1-2-3 worksheet that you can see on the twenty rows on your screen is called a window because you cannot always see all of the active part of the worksheet at one time. You must move the window to see different parts of the worksheet.

A worksheet consists of 2,097,152 cells (256 X 8,192 = 2,097,152). Although this provides a large number of theoretically available cells, most microcomputers do not have enough random access memory (main memory) to take advantage of even a large fraction of this space. New memory expansion boards make a larger number of cells accessible. Version 1A of 1-2-3 makes 524,288 cells available within 256 columns and 2,048 rows.

Inside the window, probably at cell address A1, if you did not accidentally touch a cell pointer movement key, you see a highlighted cell pointer. Movement of the cell pointer activates the cell on which it is placed. When you enter data, it is entered into the active cell.

The three lines above the highlighted column identifiers are called the control panel. The first line of the control panel is called the status line. In the left corner of this line is an address noting where the cell pointer is currently located. This is the address of the active cell. Next to the cell address may appear: (a) a notation to guide the display of a number assigned to that cell; (b) a notation to express the width of a column; (c) a notation to indicate that the cell is unprotected; and (d) the actual contents of the cell. The portion of a sample worksheet screen in Figure 1-3 displays the information that cell B2 contains the number 27.5, but the formatting notation (C2) displays the number as currency with two decimal places (i.e., $27.50).

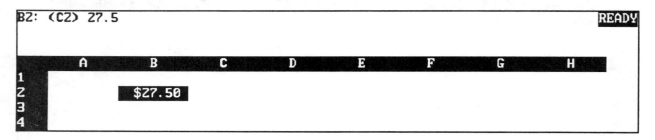

Figure 1-3.

The right side of the status line displays the word READY in a highlighted block. This is called the mode block indicator. The word in the mode block changes periodically to inform you about what 1-2-3 is doing or about the type of response that is expected.

The second line of the control panel, the entry line, is used for three different purposes. If you are typing data to be placed in a cell, this line serves as an entry line which displays what you have typed before this data is actually entered with the Enter key. If you have already entered data into a cell, this data can be recalled to the entry line with the Edit key, F2. The data can then be edited and re-entered. Figure 1-4 illustrates how part of the control panel appears when data is being entered.

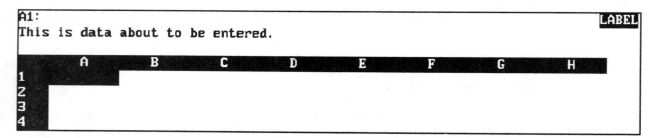

Figure 1-4.

The entry line also serves to display command menus similar to those that were seen on the 1-2-3 access menu. Command menu sequences are initiated by pressing the Slash key.

If command menus are being selected, the third line serves as a prompt line. The prompts briefly explain what actions are to be taken or what other command menus will appear if the currently highlighted menu choice is selected. Prompts may also request that you identify the cells to be affected by the command. Selection of a menu choice can be made by either typing the first letter of the command word or by moving the cursor to highlight a choice and pressing the Enter key.

A line beneath the worksheet window is reserved for the display of errors made during the execution of command sequences and for the display of indicator blocks. Indicator blocks notify you that selected key functions have been turned on. For instance, if the Caps Lock has been activated, the block with the word CAPS appears. There are indicator blocks for the Caps Lock, Num Lock, and Scroll Lock keys. Indicator blocks are eliminated when the appropriate key is pressed a second time. This line is often empty at the start of a new worksheet, except for the UNDO indicator block. This feature allows the user to press Alt-F4, the UNDO key, to cancel any changes made to a worksheet since 1-2-3 was last in READY mode. Some computers boot with the Num Lock key on, causing the indicator NUM to display.

CELL POINTER MOVEMENT KEYS

Nine keys (see Figure 1-5) located on the right side of the keyboard of your microcomputer can be used for moving the cell pointer within the worksheet.

7 Home	8 ↑	9 PgUp
4 ←	5	6 →
1 End	2 ↓	3 PgDn

Figure 1-5. Cell Pointer Movement Keys

Be sure to notice that the numbers are in the uppercase position. The lowercase positions are used by the directional arrows and the commands Home, End, PgUp, and PgDn. The uppercase numbers can be accessed by depressing the Shift key or by depressing the Num Lock key. Generally, on 80-character keyboards, having the numbers in the keypad readily available and not the directional arrows is undesirable. Use the numbers on the top row of the keyboard instead.

Many newer computers have larger, 101-key keyboards. These keyboards provide additional arrow keys, and Insert, Home, PgUp, PgDn, Delete, and End keys that are separated from the numbers on the numeric key pad. The directional keys are used in the manner shown in Figure 1-6.

KEY	ACTION
↓	Moves the cell pointer down one cell.
↑	Moves the cell pointer up one cell.
→	Moves the cell pointer right one cell.
←	Moves the cell pointer left one cell.
Home	Returns the cell pointer to the cell located at address A1, the top left corner of the worksheet.
PgUp	Moves the cell pointer up 20 cells to a new screen with no overlapping of cells.
PgDn	Moves the cell pointer down 20 cells to a new screen with no overlapping of cells.
End	When End precedes the use of any arrow key, the cell pointer moves to the next boundary position in the direction of the arrow key pressed after the End key. A boundary position is a point where one group of cells with contents (i.e., data in them) are next to cells that are empty (i.e., have no data in them).
|← →|	The Tab key (Big Right) moves the cell pointer to the column immediately to the right of the current screen. Shift and Tab (Big Right) together move the cell pointer to the left in the same fashion.

Figure 1-6. Directional Movement Keys

AN EXERCISE

Try moving the cell pointer with these directional keys. You will probably notice several things as you experiment with moving the cell pointer. You will notice that:

1.   You get a beep if you try to move the cell pointer across an edge of the worksheet. Any time you make an error 1-2-3 beeps. A beep does not make any changes to your worksheet. Rather, it calls attention to your attempt to make 1-2-3 do something that you are not allowed to do.
2.   The cell address in the control panel changes as the cell is moved around.
3.   The row numbers and column letters change as the cell pointer crosses window boundaries. The column letters advance from A to Z, to AA, AB, AC to AZ, to BA, BB, BC to BZ, and so on until they stop at IV.
4.   The End key followed by a right arrow takes you to the IV column since there are no boundaries other than a worksheet edge in a new worksheet.
5.   The End key followed by a down arrow takes you to row number 8,192 since there are no boundaries other than a worksheet edge in a new worksheet.

FUNCTION KEYS

On the left side of the keyboard are ten keys marked F1 through F10 as shown in Figure 1-7.

On some microcomputers the function keys are located across the top of the keyboard. Regardless of where these keys are physically positioned, their functions remain the same. Generally, function keys are used by computer programs to carry out relatively complicated actions quickly. This is the case with function keys in 1-2-3 also. The most commonly used function keys are further described within the context of the worksheets that are developed in this book.

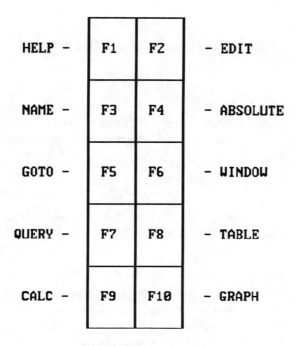

Figure 1-7. Function Keys

AN EXERCISE

If you have a dual-drive system, place the 1-2-3 Help disk in drive A. (This is not necessary on a hard drive or networked microcomputer.) Press

F1   Function key F1, the Help key

      The Help key provides fast explanations of what choices you have available to you at any point. Use of the Help key is said to be context sensitive because the information it provides changes, depending on the menu commands (described below) 1-2-3 is displaying.

      Return to 1-2-3 by pressing the Escape (Esc) key. Return the system disk to drive A, if necessary (on a dual drive system).

SPECIAL PURPOSE KEYS

Several of the remaining keys have special functions to perform.

Enter (Return)

The Enter key is used to place data that is typed on the entry line of the control panel into the cell on which the cell pointer is currently located.

Backspace

The Backspace key is used for editing data on the entry line. Use of the Backspace key deletes the character to the left of the cursor.

Space Bar

The space bar is used to enter blanks (spaces) on entry lines. A blank is a character just as are the letters a and Z. If a cell contains only blanks, a cell may appear to be empty, although it actually has contents.

Escape

The Escape key is useful because it enables you to back out of mistakes you may make in the selection of menu choices and to erase data from the entry line.

Caps Lock

The key marked Caps Lock places all of the alphabetic characters, the letters a through z, into uppercase. Setting Caps Lock "on" causes the indicator block for CAPS to appear below the worksheet window. Use of the Caps Lock key does not cause the numbered keys, the directional keys, or the keys with special operators such as . or / to shift to become uppercase. To bring these keys to uppercase requires the use of the Shift key.
   If Caps Lock is on, the use of the Shift key causes the lowercase to be typed.

Control

The Control key, marked Ctrl, is used simultaneously with another key in the same way that the Shift key is used. In 1-2-3 the most important function the Control key has is in conjunction with the key marked Break / Scroll Lock. This combination of keys cancels some operations, such as the immediate removal of the main menu from the control panel, the printing of a worksheet, or the stopping of a keyboard macro.

Alternate

The Alternate key, marked Alt, is used to give keys an alternative meaning in 1-2-3. This key is used to invoke keyboard macros, complex commands that you can build that 1-2-3 can carry out for you automatically. Macros are an advanced feature of 1-2-3 that are not dealt with in this book, although a summary of macro commands can be found in Appendix C.
   The function keys have another set of uses that become available when they are pressed simultaneously with the Alternate key. These uses are shown in Figure 1-8.

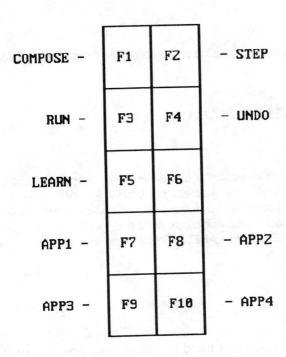

Figure 1-8. Alternate-Function Keys

The Undo key is used in this book, but the other uses are employed in advanced applications.

Number Lock

The key marked, Num Lock, puts the light-colored key pad on the right side of the keyboard in uppercase. The directional arrows and commands such as PgUp then become available only through the use of the Shift key. When Number Lock is on, an indicator block with NUM appears on the line below the worksheet window.

Scroll Lock

The Scroll Lock key changes the effect of the directional arrows and commands. Instead of the cell pointer moving over the worksheet, the worksheet seems to move under the cell pointer. The best method of understanding this difference is to actually put Scroll Lock on and employ the directional keys. When Scroll Lock is on, an indicator block with SCROLL appears on the line below the worksheet window.

Delete

The Delete key is used when data on the entry line of the control panel is being edited. The Delete key removes the character that is immediately above the cursor. This is a different effect than that of the Backspace key which deletes the character to the left of the cursor.

Although the Backspace key can be used when you are originally entering data on the entry line, the Delete key cannot be used here because it is always found to the right of any characters that have been typed. None are above it. The Delete key can only be used when you are in what 1-2-3 calls the edit mode.

Insert

The key marked Ins is used to switch between insert (default mode) and overwrite when you are editing cell contents.

ENTERING DATA INTO WORKSHEET CELLS

Labels

The term labels is used by 1-2-3 to describe character data. Labels are strings of 1 or more characters. For instance, a, Dog, Name, B69C, and Address are labels. As soon as you type a cell entry beginning with a character from A to Z (uppercase or lowercase), a space or any other character that has no mathematical meaning, the mode indicator block, which is located in the upper right corner of the control panel, changes from READY to LABEL. This means that the entire entry is treated as character data, even if it contains numbers.

AN EXERCISE

Place your cell pointer in cell address A1 using the arrow keys if necessary. If you are far from this location, remember that the Home key takes you to A1 rapidly. Then type

Jack

◄⌐

As you type, the name does not initially appear in the cell where the cell pointer is located. It appears on the entry line of the control panel. The mode block reads LABEL. Enter key. If you look in the control panel, you see that the entry line has been cleared. Now the name Jack appears in cell A1 of the window and on the status line of the control panel, next to the cell address of the currently active cell. You should also see that the name is preceded by an apostrophe. The apostrophe is automatically put in front of any label entered into a cell. The apostrophe is called a label prefix and is used by 1-2-3 to begin displaying the label from the left side of the cell it is entered into. The label prefix does not appear in cell A1. You can right-justify with a quote, ", or center the label with a caret, ^, if you choose.

After the entry is complete, the mode block indicator returns to READY.

Values

When you begin an entry with a number or with a plus, minus, multiply (the asterisk, *), or divide sign (the slash, /), or with any of the several special characters,

.   (@   # $

the mode block displays VALUE. This indicates that the entry you are creating can contain any of the following:

1. a number
2. a formula
3. a cell address

Characters that are not part of one of these entries are not permitted. If you type an illegal character, such as the letter D, and that letter is not part of a valid cell address, the entry is kept on the entry line and the worksheet is placed in edit mode when you hit the Enter key. The mode indicator block displays EDIT. You must correct the entry.

AN EXERCISE

Using your arrow keys, place the cell pointer on cell B1. Type

123	The number one hundred twenty-three (123). The mode block indicator reads VALUE.
◄⌐	Enter key. Observe the control panel. In addition to the entry line having been cleared, the number appears next to the cell address. There is no apostrophe in front of the number, however. This is because you have entered a value and not a label. Numbers are not prefixed with apostrophes. They are right-justified.
↓	Down arrow, to move your cell pointer to cell address B2
456a	The number four hundred fifty-six followed by the deliberate error of the addition of an "a."
◄⌐	Enter key. Listen for a beep that signals an error. Notice that the mode block now displays EDIT because of the presence of the character in the number. The cursor places itself underneath the a, an indication that 1-2-3 believes that this is the offending character in the formula.
Del	Delete key, to remove the a
◄⌐	Enter key. The number is accepted as legal. Stop for the moment. You shall return to the worksheet shortly.

Formulas

If 1-2-3 could only enter labels and numbers in rows and columns, it would have rather limited capabilities. It would be a poor word processor that could only help you in structuring the appearance of rows and columns of data. It does far more. You can also enter formulas that contain correctly organized combinations of any of the following:

1. numbers
2. arithmetic operators (* / - + =)
3. built-in functions
4. parentheses
5. logical operators such as #AND# and #NOT#

Discussion of the last two elements will be deferred until they are needed in the worksheet exercises.

AN EXERCISE

Type:

↓	Down arrow, to move to cell B3
+	Plus sign (if your keyboard has two plus sign keys, you may use either one), notifies

	1-2-3 that a value is being entered. Note the word VALUE in the control panel. A plus sign, a number, or some other mathematical notation must precede a cell address that begins a value entry. Otherwise the leading letter causes the entry to be treated as a label.
↑	Up arrow, to move the cell pointer to cell address B2. The mode block indicator changes to read POINT, indicating that a cell address appears on the entry line of the control panel. B2 has been entered next to the plus sign.
+	A second plus sign, to indicate that another value is to be added to the value found in cell B2. The cell pointer returns to the active cell B3. The mode block changes to VALUE.
↑	Up arrow, to move up one cell. The mode block changes to POINT and a second B2 has been placed on the entry line.
↑	Up arrow, to move one more cell to arrive at cell B1. At this point the entry line reads **+B2+B1** That is, "find the value in the cell with the coordinates B and 2 and add that value to the value in the cell with the coordinates B and 1 and enter the result in the active cell, B3."
◄⅃	Enter key, to enter the formula into cell B3, the active cell on which the cell pointer was located when you began

Upon entry of the formula into the cell, you see that cell B3 displays the result 579, which is obtained by adding 123 and 456. On the status line, however, you see the formula you created next to the cell address. 1-2-3 remembers the formula as its contents. However, in the worksheet window, 1-2-3 displays the number that is created by evaluating the formula. The distinction between a cell's display and a cell's contents is an important one. To illustrate why, do the following:

↑	Up arrow, to move to cell B2. Note that you have not begun a formula so the use of the arrow does not cause the mode block to change from READY to POINT.
↑	Up arrow, to move to cell B1
789	To create the value seven hundred eighty-nine on the entry line
◄⅃	To enter the value into cell B1, thereby replacing the value 123

1-2-3 almost immediately recalculates the results computed by the formula in cell B3 even though the change was made in cell B1. This is because the content of cell B3 is the formula, not the number it displayed earlier.

BUILT-IN FUNCTIONS

1-2-3 provides a group of techniques for carrying out complex operations on cells automatically. For instance, if you wished to add up the values found in the first ten cells of column A, you could create a formula similar to this

A1+A2+A3+A4+A5+A6+A7+A8+A9+A10

This is difficult to do, however, for several reasons. The typing of such a long formula requires many keystrokes. This takes time and you may make errors in typing. It is also not always clear whether all of the cells you wished to include are actually included. Further, you may have duplicated a cell address unwittingly. Some operations, such as finding the standard deviation for a group of values or the determination of the internal rate of return on an investment, may require writing difficult formulas that most people would not wish to create.

Functions are operations, usually mathematical or logical, that reduce or eliminate all of these problems. With a function, the lengthy formula above can be reduced to

@SUM(A1..A10)

which can be read as, "Sum up all of the values found in the cells from cell address A1 through cell address A10 and display the result." Built-in functions enable you to develop very complex worksheets rapidly and accurately.

The structure, or syntax, of a built-in function includes five elements. A function always begins with the at sign (@), which is followed by the name of the function. This is followed by an opening parenthesis.

Between the parentheses are arguments. The number of arguments in functions varies among the functions. Arguments typically are individual cell addresses, rectangular groups of cells called ranges, numbers, or a combination of ranges, numbers, and cells. A closing parenthesis terminates the function.

As you become knowledgeable about 1-2-3, you will find that built-in functions can save you considerable time and allow you to complete operations that might otherwise be very difficult to accomplish.

AN EXERCISE

Using the arrow keys if necessary, move your cell pointer to cell address B3 and type

@SUM(	Begin the summing function
B1	To add the value found in B1
..	Through
B2	Cell address B2
)	Terminate the list of cell values to be summed, as well as the function. There are no spaces allowed in formulas. The formula appears as @SUM(B1..B2).
↵	Enter key

When you entered the formula with the @SUM function into the active cell, B3, this formula calculated the same result calculated by addition.

POINTING VERSUS CELL ADDRESS NAMING

There are two ways of entering cell addresses in formulas. The first way is by pointing to cells as you type a formula on the entry line. Once a formula has been started, you point by moving any of the directional keys. As you move the cell pointer, the cell address in the formula changes to reflect its current location. This method of cell addressing is most useful when you have to search for the correct cell to be used in the formula. When pointing to cell addresses during formula building, the mode block indicator changes to POINT.

The Escape key, marked Esc, can be used to erase a cell address from the entry line if you have started to point within a formula.

The second method of entering a cell address is simply to type the cell address on the entry line. This may be the fastest method of cell address entry if you can see the cell on the screen or if you remember or have written down the address. Most of the exercises presented in this book direct you to type the cell addresses directly; however, you can interpret an instruction to enter +A20 as being equivalent to typing a plus sign and pointing to A20 by moving the cell pointer to that cell, whereas entering @SUM(A8..B10) is equivalent to typing @**SUM(**, pointing to cell A8, pressing the period, pointing to B10, pressing the Enter key, and typing **)**.

AN EXERCISE

Move your cell pointer to cell address B4 and type

+	Plus sign, to begin a formula and change the mode block from READY to VALUE
↑	Up arrow, to move to B3. Notice the appearance of the cell address on the entry line of the control panel and the word POINT in the mode indicator block.
Esc	Escape key, to remove the cell address and to exit from point mode
Esc	Escape key, to remove the plus sign and to return the mode block to READY

ENTRY LENGTHS

Whether you are entering formulas, numbers, or labels into active cells, there is a 240-character limit to the entry line. If your entry exceeds 79 characters, the entire line cannot be viewed at once. The characters move off the left side of the entry line. In edit mode, entered with function key F2, as you move back and forth on the line with the left and right arrow keys, some of the characters are lost from view. 1-2-3 does not lose track of the data that has been entered.

COLUMN WIDTHS

Whenever 1-2-3 begins with a blank worksheet, it provides an automatic columnwidth of nine characters.This is a default value. A default value is a value that is built into a computer program to take effect if the user does not explicitly change it. 1-2-3 uses other default values in other contexts. The default value for column width can be changed. Column width is important in several ways:

1. When you type alphabetic character data (labels), they are displayed continuously into the adjacent columns as long as the characters do not interfere with the display of data already present in the cells in those columns.
2. When you type numbers or formulas that result in numbers being displayed that are larger than the column width, the cell displays the number in a scientific format.
3. Later you will find that a number which is too large to appear in a cell formatted to display numbers in a particular style, for example as currency, two decimal places, is displayed as a block of asterisks (*). This forces you to see that the data cannot be displayed correctly. If 1-2-3 did not do this, it would have to truncate the number. The results would then appear to be correct, but would, in fact, be incorrect.
        When asterisks are displayed, the column width must be widened. As soon as the width is expanded sufficiently, the complete number is displayed. At no time does an inadequate display width cause the loss of data.

AN EXERCISE

Move your cell pointer to cell A5. Type

THIS IS A VERY LONG LINE ENTRY.

↵   Enter key, to enter the label. Note that the status line displays the entire entry as the contents of A5.

→   Right arrow, to move to cell B5. See that the status line shows no contents for B5, even though the label for A5 overlaps this cell.

→   Right arrow, to move to cell C5

INTERFERENCE

↵   Enter key, to enter the word INTERFERENCE into C5. Note how the label in A5 continues to be displayed in columns A and B where the word placed in C5 does not appear. The word in C5 overlaps into column D.

  Move the cell pointer to cell B7 and enter

123456789.456   A number too large for the nine-character display.

↵   Enter key. Note the scientific notation for the number, 1.2E+08, that displays the original number in the cell. But on the status line you can still see the number you entered. 1-2-3 has not forgotten the entry.

CORRECTING MISTAKEN ENTRIES

Retyping

When you are entering data into a worksheet, mistakes are inevitable. Certainly you will find that even if cell entries were made correctly, some data will have to be updated or some new information will require you to modify your formulas.

  If the original entries are short, or if these entries must be totally reworked so that there is little point in editing them, then the best way to make them correct is to simply type them over. This is accomplished by making the cell active by placing the cell pointer on it, then typing and entering the new entry.

Editing

A second and often preferred method is to edit the cell's contents. The F2 key is called the Edit key. To use the Edit key, you make the cell containing the incorrect entry active by pressing the F2 key and editing the entry line. The following keys are the basic keys used in editing:

KEY	ACTION
Del	Deletes the character above the cursor.
Backspace	Deletes the character to the left of the cursor.
→	Moves nondestructively right one character.
←	Moves nondestructively left one character.
Home	Moves nondestructively to the left-most character.
End	Moves nondestructively to the right-most character.
Esc	Deletes the entire entry. Escape must be pressed before an Enter key or directional arrow clears the entry line by placing the data in the active cell. Escaping from edit mode leaves the contents of the active cell unchanged.
Ins	Toggles between insert and overwrite. The insertion or overwriting of characters is identical to that found in WordPerfect.

Figure 1-9. Editing Keys

When the entry line has been corrected, it is re-entered with the Enter key.

AN EXERCISE

This exercise familiarizes you with the editing capabilities of 1-2-3. Move the cell pointer to cell D6 and enter

ABC CORP. BUDGET A label to be typed in. Note the entry on the entry line of the control panel.
◄┘   Enter key to place the label in the active cell. Note the apostrophe label prefix that was added to what you typed, as well as the empty entry line. The cell pointer remains on cell D6.
F2   Edit key, to put the entry back on the entry line of the control panel. The mode block changes to EDIT. The cursor is to the right of the entry.
←   Left arrow ten times, to place the cursor under the R in CORP
Del   Delete key three times, to delete the alphabetic character string RP
MPANY   Insert the letters MPANY to form COMPANY. Notice that the letters typed were automatically inserted at the location of the cursor. Characters above and to the right of the cursor were moved to the right.

Before entering the revised label, ABC COMPANY BUDGET, experiment with the other movement keys to see their effects.

Home   Home key, to go to the extreme left
End   End key, to go to the extreme right
→   Right arrow three times
←   Left arrow three times
◄┘   Enter key. This replaces the cell's previous contents with the new entry.

AN EXERCISE

Return your cell pointer to cell D6 if it was moved, then type

F2   Edit key, to recall ABC COMPANY BUDGET to the entry line
Esc   Escape key, to delete the entry. Observe the mode block. One escape does not exit you from the edit mode.
Esc   Escape key, to exit from edit mode and to return to READY. There is no change in the contents of cell D6. If you wished to delete the contents of a cell, you would use a different approach to be described below.

1-2-3 COMMAND MENUS

Thus far you have been shown how to move the cell pointer from cell to cell and how to make entries in the cells. Another major category of support comes from the 1-2-3 command menu structure. 1-2-3 commands are initiated with the Slash key. The Slash key, located to the right of the period, is not to be confused with the Backslash key, which is often but not always located immediately to the left of the space bar. The Backslash has a markedly different purpose.

AN EXERCISE

Be certain that the mode block indicator displays READY. If this indicator does not appear, strike the Escape key repeatedly until it does. Then type

/   Slash key, to invoke the initial menu. Your menu should look similar to that pictured in Figure 1-10. Notice that the mode block indicator reads MENU.

It is only permissible to make a menu choice, to press the Escape key to exit the menu, or to respond to a prompt. You may not enter data while MENU is displayed.

```
A1:                                                                    MENU
Worksheet  Range  Copy  Move  File  Print  Graph  Data  System  Add-In  Quit
Global   Insert  Delete  Column  Erase  Titles  Window  Status  Page  Learn
```

Figure 1-10. Main 1-2-3 Menu

→   Right arrow, to highlight the menu choice RANGE. Note that the prompt line of the control panel changes as the cursor moves from menu choice to menu choice. This line describes what the highlighted choice helps you to do if it is selected.

↵   Enter key, to select the Range choice. A new submenu with different choices appears.

E   Erase is chosen with the typing of the first letter

↵   Enter key, to erase the currently active cell identified in the prompt, "Enter range to erase: D6..D6." There is no change made to the other cells.

Another illustration shows how menu decisions are reversed. Move your cell pointer to B7 and enter

/   Slash, to invoke the initial menu

R   Range

Esc   Escape key, to back up to initial menu

Esc   Escape key, to clear the control panel of menus and to return to the READY mode. No change was made to the cell on which the range command was begun, but not completed.

The command menu sequences open to you are diverse and numerous. At first the variations may seem overwhelming. As you work with 1-2-3, seemingly foreign and hard to remember command sequences will become easier and easier to recall without reference to manuals or guidebooks. For now it is sufficient to know that until an action is actually initiated, you can always use the Escape key to reverse yourself.

FILES

So far we have worked, albeit awkwardly, with a worksheet that is resident in the microcomputer's random access memory (RAM). The worksheet in RAM is said to be transient because it has no permanent existence. If the computer is turned off, the results of your typing are lost. This may not seem like much of a tragedy given the screen in front of you, but in other circumstances this is important indeed.

In order to save the worksheet so that you can recall it a day or a month from now, you have to use the command structure to save it to a diskette. Again, the exercise that follows assumes that the 1-2-3 system diskette has been correctly adapted to your computer and that it appropriately saves your files to the right disk drive and, if necessary, to the correct directory. If it does not, consult your 1-2-3 manual to assure that it works correctly. Check to be certain that a formatted disk is in drive B.

AN EXERCISE

The cell pointer can be in any location on the worksheet when the worksheet is saved to disk. The following typing sequence can be initiated from any location:

/	Slash, to invoke the main menu
F	**F**ile
S	**S**ave, to save the worksheet to disk
JUNK	A filename in response to the prompt "Enter save file name:"; chose any name up to eight characters or numbers that describes the worksheet in a manner that helps you to recall its contents.
↵	Enter key. Observe that: (1) a red light appears on the disk drive receiving the permanent copy of the worksheet, and (2) the mode block indicator changes to WAIT. While the red light is on, 1-2-3 is actively writing out the file.

When saving a revised version of a worksheet, select R to replace an earlier version with the new one.

Filenames are limited to lengths of eight characters, a limitation that restricts the degree of descriptiveness the name can have. Because a floppy diskette, or to a still greater degree, a hard disk, can store a large number of files, it is important to assign each file a name that can help you to recall it without your having to search files at random looking for the one you need.

A very important point to remember regards the red light that appears when the computer is writing a file to disk. As the file is being written out, the mode block reads WAIT. WAIT is replaced by READY as soon as 1-2-3 is finished. It takes the computer somewhat longer to write the file out so the red light stays on longer. Remember: Do not turn the machine off or take the diskette out of the disk drive until the red light goes off.

The reason for this is that 1-2-3 destroys the old file before it writes out the new one. If the new file has not been completely written out, it is not recoverable by 1-2-3 in subsequent sessions. If you have lost the old file and you have an incomplete new file, you have lost all of your efforts.

WORKSHEET ERASING   / **Worksheet Erase**

Saving a file does not erase it from the worksheet window that appears on your screen. To remove the current worksheet from the window and to remove it from the computer's memory, though not from the diskette, type

/	Slash
W	Worksheet
E	Erase
Y	Yes

This command sequence clears your screen.

QUITTING LOTUS 1-2-3   / **Quit**

Before exiting from Lotus 1-2-3, be sure to save your file first. In this case there is no need to save your file. To quit 1-2-3, type

/	Slash
Q	Quit
Y	Yes, to confirm that you wish to exit 1-2-3
E	Exit

Chapter 2

Getting Acquainted with Worksheets

Chapter Outline

Some analysts cite the availability of electronic worksheets as the key reason for the initial popularity of microcomputers. Worksheet programs are useful in organizing data that are normally displayed in rows and columns. Unlike word processors that only use tab markers for aligning columns of data, worksheet programs have powerful mathematical capabilities that allow the user to manipulate data rather than simply record data. The difference is significant.

     In this chapter you will:

1. Learn the basic components of a worksheet screen;
2. Move the cell pointer around the worksheet;
3. Enter text, numerical data, and formulas into cells;
4. Execute worksheet commands;
5. Learn the difference between cell and range addresses;
6. Change the appearance of a cell's contents;
7. Copy cells;
8. Change the width of a column of cells;
9. Save and retrieve a file.

WHY WORKSHEETS?

Think about the production of a company's annual budget without a worksheet program. Someone must compute the values for a company's various expense and income categories with a calculator. Subtotals and totals must also be computed by hand. The last step in what may be a laborious process is the passing of hand-written budget sheets to a secretary for typing. If the numbers used in calculations must be changed for any reason, the entire typed copy probably will have to be redone to reflect changes necessitated throughout the budget. A change can be made and the worksheet automatically recalculates all formulas in the budget to bring it up to date.

Worksheets, also called spreadsheets, can be employed to organize and experiment with data required to solve a variety of problems. This software can help to solve problems related to producing financial statements of all types: budgets, income analyses, cash flow analyses, break even and start-up cost analyses, income tax reporting, and investment analyses. Worksheets can be especially useful in making projections of sales and income, utility costs and other expenses, and the impact of external factors on the internal financing of a company.

Not all worksheets involve monetary data. Many quantitative problems not involving money can be addressed with worksheets. Some worksheets actually use little quantitative data.

WHAT IS A WORKSHEET?

Assume that you are constructing a computer sales projection for a small manufacturing firm. The firm sells three models of microcomputers that have been introduced at different times and confront different levels of competition from other computer manufacturers. Among the factors that must be taken into account in producing a projection are the following:

1. The Hacker 1 model computer is cost-competitive and is popular with certain banking institutions. Last quarter sales of this model were at 15,500 and sales are expected to grow at 3% per sales quarter over the next year.
2. The Hacker 2 model has been discontinued, but an inventory remains. With a discounted price, the company expects to be able to sell these models at levels that decrease by 50% in each quarter. In the last quarter, 7,300 Hacker 2s were sold.

	A	B	C	D	E	F	G	H
1				HARDWARE ASSOCIATES				
2								
3				SALES FORECAST				
4								
5		LAST	1ST	2ND	3RD	4TH	YRLY	
6	MODEL	QTR.	QTR.	QTR.	QTR.	QTR.	TOTAL	
7								
8	HACKER 1	15,500	15,965	16,444	16,937	17,445	66,792	
9	HACKER 2	7,300	3,650	1,825	913	456	6,844	
10	HACKER 3	5,500	5,950	6,400	6,850	7,300	26,500	
11								
12	TOTALS	28,300	25,565	24,669	24,700	25,202	100,135	
13								
14								

Figure 2-1.

3.   The Hacker 3 model is popular due to its high speed and large hard disk subsystem. Unfortunately, the supplier of the hard disks can only gear up to provide an increase of 450 disks in each quarter. 5,500 Hacker 3s were sold in the last quarter.

Without a worksheet program, a typical approach to projecting the company's probable sales over the next four quarters would be to sit down with a pencil, paper, and calculator to do the projections manually. The result is Figure 2-1.

To construct this projection manually is not an overwhelming task although it does take time to perform the twenty-one calculations by hand. Miscalculations are possible. The major problem with manually preparing this forecast is the prospect that it may have to be changed. The supplier of hard disks could announce that it is able to increase its production by 100 each quarter. The company may begin a new relationship with a chain distributor that increases Hacker 1 sales by 200 per quarter. A new model computer might be introduced. Each of these changes requires that some, if not all, of the twenty-one calculations in this worksheet need to be recomputed.

A worksheet is a computer model that looks like the hand-produced projection shown in Figure 2-1. The worksheet is organized in a grid with rows and columns. Unlike the hand-produced projection, the computer model is easily modified to accommodate changes.

LOADING LOTUS 1-2-3

Boot your microcomputer. Follow the directions in the preceeding lesson for starting Lotus 1-2-3. This chapter assumes that you entered 1-2-3 from the access screen. Some users who do not require access to the other components of 1-2-3 choose to enter **1-2-3** rather than **lotus** to load the worksheet directly, bypassing the access screen.

DATA ENTRY

Begin to enter the data in the worksheet by placing your cell pointer on D1 and pressing

Caps Lock   To enter text in uppercase
HARDWARE ASSOCIATES   The text to be entered
◄┘   Enter key

If you enter incorrect text into a cell, you can simply edit or retype the entry. The new entry replaces the old entry. If you put the entry into the wrong cell, you can erase the contents of the cell by placing your cell pointer on the cell and typing

/   Slash
R   **R**ange
E   **E**rase
◄┘   Enter key, to empty the currently active cell

When you are entering data, you need not always press the Enter key. Pressing any of the directional keys (arrows, Enter, Tab, PgUp, PgDn) or the Home key automatically enters the data typed on the entry line before the cell pointer is moved. For example, if you are entering a column of numbers by typing a number and pressing the Down arrow, instead of typing a number, pressing Enter and then pressing the Down arrow, saves you one keystroke with each entry. If the column had 300 numbers, you would save 300 keystrokes.

Using your directional keys to change to different cell addresses, make the following text entries:

Cell Coordinate	Entry
D3	SALES FORECAST
B5	LAST
C5	'1ST
D5	'2ND
E5	'3RD
F5	'4TH
G5	YRLY
A6	MODEL
B6	QTR.
C6	QTR.
D6	QTR.
E6	QTR.
F6	QTR.
G6	TOTAL
A8	HACKER 1
A9	HACKER 2
A10	HACKER 3
A12	TOTALS
B8	15500
B9	7300
B10	5500

When entering labels that start with a numeric digit, you must enter a label-prefix character before the first label character. That is why the apostrophe is required. Other label prefixes (\, ", ^) would also work if you wish to repeat, right align, or center the label. If you enter a number with text behind it, the entry is put into edit mode.

FORMULA ENTRIES

Formulas can contain (1) numbers; (2) arithmetic operators including, but not limited to

^	Exponentiation
*	Multiplication
/	Division
+	Addition
-	Subtraction

(3) cell addresses such as A10 and B15 which are interpreted to mean the value contained in the cells located at the coordinates stated; and (4) built-in functions that result in mathematical values. An example of a relatively complex formula is

(A5*C10+@AVG(B2..B5))/2

which, if it were entered into a cell, would be read as

Multiply the value of the cell A5 by the value of the cell in C10 and

Add that result to the average of the values in the cells B2, B3, B4, and B5 and then
Divide the result by two, and
Display the result in the active cell.

Place your cell pointer on cell B12 and type the formula

+B8+B9+B10 The formula to calculate the annual sum.

After entering the formula with the Enter key, you see that the cell displays the number 28300, but its contents are seen on the status line to be a formula, **+B8+B9+B10**. The distinction between display and content is important. Move your cell pointer to B9 and type

8500   A new value for sales of the Hacker 2
↵   Enter key. Notice that the total for the column changes, seemingly immediately. The changes are made because the content of B12 is a formula that is recalculated every time a new entry is made in the worksheet.

Type and re-enter the number 7300 in B9. Your worksheet should now look like Figure 2-2.

	A	B	C	D	E	F	G
1				HARDWARE ASSOCIATES			
2							
3				SALES FORECAST			
4							
5		LAST	1ST	2ND	3RD	4TH	YRLY
6	MODEL	QTR.	QTR.	QTR.	QTR.	QTR.	TOTAL
7							
8	HACKER 1	15500					
9	HACKER 2	7300					
10	HACKER 3	5500					
11							
12	TOTALS	28300					
13							

Figure 2-2.

As long as the formula you type contains correctly formed cell addresses and numbers, the entry is treated as a value. If you press Return and the formula appears in the cell, you have made a mistake in the entry (probably a missing plus sign as the first character). At times you may hear a beep and the mode indicator block displays EDIT. This signal means that the first character began a value entry, but a later character is incorrect. Common errors that put the entry into edit mode including using the letters l and o instead of 1 and 0. Incorrect cell addresses and illegal operators also cause the entry to be put into edit mode.

CELL DISPLAYS THAT ARE TOO LARGE   **/ Worksheet Column-width**

The default width of a cell is nine characters. Although text entered in cells may overlap to adjoining columns, numbers that are too large to display correctly do not overlap columns. Whenever Lotus 1-2-3 encounters this situation, you see a number with scientfic notation or the cell is filled with asterisks (*). This is a special display. It is not an indication that the contents are incorrect. The asterisks may appear after a number has displayed correctly if you change the display. For instance, if a cell displaying 1234567 was formatted with the /Range Format command, described shortly, to display the number as currency with two decimal places, 13 characters must be displayed since the formatting adds a dollar sign, two commas, a period, and two zeros to look like $1,234,567.00. Since this entry is too large to display, the asterisks are displayed. By looking on the entry line, you can see that the original contents remain. Again, there is a difference between a cell's contents and its display.

If you wished to remove the asterisks and display the number, you would change the width of the cell by typing

/	Slash
W	Worksheet
C	Column-width
S	Set-width
14	Or any number large enough to display the number
⏎	Enter key

The **W**orksheet-**C**olumn-width command allows you to set the width in two ways. In the exercise just completed you typed 14 and pressed the Enter key. This is the approach to take when you are confident you know what the width should be. Sometimes you do not know the width you should have. When this is the case, instead of typing a new number, use the Right and Left arrow keys. As you press the arrows, the width of the column widens and contracts interactively. Expand the column to the width you desire and then press the Enter key.

CHANGING THE WIDTH OF SEVERAL COLUMNS

The command described changes the width of one column: the column the cell pointer is located in. To change the width of several adjacent columns, use the / Worksheet Column Column-range Set-width command.

USING CELL AND RANGE ADDRESSES

The cell address B6 is a reference to a single cell. The value stored in B6 is returned to a formula that references it.

The reference to B2..B5 in the sample formula is a range address. It refers to a rectangular group of cells which has the cell B2 in one corner and the cell B5 in the opposing corner and includes all the cells in the block. B2 and B5 are the end points of the range. A range address could reference

A single cell	A1..A1	with one cell
A column of cells	A1..A10	with ten cells
A row of cells	A1..G1	with seven cells
A block of cells	A1..G10	with 70 cells

Some of the command menu choices ask you to indicate which cell or range of cells is to be affected. When initiating these commands, if you can see or you know where the cells and ranges are, you can type them in response to a prompt.

In the pages that follow, you are often asked to "anchor" a range. This is accomplished with the period. Pressing the period changes a cell address like C10 to a range address,C10..C10. Use the Escape key to "unanchor" a range (i.e., to change a range address to a cell address).

THE COMMAND MENU

In addition to entering data in cells, many operations are conducted through a command menu. The main command menu is obtained by pressing the Slash key (uppercase is a question mark). Enter

/   Slash key. The main menu appears as:

```
Worksheet Range Copy Move File Print Graph Data System Add-in Quit
```

Each choice on the menu begins with a unique character. Range, for instance, is the only choice that begins with the character R. Once this menu or any submenu appears, you make choices by typing the first letter of the menu choice you wish to select, or by responding to prompts (questions) that some of the choices lead to.

The commands included in the command menu serve the functions noted in Figure 2-3.

You will use the command menu shortly. To exit from the menu whenever you are finished using it, or whenever you enter it in error, press

Esc   Escape key

WORKSHEET	Inserts and deletes rows and columns, erases the worksheet, creates windows and titles, sets global worksheet characteristics, and records keystrokes in a worksheet.
RANGE	Changes the display of cell ranges, erases, protects, and unprotects cells.
COPY	Duplicates a cell or range of cells.
MOVE	Relocates a cell or range of cells.
FILE	Saves, erases, retrieves, combines, and links worksheets.
PRINT	Prints a file and specifies the printout's range, margins, and other characteristics. Also used to write the file to disk.
GRAPH	Creates bar, stacked bar, X-Y, line, and pie charts from worksheet data.
DATA	Sorts rows, carries out database operations such as find, extract, and deletion, frequency counting, regression.
SYSTEM	Invokes DOS to manage files, format disks, or perform other activities.
ADD-IN	Attaches, detaches, invokes, or clears memory add-in programs.
QUIT	Exits from Lotus 1-2-3.

Figure 2-3. Lotus 1-2-3 Commands

TEXT JUSTIFICATION AND FORMATTING

/ **Range Label-Prefix**
/ **Range Format**

As numbers are entered, they are right-justified; text is left-justified. Often it is necessary, for better appearance, to change the justification of either numbers or text. Change the justification of the column headings in columns B through G by placing the cell pointer on cell B5 and typing

/   Slash, to call up the command menu
R   **R**ange

L	Label-Prefix
R	Right, to set right-justify
→	Right arrow five times, to highlight the range B5 through G5
↓	Down arrow once, to highlight B5 through G6
◄┘	Enter key, to complete the range designation

Use the formatting procedure to change the appearance of the numbers given as the sales for the last quarter and for future quarters by placing the cell pointer on cell B8 and typing

/	Slash, to call up the command menu
R	Range
F	Format, to change the display of a cell's contents
,	Comma
0	0, for the number of decimal places
◄┘	Enter key
→	Right arrow five times, to highlight B8 through G8
↓	Down arrow four times, to expand coverage to B8 through G12
◄┘	Enter key

The cells B8 through G10 have now been formatted to display numbers in a currency format. New numbers entered in these cells and numbers created by formulas follow this formatting and not the general format provided by default by Lotus 1-2-3.

CREATING AND USING FORMULAS

You have already created one formula that summed the sales for the last quarter. Now you must create a formula for summing the first quarter sales. For each model of computer sold, a different assumption is used to project (guess) the sales. To project the sales for the Hacker 1, place your cell pointer on C8, and without entering any spaces in the formula, type

+B8	The cell address for the value representing the sales of the Hacker 1 computer in the last quarter
*	The multiplication symbol
1.03	Increase previous sales by 3%
◄┘	Enter key, to enter the formula **B8*1.03** currently on the entry line into the active cell, C8, giving the projected sales of $15,965

Now project the sales for the Hacker 2. Move the cell pointer to C9 and enter

+B9/2	To reduce the value in B9, the last quarter sales for the Hacker 2, by 50%
◄┘	Enter key, to enter the formula which produces the value $3,650

Project the sales of the Hacker 3. Move the cell pointer to C10 and type

+B10+450	Increase the last quarter sales of the Hacker 3 by a fixed amount of 450 units
◄┘	Enter key, to enter the formula created. This produces the value 5,950.

COPYING   **/ Copy**

These three formulas provide you with the first quarter's projected sales. You could (but don't) continue to create additional formulas of the same type throughout the remaining columns for quarterly sales. You could also type a formula for totaling the last quarter's sales at the bottom of each column. In each case, you would use the same formula, but you would adjust the cell addresses. To project the second quarter's sales, for illustration, you could type C8*1.03, instead of B8*1.03. This duplication of formulas could lead to mistakes, however. The time that it takes to duplicate the formulas could be substantial if a worksheet is large.

Lotus 1-2-3 provides a command for copying these formulas that saves you time and assures you that the formulas have been copied correctly. To copy the formulas, place the cell pointer on cell C8 and type

/	Slash
C	Copy
↓	Down arrow twice, to enter the range to copy from as C8..C10
↵	Enter key
.	Period, to anchor the range. The cell address is converted to a range address.
→	Right arrow three times, to enter horizontal range which highlights C8 through F8
↵	Enter key, to complete the copy

USING BUILT-IN FUNCTIONS

The total annual sales for each model of computer are to be computed in column G. You could follow the approach taken in totaling the last quarter's sales by adding the individual cells to one another. A formula such as C8+D8+E8+F8 is awkward to use because it takes time to type, you may mistype, omit, or duplicate a cell address, or a new column may be added and the formula would have to be retyped. Lotus 1-2-3 provides a group of operations called functions that enable you to carry out complex operations easily. To compute the annual total, place your cell pointer on G8 and type

@SUM(C8..F8)
↵	Enter key

which uses the @SUM function to sum the values in the cells C8, D8, E8, and F8, all the cells between and including C8 and F8. The result is 66,792 (includes a roundup of one). The range address could include a large group of cells, for instance, C8 through Z8, yet it takes no more effort to create a formula with this range than with a small range.

@SUM is only one built-in function. Others are used in later chapters.

MORE COPYING   **/ Copy**

Now you should copy the formula by placing your cell pointer on G8 (if it has been moved) and typing

/	Slash
C	Copy
↵	Enter key, to accept G8 as the default from range of cells to be copied. It is legal to type a cell address, to type a range address, or to press the Enter key to accept the active cell as the default address.
.	Period, to anchor the copy-to range

| ↓ | Down arrow twice, to set the range to G8 through G10 |
| ◄┘ | Enter key |

Complete the worksheet by copying the formula in B12 so the totals for the remaining columns are also displayed. Place the cell pointer on cell B12 and type

/	Slash
C	**C**opy
◄┘	Enter key
.	Period, to anchor the range
→	Right arrow five times
◄┘	Enter key

Your worksheet should now look like Figure 2-4.

	A	B	C	D	E	F	G	H
1				HARDWARE ASSOCIATES				
2								
3				SALES FORECAST				
4								
5		LAST	1ST	2ND	3RD	4TH	YRLY	
6	MODEL	QTR.	QTR.	QTR.	QTR.	QTR.	TOTAL	
7								
8	HACKER 1	15,500	15,965	16,444	16,937	17,445	66,792	
9	HACKER 2	7,300	3,650	1,825	913	456	6,844	
10	HACKER 3	5,500	5,950	6,400	6,850	7,300	26,500	
11								
12	TOTALS	28,300	25,565	24,669	24,700	25,202	100,135	
13								
14								

Figure 2-4.

SAVING A FILE   / File Save

The worksheet you have been building is in the computer's RAM, or main memory. It has not yet been stored on the diskette where it can be recalled later. Be sure to save your work when it has been completed. When you are constructing a large worksheet, you should save your file periodically to avoid the possibility of accidental loss through a power loss or through a failure to save the file before the machine was turned off. Save your worksheet by typing

/	Slash
F	**F**ile
S	**S**ave
Computer	Or any filename you chose
◄┘	Enter key

Saving a worksheet does not exit you from Lotus 1-2-3. You can save a worksheet and then continue working on it.   Replace the diskette in drive B with your backup diskette and repeat the save procedure. Do not use the **Backup** option. The backup option on the save menu copies the worksheet file already saved on disk to a backup file with the same file name but the extension .BAK. The current worksheet is saved with the same name and the extension .WK1. This option would be useful for keeping a copy of an unrevised worksheet.

LISTING WORKSHEET FILENAMES   / File List

To determine which files are on your data disk, press

/	Slash
F	File
L	List
W	Worksheet, to see worksheets and not graph, print, or other files. A list of filenames appears.
◄┘	Enter key, to return to READY when you have viewed the list

RETRIEVING A FILE   / File Retrieve

If you wish to return to the file COMPUTER to work on it at a later time, do so with the following command sequence:

/	Slash
F	File
R	Retrieve. The execution of this command displays a menu of filenames on the default drive. You can retrieve a file by using the right and left arrow keys to highlight the filename you want and then pressing Return. You see that Lotus has appended the file extension .WK1 to the filenames. You can simply type the filename you want, without the extension. If your diskette for saving files is not in the default drive, you have to use the command sequence / **File Directory A**: ◄┘ to change the default.
COMPUTER	The filename for the saved worksheet
◄┘	Enter key

When a worksheet file is retrieved, it replaces any other worksheet that is in the computer's memory. If a worksheet you have been working on is to be saved, it must be saved before a second worksheet is retrieved.

PRINTING   / Print

To print your worksheet, type

/	Slash
P	Print
P	Printer. Notice that the current print settings are displayed here.
R	Range
Home	Home key
.	Period, to anchor the range at A1
↓	Down arrow 11 times, to highlight a vertical range A1 through A12
→	Right arrow six times, to highlight a horizontal range A1 through G12
◄┘	Enter key, to close the range
A	Align, to print top of worksheet at the top of page. Check the printer to see that the

	paper is at the top of the printer head.
G	**G**o, to execute the printing
P	**P**age, to eject the paper
Q	**Q**uit the print menu

Printing Cell Contents

Often, it is desirable to print out the contents of the cells so formulas can be checked for accuracy. This can be done with the sequence

/	Slash
P	**P**rint
P	**P**rinter
R	**R**ange. The print range used previously is a remembered range. You can skip this step by pressing the Enter key if the print range has been defined and need not be changed.
O	**O**ptions, to change or modify the usual print characteristics
O	**O**ther
C	**C**ell-Formulas, to print the cells' contents, not the cells' displays
Q	**Q**uit, to return to the next higher menu. Escape would return you to the same menu.
A	**A**lign
G	**G**o
P	**P**age, to eject to the next page
Q	**Q**uit the print menu

STOPPING THE PRINTER

If you initiate the printing of a worksheet and decide to abort the printing, hold down the Control key and press the Break key.

QUITTING LOTUS 1-2-3   / Quit

Now that you have saved and printed your worksheet, exit the Lotus 1-2-3 program, by typing

/	Slash
Q	**Q**uit, to quit 1-2-3
Y	**Y**es, to confirm exit
E	**E**xit, to exit the Lotus program

A hard drive microcomputer returns the prompt. For a dual drive computer, you need to place the DOS disk in drive A to continue.

EXERCISES

A. A small book company produces specialty cookbooks for local bookstores. Last year's sales are already known, but only estimates can be made of the future sales for each volume. *Cooking With Gas*, is expected to increase in sales annually by 15%. *Serving Cold Foods* is expected to drop to 90% of each previous year's sales. *Fish & Fowl* will increase its sales by 45 copies per year, while *Meat & Potatoes* is anticipated to sell 300 fewer copies per year. The publisher prepared the following worksheet to illustrate the results of a two-year projection.

	A	B	C	D	E	F	G
1	BOOK SALES						
2							
3		LAST	THIS	YEAR	3-YEAR		
4	TITLE	YEAR	YEAR	AFTER	TOTAL		
5	==						
6	COOKING WITH GAS	2,578	2,965	3,409	8,952		
7	SERVING COLD FOODS	1,145	1,031	927	3,103		
8	FISH & FOWL	980	1,025	1,070	3,075		
9	MEAT & POTATOES	1,577	1,277	977	3,831		
10							
11	TOTALS	6,280	6,297	6,384	18,961		
12							
13							

Use the / Range Format , command to format the numbers with commas.

Reproduce the results obtained by the publisher.

B. An oil producing company has four oil fields that have different prospects for continuing to yield oil. The Great Gusher field has not reached its peak and will be increasing by 7% each year. Oilmen's Acres will increase by 1,300 barrels per year as new wells are drilled. Black Gold Hills will drop production by 1,400 barrels per year and Well Mountain will decrease by 12% per year. The chief geologist produced the following worksheet. Reproduce it using appropriate formulas and formatting. Use the / Range Format , command to format the numbers with commas.

	A	B	C	D	E	F	G
1		OIL OUTPUT					
2		(IN BARRELS)					
3		============					
4							
5		CURRENT	NEXT	YEAR	3-YEAR		
6	OIL FIELD	YEAR	YEAR	AFTER	TOTAL		
7							
8	GREAT GUSHER	20,500	21,935	23,470	65,905		
9	OILMEN'S ACRES	15,800	17,100	18,400	51,300		
10	BLACK GOLD HILLS	19,700	18,300	16,900	54,900		
11	WELL MT.	29,500	25,960	22,845	78,305		
12							
13	TOTALS	85,500	83,295	81,615	250,410		
14							

C.   A small city school district has four high schools that have been experiencing different growth patterns. East High had 2,101 students in 1987 and was expected to increase its enrollment by 7% in each of the next three years. In the same period West High would increase its enrollment of 3,224 students by 5% each year. North High will increase from 2,768 at a 2% annual rate. South High will experience a decline of 3% each year from its 1987 level of 2,346. Prepare a worksheet that displays the expected enrollment for each of the high schools and a yearly total for the combined schools.

D.   In the first quarter of a year, a manufacturer of computer hardware sold 210, 356, 275, 156, and 142 units each of printers, tape drives, disk drives, card punches, and card readers. Printers, tape drives, and disk drives are expected to increase by 5%, 5%, and 3% respectively each of the following three quarters. Card punch sales will decrease by 15% and card reader sales will decrease by 11%. Prepare a worksheet that projects the sales for each device each quarter and that displays the total sales for each device over the one-year period.

Chapter 3

Using Worksheets: A Sales Analysis

Chapter Outline

Worksheets like Lotus 1-2-3 make a wide range of techniques available for calculating and displaying data in a form that is useful to decision-makers. Keeping a worksheet useful often means that the worksheet must be changed as demands change. Usefulness also requires that complex formulas be developed to address complex problems. In this chapter, you will apply previously learned skills and will:

1. Utilize built-in functions for analyzing data;
2. Add and delete rows and columns;
3. Examine the need to adjust cell formulas when the number of rows and columns change;
4. Edit, rather than retype, a cell's contents;
5. See the need for distinguishing between absolute, mixed, and relative cell and range addresses during the copying process.

THE PROBLEM

The manufacturing company that produces the three Hacker model computers distributes its machines through regional sales offices. The president of the company needs to see sales statistics on the relative productivity of these offices. These statistics help top management to evaluate the degree to which staffing changes are needed, additional promotion and publicity campaigns should be mounted, and marketing analyses should be undertaken. The assistant to the president assembles these statistics from quarterly reports submitted by the managers of each of the regional offices. Unlike the first worksheet, which projected sales based on assumptions made by management, this report is more analytical. The assistant wishes to produce a report that looks like Figure 3-1.

```
        A           B           C           D           E           F           G
1                       HARDWARE ASSOCIATES
2                       ===================
3
4               QUARTERLY SALES BY SALES OFFICE
5                                                           YEARLY   PERCENT
6   OFFICE          QTR 1       QTR 2       QTR 3       QTR 4   TOTAL  OF TOTAL
7   --------------------------------------------------------------------------
8   SOUTHWEST       10,329      8,790       7,834       7,903   34,856      31%
9   SOUTHEAST        2,900      4,376       4,502       4,678   16,456      14%
10  NORTHWEST        4,567      4,500       4,325       5,605   18,997      17%
11  NORTHEAST       10,654     10,834      10,839      10,854   43,181      38%
12
13  TOTAL SALES     28,450     28,500      27,500      29,040  113,490
14  MINIMUM          2,900      4,376       4,325       4,678   16,456
15  MAXIMUM         10,654     10,834      10,839      10,854   43,181
16  AVERAGE          7,113      7,125       6,875       7,260   28,373
17
18
```

Figure 3-1.

The report should be created on a worksheet like Lotus 1-2-3 because this reporting format could be reused every year. Also, the assistant believes that once the report is shared with the regional managers, they may have corrections to make in the sales data. By using a worksheet, the formulas will automatically update the calculations based on revisions of the reported sales.

INITIAL ENTRIES

After loading Lotus 1-2-3, make the following numerical and text entries:

Cell Coordinate	Entry
C1	HARDWARE ASSOCIATES
C2	'= (Apostrophe, 19 Equal Signs)
B4	QUARTERLY SALES BY SALES OFFICE
F5	YEARLY
G5	PERCENT
A6	OFFICE
B6	QTR 1
C6	QTR 2
D6	QTR 3
E6	QTR 4
F6	TOTAL
G6	OF TOTAL
A7	'- (Apostrophe, 66 Minus Signs)
A8	SOUTHWEST
B8	10329
C8	8790
D8	7834
E8	7903
A9	SOUTHEAST
B9	2900
C9	4376
D9	4502
E9	4678
A10	NORTHWEST
B10	4567
C10	4500
D10	4325
E10	5605
A11	NORTHEAST
B11	10654
C11	10834
D11	10839
E11	10854
A13	TOTAL SALES
A14	MINIMUM
A15	MAXIMUM
A16	AVERAGE

FORMATTING   / Range Label-Prefix

The column headings can be right-justified to align the headings with the numbers beneath by placing the cell pointer on cell B6 and typing

/	Slash
R	Range
L	Label-Prefix, to alter the display of a label
R	Right

↑	Up arrow once, to highlight B6 through B5
→	Right arrow five times, to highlight B6 through G5
◄┘	Enter key, to complete the Range Label-Prefix command

/ Worksheet Column-width

The text entries in column A, especially A13, are too wide to display properly in a nine-character cell. Widen this column by placing your cell pointer anywhere in column A and typing

/	Slash
W	Worksheet
C	Column
S	Set-Width; a return here will suffice since the command cursor is already on Set-Width
→	Right arrow three times, the column expands to a width of 12
◄┘	Enter key, to complete the Worksheet-Column command

The Range Format command is used to alter the display of numbers. Since the sales figures represent the number of units sold, they should be displayed with commas, but no decimal places. Do this by placing your cell pointer on B8 and typing

/	Slash
R	Range
F	Format
,	Comma, to select the comma formatting style. The comma is needed because the typing of a C would have formatted the range of cells as Currency.
0	Zero, no decimal places
◄┘	Enter key, to accept the zero. The prompt **Enter range to format:** displays B8..B8.
↓	Down arrow eight times, to highlight B8 through B16
→	Right arrow four times, to highlight B8 through F16
◄┘	Enter key, to complete the command

USING BUILT-IN FUNCTIONS

The first worksheet you constructed was a projection of sales that illustrated some of the primary features of worksheet software. In that model, you used the @SUM function to total the values in each row of sales figures. The @SUM function is similar to other Lotus 1-2-3 functions. The built-in function @AVG, for instance, could be used to average the sales in each year and the function @MIN could be used to determine what the lowest number was in each year. To use these functions on identical ranges, you need only alter the function name and retain the range addresses that appear in the totals column. @SUM(C8..F8) displays a total of the values in the four cells C8, D8, E8, and F8, whereas AVG(C8..F8) displays the average of the same cells.

To address the current problem, the development of a sales analysis model will involve the @SUM function and several additional, similar built-in functions. Place your cell pointer on B13 and type

| **@SUM(B8..B11)** | The formula |
| ◄┘ | Enter key |

which displays 28450, the sum of the sales for the four offices for the first quarter. The determination of the minimum, maximum, and average sales per office per quarter will be similar. Type

CELL COORDINATE	ENTRY	DISPLAYS
B14	@MIN(B8..B11)	2,900
B15	@MAX(B8..B11)	10,654
B16	@AVG(B8..B11)	7,113

The yearly total column (F) utilizes the @SUM function, but the range of cells being summed is horizontal, rather than vertical. Place your cell pointer on F8 and type

@SUM(B8..E8)
↵   Enter key, which produces 34,856

in months

Selected Built-In Functions

Lotus 1-2-3 has many built-in functions that can assist you in developing sophisticated worksheets. Figure 3-2 identifies twelve of these functions. Others are described in the Lotus 1-2-3 manuals and in Help screens.

@ABS(number)	Returns the absolute value of a number.
@AVG(list)	Returns the average of all values in a list; does not count empty cells.
@COUNT(list)	Returns a count of the number of nonempty cells, including labels, in a list.
@IF(logical expression,result1,result2)	
	Returns result1 if the logical expression is true or returns result2 if the logical expression is false.
@INT(number)	Returns the integer portion of a number.
@HLOOKUP(key,range,offset)	
	Looks up the key value in the horizontal lookup range and returns the value in the cell above or below specified by the offset.
@VLOOKUP(key,range,offset)	
	Looks up the key value in the vertical lookup range and returns the value in the column in the cell to the right specified by the offset.
@MAX(list)	Returns the largest value in a list.
@MIN(list)	Returns the smallest value in a list.
@ROUND(number,places)	
	Returns the value of a number rounded to a specified number of decimal places.
@SQRT(number)	Returns the square root of a number.
@STD(list)	Returns the standard deviation for all numbers in a list.
@SUM(list)	Returns the sum of a list of numbers.

Figure 3-2. Selected Lotus 1-2-3 Built-In Functions

COPYING   **/ Range Copy**

Copy the formulas for total, minimum, maximum, and average sales per quarter in column B across the next four columns by placing the cell pointer in cell B13, followed by the command sequence

/   Slash
C   Copy

↓	Down arrow three times
↵	Enter key, to define the range to copy-from as B13..B16
.	Period to anchor the copy-to range
→	Right arrow four times, to highlight the cells B13 through F13
↵	Enter key to execute the copy command

Copy the formula for the annual total of sales found in F8 for the other three offices by placing your cell pointer on F8 and typing

/	Slash
C	Copy
↵	Enter key, to accept the current cell as the single cell to be copied. Since the range address F8..F8 was shown, only a single cell composes the range.
.	Period, to anchor the copy-to range
↓	Down arrow three times
↵	Enter key, to execute the copy command

Look at the formulas that were created in F9 by moving your cell pointer to F9. Observe on the status line how the cell addresses in the formula that was copied were changed from B8 to B9 and from E8 to E9.

ABSOLUTE AND RELATIVE CELL ADDRESSES

Lotus 1-2-3 allows for three types of cell addresses: relative, absolute, and mixed. When a cell address in a copied formula is adjusted, the row and column coordinates are changed relative to the direction in which the cell address is copied. For instance, if cell address C10 is contained in a formula found in D20 and this formula is copied to E21, and if C10 is allowed to be adjusted because it is a relative address, it will be changed to D11. The C is adjusted to D because the formula was copied one column to the right. The 10 is changed to 11 because the formula was copied one row down.

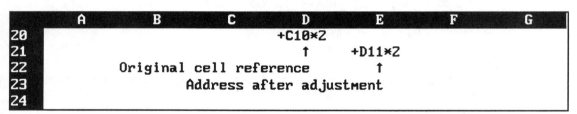

Figure 3-3. Relative Addressing

Cell addresses are made absolute by placing a dollar sign in front of both the row and column coordinates. If an absolute cell address is copied from one cell to another, the cell address is copied unchanged. An absolute cell address prevents adjustment so that the cell "absolutely" refers to the same cell it did before copying. If the formula $C$10*2 is copied, no adjustment is permitted, and the cell address will remain unchanged regardless of the number of rows or columns that separate the original cell from the copy.

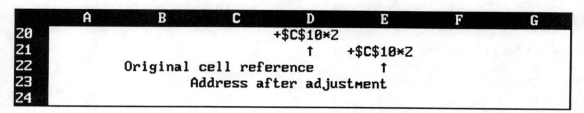

	A	B	C	D	E	F	G
20				+$C$10*2			
21				↑	+$C$10*2		
22			Original cell reference		↑		
23			Address after adjustment				
24							

Figure 3-4. Absolute Addressing

The dollar sign in front of the column coordinate C means "if this formula is copied, absolutely do not adjust the column coordinate." The dollar sign in front of the row number has a similar meaning, but holds the row coordinate constant. If a cell address will not allow either the column or row to be adjusted, copies of it will always refer to the same location.

A mixed cell address holds either the column or the row absolute but not both. $C10 and C$10 are mixed addresses.

The differences among relative, absolute, and mixed cell addresses are critical to the successful development of worksheets. In many formulas, there will be addresses of each type. After copying formulas, you should always examine the products of the formulas copied to be sure that they are returning the correct answers; don't assume that they are! If the correct answers are not present, but the original formula was correct, look closely at the formulas in the cells to which the formula was copied and check the cell references to be sure that they refer to the appropriate cells. If they do not, reset the cell addresses correctly.

Column G calculates each office's sales as a percentage of the total sales for the company. To create this combination absolute and relative formula for the first office, place your cell pointer on G8 and enter

+F8/$F$13

This divides the Southwest office's relative sales by the company's absolute sales. The dollar signs imbedded in the column and row address F13 designate an absolute reference to the total sales cell for the year. In addition to typing in the dollar signs to create absolute addresses, you can use function key F4 to set absolute references to a cell. The formula in G13 has been typed directly into the worksheet with the dollar signs having been added with the $ key, not with F4. For illustrative purposes, you will enter the formula again to see how the F4 key works. Place your cell pointer on G8 and type

+	Plus sign, to designate the entry as a value
←	Left arrow, to start the formula as +F8
/	Slash, to divide the Southwest office's relative sales by the company's absolute yearly sales
←	Left arrow
↓	Down arrow five times, to place the cell pointer on cell F13
F4	Function key F4, the Absolute key, which changes the cell address to $F$13. If you continue to press the F4 key, the cell address will be changed to the two forms of mixed addressing and to the completely relative form as well. If you try pressing the key again, make sure that before you proceed, the address is absolute. The formula on the status line now appears as +F8/$F$13.
↵	Enter key, to complete the entry of the formula

FORMATTING

To format this number as a percentage, type

/	Slash
R	Range
F	Format
P	Percent
0	To suppress the display of any fractional parts
◄⌐	Enter key
◄⌐	Enter key, to execute the Range Format command which displays 31%

COPYING

Copy the formula in G8 by leaving your cell pointer on G8 and typing

/	Slash
C	Copy
◄⌐	Enter key, to accept the current cell as the cell to be duplicated
.	Period, to anchor the copy-to range
↓	Down arrow three times
◄⌐	Enter key, to execute the copy command

Since the formula in G8 is referencing both absolute and relative columns and rows, the formulas in G9 through G11 will adhere to the same addressing modes.

Your worksheet should now look like that shown in Figure 3-5.

```
          A            B          C          D          E          F          G
        ┌─────────────────────────────────────────────────────────────────────
1       │            HARDWARE ASSOCIATES
2       │            ====================
3       │
4       │       QUARTERLY SALES BY SALES OFFICE
5       │                                              YEARLY  PERCENT
6       │OFFICE       QTR 1      QTR 2      QTR 3      QTR 4    TOTAL OF TOTAL
7       │─────────────────────────────────────────────────────────────────────
8       │SOUTHWEST    10,329     8,790      7,834      7,903    34,856      31%
9       │SOUTHEAST     2,900     4,376      4,502      4,678    16,456      14%
10      │NORTHWEST     4,567     4,500      4,325      5,605    18,997      17%
11      │NORTHEAST    10,654    10,834     10,839     10,854    43,181      38%
12      │
13      │TOTAL SALES  28,450    28,500     27,500     29,040   113,490
14      │MINIMUM       2,900     4,376      4,325      4,678    16,456
15      │MAXIMUM      10,654    10,834     10,839     10,854    43,181
16      │AVERAGE       7,113     7,125      6,875      7,260    28,373
17      │
18      │
```

Figure 3-5.

ADDING ROWS

Adding Rows Within Ranges

One of the great values of worksheets is the rapidity with which they can be modified. Suppose that after the assistant to the president completed the annual sales analysis model, it was found that the company had actually sold 2,205 more computers than were reflected in the sales in each region. The difference is found to be the failure to include sales by two sales representatives who report to the main office of Hardware Associates, rather than to a regional office. One of these salespeople is in Alaska and the other is based in Kansas City. Since the company is contemplating opening full-scale offices in both locations, the assistant decides to add two new rows to the worksheet.

For illustrative purposes, the two rows will be added in two separate locations. To create the first entry for the Central office in Kansas, place your cell pointer on A10 (although the cell pointer could be anywhere on this row), and type

/	Slash
W	Worksheet
I	Insert, to create a new row 10 and to move row 10 and other rows below it underneath the new row
R	Row
↵	Enter key, to choose row 10 as the location at which a new row will be inserted. If you wished to insert more than one row, you would press the Down arrow key once for each additional row needed.

The new row appears, but more changes have been made to the worksheet than are apparent. Move your cell pointer to B14 and look at the contents of the cell as they appear next to the prompt line. The range of cells being summed, which you entered as B8..B11, is now shown as B8..B12. The end points of the range of cells were automatically adjusted by Lotus 1-2-3 to include the inserted row. This is because the new row was located between the two range corner cells B8 and B11. This adjustment was made to all the formulas that are now found in rows 14 through 17. Had a column been inserted, the ranges found in column F would also have been adjusted.

The information you should now enter in the blank row is

Cell Coordinate	Entry
A10	CENTRAL
B10	379
C10	334
D10	311
E10	323

Entries in this row change the column totals, averages, and minimums. These data are taken into account by the formulas on rows 14 through 17 as soon as they are entered. The yearly total and the percent of total columns for Central remain empty because no formulas have been put in them. The formulas will be added shortly.

Adding Rows Outside Ranges

The assistant to the president decides to add the Alaskan entry at line 13, a line that is currently blank. A blank line is still needed to separate the data from the results of the analysis. To add the new row, place your cell pointer on row 13, and type

/	Slash
W	Worksheet
I	Insert, to create a new row 13 and to move row 13 and other rows below it down
R	Row
◄┘	Enter key, to choose row 13 as the location of the row to be inserted

Make the following entries:

Cell Coordinate	Entry
A13	**ALASKA**
C13	**256**
D13	**295**
E13	**297**

ADDING COLUMNS
/ Worksheet Insert

This exercise demonstrated how rows are inserted in worksheets. The insertion of a column is essentially the same. The completion of the insertion command causes a new column to be inserted at the location of the cell pointer. The column the cell pointer was on is pushed to the right, along with any other columns to the right of the cell pointer. When columns or rows are inserted, you should examine relevant formulas closely to be sure that the new column is included in the intended formula ranges.

DELETING ROWS AND COLUMNS
/ Worksheet Delete

The command sequence for deleting columns and rows can also affect the validity of formulas contained in other columns and rows. For instance, the deletion of column F can cause a formula in column G that reads @SUM(A8..F8) to display an error. Lotus 1-2-3 keeps track of the two end points of a range, but not the entire range. Thus, when one of the end points is eliminated, Lotus 1-2-3 does not assume that there is a new end point such as E8. An error is displayed.

The deletion of a row or column in the middle of a range is automatically accommodated by formulas that had that row or column in the middle of its range.

EDITING CELL CONTENTS
F2

Notice that total sales for the last three quarters have not changed even though there were sales in Alaska. Neither have the minimum or the average sales changed. Move your cell pointer to B15 and look at the range address on the contents line. The range being summed is still defined as B8..B12 so the row that was just added was not included in this or in any of the formulas on rows 15 through 18. The formulas must all be edited to reflect the inclusion of this row.

It is not necessary to retype a cell's contents completely if much of them are correct. Retyping might introduce new errors. Edit the contents with the Edit key, F2, instead. With your cell pointer on B15, type the following:

F2	Edit key
←	Left arrow, to place the cursor under the)
Backspace	Backspace key, to remove the 2
3	To insert a 3 to make the range B8..B13
↵	Enter key

The total does not change because B13 is blank. An empty cell is not treated as a zero. It is ignored. Notice that an empty cell is not treated as a zero by the minimum function. An empty cell is different from a cell with a zero in it. A zero would be evaluated in all four functions used here.

Edit the cells in B16 through B18 with the same keystrokes.

The formulas in the total column (F) and the four analytical rows (B15 through B18) must be recopied. Do this by placing the cell pointer on B15 and typing

/	Slash
C	Copy
↓	Down arrow three times, to set the copy-from range
↵	Enter key
.	Period, to anchor the copy-to range
→	Right arrow four times, to set the copy-to range
↵	Enter key, to complete the Copy command

Recalculate the annual totals and the percent of totals figures for each of the offices by placing your cell pointer on F8 and entering

/	Slash
C	Copy
→	Right arrow, to set the copy-from range
↵	Enter key
.	Period, to anchor the range
↓	Down arrow five times, to set the copy-to range
↵	Enter key, to execute the Copy command

Your worksheet is complete and should look like Figure 3-6.

	A	B	C	D	E	F	G
1			HARDWARE ASSOCIATES				
2			====================				
3							
4		QUARTERLY SALES BY SALES OFFICE					
5						YEARLY	PERCENT
6	OFFICE	QTR 1	QTR 2	QTR 3	QTR 4	TOTAL	OF TOTAL
7	---						
8	SOUTHWEST	10,329	8,790	7,834	7,903	34,856	30%
9	SOUTHEAST	2,900	4,376	4,502	4,678	16,456	14%
10	CENTRAL	379	334	311	323	1,347	1%
11	NORTHWEST	4,567	4,500	4,325	5,605	18,997	16%
12	NORTHEAST	10,654	10,834	10,839	10,854	43,181	37%
13	ALASKA		256	295	297	848	1%
14							
15	TOTAL SALES	28,829	29,090	28,106	29,660	115,685	
16	MINIMUM	379	256	295	297	848	
17	MAXIMUM	10,654	10,834	10,839	10,854	43,181	
18	AVERAGE	5,766	4,848	4,684	4,943	19,281	
19							

Figure 3-6.

The percentage column does not add up correctly because of round-off error. The percentages could be displayed to reflect a 100% total if fractional parts were displayed.

SAVING YOUR WORKSHEET   / File Save

Save your worksheet by typing

/	Slash
F	**F**ile
S	**S**ave
SALES	To assign **SALES** as the filename. If you have already saved SALES once, the name will automatically appear. You need not retype the name. Go on to the next step instead.
↵	Enter key, to enter the save filename

Replace the diskette in drive B with your backup diskette and repeat the file save procedure used in earlier chapters. Do not use the backup option that is used for keeping a copy of the file before changes are made.

PRINTING YOUR WORKSHEET   / Print Printer

To print your worksheet, type

/	Slash
P	**P**rint
P	**P**rinter
R	**R**ange

Home	Home key
.	Period, to anchor the copy to range
↓	Down arrow 17 times, to set the vertical range
→	Right arrow six times, to set the horizontal range
◄┘	Enter key, to complete the print range
A	**A**lign. Set the paper crease at the top of the print head.
G	**G**o, to execute the printing of the worksheet
P	**P**age, to advance to the top of the next page
Q	**Q**uit, to return to Lotus 1-2-3

PRINTING A WORKSHEET TO DISK / **Print File**

Normally, to say that you are printing a file implies that you are sending the file to the printer to get hard copy output. It is also possible to print a file to the disk. When you do this, a line-by-line image of the worksheet is sent to a new file. Unlike the worksheet file, in which all of the formatting commands, column widths, and cell contents are known, the printed disk file contains only the characters that you see on the screen inside of the worksheet. For example, a single cell that contains a formula B2*C3/20 might display $20.13 because the number created by the formula is displayed as currency, two decimal places. A print file contains only leading spaces, if any, the dollar sign, the period, and the numerals as part of a larger line. There is nothing to indicate how these characters came to become part of the line printed within the file.

   Print-to-disk files are primarily used to create files that are accessible to word processing and other programs. Worksheet files by themselves cannot be read into most other programs directly. Worksheet files contain information and control characters that the user does not want to become a part of the receiving file and that the receiving program does not know how to handle. By creating a print file, only the display of the worksheet is saved. These print lines can be added to a word processing or other program file later.

   To print a file to disk, type

/	Slash
P	**P**rint
F	**F**ile
SALES	The filename to be used. The extension .PRN will be added to the filename automatically.
◄┘	Enter key
G	**G**o, to print the worksheet image to a file
Q	**Q**uit, to return to Lotus 1-2-3

PRINTING WORKSHEETS AS FORMULAS / **Print Printer Options Other**

At times it is necessary to examine the contents of cells rather than the displays of the cells. If results are inaccurate, it may be that the formulas contained in some of the cells are incorrect. It may be difficult to evaluate all of the formulas if you are restricted to a single screen of the worksheet since many worksheets contain hundreds of formulas which are found throughout thousands of cells. Printing the formulas allows you the flexibility of having the formulas close at hand while you examine a printout of the display organized by rows and columns to see whether correct references are being made to cell and range addresses. Print out the formulas for this worksheet by typing

/	Slash

P	**P**rint
P	**P**rinter
O	**O**ptions
O	**O**ther
C	**C**ell-Formulas
Q	**Q**uit, to return to a higher command level
A	**A**lign
G	**G**o, to print out the cell formulas
P	**P**age, to advance to the top of the next page
Q	**Q**uit, to return to Lotus 1-2-3

ENHANCING PRINTED WORKSHEETS   / **Add-in**

Lotus provides a main menu command for loading supplementary programs into RAM that enhance Lotus's capabilities. This is accomplished using add-in programs which have the extension .ADN. Lotus supplies two add-in programs, Macro Library Manager and Always. Always is used to produce presentation style worksheets. In order to use add-in programs, your computer must have a hard drive as well as at least 512K memory. Always will be used for this exercise. Before a worksheet's appearance can be enhanced, the add-in program must be brought into memory or attached. Do this by typing

/	Slash
A	**A**dd-in
A	**A**ttach; available programs are displayed. Highlight ALWAYS.ADN
↵	Enter key, to select Always
↵	Enter key, to select No key. Keys can be used to invoke an add-in program assigned to it. An introductory screen will appear briefly, then the worksheet screen will return. The add-in program Always is now in memory and is ready to be used (invoked).
I	**I**nvoke, to place the program into use. Make sure Always is highlighted.
↵	Enter key, to invoke Always. The worksheet screen will change in appearance. The mode indicator will display Always and the current font will be listed at the top of the window.

Fonts can be changed with regard to type and size. The text of the entire worksheet can be changed or just a letter can be changed. To change the font style of the first title, place the cursor on cell C1. Enter

/	Slash
F	**F**ormat
F	**F**ont. A menu will appear with the available fonts.
7	To highlight TIMES 14 point
↵	Enter key, to select the font style
→	Right arrow twice, to set the range to C1..E1
↵	Enter key, to accept the range. Notice the change in the titles' appearance.

Change the appearance of the column headings by placing the pointer on cell B6 and typing

/	Slash
F	**F**ormat
B	**B**old

S	**S**et
→	Right arrow six times
↑	Up arrow, to set the range A6..G5
↵	Enter key, to accept the range. The column headings appear boldfaced.

The report totals would look better if they were standardized with a double underline before them. This is done by placing the pointer on B13 and typing

/	Slash
F	**F**ormat
U	**U**nderline
D	**D**ouble
→	Right arrow four times, to specify the range B13..F13
↵	Enter key; notice the double underline is directly under the column numbers, not on the next row.

The row beneath the main heading does not appear as intended while in the Always mode so this row should be removed. Editing cell contents cannot be performed within an add-in program, so return to the Lotus Ready mode. Type

/	Slash
Q	**Q**uit

Place the pointer on cell C2 and type

/	Slash
R	**R**ange
E	**E**rase
→	Right arrow three times, to highlight the range C2..E2
↵	Enter key, to complete the erase
/	Slash
A	**A**dd-in
I	**I**nvoke; insure that ALWAYS is highlighted.
↵	Enter key

Now that the worksheet has been changed to look more professional, it can be printed. Place the cursor on cell A1 (Home) and type

/	Slash
P	**P**rint
R	**R**ange
S	**S**et
→	Right arrow six times
↓	Down arrow 17 times, to highlight the range A1..G18
↵	Enter key; notice the dotted box around the range to print
G	**G**o, to send the report to print. At the top of the screen the current row printing is displayed.

After the enhanced worksheet is finished, control is returned to the worksheet. No more enhancements will be made to this worksheet. Exit the add-in program by typing

/	Slash
Q	**Q**uit

Control is returned to the 1-2-3 worksheet. Always remains in memory until it is removed by (1) / **A**dd-in **D**etach, (2) / **A**dd-in **C**lear, or (3) leaving the work session. To save the add-in program's formatting, the worksheet must be saved before exiting the worksheet. Since this file will not be used again in this text, it is not necessary to save the Always formatting. However, if you wish to save the file with the Always settings, use the / File Save procedure now. Then continue.

QUITTING LOTUS 1-2-3   / **Quit**

Exit the Lotus 1-2-3 program. Type

/	Slash
Q	**Q**uit
Y	**Y**es, to confirm exit

and load the DOS diskette if prompted to do so.

EXERCISES

A.   A college professor is keeping student grades in a Lotus 1-2-3 worksheet. Copy the following seminar class grade book. The cumulative total column represents the sum of each student's grades for the semester, while the average column is an average of all the grades.

	A	B	C	D	E	F	G	H
1			GRADE BOOK					
2			CIS 450					
3			========					
4								
5							CUM.	
6	STUDENT NAME	TEST 1	TEST 2	TEST 3	TEST 4	FINAL	TOTAL	AVERAGE
7	--							
8	SMITH, S.	89	92	90	92	99	462	92
9	JONES	78	85	82	70	80	395	79
10	BLACK, B.	98	93	92	90	91	464	93
11	WHITE, W.	77	80	86	78	88	409	82
12	THOMAS, T.	85	87	87	83	90	432	86
13	WRIGHT, W.	85	73	84	87	84	413	83
14								
15	AVERAGE	85	85	87	83	89	429	
16	MINIMUM	77	73	82	70	80	395	
17	MAXIMUM	98	93	92	92	99	464	
18								

Print out this worksheet as it appears and as formulas. Also print this worksheet to a file with the filename GRADES.PRN (Lotus appends the .PRN).

B.   A motor vehicle sales office manager breaks down the revenues from the sale of vehicles into four categories: sedans, station wagons, vans, and trucks. In addition to totaling the sales, the manager wishes to determine the percentage of the total each amount represents. The sales for each half-year and the percentage of the total for each is shown below. Reconstruct the worksheet.

	A	B	C	D	E
1		REVENUE ANALYSIS			
2					
3		FIRST	% OF	SECOND	% OF
4	PRODUCT	HALF	TOTAL	HALF	TOTAL
5					
6	SEDANS	$2,456,686	43.91%	$3,112,800	45.59%
7	STA. WAGONS	$1,233,345	22.05%	$1,577,380	23.10%
8	VANS	$114,567	2.05%	$134,677	1.97%
9	TRUCKS	$1,789,655	31.99%	$2,003,456	29.34%
10					
11	TOTALS	$5,594,253	100.00%	$6,828,313	100.00%
12					

The dollar signs are displayed with the use of the Range Format command. Select C to display the dollar sign and the comma for the specified range.

The sales office began to sell subcompact cars in the second half of the year. Modify the worksheet to reflect $57,657 of revenue realized from the sale of subcompacts as a fifth category.

Print out this worksheet as it appears and as formulas. Also print this worksheet to a file with the filename INCOME.PRN.

C.   A superintendent of a small rural school district has been asked to prepare a table that reflects the number and percent of the total of males and females employed at each school level in the district. At the elementary school level, there are 26 males and 67 females. At the middle school level, there are 28 males and 24 females. At the high school level, there are 32 males and 24 females. Prepare a worksheet that displays this information, the totals for each school level, and the percentage each sex contributes to the total of 100% for each school level. For instance, the 26 males at the elementary school level are 27% of the total of 93 teachers employed at the elementary level. Also display the total numbers of males and females for the district and each group's composite percentage of the total. Print this worksheet as it appears and as formulas. Also print the worksheet to a file named MFRATIO.PRN.

D.   The Watson County School district's budget is composed of expenditures of $1,609,370 for instruction, $327,058 for administration, $346,600 for maintenance, and $172,630 for transportation. A comparative study of ten other school districts showed their average expenditures for the same items to be $1,472,300, $313,980, $256,780, and $142,890 respectively. Build a worksheet that displays each item's percent of the total for both the school district and the comparative sample. Display the four items in thousands of dollars (e.g., $313,980 is displayed as $313.98).

E.   The Ace Taxicab Company has five vehicles. The mileage for each vehicle is tracked carefully. The mileages for one quarter are:

VEHICLE	JAN.	FEB.	MAR.
123-ABH	2,056	3,004	2,768
345-XYG	2,344	3,021	2,856
455-XYH	1,589	1,468	1,290
231-ABH	2,788	2,234	1,121
346-XYG	2,700	2,344	1,903

Create a worksheet that identifies the average, total, minimum, and maximum mileages for each month, as well as for the quarter. Also, display the percent of the total that each cab was driven.

A sixth vehicle with the license plate 311-BMW is acquired in March. Add this vehicle to the list as well as its March mileage of 1,250 miles. Adjust the formulas to accurately reflect this addition.

Chapter 4

Lotus Graphing

Chapter Outline

Numerical presentations like those of the projected sales for each regional office of Hardware Associates are useful to management in that the data presented offer a quantitative basis for planning. Discussion of the assumptions made in the projection enable managers to question whether the projections are realistic or not. If data need to be changed, this can be done quickly and easily. Unfortunately, it is difficult for many people to fully grasp the implications of the projections. Which of the several regions are increasing their sales? Are overall sales increasing or decreasing? Graphs and charts portraying numerical data are often more useful in presenting data in a form that is suitable for human understanding than are raw numbers. In this chapter, you learn how to

1. Construct and save 1-2-3 graphs;
2. Save and print graphs;
3. Name graph settings so the graph can be recalled for adjustment in the future;
4. Use the Graph key;
5. Reset graph settings to facilitate the development of new graphs.

RETRIEVING A WORKSHEET   / **File Retrieve**

In the last chapter, you created a worksheet with the filename SALES. If you have been working with Lotus 1-2-3, you should save the file you are working with before you retrieve the file SALES because this file totally replaces the worksheet currently in view. If you are starting anew, boot the computer with DOS and type

lotus   To load Lotus 1-2-3

　　　Before pressing the Enter key, notice the choice **PrintGraph** on the access menu. You will return to this choice later in the chapter when you print the graphs you create in 1-2-3. Press

◄┘   Enter key

When you have obtained the blank worksheet screen, retrieve the worksheet SALES by typing

/   Slash
F   **F**ile
R   **R**etrieve
SALES   The name of the file to be retrieved
◄┘   Enter key

　　　The graph to be created first is a pie chart that displays the first quarter's sales. Each sector, or pie piece, represents the sales by one sales office. Together, the sales of all of the offices total 100% of the sales.

THE GRAPH COMMAND   / **Graph**

Before initiating the Graph command, place your cell pointer on A8, the label SOUTHWEST. Once you have begun to execute a command sequence, it is awkward or impossible to move the cell pointer to a desired location. You are restricted to making choices from the menu or to responding to prompts. The prompts frequently assume that the currently active cell is the starting point for a range. If the current cell is not the starting point, you must relocate the cell pointer to the new location. The Graph command is initiated by typing

Caps Lock   Put Caps Lock on
/   Slash
G   Graph, which displays the current graph settings and the following menu:

Type	X	A	B	C	D	E	F	Reset	View	Save	Options	Name	Group	Quit

　　　The default choice, Type (default because it is already highlighted), is used to select the style of graph you would like to prepare. Press

◄┘   Enter key, to select Type. Notice that five types charts can be created: line, bar and
　　　　　　　　　stacked bar charts, XY, and pie charts.
P   **P**ie, to create a pie chart

　　　Notice that after 1-2-3 accepted the pie chart choice, the Graph menu returned to the control panel. This is a sticky menu that assumes that you need to continue working with it since the

construction of a graph is a multistep process. A sticky menu saves you the trouble of retyping the /
and G to return to this menu many times.

The X on the menu represents the choice with which to identify cell range that contains the
identifying labels for the pie's sectors. In this graph, you would like to have the office names
(Southwest, Southeast, etc.) be these labels. The letters A through F are used to designate data ranges
that are used to construct the graphs. In a pie chart, you need only set the X and A ranges. 1-2-3
allows only one chart per screen. Therefore, only one set of data can be graphed. To set the two
ranges, type

X	To select the X range. A prompt shows the default cell to be A8. A8 is a free cell address because it is not anchored. If necessary, you could move the pointer and only highlight the currently active cell. This is the correct cell to begin with since the X range should highlight the office names.
.	Period, to anchor the range and to display A8..A8
↓	Down arrow five times, to highlight the office names and to display the X range as A8..A13
◄┘	Enter key, to complete selection of the X labels range

A data range must now be set. The A data range is used to capture the values for the pie chart.

A	To select the A range. Again, the default cell is A8, which is not correct.
→	Right arrow, to begin the A data range at B8
.	Period, to anchor the range and to display B8..B8
↓	Down arrow five times, to highlight the sales figures and to display the A data range as B8..B13. It is important to note that the X and A data ranges parallel one another. 1-2-3 makes the association between Southwest and the number 10,329, as well as between the other office names and their corresponding sales figures.
◄┘	Enter key
V	**V**iew, to see the pie chart. Observe the labels that were selected as the X range. The numbers of the A range were automatically converted to percentages, which are also displayed.

GRAPH OPTIONS   / Graph Options

Titles

The pie chart is accurately produced, but it lacks some vital information. Namely, there are no titles
indicating what the graph portrays. Add titles by pressing

Esc	Escape key, to cancel the graphic display
O	**O**ptions, to enhance the graph with some additional information
T	**T**itles, to incorporate one of the possible titles on the graph
F	**F**irst, to create a banner title at the top of the graph

HARDWARE ASSOCIATES

	The main title
◄┘	Enter key, to enter the title
T	**T**itles, to select another title which appears below the main title
S	**S**econd, to enter a subtitle just beneath the main title
Caps Lock	Toggle Caps Lock off

First Quarter Sales
	The subtitle
◄⌐	Enter key. A pie chart does not use X-axis and Y-axis titles so these choices will not be selected.
Q	**Q**uit, to return to the graph menu
V	**V**iew, to see the graph with the titles
Esc	Escape, to return to the graph menu

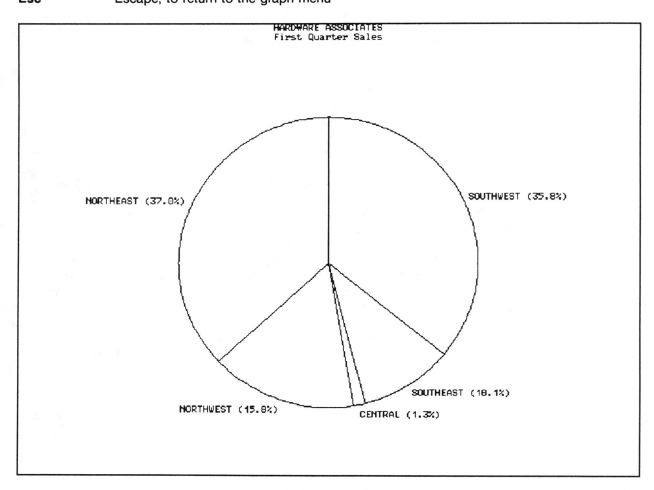

Figure 4-1. Pie Chart

SAVING THE GRAPH   / Graph Save

Selection of the Save menu choice creates a new file on the diskette. The new file is not a worksheet with the extension .WK1, which is automatically assigned to Lotus worksheets. Rather, the file is a representation of the picture that is readable and printable only with the 1-2-3 PrintGraph diskette. The new file has the extension .PIC.

The graph file that is saved cannot be retrieved by 1-2-3, nor can it be modified since it is a picture. It can be replaced by saving a new picture with the same filename. PrintGraph can make some changes to type styles used to reproduce text and to the size of the graph, but the basic graph must be reproduced as it was saved. To save the graph, type

S	Save, to initiate the save process
QTR1A	The graph filename. The filename could be the same as the worksheet filename. Since the extensions are different, 1-2-3 and DOS recognize them as being unique.
◄┘	Enter key. Notice the red light go on as the file is written to disk, an indication that a file is being created. The control panel redisplays the Graph menu.

NAMING THE GRAPH   / Graph Name

Another choice on the Graph menu is Name. This command is easily confused with the Save command since it too deals with your ability to recall previously designed charts. Unlike the Save command, use of the Name command does not save a picture, neither does it create a separate file. It is used to identify and retain for future use the settings that can reproduce graphs on the screen. By naming a graph, you associate a series of graph settings with the name selected. Name the graph by typing

N	Name
C	Create
QTR1A	The graph settings name
◄┘	Enter key. Notice how quickly control returns to the Graph menu and that the red light did not go on. No new files were created.

Once the graph settings have been named, you can reuse the graph name and recall the graph at any time. You will do this shortly.

MODIFYING THE GRAPH

The pie chart is only one of the possible displays available. Change the chart type by pressing

T	Type, or Enter, to select a new style
B	Bar, the new style (displayed in Figure 4-2)
V	View, to see the altered graph style
Esc	Escape key, to cancel the graph's display

Save the graph as described in the Saving the Graph section above, using the graph filename, QTR1B. Again, note the disk drive writing the file to the diskette. Name the graph settings with the name QTR1B also.

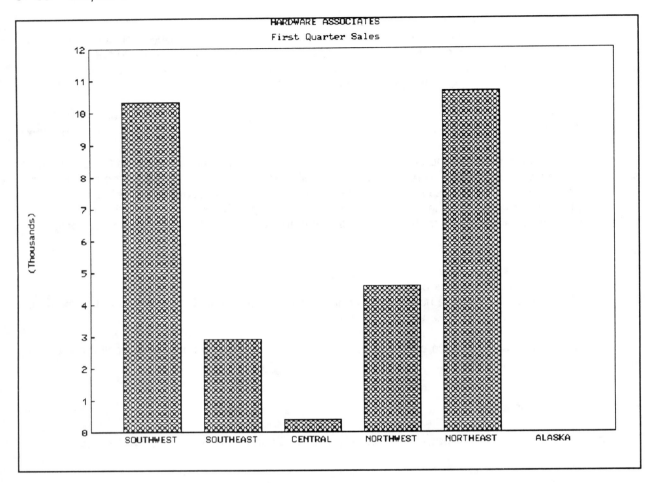

Figure 4-2. Bar Chart

THE GRAPH KEY   **F10**

Lotus keeps track of the last settings used in a graph display. The function key F10 is called the Graph key because it recreates a graph from the READY state with the last graph settings used. This allows you to change the specific values in the X and A ranges, for instance, and to reproduce the graph without re-entering the Graph menu. The graph displayed shall be reorganized to reflect the changes. Obtain a clear control panel and change the mode block to READY by pressing

Q   **Q**uit

Before proceeding, it is necessary to convert the office names to their abbreviations. The graphs that are produced by Lotus have a limited capacity to compress and reduce the size of type used for labels. Sometimes labels like NORTHWEST are too large to appear on the screen. At other times, long labels may appear on the screen, but are truncated. Simply replace each of the office names with the abbreviations SW, SE, CNT, NW, NE, and AK by entering the abbreviations in the appropriate cells (A8 to A13). Then see the difference this makes by pressing

| **F10** | The Graph key, to see the revised graph |
| **Esc** | Escape key, to remove the graph and to return to the command menu |

RECALLING NAMED GRAPHS   **/ Graph Name**

Having seen the new display of the first quarter's sales, you may wish to see the original graph again. Simply type

/	Slash
G	**G**raph
N	**N**ame
U	**U**se
QTR1A	The first graph's named settings
↵	Enter key, to see the first graph. You do not have to re-enter the range settings and titles.

Repeat the recalling sequence and display the second graph, QTR1B. By having named the settings, you can reuse them and not have to reset all of the ranges and titles.

SAVING NAMED GRAPHS

There is another significant difference between saving a graph and naming a graph that has not been mentioned. When a graph is saved, a file resides on the diskette whether or not the worksheet it is based on is saved to the disk. A named graph is not saved unless the worksheet is also saved to the diskette. The named graph is similar to, for example, a Range Format command setting.

Suppose that you retrieve a file that has a column of numbers that are displayed in the general format. If you alter the display to be currency, zero decimal places, the change will not be present the next time you use the worksheet if you do not save it with the new display. A named graph is part of the current worksheet, also.

QUITTING THE GRAPH MENU

To return to the main menu, you can either press the Escape key three times, or press

| **Q** | **Q**uit |

If you do not save the worksheet after naming a graph, the graph names will not be present when the worksheet is retrieved.

ADDING DATA RANGES

The two graphs used have used only one column of numbers: that for the first quarter. The values in column B were used for the A data range. The values in column C are the B data range and the values in column D are the C data range. Perhaps the directors of Hardware Associates would like to see a full year's projections. Place the cell pointer on C8. Return to the Graph menu and select additional data ranges by typing

/	Slash
G	**G**raph, which displays the Graph menu
B	To set the second data range and which displays the cell address, C8
.	Period, to anchor the range and to display C8..C8
↓	Down arrow five times, to highlight the office names and to display the B range as C8..C13
↵	Enter key

Repeat this sequence for the C and D data ranges, not data columns, remembering to move the cell pointer before you press the period, which anchors the range.

UNANCHORING A DATA RANGE

If you mistakenly press the period, you can unanchor the range by pressing the Escape key. Also, if you set a range incorrectly, you can cause Lotus to forget a remembered, incorrect range, by pressing the Escape key.

VIEWING THE GRAPH

When you have set the four data ranges, change the graph style and view the graph by typing

T	**T**ype
B	**B**ar
V	**V**iew, to see the graph. Notice that with four data ranges, four different patterns are used to display the data.
↵	Enter key, to return to the Graph menu

ADDING TITLES AND LEGENDS   / Graph Options

The new graph has two ambiguities associated with it. First, it is not immediately obvious what the four patterns stand for. Second, the height of the bars is marked by numbers on the vertical dimension (the Y-axis) and each group of bars is labeled with two-letter abbreviations. If you had not constructed the graph, would you know what the numbers and the abbreviations represented? In three months will you remember? Identify these labels more accurately by typing

O	**O**ptions, to enhance the graph with some additional information
T	**T**itles, to incorporate additional titles
S	**S**econd, to change the original subtitle

Quarterly Sales

	The new subtitle
↵	Enter key
T	**T**itle
X	**X**-axis, to create a title centered at the bottom of the graph

Regional Offices

	The X-axis title, to identify the X-range labels
↵	Enter key, to enter the title

T	Titles, to create another title to appear beneath the main title
Y	**Y**-axis, to enter a title that appears vertically along the left side of the graph to identify the significance of bar heights

Level of Sales

	The title
◄┘	Enter key
L	Legend, to identify the data range patterns
A	The legend title for the A data range
1st	The title
◄┘	Enter key
L	Legend, to identify the data range patterns
B	The legend title for the B data range
2nd	The title
◄┘	Enter key
L	Legend, to identify the data range patterns
C	The legend title for the C data range
3rd	The title
◄┘	Enter key
L	Legend, to identify the data range patterns
D	The legend title for the D data range
4th	The title
◄┘	Enter key
Q	**Q**uit, to return to the Graph menu
V	**V**iew, to see the graph with the new titles and legends (displayed in Figure 4-3)
Esc	Escape, to return to the Graph menu

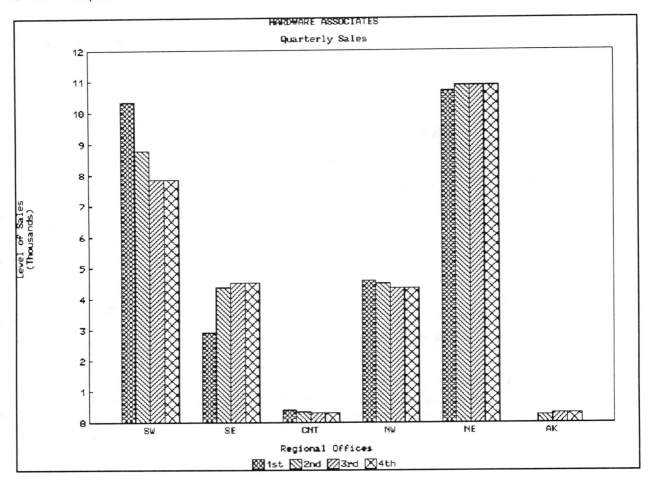

Figure 4-3. Clustered Bar Chart

Save the graph as a picture with the following commands:

S	**S**ave
ANNUAL	The .PIC filename
◄┘	Enter key, to save the file

Name the settings with the following commands:

N	**N**ame
C	**C**reate
ANNUAL	The graph settings name
◄┘	Enter key
Q	**Q**uit, to exit the Graph menu

SAVING YOUR WORKSHEET   / **Graph Save**

Save your worksheet by typing

/	Slash
F	**F**ile
S	**S**ave
◄┘	Enter key, to accept **SALES** as the filename. Since you have already saved SALES once, the name automatically appears. You need not retype the name.
R	**R**eplace, to overwrite the old file with the new file

Replace the diskette in drive B with your backup diskette and carry out the file save procedure. Do not use the backup option on the save menu.

PRINTING GRAPHS   **PrintGraph**

You will not print the worksheet since the worksheet has not been changed significantly. It has had named graphs added to it, however. You cannot print the graphs you saw on the screen with 1-2-3 commands or with the PrtSc key. To print the graph files you saved, QTR1A, QTR1B, and ANNUAL, you must quit 1-2-3 and enter PrintGraph. The installation process must have correctly identified the printer or plotter for producing graphs. Start the process by typing

/	Slash
Q	**Q**uit
Y	**Y**es. If you loaded Lotus with the command **lotus**, the remaining sequence will function correctly. If you loaded Lotus with the command, **123**, you bypassed the access menu, so you will receive the DOS prompt instead. In this case you will have to reload Lotus with the **lotus** command.
P	**P**rintGraph. A prompt requests that you insert the PrintGraph diskette in drive A. Do so and leave your Lotus files diskette in drive B.
◄┘	Enter key, to load PrintGraph

Hardware Settings

Before proceeding, check the information displayed under HARDWARE SETTINGS. Your graph files should be in drive B, so the Graphs Directory should be B:\. The PrintGraph disk should be in drive A, so the Fonts directory should be A:\. The paper size should be the same as that for the paper in your printer.

If the ACTION SETTINGS specifies No for Pause, it means that if you select several graphs for printing, there will be no time break between graph printings during which you can adjust the paper. Similarly, if Eject is set to No, the paper will not be automatically advanced to the next sheet when a graph has been printed. If you are printing more than one graph, both of these options should be changed to Yes.

Only when, and if, you need to make adjustments, enter the menu for making these changes by typing S for Settings and then either H for hardware settings changes or A for action settings changes. Press

Q	**Q**uit
Q	**Q**uit, to return to the PrintGraph menu

Image Select

The first step in using the PrintGraph commands is to select one or more graph files that are to be printed. The prompt line

```
┌─────────────────────────────────────────────────────────────────────┐
│ Image-Select  Settings  Go  Align  Page  Exit                         │
└─────────────────────────────────────────────────────────────────────┘
```

is in the PrintGraph control panel with Image-Select highlighted. Press

◄┘   Enter key, to choose Image-Select. A list with the three graph filenames and information about these files appears.

   Read the instructions in the right-hand column. By pressing the space bar, a # is toggled on and off in front of the graph filename, which is highlighted. When the # is present, the file has been selected for printing, but printing has not yet been started. You can highlight any of the filenames by moving the highlighting bar with the Up and Down arrow keys. When you have selected all of the files that you wish to print, press the Enter key. For this exercise, highlight ANNUAL and press

Space Bar To select ANNUAL. A number sign (#) appears to indicate that the file has been selected.
◄┘   Enter key, to select this and no other files. Check the paper in your printer to see that it is in the correct starting point.
A   Align the printer with PrintGraph
G   Go

Colors

Many computer systems have color monitors that give dramatic displays of Lotus graphs. If you were experimenting with the color option and happened to save your graph with this option turned on, all of the bars printed may be printed solid black. Unless you have a color printer or plotter, most printers cannot reproduce the colors you saw on the screen. Since you are trying to reproduce a picture, you have to return to the original worksheet, enter the Graph menu, set the black-and-white option (B&W) on, and save the file again.

Settings

Often the default settings are unsatisfactory because they overdistort the appearance of the graph in the vertical dimension. The main menu choice, Settings, allows you to adjust the appearance of the graph in many ways. Press

S   Settings
I   Image, to change the size of the graph
S   Size, to alter the dimensions
H   Half, to reduce the graph to half-size. The next two steps can be skipped if the value for Rotate under Size is .000.
M   Manual, to change the placement of the graph on the page
R   Rotation, to rotate the image so it is positioned vertically rather than horizontally on the page
.000   The number of degrees the image is to be rotated in a counter-clockwise direction
◄┘   Enter key
Q   Quit option, to return to the main menu
P   Page, to eject the paper to the next page
G   Go, to execute the Print command

After the graph has been printed a second time, press

S	Settings
I	Image, to change the size of the graph
S	Size, to alter the dimensions
F	Full, to return the graph to full-size
Q	Quit, to return to the previous menu

Font Changes

Before printing the last graph, adjust the fonts for printing the titles on the graph by pressing

F	Font
1	To set the font style for the main (first) title
↓	Down arrow twice, to highlight Bold
Space Bar	To select Bold
◄┘	Enter key
F	Font
2	To set the font style for all other titles
↓	Down arrow four times, to highlight Italic1
Space Bar	To select Italic1
◄┘	Enter key
Q	Quit, to return to the settings menu
I	Image
S	Size
F	Full, to return to a full-size image
M	Manual, to change the placement of the graph on the page
R	Rotation, to rotate the image so it is positioned horizontally rather than vertically on the page
90.00	The number of degrees the image is to be rotated in a counter-clockwise direction
◄┘	Enter key
Q	Quit options until return to the main menu
P	Page, to eject the paper to the next page
A	Align the printer with PrintGraph
G	Go, to execute the Print command

EXITING PRINTGRAPH   **/ Exit**

Exit from PrintGraph by typing

E	Exit
Y	Yes, after which you see the main access menu

At this point you can either press E and Y to exit from Lotus entirely or you can press 1 and replace the PrintGraph diskette in drive A with the 1-2-3 system diskette and continue.

EXERCISES

A.   Using the SALES worksheet, create and print pie graphs for quarters 2, 3, and 4. Add titles and legends. Rotate the graphs 90 degrees.

B.   Retrieve the file GRADES and produce a bar chart displaying the class's average grades over the semester. Add titles and legends. Create line charts displaying the minimum and maximum grades. Print the charts in both the default and rotated formats.

C.   Retrieve the file INCOME and produce a pie chart displaying the sales of the four vehicle types in the first half of the year. Add titles and legends. Create a bar chart with titles and legends displaying the two half-years' sales.   Print the charts in both the default and rotated formats.

Chapter 5

Using Built-In Functions and Formulas:
A Project Costing Model

Chapter Outline

The worksheet in this chapter will extend your knowledge of how to employ a worksheet program effectively. You will see how a worksheet can be used to test out what a project will cost given assumptions about costs for various project tasks. In doing this worksheet, you

1.   Set column widths;
2.   Justify and format cell displays;
3.   Utilize the powerful @VLOOKUP function;
4.   Alter cost assumptions to see what impact staffing decisions have on a project's costs.

THE PROBLEM

The worksheet focuses on the need for a manager to determine the costs involved in undertaking a project that has been proposed. The project involves eight activities: (1) writing specifications for a computer program; (2) writing and testing of computer program code; (3) gathering data; (4) entering data into the program; (5) revising and correcting data; (6) editing a final report; (7) printing a catalog; and (8) distributing the catalog. Each phase of the project involves different types of employees who earn different salaries.

      The manager has a good idea about how the project's financial requirements could be estimated. Several other projects are being discussed that must also be evaluated carefully before they are implemented. Consequently, the manager has decided to build a worksheet model that could also be used to examine these projects as they arrive.

INITIAL ENTRIES

Figure 5-1, part A outlines the basic appearance of the model. To cost out a project requires that the manager identify, for each phase of the project, what type of employee is to be involved, how many days that type of employee is involved, how much those employees are to be paid, what other non-personnel related costs are required (paper, travel, books, etc.), and finally, how much the personnel and nonpersonnel costs total. Once the model has been constructed, data specific to each of the coming project proposals can be inserted in the model so she can evaluate the costs accordingly.

Part B of the model is an employee charge schedule. The table identifies some of the firm's employee categories and, on the same line as each job title, is a number which identifies each type of position, an average annual salary and compensation cost for the position, and a daily rate at which the time for a person in that category could be charged.

Begin to set up the worksheet shown in Figure 5-1 by loading Lotus 1-2-3 and making the following cell entries. The entries in column A will not appear in their entirety now.

Cell Coordinate	Entry
C1	PROJECT COST MODEL
C2	PART A
B4	EMP.
C4	TASK
D4	DAILY
E4	PERS.
F4	OTHER
G4	TOTAL
A5	ACTIVITY
B5	TYPE
C5	DAYS
D5	RATE
E5	COST
F5	COST
G5	COST
A7	PREPARE SPEC'S
B7	3
C7	3
A8	WRITE & TEST CODE
B8	4
C8	6
A9	GATHER DATA
B9	1
C9	20
A10	DATA ENTRY
B10	2
C10	15
A11	REVISE ENTRIES
B11	5

	A	B	C	D	E	F	G
1			PROJECT COST MODEL				
2			PART A				
3							
4		EMP.	TASK	DAILY	PERS.	OTHER	TOTAL
5	ACTIVITY	TYPE	DAYS	RATE	COST	COST	COST
6							
7	PREPARE SPEC'S	3	3	128	384	250	634
8	WRITE & TEST CODE	4	6	116	696	150	846
9	GATHER DATA	1	20	64	1,280	150	1,430
10	DATA ENTRY	2	15	80	1,200	50	1,250
11	REVISE ENTRIES	5	5	98	490	50	540
12	EDIT FINAL COPY	6	2	126	252	50	302
13	PRINT CATALOG	0	0	0	0	2,500	2,500
14	DISTRIBUTE	1	2	64	128	200	328
15							7,830
16	====================						
17							
18			EMPLOYEE CHARGES SCHEDULE				
19			PART B				
20							
21		EMP.	ANN.	DAILY			
22	DESCRIPTION	TYPE	SAL.	RATE			
23							
24	NO. PERSONNEL	0	0	0			
25	HOURLY WORKER	1	16,000	64			
26	DATA ENTRY CLERK	2	20,000	80			
27	SYSTEMS ANALYST	3	32,000	128			
28	PROGRAMMER	4	29,000	116			
29	JR. EDITOR	5	24,500	98			
30	SR. EDITOR	6	31,500	126			
31	TEAM LEADER	7	29,000	116			
32							
33							

Figure 5-1.

Cell	Content
C11	5
A12	EDIT FINAL COPY
B12	6
C12	2
A13	PRINT CATALOG
B13	0
C13	0
A14	DISTRIBUTE
B14	1
C14	2
A16	\= (Backslash, Equal Sign)
C18	EMPLOYEE CHARGES SCHEDULE
C19	PART B

B21	EMP.
C21	ANN.
D21	DAILY
A22	DESCRIPTION
B22	TYPE
C22	SAL.
D22	RATE
A24	NO. PERSONNEL
B24	0
C24	0
D24	0
A25	HOURLY WORKER
B25	1
C25	16000
A26	DATA ENTRY CLERK
B26	2
C26	20000
A27	SYSTEMS ANALYST
B27	3
C27	32000
A28	PROGRAMMER
B28	4
C28	29000
A29	JR. EDITOR
B29	5
C29	24500
A30	SR. EDITOR
B30	6
C30	31500
A31	TEAM LEADER
B31	7
C31	29000

FORMATTING THE WORKSHEET

Setting Column Widths   **/ Worksheet Column-Width**

Lotus 1-2-3 uses a default column width of nine characters to display cell entries. The first column is too narrow to display the labels contained in its cells. The other columns will be reduced to a width of eight. There are three methods of changing column widths: globally, individually, and changing a range of column widths.

Columns D, E, F, and G should be eight characters wide. These columns can be set all at once. The remaining column widths can be set individually. To set the this range of widths, position the cell pointer to any cell on column D and type

/	Slash
W	**W**orksheet
C	**C**olumn
C	**C**olumn-Range
S	**S**et-Width

D1..G1	The range of columns to be altered
◂┘	Enter key
8	To set column width to eight
◂┘	Enter key

In addition to setting column widths column by column, the / **W**orksheet, **G**lobal, **C**olumn-Width command can be used to alter the width of all columns using the default column width simultaneously. This command does not change the width of columns whose width was specified by the / **W**orksheet **C**olumn command.

Column A is too narrow to display the complete text placed in the column of cells. It should be widened by placing the cell pointer in column A and typing

/	Slash
W	Worksheet
C	Column
S	Set-Width
18	To set column width to 18, the width of WRITE & TEST CODE plus 1
◂┘	Enter key

Justifying Labels   **/ Range Label**

The headings would look better if those in columns B through G were right-justified. The headings will then have the same justification as the numbers that appear beneath them. Justify the headings in part A by moving your cell pointer to B4 and typing

/	Slash
R	Range
L	Label
R	Right, to right-justify
↓	Down arrow
→	Right arrow five times, to set range
◂┘	Enter key

Justify the Employee Charges Schedule headings by moving your cell pointer to B21 and typing

/	Slash
R	Range
L	Label
R	Right, to right justify
↓	Down arrow
→	Right arrow twice, to set the range
◂┘	Enter key

USING FORMULAS AND BUILT-IN FUNCTIONS

To have Lotus 1-2-3 compute the daily rate of pay in column D of the Employee Charges Schedule, you need to divide the annual salary by the number of working days in a year (250). Place your cell pointer on D24 and enter

+C24/250

which returns the value of 0. Next, copy the formula down the column by keeping the cell pointer on D24 and using the Copy command.

/	Slash
C	**C**opy
↵	Enter key, to accept D24 as the default cell to be duplicated
.	Period to anchor the range
↓	Down arrow seven times, to complete the copy-to range
↵	Enter key

Column D of part A, the daily rate column, presents a more difficult cell entry to develop. If you were filling in the column by hand, you would look in the employee type column (B) to see what job category number was assigned to the position responsible for that phase of the project. Then you would visually find the employee type number in the Employee Charges Schedule and search across to

	A	B	C	D	E	F	G
1			PROJECT COST MODEL				
2			PART A				
3							
4		EMP.	TASK	DAILY	PERS.	OTHER	TOTAL
5	ACTIVITY	TYPE	DAYS	RATE	COST	COST	COST
6							
7	PREPARE SPEC'S	3	3				
8	WRITE & TEST CODE	4	6				
9	GATHER DATA	1	20				
10	DATA ENTRY	2	15				
11	REVISE ENTRIES	5	5				
12	EDIT FINAL COPY	6	2				
13	PRINT CATALOG	0	0				
14	DISTRIBUTE	1	2				
15							
16	====================						
17							
18			EMPLOYEE CHARGES SCHEDULE				
19			PART B				
20							
21		EMP.	ANN.	DAILY			
22	DESCRIPTION	TYPE	SAL.	RATE			
23							
24	NO. PERSONNEL	0	0	0			
25	HOURLY WORKER	1	16,000	64			
26	DATA ENTRY CLERK	2	20,000	80			
27	SYSTEMS ANALYST	3	32,000	128			
28	PROGRAMMER	4	29,000	116			
29	JR. EDITOR	5	24,500	98			
30	SR. EDITOR	6	31,500	126			
31	TEAM LEADER	7	29,000	116			
32							

Figure 5-2.

the daily rate column to find the per day charge. This amount would then be entered in the daily rate column for Part A. You would repeat this for each of the phases.

Before proceeding, check to see that your worksheet looks like Figure 5-2.

The Vertical Lookup Function   @VLOOKUP

The manual operation described would suffice for some purposes, but since the manager wishes to use the worksheet again for other projects and since the type of employees used for some phases might change, it is preferable to insert a formula with a built-in function to complete this operation automatically and, perhaps, more accurately. The built-in function for this purpose is the @VLOOKUP function. This function has these parts:

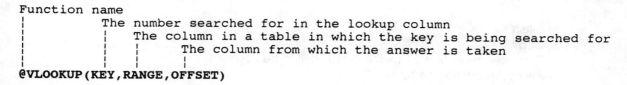

```
Function name
|           The number searched for in the lookup column
|           |      The column in a table in which the key is being searched for
|           |         The column from which the answer is taken
|           |         |
@VLOOKUP(KEY,RANGE,OFFSET)
```

Figure 5-3. VLOOKUP Syntax

To illustrate with an example, place your cell pointer on D7 and type the following entry without blanks:

@VLOOKUP(	The name of the function
B7,	The cell with the number for the first employee type
$B$24..$D$31,	The range of cells to be searched (employee type). Remember the absolute addressing of cells discussed in Chapter 3: Using Worksheets: A Sales Analysis, with the F4 function key; don't forget to type the commas separating the three elements within the parentheses.
2)	Return the number found in the second column to the right of the index range
◄┘	Enter key, which returns the daily rate of 128

The function entered looks up the number 3 (found in B7) by searching down the range. The numbers in the range are, and must be, in ascending order. When the function finds the first entry in the search range that is larger than the number being searched for, it "looks" across from the previous entry. @VLOOKUP searches down until it finds a 4, a number larger than the 3 being searched for, and then searches across the previous row by the amount of the offset.

@VLOOKUP does not find that 3 is equal to 3. The method of searching used by @VLOOKUP allows you to search for an 18 in a list that increments by 5 (0, 5, 10, 15, 20 ...) and return a value from the row beginning with 15, the last number that was not larger than 18.

The offset column is the number of the column to the right of the index range. The index column is considered to be column number 0. The column to the right is column 1, the next is column 2, and so on. In this example, Lotus 1-2-3 searches the second column to the right of the index range.

Copy this formula, keeping the cell pointer on D7, by typing

/	Slash
C	Copy
◄┘	Enter key, to accept D7 as the default cell to be duplicated
.	Period to anchor the range
↓	Down arrow seven times, to complete the copy-to range
◄┘	Enter key

The absolute references of the range of cells in the lookup table kept the copied formulas from changing. If you allowed Lotus 1-2-3 to adjust the addresses by using relative cell addresses, the first copy of the formula would reference B25 through B32, the second would reference B26 through B33, and so on. Incorrect answers or error messages would be returned as the top of the list, and eventually the entire list would be lost. The personnel cost for each phase is computed by multiplying the daily rate (column D) by the number of days each type of employee is involved. Place your cell pointer on E7 and enter

+C7*D7
◄┘   Enter key

which returns 384. Copy this formula by keeping the cell pointer on E7 and typing the command sequence

/	Slash
C	**C**opy
◄┘	Enter key, to accept E7 as the default cell to be copied
.	Period, to anchor the range
↓	Down arrow seven times, to complete the copy-to range
◄┘	Enter key

You may begin to notice that as the worksheet contains more data in cells and as the number of formulas increases, it takes Lotus 1-2-3 longer to update the worksheet. The nonpersonnel costs are estimated, rather than computed costs, and must be entered as follows:

Cell Coordinate	Entry
F7	250
F8	150
F9	150
F10	50
F11	50
F12	50
F13	2500
F14	200

The next task is to compute the cost for each phase of the project. The cost for each phase is the total of the personnel and nonpersonnel costs. Place your cell pointer on G7 and enter

+E7+F7
◄┘   Enter key

which creates the value 634. Copy the formula with the command sequence

/	Slash
C	**C**opy
◄┘	Enter key, to accept G7 as the default cell to be copied
.	Period, to anchor the range
↓	Down arrow seven times, to complete the copy-to range
◄┘	Enter key

The total cost of the project is computed in G15. The entry to this cell is

@SUM(G7..G14)

which returns 7830.

FORMATTING   / **Range Format**

Many of the columns contain numbers that represent currency. The use of the Range Format command changes the appearance of numbers. If a cell with a label is formatted as a number, the display is left unchanged. Place your cell pointer on cell G7 and enter

/	Slash
R	Range
F	Format
C	Currency
0	Zero
◄┘	Enter key, to accept the zero
←	Left arrow three times
PgDn	Page Down key, to rapidly highlight G7 through D27. The highlighting covers some cells with text but these cells are not be affected by the formatting change. Do not move the cell pointer to column C. Movement of the cell pointer to column C also highlights the number of days for each task in part A.
↓	Down arrow four times
◄┘	Enter key

Use of the End Key   **End**

The End key is one means of rapidly moving the cell pointer through cells in order to relocate it. The End key is used to format cells C24 through C31. Place your cell pointer on C24 and enter

/	Slash
R	Range
F	Format
C	Currency
0	Zero
◄┘	Enter key, to accept the zero. The range is displayed as C24 through C24.
End	End key. Note the End block in the lower left corner of the screen.
↓	Down arrow once. The highlighting covers all of the cells up to the boundary where filled cells abut an empty cell.
◄┘	Enter key, to complete the formatting

The model as it appears in Figure 5-4 is now complete.

WHAT IF?

The great advantage of using a worksheet is that as conditions change, data in the model can be changed and the computer can recalculate the formulas immediately to give you revised projections. For instance, suppose that it was determined that the gathering of data could not be handled by unskilled, hourly-paid workers, but had to be conducted by systems analysts. Change the employee type in B9 from 1 to 3. Note the changes throughout your worksheet.

Experiment with other possible changes, but be careful. You can replace numbers with numbers and character strings with strings. If you replace a formula with a number, you are likely to lose some of the accuracy of the model.

	A	B	C	D	E	F	G
1			PROJECT COST MODEL				
2			PART A				
3							
4		EMP.	TASK	DAILY	PERS.	OTHER	TOTAL
5	ACTIVITY	TYPE	DAYS	RATE	COST	COST	COST
6							
7	PREPARE SPEC'S	3	3	$128	$384	$250	$634
8	WRITE & TEST CODE	4	6	$116	$696	$150	$846
9	GATHER DATA	1	20	$64	$1,280	$150	$1,430
10	DATA ENTRY	2	15	$80	$1,200	$50	$1,250
11	REVISE ENTRIES	5	5	$98	$490	$50	$540
12	EDIT FINAL COPY	6	2	$126	$252	$50	$302
13	PRINT CATALOG	0	0	$0	$0	$2,500	$2,500
14	DISTRIBUTE	1	2	$64	$128	$200	$328
15							$7,830
16	====================						
17							
18			EMPLOYEE CHARGES SCHEDULE				
19			PART B				
20							
21		EMP.	ANN.	DAILY			
22	DESCRIPTION	TYPE	SAL.	RATE			
23							
24	NO. PERSONNEL	0	$0	$0			
25	HOURLY WORKER	1	$16,000	$64			
26	DATA ENTRY CLERK	2	$20,000	$80			
27	SYSTEMS ANALYST	3	$32,000	$128			
28	PROGRAMMER	4	$29,000	$116			
29	JR. EDITOR	5	$24,500	$98			
30	SR. EDITOR	6	$31,500	$126			
31	TEAM LEADER	7	$29,000	$116			
32							

Figure 5-4. Completed Project Cost Model

SAVING YOUR WORKSHEET   **/ File Save**

The worksheet is now complete. Save the file with the following command sequence:

/	Slash
F	File
S	Save

PROJECT   The drive destination and filename of the worksheet
◄┘   Enter key

Back up your worksheet by placing your backup diskette in drive B and repeating the save procedure. Do not use the backup option on the save menu.

PRINTING YOUR WORKSHEET   / Print Printer

Print your file with the command sequence

/	Slash
P	**P**rint
P	**P**rinter, or Enter key, since the cursor is located on Printer by default
R	**R**ange
Home	**Home** key
.	Period, to anchor the range
↓	Down arrow 30 times, to cover the vertical range
→	Right arrow six times, to highlight the horizontal range
◄┘	Enter key, to specify the entire worksheet
A	**A**lign
G	**G**o, to execute to printing
Q	**Q**uit, to return to Lotus 1-2-3

ERASING YOUR WORKSHEET   / Worksheet Erase

The file PROJECT has been safely stored on the diskette. The next command sequence should be used only if you have carefully considered whether the file is still useful to you and has been saved, or whether it can be erased from the computer's RAM memory because it is either not needed or a more desirable version already exists on the diskette.

The Worksheet-Erase command erases the worksheet seen on your monitor from RAM. It does not delete the worksheet file from the diskette if it has been saved. Erasing a worksheet erases the contents of the cells and returns all default values of the worksheet to the state they would be in if you entered Lotus 1-2-3 from DOS. All column widths would be reset to nine.

Erase your file to see the effect with the sequence

/	Slash
W	**W**orksheet
E	**E**rase
Y	**Y**es

QUITTING LOTUS 1-2-3   / Quit

Exit from Lotus 1-2-3 by typing

/	Slash
Q	**Q**uit
Y	**Y**es

and replace the Lotus 1-2-3 disk in drive A with the DOS disk and hit any key to return to the DOS prompt.

EXERCISES

A.   A corporate accountant has developed a table for determining the cost for a motor vehicle's depreciation in a given year. Knowing the cost and age of a vehicle, the depreciation table can be used to determine the cost to be deducted from corporate taxes that year. The cell displaying the depreciation cost contains a formula with a lookup function multiplied by the original cost of the vehicle. Whenever the age and cost of a vehicle are entered, the depreciation costs are recalculated. The appearance of the accountant's worksheet is shown.

	A	B	C	D	E	F	G
1			VEHICLE DEPRECIATION CALCULATOR				
2							
3				DEPRECIATION TABLE			
4	YRS. OLD		3	------------------			
5	ORIG. COST	$12,200		VEHICLE AGE			
6							
7	DEPRECIATION	$2,440		1	30%		
8				2	25%		
9				3	20%		
10				4	15%		
11				5	10%		
12							

Reproduce this worksheet and test it for a vehicle one year old and costing $15,327. For a four-year-old vehicle costing $11,287.

B.   A sales manager computes the monthly commission for the company's sales personnel with the help of a sales commission lookup table. A salesperson's commission is based on the length of time the person has worked for the company. The worksheet used for this assessment is shown below.

	A	B	C	D	E	F
1			SALES COMMISSIONS CALCULATOR			
2						
3				COMMISSION TABLE		
4				------------------		
5	YRS. OF SERVICE		7	YEARS	RESPONSIBILITY	
6	SALES TOTAL	$24,000		SERVICE	LEVEL	
7						
8	COMMISSION RATE	5.0%		0	4.5%	
9				5	5.0%	
10	COMPUTED COMMISSION	$1,200		10	5.5%	
11				15	6.0%	
12				20	6.5%	
13						

Prepare the worksheet so that when new years of service and sales total entries are made, the worksheet automatically computes the commission earned. Test the worksheet with three different sets of values for sales totals and years of service. Note that the years of service entry of 0 includes all persons with between 0 and 4.9 years of service.

C.   The personnel office secretary is often asked for the total cost of compensation for hiring a new employee at any one of 16 ranks of pay. Total compensation consists of the salary plus the fringe benefits. The lowest salary is $10,000 and each rank receives an increase of $1,000 over the preceding rank. Fringe benefits are computed as being 28% of the salary. Prepare a worksheet with lookup table in which there are three columns: the lookup column which contains the ranks 15 through 30, the salary column with salaries ranging from $10,000 through $25,000, and the fringe benefits column computed at 28% of the salary. Identify a cell in which the rank is entered, a cell in which the salary is looked up, and a cell in which the fringe benefits are looked up. Add a cell in which the total compensation is computed.

D.   A heavy equipment sales organization pays a commission to the salesperson, the salesperson's local sales agency, and the regional sales agency on every order placed. The commissions vary with the size of the order. The table involved looks like the following:

	B	C	D	E	F	G	H
13							
14		AMT. OF	LOCAL	LOCAL	REGIONAL		
15		SALE	SALESPER.	AGENCY	AGENCY		
16		---					
17		$25,000	3.00%	1.00%	0.50%		
18		$50,000	3.50%	1.50%	1.00%		
19		$75,000	4.00%	2.00%	1.50%		
20		$100,000	4.50%	2.50%	2.00%		
21		$125,000	5.00%	3.00%	2.50%		
22							
23							

Construct a worksheet that uses a sale amount entered in one cell as the lookup amount. Three separate cells should display the amount of commission paid to each entity (looked-up commission times the amount of sale), as well as the total amount of the commissions paid.

Chapter 6

What If . . . ?

Chapter Outline

This chapter provides you with another worksheet designed to demonstrate how managers can test "what if" changes in a worksheet model. The results of the changes can be analyzed and assessed for decision making. In particular, this worksheet will enable you to

1. See how including a filename inside a worksheet can help you to identify a file when you do a directory listing from DOS;
2. Set aside assumptions in identifiable locations so various alternatives can be examined without your having to modify or add formulas to the worksheet;
3. Examine the use of the @IF function;
4. Protect cells from inadvertent changes.

A PROJECT BUDGET

The director of the management information systems (MIS) department of a medium sized firm was asked by the firm's vice president for finance to develop a microcomputer literacy project for key people in each of the firm's departments. The MIS director agreed to put together a cost estimate. Arriving at a definitive cost estimate proved to be difficult as the director thought about the problem. The difficulty was not only due to the lack of information about the cost of particular items, but also to the lack of clarity about how many people would participate, how much the departments would be willing to pay toward the project, and how many days of training would be involved.

    The MIS director also knew that after a project budget was prepared, the vice president and others would make suggestions for changes that would affect the budget. The director decided to put the budget together with Lotus 1-2-3 so that the effect of suggested changes could be analyzed.

SOME INTERNAL DOCUMENTATION

Filename

After booting up the microcomputer and loading Lotus 1-2-3, begin to create the worksheet by entering

Cell Coordinate	Entry
A1	PRJTBDGT
A2	DISK # 1

These two cell entries are used for internal documentation. Many users of worksheets produce a variety of models that are stored on many diskettes. It can be difficult to remember where a file is stored when you need to use it again. Since DOS allows the user to use only eight characters in a filename, many worksheet names are cryptic. These two cells, if they are printed out along with the key portions of the worksheet, will provide you with the documentation you need to find the worksheet again. A1 gives the name of the file as it is known to DOS and to Lotus 1-2-3. You can use this name to retrieve it. A2 gives the number of the diskette on which the file is stored so you can avoid searching through one diskette after another looking for the file.

Parameters

In constructing formulas within the worksheets completed in earlier chapters, it was difficult, once the worksheet was completed, to see how a number was arrived at. This ambiguity is frequently the case. For instance, a formula in a worksheet might be +C6*B8*.07. Simply looking at the formula is no assurance that you can tell what the formula is attempting to do, so there is no way to be certain that the formula is arriving at a correct answer. When part of the formula is .07, there is no clear indication of why .07 was chosen and not some other percentage. If you knew that somewhere within a worksheet there were references to the inflation rate, you would have no way to tell whether this percentage represented an inflation rate, the expected increase in the Consumer Price Index, the anticipated growth in base salaries, or growth in the projected value of the dollar overseas.

This ambiguity in formulas gets worse over time as you forget how you constructed a worksheet. It is made even worse when the worksheet is used by someone else. You can see why some analysts suggest that as many as 30% of the worksheets used to make major decisions are incorrect, but decision makers do not know it because the displays hide the formulas that create the displays. Often all they see is the printed worksheet.

To lessen some of the problems, divide the worksheet into two primary parts: a parameter portion and a projection portion. The parameter portion will consist of the most basic pieces of the problem and their values. For this worksheet, enter

Cell Coordinate	Entry
B3	PROJECT BUDGET
B4	\= (Backslash, Equal Sign)
C4	\= (Backslash, Equal Sign)
A6	PARAMETERS
A7	\- (Backslash, Minus Sign)
B6	PARAMETER VALUES
B7	\- (Backslash, Minus Sign)
A8	NO. OF PARTICIPANTS

B8	15
A9	DAILY PARTICIPANT EXPENSES
B9	20
A10	NO. OF TRAINING DAYS
B10	10
A11	COMPUTER COSTS
A12	MICROCOMPUTER
B12	2000
A13	PRINTER
B13	450
A14	FURNITURE
B14	400
A15	SOFTWARE
B15	750
A16	TRAINER FEE PER DAY
B16	500
A17	TRAINING ASSISTANT
B17	200
A18	DEPT. CHARGE-BACK
B18	1500

These cells document the assumptions the director is making about the project. There are ten basic building blocks for determining the costs of the project. The specific values that are entered into column B are not especially important because they can easily be changed. It is much more important to identify all the elements that go into the training project and then to determine how these elements relate to one another. For example, it is important to know that the number of days of training will affect the cost of hiring a trainer who is paid on a per day basis, as well as the total of the daily costs for the participants. It is less important to know precisely how much the trainer will be paid, than that a trainer will be paid on the number of days worked.

Notice that the entries in column B are all numbers. No calculations are made here. The director will be able to change these numbers to test different cost alternatives without having to worry that an important formula is being overwritten.

Projections

The second portion of the worksheet will be the cost projection for the project. The entries in column B of this portion of the worksheet will avoid the use of typed-in numbers. Instead cell addresses will be used. This will enable the director to avoid having to revise and copy the formulas continuously. For example, if a cell is to compute the cost for the trainer, its contents will not be +10*500. Instead, its contents should be +B10*B16. Then the director can try out different numbers of days and different daily pay rates as these are suggested; Lotus 1-2-3 will redo the calculation.

Enter the following:

Cell Coordinate	Entry	Meaning
A21	COST PROJECTION	
A22	\- (Backslash, Minus Sign)	
B22	\- (Backslash, Minus Sign)	
A23	TRAINER	
B23	+B10*B16	NO. OF TRAINING DAYS x TRAINER FEE PER DAY, Displays 5000

A24	TRAINING ASSISTANT	
B24	@IF(B8 > = 10,B17*B10,0)	If the NO. OF PARTICIPANTS is greater than or equal to 10, then display the result of multiplying the NO. OF TRAINING DAYS x TRAINING ASSIST., Displays 2000
A25	COMPUTER COSTS	
B25	@SUM(B12..B15)*B8	The total cost for a MICROCOMPUTER, a PRINTER, FURNITURE, and SOFTWARE x the NO. OF PARTICIPANTS, Displays 54000
A26	DAILY EXPENSES	
B26	+B8*B9*B10	The NO. OF PARTICIPANTS x DAILY PARTICIPANT EXPENSES x NO. OF TRAINING DAYS, Displays 3000
B27	\- (Backslash, Minus Sign)	
A28	TOTAL EXPENSES	
B28	@SUM(B23..B26)	The total of the expenses computed for TRAINER, TRAINING ASSISTANT, COMPUTER COSTS, and DAILY EXPENSES, Displays 64000
A29	TOTAL CHARGE-BACK	
B29	+B18*B8	The DEPT. CHARGE-BACK x NO. OF PARTICIPANTS. Displays 22500
A30	TOTAL TO CENTRAL OFFICE	
B30	+B28-B29	TOTAL EXPENSES - TOTAL CHARGE-BACK. Displays 41500

Alter the width of column A to display all the text it contains by placing the cell pointer in column A and typing

/	Slash
W	Worksheet
C	Column
S	Set-Width
26	A number large enough for the widest entry
↵	Enter key

Your worksheet should now look like Figure 6-1.

```
              A              B        C        D        E        F
1  PRJTBDGT
2  DISK # 1
3                      PROJECT BUDGET
4                      ==================
5
6  PARAMETERS              PARAMETER VALUES
7  ---------------------------------------
8  NO. OF PARTICIPANTS          15
9  DAILY PARTICIPANT EXPENSES   20
10 NO. OF TRAINING DAYS         10
11 COMPUTER COSTS
12 MICROCOMPUTER              2000
13 PRINTER                     450
14 FURNITURE                   400
15 SOFTWARE                    750
16 TRAINER FEE PER DAY         500
17 TRAINING ASSISTANT          200
18 DEPT. CHARGE-BACK          1500
19
20
21 COST PROJECTION
22 ---------------------------------------
23 TRAINER                    5000
24 TRAINING ASSISTANT         2000
25 COMPUTER COSTS            54000
26 DAILY EXPENSES            3000
27                          ---------
28 TOTAL EXPENSES           64000
29 TOTAL CHARGE-BACK        22500
30 TOTAL TO CENTRAL OFFICE  41500
31
```

Figure 6-1.

For illustrative purposes, the cell in B24 uses the @IF function, to be described below, and contains the number 10. This is the only "hard" number in the projection of expenses. Even this number could be replaced with a parameter address. The other formulas that have gone into producing the worksheet only utilize cell addresses. If it was decided that an assistant trainer would be needed only if the number of participants was 12, the formula in B24 would have to be edited. The other cells from B23 to B26 would need to be edited only if the formulas they contain were incorrect in their cell references or if new parameters were added later.

FORMATTING   **/ Range Format**

The numbers in column B should virtually all be formatted as currency with no decimal places. Format most of these numbers by moving the cell pointer to B8 and typing

/   Slash

R	Range
F	Format (or Enter key, since Format is highlighted by the cell pointer)
C	Currency format
0	The number of decimal places
↵	Enter key
PgDn	Page Down key, to highlight the entire column
↓	Down arrow twice
↵	Enter key

```
          A               B        C      D       E       F
1  PRJTBDGT
2  DISK # 1
3                     PROJECT BUDGET
4                     ==================
5
6  PARAMETERS          PARAMETER VALUES
7  ---------------------------------------
8  NO. OF PARTICIPANTS        15
9  DAILY PARTICIPANT EXPENSES  $20
10 NO. OF TRAINING DAYS       10
11 COMPUTER COSTS
12 MICROCOMPUTER          $2,000
13 PRINTER                  $450
14 FURNITURE                $400
15 SOFTWARE                 $750
16 TRAINER FEE PER DAY      $500
17 TRAINING ASSISTANT       $200
18 DEPT. CHARGE-BACK      $1,500
19
20
21 COST PROJECTION
22 ---------------------------------------
23 TRAINER                $5,000
24 TRAINING ASSISTANT     $2,000
25 COMPUTER COSTS        $54,000
26 DAILY EXPENSES         $3,000
27                      ---------
28 TOTAL EXPENSES        $64,000
29 TOTAL CHARGE-BACK     $22,500
30 TOTAL TO CENTRAL OFFICE $41,500
31
```

Figure 6-2.

Cells B8 and B10 should not be formatted as currency. Place the cell pointer on B8 and type

/	Slash
R	Range
F	Format (or Enter key, since Format is highlighted by the cell pointer)
,	Comma

0	The number of decimal places
◄┘	Enter key
◄┘	Enter key, to accept cell B8 as the format range and to execute the format change

Repeat this series of keystrokes on B10 also. Your worksheet should now look like Figure 6-2.

THE @IF FUNCTION   @IF

The formula in B24 uses the @IF function. The general structure of the @IF function involves three elements, or operands, that are found between the parentheses. The first operand is a logical condition. This condition is evaluated as being either true or false. Examples of possible conditions that could appear in an @IF function are:

1 = 10	An obviously false relation since 1 does not equal 10
A1 < 3	True if the value of A1 is less than 3, but false if the value in A1 is 3 or greater

The equal sign and the less than sign are called relational operators. The relational operators that can be used in the @IF statement are:

Symbol	Meaning	Example	Value
=	Equal to	A1 = 10	True if A1 equals 10
>	Greater than	A2 > 5	False if A2 equals 3
<	Less than	A3 < 9	True if A3 contains 2
> =	Greater than or equal to	A4 > = 14	True if A4 contains 14
< =	Less than or equal to	A5 < = 16	True if A5 contains 16
< >	Not equal to	A6 < > 20	False if A6 contains 20

The second element in the @IF function is the value the function will return (display in the cell) if the logical condition is evaluated as being true. In B24, the formula returns the value calculated by multiplying B17 by B10. The value returned can be a number, a value obtained from a cell address, a character string, another function that returns a numerical value, or a formula.

The third element in the @IF function is the value the function will return if the logical condition is evaluated as being false. In B24, the formula returns a 0. The value returned could also be a number, a numerical value obtained from a cell address, a character string, another function that returns a numerical value, or a formula. The formula in B24

   @IF(B8 > = 10,B17*B10,0)

is read as "If it is true that the value of B8 is greater than or equal to 10, then return the value calculated by multiplying the values in B17 and B10, else return the value 0." If the number of participants changes to less than 10, then the cost for a training assistant will be zero (i.e., one is not needed).

Other examples of @IF functions are:

@IF(C10 < > 45,5,9)	If C10 is not equal to 45, return 5, else return 9
@IF(C1 = Z15,@SUM(B1..B3),0)	If C1 is equal to the value of Z15, return the sum of cells B1, B2, and B3, else return 0
@IF(W3 < 500,A1,A2)	If W3 is less than 500, return the value of A1, else return the value of A2

PROTECTION

/ Range Protect
/ Worksheet Global Protection

By default, Lotus 1-2-3 leaves cells unprotected. You, or whoever uses your worksheet, can change any or all cells at will. When you have developed a worksheet, however, you may wish to be sure that certain cells are not changed inadvertently. Changes made may well make the results displayed dangerously inaccurate. Since you are primarily aware of the displays of cells, if an underlying formula is changed or replaced by a number, you may never know that an improper change has been made.

You want to be able to change the parameters, but you also want to be sure that you cannot change cells B23 through B30 since these cells contain formulas that should remain unchanged unless you decide to edit them. First, protect every cell in the worksheet by typing

/	Slash
W	Worksheet
G	Global
P	Protection
E	Enable

Second, unprotect the parameters sections of the worksheet by placing the cell pointer on B8 and typing

/	Slash
R	Range
U	Unprotect
↓	Down arrow ten times, to cover the range to be unprotected
◄┘	Enter key. The color intensity changes to reflect the unprotected nature of cells B8 through B18

Move your cell pointer over the cells from B23 through B30. Try to change one of these cells by trying to replace the contents with some other entry. You will not be allowed to do so.

WHAT IF?

A major advantage of creating this type of worksheet is the ability a decision maker gains to test various alternatives. The initial worksheet displays the costs involved in one possible scenario. Hundreds of others can be tested by changing the values for each of the parameters.

Try changing any of the values in B8 through B18 to see what effect a change has on the total expenses, the total charge-back, and the total cost to the central office. Use the PgUp and PgDn keys to move back and forth. Notice that even though you protected cells B23 through B30, their displays change. The contents of the cell are not permitted to change, but the display is allowed to change.

Find a cost alternative (there are many possibilities) in which the number of participants is greater than 20 and the cost to the central office is less than $40,000.

PRINTING YOUR WORKSHEET

Print the alternative cost estimate you locate by typing

/	Slash
P	Print

P	**Printer**
R	**Range**
Home	Home key, to find the top of the worksheet
.	Period, to anchor the range
↓	Down arrow 29 times, to cover the vertical range of the worksheet
→	Right arrow, to cover both columns of the worksheet
◄┘	Enter key, to submit the range just set
A	**A**lign
G	**G**o, to print the worksheet
Q	**Q**uit, to return to Lotus 1-2-3

SAVING YOUR WORKSHEET

/ **File Save**

Save the file with the command sequence

/	Slash
F	**F**ile
S	**S**ave
PRJTBDGT	The filename of the worksheet
◄┘	Enter key

Make a backup copy of your file by putting your backup files diskette in drive B and repeating the save process. Do not use the backup option on the save menu.

QUITTING LOTUS 1-2-3

/ **Quit**

Exit the Lotus 1-2-3 program. Type

/	Slash
Q	**Q**uit
Y	**Y**es

and load the DOS diskette if necessary and when prompted to do so.

EXERCISES

A.   A store manager wishes to use a daily inventory of stock on hand to determine whether any items have to be reordered. The manager has determined, for each item in stock, what the minimum number on hand should be for each item in inventory. An assessment has also been made to determine the maximum number of each item that the store should have on hand at any one time. This maximum allows the manager to place an order that is an economically desirable, but it prevents the ordering of stock that will simply sit on a shelf. An order is made whenever the stock on hand is less than the minimum. If an order is made, the amount ordered is the maximum amount allowed minus the amount on hand.

Develop an order quantity worksheet for the manager using the following data as your test case:

	A	B	C	D	E	F
1	FILE: EOQ1					
2	DISK # 1					
3						
4	ORDER QUANTITY CHART					
5	====================================					
6						
7	NO. NAME		ON-HAND	MIN	MAX	ORDER
8	--					
9	100 5 1/4" DISKETTES SS/SD		30	100	500	470
10	101 5 1/4" DISKETTES SS/DD		100	100	500	0
11	102 5 1/4" DISKETTES DS/SD		210	100	500	0
12	103 5 1/4" DISKETTES DS/DD		500	100	500	0
13	104 8" DISKETTES		49	50	300	251
14	105 3 1/2" HARD DISKETTES		25	25	100	0
15	106 10 DISKETTE FILE BOX		10	15	35	25
16	107 25 DISKETTE FILE BOX		15	15	35	0
17	108 50 DISKETTE FILE BOX		25	15	35	0
18	109 8 1/2 X 11" COMPUTER PAPER PLAIN		35	25	50	0
19	110 8 1/2 X 11" COMPUTER PAPER LINED		45	25	50	0
20	111 11 X 8 1/2" COMPUTER PAPER PLAIN		15	25	50	35
21	112 11 X 8 1/2" COMPUTER PAPER LINED		22	25	50	28
22	113 11 X 14" COMPUTER PAPER PLAIN		27	25	50	0
23	114 11 X 14" COMPUTER PAPER LINED		35	25	50	0
24	115 RIBBONS - OKIDATA		6	10	40	34
25	116 RIBBONS - EPSON		12	10	40	0
26						

B.   A motor bicycle company produces three different motor bicycles that have different levels of capability. Consequently, the three models have their own sales history, sales picture, and pricing. The basic model sells for $1,500 and sold 20,150 units last year. Its sales are expected to increase by 15%. The enhanced model sells for $1,850 and sold 24,345 units last year. Its sales in each of the next two years are expected to decrease by 5% in each subsequent year. The luxury model, which sold 15,575 units last year, is expected to sell 25% more units in each of the next two years. The price of the luxury model is $2,200. The worksheet described below presents one projection of the company's revenue based on sales projections that use all three factors (units sold + expected increase * price). Recreate this worksheet. When you write formulas, remember that some references to cells should not be absolute so they do not change when they are copied.

	A	B	C	D	E
1		SALES INCOME FORECAST			
2					
3	PARAMETERS				
4	==================				
5	MOTOR BIKE SALES (THIS YEAR)				
6	BASIC	20,150			
7	ENHANCED	24,345			
8	LUXURY	15,575			
9	EXPECTED CHANGES (NEXT TWO YEARS)				
10	BASIC	0.15			
11	ENHANCED	-0.05			
12	LUXURY	0.25			
13	PRICE PER UNIT				
14	BASIC	$1,500			
15	ENHANCED	$1,850			
16	LUXURY	$2,200			
17					
18	PROJECTED SALES INCOME				
19	=================================				
20		THIS YR.	NEXT YR.	YR. AFTER	
21	BASIC	$30,225,000	$34,758,750	$39,972,563	
22	ENHANCED	$45,038,250	$42,786,338	$40,647,021	
23	LUXURY	$34,265,000	$42,831,250	$53,539,063	
24		---------	---------	---------	
25		$109,528,250	$120,376,338	$134,158,646	
26					

Check the effect on revenue of a price rise of $150 per model and for a price rise of $75 per model.

C.   A software production firm produces three pieces of software under the names, Word Processor, Worksheetor, and Communicator. The firm has prepared the following worksheet displaying the sales for each software package in the current year, the cost of each package, and the expected increase or decrease in sales in each of the next several years. The first column of the projected income is composed of formulas that compute the actual income realized in the current year. Recreate this worksheet by producing the formulas for the current year's revenue and for computing the sales income for the following year. Through the use of absolute cell addresses, the formulas in the second column can be copied to the final column.

	A	B	C	D	E
1	SOFTWARE SALES				
2					
3	SALES BY PACKAGE TYPE				
4	WORD PROCESSOR	770			
5	WORKSHEETOR	2,541			
6	COMMUNICATOR	980			
7	EXPECTED CHANGES (NEXT TWO YEARS)				
8	WORD PROCESSOR	-0.12			
9	WORKSHEETOR	0.15			
10	COMMUNICATOR	0.33			
11	PRICE PER UNIT				
12	WORD PROCESSOR	$89.50			
13	WORKSHEETOR	$49.50			
14	COMMUNICATOR	$32.50			
15					
16	PROJECTED REVENUE BY PACKAGE TYPE				
17	===				
18		THIS YR.	NEXT YR.	YR. AFTER	YR. AFTER
19	WORD PROCESSOR	$68,915	$60,645	$53,368	$46,964
20	WORKSHEETOR	$125,780	$144,646	$166,343	$191,295
21	COMMUNICATOR	$31,850	$42,361	$56,339	$74,931
22		------------	------------	------------	------------
23		$226,545	$247,652	$276,051	$313,190
24					

What is the effect on sales if Word Processor is repriced at $79.50 and Communicator is repriced at $35.50?

D.   A manufacturer of electric mixers is attempting to estimate the amount of money that would be received if either of two factors is varied. The sale price of a mixer is currently at $30 and will be varied by $2 per unit. The current level of sales is 5,000 per year and will be varied in increments of 250. The worksheet results are shown below:

	A	B	C	D	E	F
1	ELECTRIC MIXER REVENUE SCENARIOS					
2						
3	# UNITS	CURRENT				
4	SOLD	UNIT PRICE				
5	5,000	$30				
6						
7		$30	$32	$34	$36	$38
8	5,000	$150,000	$160,000	$170,000	$180,000	$190,000
9	5,250	$157,500	$168,000	$178,500	$189,000	$199,500
10	5,500	$165,000	$176,000	$187,000	$198,000	$209,000
11	5,750	$172,500	$184,000	$195,500	$207,000	$218,500
12	6,000	$180,000	$192,000	$204,000	$216,000	$228,000
13	6,250	$187,500	$200,000	$212,500	$225,000	$237,500
14	6,500	$195,000	$208,000	$221,000	$234,000	$247,000
15	6,750	$202,500	$216,000	$229,500	$243,000	$256,500
16	7,000	$210,000	$224,000	$238,000	$252,000	$266,000
17	7,250	$217,500	$232,000	$246,500	$261,000	$275,500
18	7,500	$225,000	$240,000	$255,000	$270,000	$285,000
19	7,750	$232,500	$248,000	$263,500	$279,000	$294,500
20	8,000	$240,000	$256,000	$272,000	$288,000	$304,000
21	8,250	$247,500	$264,000	$280,500	$297,000	$313,500
22						

Except for the initial statement of the number of mixers sold and of the initial price, the numbers, including the column headers and row headers, are created by formulas. Recreate the worksheet. When you create the initial sales formula ($30*5,000 = $150,000), this formula can be copied in several steps to fill the table. Do not create a new formula in each cell.

The product manager for electric toasters asks to see the results produced by this worksheet when the number of toasters sold is 8,950 and the starting price is $12.50 per unit. The $2 difference between columns can remain.

Appendix A

Summary of Lotus 1-2-3 Commands

WORKSHEET COMMANDS

Global	Changes affecting the entire worksheet.
Format	Changes default display for values.
Label-Prefix	Changes default display for labels.
Column	Changes default column width.
Recalculation	Switches between (Natural, Columnwise, Rowwise) and between (Automatic, Manual, Iteration).
Protection	Enables or disables cell protection.
Default	Defaults for printer and directory, to determine existing settings (status), to update startup defaults.
Zero	Hides the display of zeros.
Insert	Inserts a column or row.
Delete	Deletes a column or row.
Column	Alters column widths.
Erase	Erases the current worksheet and resets all settings.
Titles	Freezes row and/or column titles in place.
Window	Creates or clears a horizontal or vertical window.
Status	Displays available memory, recalculation method, circular reference, and defaults in use.
Page	Inserts a page break

RANGE COMMANDS

Format	Changes the display of values.
Label	Left-, right-, or center-justifies labels.
Erase	Erases a range.
Name	Assigns a name to a range.
Justify	Constrains the display of labels to a restricted range.
Protect	Prevents changes to cell/range contents.
Unprotect	Permits changes to cell/range contents.
Input	Restrains cell pointer to unprotected cells.
Value	Converts formulas to their numeric values.
Transpose	Transposes a range on its axis, making the rows, columns and the columns, rows.

COPY

Copy	Replicates a range of cells.

MOVE

Move	Repositions a range of cells.

FILE COMMANDS

Save	Writes a worksheet to a .WK1 file.
Retrieve	Recalls a worksheet from disk.
Combine	Incorporates all or part of the data from a worksheet into the current worksheet.
Copy	Replaces the contents of the current worksheet with those of the incoming range.
Add	Adds the incoming values to those already in the range.
Subtract	Subtracts the incoming values from those already in the range.
Xtract	Writes part of the current worksheet to a .WK1 file.
Erase	Removes a file from the default drive/directory.
List	Lists the names of files in the default drive/directory.
Import	Reads in a text file as text or numbers.
Directory	Resets the default drive/directory.

PRINT COMMANDS

Printer	Prints the file on the default printer.
Range	Sets the range of cells to be printed.
Line	Advances the paper one line.
Page	Advances the paper to the top of the page.
Options	Sets borders, headers and footers, font size, margins, and other settings.
Clear	Removes print settings.
Align	Synchronizes the printer with 1-2-3.
Go	Starts the printing.
Quit	Clears the print menu from the control panel.
File	Prints the file to a .PRN text file. Uses the same options as / Print Printer.

GRAPH COMMANDS

Type	Sets the type of graph (bar, stacked bar, pie, XY, line).
X	The labels range.
A-F	Data (values) ranges.
Reset	Voids previous graph settings.
View	Displays the graph.
Save	Saves the graph as a .PIC file.
Options	Adds graphic enhancements.
Legend	Legends for data ranges.
Format	For XY graphs, display as symbols or lines.
Titles	Sets four titles.
Grid	Overlays the graphic lines on the chart.
Scale	Controls over axis scales.
Color	Displays in color.
B&W	Displays in black and white.
Data-Labels	Labels for data points.
Quit	Escapes to previous (graph) menu.
Name	Names the settings for a graph for use at a later time.
Quit	Clears the graph menu from the control panel.

DATA	**COMMANDS**
Fill	Fills a range with a sequence of values.
Table	Creates tables of values using formulas.
1	A table with one input cell.
2	A table with two input cells.
Reset	Voids previous table settings.
Sort	Organizes rows in ascending or descending order.
Data-Range	The range to be sorted.
Primary-Key	The column (key field) on which the sort is based.
Secondary-Key	The column used to continue the sort if there are ties in the primary key.
Reset	Voids the previous sort settings.
Go	Executes the sort procedure.
Query	Selects records (rows) from a database.
Input	The range containing the records.
Criterion	The range containing bases on which to select records.
Output	The range in which records meeting the criterion are placed.
Find	Locates records in the database meeting the criteria.
Extract	Reproduces, in the output range, records in the database meeting the criteria.
Unique	Reproduces records that are not duplicated.
Delete	Deletes records that meet the criteria.
Reset	Voids the previous query settings.
Distribution	Creates a frequency distribution.
Matrix	Matrix operations.
Invert	Inverts a matrix.
Multiply	Multiplies two matrices.
Regression	Linear regressive formula calculation.
Parse	Converts rows of ASCII text to 1-2-3 recognizable columns of values and labels.

SYSTEM

System	Temporarily exits to DOS shell.

QUIT

Quit	Exits 1-2-3.

Appendix B

Summary of Lotus 1-2-3 Functions

FUNCTION	RETURNS
@@(cell address)	Retrieves the contents of the cell address.
@ABS	Absolute (positive) value of a number.
@ACOS	Arc cosine.
@ASIN	Arc sine.
@ATAN	Two-quadrant arc tangent.
@ATAN2	Four-quadrant arc tangent.
@AVG	Finds the average for a list of values.
@CELL	Returns attribute data about the upper left corner of a range.
@CELLPOINTER	Returns attribute data about the active cell.
@CHAR	ASCII character represented by a value.
@CHOOSE	Selects the nth item in a list.
@CODE	The code value of the first character in a string.
@COLS	Number of columns found in a range.
@COS	Cosine.
@COUNT	Number of nonempty cells in a list of cells.
@CTERM	Number of compounding periods for an investment, given a present value, a future value, and a fixed periodic interest rate.
@DATE	The serial date number for a day represented by digit pairs of YY, MM, and DD.
@DATEVALUE	Serial date value of a datelike character string.
@DAVG	Selective average of values in an offset column, within a table meeting specified criteria.
@DAY	Day number represented by a serial date number.
@DCOUNT	Selective count of non-empty cells in an offset column within a table meeting specified criteria.
@DDB	Double declining depreciation.
@DMAX	Identification of largest value in an offset column according to specified criteria within a table.
@DMIN	Identification of smallest value in an offset column according to specified criteria within a table.
@DSTD	Standard deviation of a list of values in an offset column according to specified criteria within a table.
@DSUM	Selective summation of values in an offset column according to specified criteria within a table.
@DVAR	Variance of a list of values in an offset column according to specified criteria within a table.
@ERR	Value of ERR (error).
@EXACT	Compares two strings for identity.
@EXP	Raises a number to its exponential value.
@FALSE	Value of FALSE (0).
@FIND	Locates the position of a character in a string.
@FV	Future value.
@HLOOKUP	Horizontal table lookup.
@HOUR	Hour number in a number.

@IF	Returns one value if a comparison is true, a second value if the comparison is false.
@INDEX	Returns the contents of the cell found at specific cell coordinates.
@INT	Integer value of a number.
@IRR	Internal rate of return.
@ISERR	True if the item evaluated is ERR, false if not.
@ISNA	True if the item evaluated is NA, false if not.
@ISNUMBER	True if the item evaluated is a value, false if not.
@ISSTRING	True if the item evaluated is a string, false if not.
@LEFT	Returns the specified number of leading characters in a string.
@LENGTH	Returns the length of a string.
@LN	Natural log.
@LOG	Log.
@LOWER	Converts a string to all lowercase.
@MAX	The maximum value in a list.
@MID	Returns a specified number of characters from the middle of a string.
@MIN	The smallest value in a list.
@MINUTE	The minute number represented by a number.
@MOD	Remainder of a number when divided by another number.
@MONTH	The month number represented by a number.
@N	The value of the cell in the upper left corner of a range.
@NA	The value of NA (Not Available).
@NOW	Current date and time.
@NPV	Net present value.
@PI	The value of Pi (3.1415...).
@PMT	Payment needed given principal, periodic interest rate, and number of payments in term.
@PROPER	Converts words in a string to a leading uppercase character and remaining characters to lowercase.
@PV	Present value.
@RAND	Random number between 0 and 1.
@RATE	Periodic interest rate given present value, future value, and compounding periods.
@REPEAT	Replicates a string a specified number of times.
@REPLACE	Replaces all or part of a string with another string.
@RIGHT	Returns the specified number of trailing characters in a string.
@ROUND	Rounds a value to a specified number of decimal places.
@ROWS	Number of rows found in a range.
@S	The string value of the cell in the upper left corner of a range.
@SECOND	The second number represented by a number.
@SIN	Sine.
@SLN	Straight-line depreciation.
@SQRT	Square root.
@STD	Standard deviation of a list of values.
@STRING	Converts a string to its numeric value, including decimal places.
@SUM	The summed value of a list.
@SYD	Sum-of-years'-digit depreciation.
@TAN	Tangent.
@TERM	Term given number of periods, amount of each payment, the periodic interest rate, and future value.
@TIME	Serial time number represented in the format hours, minutes, seconds.

@TIMEVALUE	Converts a string to its time equivalent.
@TODAY	Returns the system date.
@TRIM	Removes leading and trailing spaces from a string.
@TRUE	Value of TRUE (1).
@UPPER	Converts a string to all uppercase.
@VALUE	Converts a string to its numeric value.
@VAR	Variance of a list of values.
@VLOOKUP	Vertical table lookup.
@YEAR	The year number represented by a number.

Appendix C

Summary of Lotus 1-2-3 Macro Commands

SPECIAL KEY MACROS

MACRO NAME	KEY REPRESENTED
{ABS}	F4
{BACKSPACE} or {BS}	Backspace
{BIGLEFT}	Shift-Tab or Ctrl-Left arrow
{BIGRIGHT}	Tab or Ctrl-Right arrow
{CALC}	F9
{DELETE} or {DEL}	Delete
{DOWN}	Down arrow
{EDIT}	F2
{END}	End
{ESCAPE} or {ESC}	Escape
{GOTO}	F5
{GRAPH}	F10
{HOME}	Home
{LEFT}	Left arrow
{NAME}	F3
{PGDN}	PgDn
{PGUP}	PgUp
{QUERY}	F7
{RIGHT}	Right arrow
{TABLE}	F8
{UP}	Up arrow
{WINDOW}	F6
~	Enter
{~}	Tilde as a character
{{}	Opening brace as a character
{}}	Closing brace as a character

MACRO COMMAND KEYWORDS

MACRO COMMAND	PURPOSE
{?}	Requests user input.
{ROUTINE-NAME}	Subroutine call.
{BEEP}	Produces an audible beep.
{BLANK}	Empties a cell or range.
{BRANCH}	Transfers macro execution to named location.
{BREAKOFF}	Disables use of Break key while macro executes.
{BREAKON}	Restores use of Break key while macro executes.
{CLOSE}	Closes a file.
{CONTENTS}	Replicates contents of a cell in another cell.
{DEFINE}	Specifies the arguments expected by a subroutine.

{DISPATCH}	Indirect branch.
{FILESIZE}	Ascertains the size of the currently open file in bytes.
{FOR}	Iterative loop structure.
{FORBREAK}	Cancels a FOR loop.
{GET}	Pauses for user input, places response in a specified cell.
{GETLABEL}	Pauses for user input of a string; places response in a specified cell.
{GETNUMBER}	Pauses for user input of a value; places response in a specified cell.
{GETPOS}	Determines location of the file pointer in the currently open file.
{IF}	Conditional execution of a command string.
{INDICATE}	Alters the string in the mode indicator block.
{LET}	Stores a number or label in a specified cell.
{LOOK}	Checks to see if a character has been typed while a macro is executing.
{MENUBRANCH}	Transfers control to a user-created menu range.
{MENUCALL}	Calls a subroutine from a menu.
{ONERROR}	Transfers control to a new location if an error is detected.
{OPEN}	Opens a file.
{PANELOFF}	Suppresses control panel changes until macro has executed.
{PANELON}	Reinitiates control panel changes.
{PUT}	Stores a number or label in a specific cell within a specified range.
{QUIT}	Terminates the macro.
{READ}	Reads characters from the open file.
{READLN}	Copies a line of characters from the open file.
{RECALC}	Recalculates formulas in a specified range.
{RECALCCOL}	Recalculates formulas in a specified group of columns.
{RESTART}	Cancels a subroutine.
{RETURN}	Transfers control back to the macro that called a subroutine.
{SETPOS}	Resets the position of the file pointer.
{WAIT}	Suspends macro execution for a specified period.
{WINDOWSOFF}	Suppresses changes in the 1-2-3 window while a macro is executing.
{WINDOWSON}	Reinitiates changes in the 1-2-3 window.
{WRITE}	Writes characters into the open file.
{WRITELN}	Writes a line of characters into the open file.

THE /X MACRO COMMANDS

MACRO COMMAND	PURPOSE
/XC	Transfers macro flow of control to a specified location; return is expected.
/XG	Transfers macro flow of control to a specified location; no return is expected.
/XI	Conditional evaluation with action if the condition evaluated is true.
/XL	Solicits a label response through a control panel message.
/XM	Transfers macro control to a location at which a user-created menu is present.
/XN	Solicits a value response through a control panel message.
/XQ	Terminates macro execution.
/XR	Returns macro flow of control to the calling macro.

Glossary

#AND# A 1-2-3 keyword that combines two logical conditions into one such that both conditions must be true for the combination of the conditions to be true.

#NOT# A 1-2-3 keyword that reverses the truth or falsity of a logical condition.

#OR# A 1-2-3 keyword that combines two logical conditions into one such that either of the conditions will make the combination of the conditions true.

A

Absolute cell address A cell address that, if relocated, always refers to the same cell. A dollar sign ($) precedes the column letters and row numbers ($A$4 or $IV$270).

Absolute key In 1-2-3, function key F4, which converts cell and range addresses into absolute, relative, or mixed forms.

Absolute reference A cell address that will not be adjusted when it is copied.

Absolute value The magnitude of a number without regard to sign.

Access system The 1-2-3 menu offering access to 1-2-3, Install, PrintGraph, Translate, and View.

Active area That portion of a worksheet that contains cell entries or cell settings. This area begins at A1 (Home) and ends at the cell found by moving down the column containing the cells farthest to the right and stopping at the row with lowest cells.

Active cell The cell highlighted by the cell pointer.

Alignment The placement of a label in a spreadsheet cell or database field. A label can be left- or right-justified or centered. Alignment is determined by label-prefix characters.

Alphabetic keys The keys on the computer's keyboard that are arranged just as they are on a typewriter keyboard.

Alphanumeric characters Any combination of letters, numbers, symbols, and spaces.

Alternate key The key marked Alt and used for initiating macros in Lotus 1-2-3.

Anchoring Conversion of a 1-2-3 cell address to a range address by pressing the period.

Application The product of a generalized application program such as a document from a word processor, a budget projection from a spreadsheet, or an inventory from a database manager.

Application program A program for producing user-specific applications.

Arguments Values, labels, cell references, ranges, or other functions used in the calculations of built-in functions. Function arguments are separated by commas or semicolons.

Arithmetic (mathematical) operators The arithmetic signs (/, *, +, -, ^).

Ascending order Arranging data such that lower values come first and higher values come last.

ASCII American Standard Code for Information Interchange; the coding scheme whereby every character, number, or symbol is represented by an integer code between 0 and 255.

ASCII files Files saved in a text format specified by the American Standard Code for Information Interchange. Files saved in this format often can be used by other programs or transmitted by modem because they have a standard format.

Automatic recalculation The process of re-evaluating all formulas in a worksheet whenever the contents of any cell change.

Automatic repeat The characteristic of keys, if held down, to continue to enter the symbol they represent after the first entry of the character and a brief pause.

B   **Back up** A process of making a second copy of a file to avoid loss of data. Backups may be created automatically by some applications programs.

Backup copy A duplicate of a file or disk that is saved in case the original file or disk is damaged.

Beep A method of notifying the user that an erroneous command has been issued.

Big Left In 1-2-3, Shift-Tab or Control-Left arrow keys pressed simultaneously to move the window to the left by complete screens.

Big Right In 1-2-3, the Tab or Control-Right arrow keys pressed simultaneously to move the window to the right by complete screens.

Boolean A form of algebra created by George Boole to manipulate logical conditions and evaluations.

Border The reverse video bars on a 1-2-3 screen that contain the column letters (A through IV) and the row numbers (1 through 8,192).

Borders A 1-2-3 printing option that repeats an identified range of cells on each page of a report.

Boundary The edge of a worksheet (columns A or IV, rows 1 or 8,192) or the point at which cells with contents abut empty cells.

Bug A program error.

Built-in functions Software-provided operations to carry out specific computational activities.

Byte A unit of representation constructed from eight bits. One byte represents a single character.

C   **CALC indicator** An indicator block that appears when recalculation is set to manual and after a cell's contents have changed.

Calc key Function key F9. Used to recalculate a worksheet when recalculation is set to manual.

Cancel To abort a program or command.

Case The shape and size of a letter. Letters in a type style may be uppercase or lowercase.

Cell A spreadsheet unit identified by specifying its column letter and row number coordinates.

Cell address The position of a cell in a worksheet, specified by a column letter and row number (e.g., A1).

Cell contents The actual value or label entered into the cell, as opposed to the cell display.

Cell display The formatted appearance of a cell's value, as opposed to the cell's contents.

Cell entry A cell's contents. May be a value or a label.

Cell formula A value in 1-2-3 that is constructed from cell addresses, numbers, and built-in functions.

Cell pointer The reverse video block highlighting the currently active cell. The cell pointer expands to highlight ranges.

Cell protection A 1-2-3 cell attribute that prevents the entry of data into the protected cell.

Center In 1-2-3, the alignment of a label in the center of a cell.

Character A symbol (numeric, alphabetic, punctuation, or mathematic) represented by one byte.

Character string See String.

Circular reference (CIRC) A formula references a cell that contains another formula that, either directly or indirectly, references the initial cell. 1-2-3 displays the CIRC indicator when a circular reference is entered.

Clear Reset previously specified settings, ranges, or values for 1-2-3 commands.

Column A vertical block of cells in a worksheet. For example, column B contains cells B1 through B8192. There are 256 columns in a worksheet.

Column letters The letters (labels) A through IV identifying columns.

Column width In 1-2-3, the number of characters (1-240) that a column displays on the screen. The number of characters stored as a cell's contents may exceed the display width.

Command An instruction to a computer that can be executed.

Commercial software Software that has been copyrighted and licensed, is supported by the developer, and that must be paid for in advance of its usage.

Compound condition A logical condition composed of two conditions united with an AND or an OR operator.

Compressed type Small type size. For example, a type size of 17.5 cpi as opposed to 10 or 12 cpi.

Configuration The currently active default values for an operating system or for an applications program. These values may be modifiable during operation.

Constants Values or strings that do not change when they are entered in cells or that are contained in formulas.

Control panel The top three lines of the 1-2-3 screen.

Coordinates The column letters and row numbers used to identify the location of a cell.

Copy command In 1-2-3, the menu choice to replicate the contents of a cell or range.

Copy protection Any of several techniques designed to prevent the copying of software.

Corner cell A 1-2-3 cell at the corner of a range.

Crosshatching Graphic display patterns for black-and-white graphs in 1-2-3.

Current cell See Active cell.

Current directory The default DOS or Lotus directory. The directory that is employed first when DOS searches for files and executable commands unless otherwise directed.

Current drive The drive containing the disk on which DOS and Lotus look to for a directory or file unless otherwise instructed.

Cursor The underscore character that indicates where characters will be entered or where commands will be carried out.

Cursor block Reverse video blocks that highlight choices on menus.

D   **Data** Alphanumeric and graphic input or output.

Data commands In 1-2-3, the menu choice to sort, extract, and otherwise manipulate data in a database.

Data disk The disk used to store files.

Data file A file that contains the data used by an applications program.

Data labels Identifying labels for data points on a 1-2-3 graph.

Data range One of the six possible 1-2-3 ranges (A through F) for values used to construct graphs.

Database function The built-in functions in 1-2-3 that begin with @D and that selectively carry out database operations according to user-specified criteria.

Date arithmetic The representation and manipulation of dates as values rather than as character strings.

Debug To discover and correct syntactic and semantic errors in a program, function, macro, batch file, or subroutine.

Default configuration The initial defaults used to establish the operating characteristics of an operating system or applications program.

Default directory See Current directory.

Default drive See Current drive.

Default value The value used or the action taken when an acceptable alternative has not been specified.

Delete The Data Query command to remove records from a database in 1-2-3.

Descending order Arranging data such that higher values come first and lower values come last.

Directory A logical grouping of files and subdirectories on a disk. A directory's filenames, extensions, and subdirectory names are displayed together along with the file's size, creation time, and date.

Disk drive The device that reads and writes files to disks.

Diskette A secondary storage medium for a computer. Diskettes come in floppy, rigid, and semirigid cases.

Display The monitor screen.

DOS Disk Operating System. The software that makes computer hardware usable.

E   **Edit key** In 1-2-3, function key F2. Returns a cell's contents to the entry line for revision.

Empty cell A cell with no contents.

End key A key that moves the 1-2-3 cell pointer to the next boundary in the direction indicated by the cell pointer movement key that follows.

Enter key Synonymous with Return key. Represented by a broken arrow on some keyboards. The Enter key inserts a carriage return and a line feed.

Entry line The second line of the 1-2-3 control panel.

Escape key The key used to back out of command sequences or from data entry in 1-2-3.

Expression A legal combination of operators, constants, and variables.

Extension Up to three characters that are added to a filename to identify the contents of the file.

Extract In 1-2-3, the Data Query command to display selected records from a database in an output range.

F   **File** A collection of data stored in a named and dedicated portion of a disk. Files can contain graphs, documents, databases, worksheets, programs, and other collections of data.

File commands In 1-2-3, the menu choice used to save, list, erase, and retrieve files.

File extension See Extension.

File specification The complete specification of a file including a drive letter, a pathway, a filename, and an extension. Also, abbreviated to filespec.

Filename The identifier that uniquely describes a file. Consists of from one to eight characters.

Find The Data Query command to locate records in a 1-2-3 database.

Floppy disk Diskettes that allow some physical flexibility, especially of the 3 1/2" and 5 1/4" size.

Formatting attribute The directive describing how values are to be displayed in a 1-2-3 cell.

Formatting Initializing and preparing a disk so that it can record and store files produced by a particular computer system. Also, the appearance of text in a document or worksheet.

Free cell Either an unanchored cell or the corner cell of a range that is diagonally opposite the anchored cell.

Freeze To lock in place. In 1-2-3, to lock some columns or rows in place while panning to view other areas of the worksheet or database.

Function keys Keys marked F1 through F10 (or F12) that carry out specialized macro operations in DOS and in applications software.

G **Global protection** Setting the protection attribute of 1-2-3 cells to enable or disable throughout the worksheet.

Global settings See Default configuration.

Goto key In 1-2-3, function key F5, which prompts the user for a cell, range name, or address to which to move the cell pointer.

Graph commands In 1-2-3, the menu choice to create, name, save, and display graphs.

Graph key In 1-2-3, function key F10, which repeats the viewing of the last graph displayed from the Graph command menu.

Graphics The use of pictures in an applications program.

Grid A matrix composed of rows and columns.

H **Help** An on-line program for providing assistance.

Help key The key that recalls Help screens (F1 in 1-2-3).

Hidden cell A 1-2-3 cell that has been formatted as hidden so that it will not appear in the window or in printed reports.

High-density disk See Quad-density disk.

Highlighting The process of specifying a range to be copied, moved, formatted, etc.

Home In Lotus 1-2-3 and many other programs, the upper left corner of the worksheet or document.

Home key The key that returns the cell pointer to cell A1 in 1-2-3.

I   **Indicator blocks**   Highlighted blocks in 1-2-3 that provide information about selected keys or the program's status.   Also called indicator blocks.

Insert mode   A mode of data entry in which new text is inserted into existing text rather than overwriting it.   Opposite of overwrite mode.

K   **Keyboard, extended**   101 keys.

Keyboard, standard   80 keys.

Keyword   A word that is reserved by an applications program for special meaning and that often cannot be used in an application.

Kill   Terminate an executing program.

L   **Label**   An alphanumeric entry in 1-2-3.   An entry with no numeric value.   Character strings that are preceded by a label-prefix character.   Also, the mode of data entry in 1-2-3 when text is being entered.

Label justification   The alignment of a label in a cell: left-justified, right-justified, centered, or repeating. The label-prefix characters apostrophe, quote, caret, and backslash control generate these alignments, respectively.

Label prefix   The characters that align labels in a cell.   See Label justification.

Legend   The patterns or symbols used to identify values shown in a graph.

List   A type of argument for 1-2-3 functions.   A list is any legally constructed combination of values, cell addresses, ranges, range names, and built-in functions.

Logical condition   A condition that evaluates to either true or false, or alternatively, to yes or no.

Logical fields   Also called Boolean fields.   Fields in a database whose value is either true or false, or alternatively, yes or no.

Logical operator   An operator that tests the truth or falsity of a comparison.   The logical operators commonly available are $=$, $<>$, $<$, $<=$, $>$, $>=$.

Lookup table   A range containing data that lookup functions like @VLOOKUP and @HLOOKUP can use to find a value associated with a lookup value.

M   **Macro**   A set of instructions that can be executed as if they were one instruction.

Macro language   Key words and instructions that can be used to construct macros.

Main menu   The menu retrieved by pressing the Slash key in ready mode in 1-2-3.

Manual recalculation   Setting a worksheet to re-evaluate cell formulas only when the Calc key (F9) is pressed.

Margin   The blank space borders at the top, bottom, left, and right of a printed document, worksheet, or database report.

Mega   A prefix meaning approximately one million.

Menu   A series of choices from which the user is to make selections.

Mixed cell address   A 1-2-3 cell address that consists of one relative and one absolute coordinate. It contains one dollar sign in front of either the column letter or row number.

Mode   The state of an operation.

Mode indicator   See Indicator blocks.

Move command   In 1-2-3, the menu choice to relocate a cell or a range without adjusting cell addresses.

MS-DOS   Abbreviation for Microsoft-Disk Operating System. The operating system used on IBM PC-compatible computers.

N   **Name key**   In 1-2-3, function key F3 that, in point mode, displays the range names created in the current worksheet.

Named graph   Graph settings that have been retained as part of a worksheet so the graph can be displayed again without reconstructing the settings.

Named range   A range of cells identified by name.

Natural recalculation   The process by which 1-2-3 normally recalculates a worksheet. Constants are determined first, then formulas that depend on these constants are calculated, then formulas based on the previous formulas are calculated, and so on.

Num Lock key   The key used to toggle the numeric key pad between lowercase and uppercase.

Numeric keypad   The block of ten keys holding numbers as uppercase and cursor movement keys as lowercase.

O   **Operator**   A symbol to indicate the action to be performed on operands or to test the relationship of the operands.

Order of precedence   See Precedence.

Overwrite mode   The mode of data entry in which typed characters type over and replace existing text. Opposite of insert mode.

P   **Page**   A 1-2-3 command that inserts the symbol :: in a worksheet and that sends a form feed command to the printer during printing.

Parent directory   The directory above a subdirectory.

PC-DOS   Abbreviation for Personal Computer - Disk Operating System. The operating system used on IBM personal computers. Comparable to MS-DOS.

Point   In 1-2-3, to use the cell pointer to insert a cell or range address in a formula.

Precedence The sequence in which operators in formulas are evaluated. Operations with higher precedence numbers, such as multiplication, are carried out before operations with lower precedence numbers such as subtraction. Parentheses can be used to enforce a different order of evaluation of operators.

Print commands In 1-2-3, the menu choice to define a print range, printing options, and to print the current worksheet on a printer or to a print file.

Print file An ASCII file with the file extension .PRN produced by 1-2-3 when a worksheet is printed to disk.

Print to disk Transferring the image of a document or worksheet to a file that is distinct from the original document or worksheet. The "printed" file loses formatting and control codes and consists solely of lines of ASCII characters.

PrintGraph The portion of Lotus 1-2-3 that prints graph files created with 1-2-3.

Program A sequence of instructions that a computer can execute to accomplish a task.

Program disk The disk that contains the main program for an application. Also called a system disk.

Prompt The signal that control has been passed to the user and that the system is awaiting a command or data entry.

Prompt line The third line of the 1-2-3 control panel.

Public-domain software Software that is not copyrighted or supported by the developer.

Q   **Quad-density disk** A 5 1/4" diskette that stores 1.2 Mb of data.

Query key In 1-2-3, the key that repeats the last Data Query command.

R   **Random Access Memory (RAM)** The portion of the computer's memory that stores the internal DOS commands, programs, and data. Also called main memory or primary memory.

Range A rectangular block of cells identified by a range address in a worksheet program.

Range address The location of a range in the worksheet defined by cell addresses in opposing corners.

Range commands In 1-2-3, the menu choice to manipulate ranges of cells. Includes formatting, changing label prefixes, and protecting ranges.

Range name A name identifying a range in a worksheet.

Range protection/unprotection The 1-2-3 command for toggling the protection attribute of cell ranges to protection on or off.

Recalculation The process of re-evaluating formulas in a worksheet with current cell values.

Relational operator See Logical operator.

Relative cell address A cell address in a formula that can be adjusted relative to the direction in which it is copied.

Remembered range A range setting created in a 1-2-3 command that is retained as part of the worksheet for repeated use.

Repeat label prefix A label prefix that repeats a character string across the width of a cell. The backslash is the repeat label prefix character in 1-2-3.

Reset Clear previous settings or restore default settings.

Retrieve Load a worksheet into RAM.

S   **Save** To write a file to secondary storage.

Saved graph A graph created by 1-2-3 for printing by PrintGraph and saved in a DOS file with the extension .PIC.

Scale The determination of the units by which the X and Y dimensions of 1-2-3 graphs will be displayed.

Setup string A character string entered in 1-2-3 that controls printer settings. Setup strings are unique to each printer. Consult the printer manual for appropriate strings to control type size, type style, and so on.

Shareware Software that has been copyrighted but is distributed on a try-it-first basis. Then, if it is useful, the user contributes a recommended amount to the developer basis.

Shift-state keys The Alternate, Control, and Shift keys. Keys that change the state of the other keyboard characters.

Software Programs that are used with a computer system. (In contrast to hardware.)

Sort To order the records in a database in ascending or descending order according to the contents of one or more fields.

Source disk The disk from which data is read or copied.

Source file The file from which data is read or copied.

Status In 1-2-3, the current state of the worksheet.

Status line The first line of the 1-2-3 control panel.

Sticky menu A menu that returns to the control panel after one of its choices has been executed.

String One or more connected characters that are used as a unit for some computer operation.

Suspend Cause a program to pause in its execution.

Synchronized windows Windows that are linked together so they display the same columns or rows.

System disk A disk containing the files needed for booting a booting system. Sometimes used to refer to the main program disk for an applications program.

T

Table key In 1-2-3, function key F8, which repeats the last Data Table command.

Text file See ASCII files.

Text Readable characters including the alphanumeric characters, the numerals, and punctuation marks. Opposite of nonvisible control codes. Also, the words in a message.

Titles Rows or columns "frozen" in place above or to the left of the cell pointer on a worksheet. Also, identifiers that describe the meanings assigned to four graph elements.

Toggle The process of switching between two states. Also, any device, command, or command switch that has two states, on and off.

Translate The portion of 1-2-3 that is used to import and export files to and from other application software packages.

Typeover mode See Overwrite mode.

U

Unanchoring Converting a range address to a cell address by pressing the Escape or Backspace keys.

Unformatted disk An uninitialized disk. The condition of the disk when first shipped.

Unformatted worksheet A worksheet whose cells are using the default formatting attribute, typically General.

Unsynchronized windows Windows that are not linked so they can display different columns and rows.

V

Value A number, formula, or function that produces a number that can be used in calculations.

View The Graph command to see a graph on the monitor screen.

Volume label A name or character string of up to eleven characters that can be assigned to any disk during formatting. Volume labels can be changed with the Label command.

W

What if analysis The testing of alternative values as dependent variables to see what effect the alternative values have on the results of a computation or series of computations.

Window A partial view of a larger document, worksheet, or database.

Window key In 1-2-3, function key F6, which moves the cell pointer between windows.

Work area The grid portion of a 1-2-3 screen that contains cells.

Worksheet A spreadsheet. A file used by an applications program that organizes and manipulates values and labels in rows and columns.

Worksheet commands   In 1-2-3, the menu choice to initiate changes that affect settings for the entire current worksheet.

Write   The process of copying data from RAM to a file.

X   **/X commands**   1-2-3 commands that can be used only within a macro.

X data range   The data range that contains labels to identify values in the A through F data ranges in 1-2-3 graphs.

Z   **Zero suppression**   In 1-2-3 and other programs, the hiding of insignificant zeros.

INDEX

Contents

Chapter 7: dBASE Functions DB-99

Preface

This book has been written to teach introductory readers to use dBASE IV software effectively. It offers practical, hands on instruction in the use of a highly successful, commercial quality database manager. This package is widely used in in business and education. This software is fully-functioned and capable of illustrating most of the major applications that one can develop with other commercial software packages of a similar nature.

Intended to meet several needs, *Beginning dBASE IV* can be useful in many settings. It can be used as a supplemental laboratory manual for courses that introduce students to computers and their applications, such as Introduction to Computing in Business, Computer Literacy, and Introduction to Microcomputer Software.

This book can also be used as a stand-alone text for short courses that focus on educating students in the main uses of microcomputers. The tutorial orientation of this book allows it to be used by a learner who wishes to work independently. The instructional approach utilized is entirely hands-on and step-by-step. Exercises are presented with detailed instructions on moving from the identification of a computing problem to its solution.

Each chapter concludes with a group of exercises that reinforce the techniques learned in that chapter. The exercises closely parallel the design of the database file presented in the chapter. In many cases, exercises are reused in subsequent chapters to enhance the student's product and to enable students to practice new techniques without unnecessary data entry.

A summary of dBASE IV commands is included for instructors who wish to cover material beyond the scope of this book. A glossary of terminology is also provided.

Fritz H. Grupe

Chapter 1

Database Management: Introduction to dBASE IV

Chapter Outline

In addition to word processors and spreadsheets, database management programs are the third type of program commonly found on microcomputers. This chapter introduces you to the basic techniques for utilizing the database management program dBASE IV. Specifically, you will

1. Learn what databases are;
2. Explore some of the features of dBASE IV that are available from a menu-driven set of commands called the Control Center;
3. Create a database, display a simple listing of the records contained in the database on the screen, and print the listing;

4. Add new records to the existing database;
5. Edit the contents of selected records;
6. Delete selected records;
7. Print the records in the database;
8. Back up your database.

WHAT ARE DATABASES?

A database is a collection of records that contain comparable types of data about people, events, or objects. A telephone directory, for instance, is a database that provides a name, an address, and a telephone number for each person listed. The directory entries follow some rules, even though variations are accepted. There must always be a name, even though a company name and an individual's name may be treated as being equal. Similarly, there must always be a telephone number listed. It would not make sense to show either a name or a telephone number, but not both. To make the directory useful, the names must appear in the same column each time and the telephone numbers must appear in their own column; otherwise, searching for an entry would be difficult. Addresses, on the other hand, are optional.

Databases are useful for many purposes. Other examples of databases include:

1. inventories of stock, supplies, or equipment
2. records on employee hiring, salaries, and training
3. facilities and vehicle records related to maintenance and repair
4. mailing list records
5. sales history and billing databases
6. school and voter registration lists
7. airplane reservation and seating assignments
8. library book catalogs

Many databases are kept by hand, not on a computer. Computerized databases are easier to manipulate and to keep up to date, however.

In a telephone directory, a single entry is a record. Each entry consists of three columns: a name, an address, and a telephone number. Each of those pieces of information is referred to as a **field**. Each complete entry is called a **record**. The telephone directory is a **database**.

WHAT ARE DATABASE MANAGERS?

There are many database managers that are available. Software in this group is primarily identified by the use of a records in which the user specifies how data is to be collected for each item in the database. The primary operations that are fundamental to a database usage are:

1. Creating and appending records to the database.
2. Editing and changing the records that already exist.
3. Deleting records that are no longer needed.
4. Sorting and indexing (another technique for organizing the records) the records to put them in an order of utility to the user.
5. Locating records with specific contents.
6. Reporting on the contents of the database either in detail or in summary. For instance, one might wish to print all records for persons who are over age 21, or one might wish to total the values for all stocks held by a given stockholder.

DIFFERENCES AMONG DATABASES

There is a wide variety among database managers in how they function and what types of features are available. Beyond the core of functions noted above, there many features that may or may not be present in a given package.

1. **Database Size.** Some databases can maintain databases with a few thousand records, adequate for many users, while others can maintain databases of a million records.
2. **Data Types.** While all databases can handle numeric and character data, not all databases can handle dates and logical (true or false) fields. Some databases can provide memo or super fields that allow the user to enter additional information of variable size that is attached to selected records.
3. **Programming Language.** Most databases provide a menu of commands that are available. Many do not provide a programming language similar to BASIC or Pascal which gives the sophisticated user sophisticated methods of manipulating the data.
4. **Security.** When confidentiality is required, users may have to enter passwords to open a database. Some database managers may wish to encrypt files so they cannot be read by unauthorized personnel. Most importantly, businesses that wish to allow several people to use the same database simultaneously must have a feature called **record locking** that prevents users from using the same record simultaneously.
5. **Fourth Generation Language Tools.** Does the database offer programs that produce standard reports easily? Does it offer a program generator that allows the user to specify what is to be accomplished by the program and the generator produces the program? The more sophisticated these user friendly tools are, the more productive are the users of the system.
6. **Method of Organization.** Some databases are only capable of handling records in a "flat file" that is awkward to organize and inefficient to access. Others use sophisticated methods of organization that make access efficient and re-organization easy to accomplish.
7. **Access to Multiple Databases.** A key principle underlying database administration is that data should only be entered once. A person's address should only be maintained in one database so changes can be made in that database. To implement this principle means that data from several databases may need to be combined in order to produce useful reports. Some databases may not permit the user to "join" databases in this manner.

AN EXAMPLE OF A DATABASE

Computer Software Associates is a company that employs part-time programmers to take on software projects that the company has contracted to produce for its client companies. The part-time programmers are paid from reports filed with the company manager. Each report has space for the following items:

1. the billing number
2. the programmer's name
3. the programmer's proficiency level, a company assigned number that is used to calculate the charge-back cost to the client and the pay-rate for the programmer
4. a client identification number
5. a job identification number (any client may have several projects in progress)
6. a job title
7. the hours of programming used on the project
8. the date during which the hours were completed
9. a note to indicate whether the job was completed
10. comments about the work referenced

Computer Software Associates has been increasingly successful in locating clients and is finding that it should computerize its own records. The reports submitted by the programmers is a good place to begin. To this point, work file record reports have been handwritten and look like Figure 1-1.

```
┌─────────────────────────────────────────────────────────────┐
│              ╔═══════════════════════════════╗               │
│              ║      Computer Associates       ║               │
│              ║      Jobs Data Form            ║               │
│              ╚═══════════════════════════════╝               │
│                                                               │
│    Date 06/12/90              Job ID   1502                   │
│                                                               │
│    Prog. Name     Jones, M.                                   │
│                                                               │
│    Client ID      127                                         │
│                                                               │
│    Job Title      Accounts Payable                            │
│                                                               │
│    Hours Spent    7.50        Completed   Y                   │
│                                                               │
│    Notes: Should the client ask, 4.5 hours of work            │
│    were completed on a home computer.  Three hours were       │
│    completed at customer site.                                │
│                                                               │
└─────────────────────────────────────────────────────────────┘
```

Figure 1-1. Work File Record Report.

Since the reports are filed on cards, the manager sorts the cards in order of programmer ID at the end of each pay period as the basis for computing the programmer's pay. At the end of each billing cycle, the cards are sorted by client ID and job ID to determine the cost per job per client. As the number of jobs has increased, so has the number of programmers. Keeping accurate records has become a problem. Consequently, the manager of the programming group has asked that a computerized database be developed that could be used to facilitate the preparation of these reports and to aid in other analyses.

ABOUT dBASE IV

dBASE IV is a powerful and flexible database management program. dBASE's flexibility is due in part to the Control Center menus that perform many complex activities, and to its command language that can be used to write specialized programs utilizing additional built-in features. With the use of the menu-driven mode, you are able to utilize dBASE's power without programming.

The Control Center and the Dot Prompt

dBASE runs in two modes, command-driven or menu-driven. Commands can be typed at the dot prompt (dBASE's prompt) or actions can be chosen from the Control Center's menus. In this book, you concentrate on the use of the Control Center.

Field Names

As mentioned above, the elements composing a database are called fields. Each field must have a name that can be referenced. Because of the way a computer stores information, the type and maximum amount of data to be stored in each field must also be specified.

In dBASE IV, records have a structure. The structure of a database consists of a complete list of the field names found in each record, the types assigned to each of the fields (the kinds of data they can hold), and the lengths of the fields.

Field names are selected by the user. A field name can be up to ten characters in length. The characters may be alphabetic, numeric, or the underscore characters. The name must begin with a letter and may not contain any embedded blank spaces. Characters typed in lowercase are converted to uppercase by dBASE IV.

Since fields are referenced extensively by name, it is a good idea to use descriptive names that indicate what is being stored. For example, the information in fields named FIRSTNAME, LASTNAME, and AGE are more easily called to mind than is possible with field names such as FIELD1, FIELD2 and FIELD3. In the database to be constructed for Computer Associates, the fields to be used are: BILLING_NO, NAME, CLIENT_ID, JOB_ID, JOB_TITLE, WORK_DATE, HRS_WORKED, COMPLETED and NOTES.

Field Types

To make database manipulations as efficient as possible, dBASE IV has six types of fields available: character, numeric, float, date, logical, and memo. One field type may be more appropriate than another depending on the manner in which the stored data is to be used. Technically, every field could be of the character type. Since you would not carry out mathematical operations on telephone numbers, storage of this information as character data is not a serious limitation. However, that is not always the best choice. For example, performing mathematical calculations on numbers stored in a character field can be difficult.

As alluded to above, **character** fields can store any printable character (alphabetic, numeric, blank spaces, and other symbols). For example, a field to hold a telephone number that uses parentheses around the area code and a dash to set off the prefix would need to be of type character. Character fields place entries on the left side of the field. The fields NAME, CLIENT_ID, JOB_ID, and JOB_TITLE store character data for Computer Associates.

Both **numeric** and **float** fields hold numbers. Unlike data in character fields, calculations can be performed on data stored in these fields. For instance, an inventory database would use fields that permitted addition and subtraction so stock quantities could be adjusted at any given time. Numeric and float fields hold numbers that are placed on the right side of the field. The Computer Associates database uses BILLING_NO, and HRS_WORKED as numeric fields. Float fields store floating point numbers and can speed up operations involving multiplying and dividing. Float fields are usually used in scientific applications where numbers are either very large or very small. Numeric fields are automatically summed in some listing of file operations

Date fields are used to store dates that appear as **11/10/88**. The field width is eight by default. The default format is mm/dd/yy where mm, dd, and yy stand for two digit numbers representing the month, date, and year respectively. Two places are held for the slashes. Limited calculations can be performed on dates. One date can be subtracted from another giving the number of days between them. A number may be added or subtracted from a date to give a new date. WORK_DATE is a date field in Computer Associates' database.

Logical fields store a single character representing either true or false. A true value can be entered by a T or t for true, or Y or y for yes. Likewise, a false value is entered with an F or f for false, or N or n for no. This type of field can be very useful. Take, for example, an inventory tracking database. A field indicating whether a particular item has been reordered or not can be invaluable to the purchasing department. Imagine the repercussions of reordering some items twice and others not at all because there was no way of seeing whether it was true or false that an item had been reordered. Computer Associates uses the field COMPLETED as a logical field.

The last type of field is a **memo** field which stores a block of text. This is an area to enter miscellaneous notes that pertain to the particular record. Memo fields are especially useful when only a small number of records in a database require the addition of supplementary notes. The text is actually stored in an auxiliary file. For this reason, the field length is variable. Unlike the other field types which have the same size for every record in the file, memo fields grow to hold whatever text is entered. That means if one record has no entry in a memo field, the field length for that record is 10. In another record, that memo field may have a length of 83. The field name NOTES has been given to a field in Computer Associates' database. This field holds comments that the programmers need to make about their time record reports, but that are not able to be included in the other fields.

Field Lengths

The user defines the field lengths of character, numeric, and float fields; the others are set by dBASE. Field lengths should be defined carefully. If a field is declared to be too short, all of your data cannot be stored. For instance, a last name field length of eight could not hold all of the characters in names like Brownstone or Quackenstein.

The length of a numeric or float field should be the maximum number of digits to be stored. This count needs to include the decimal point and the negative sign if either is to be used.

More About Fields

On the other hand, don't be extravagant with the length. During printing, columns are normally be made as wide as the field length. Thus, a field to store a name that has a length of 20 uses up about one fourth of your paper's width even if there are no names that long. Also, as records are created and stored on the diskette, each field stores the full field length even though a shorter length is adequate. In a large database, this can be significant. For example, if the name Doe is stored within a field of length 20, there are 17 blanks stored in addition to the 3 necessary letters. In a database of 1,000 records, if there are 5 extra letters in each last name field, 5,000 unnecessary blank characters are stored. If there were 10 fields, each of which stored 5 extra characters, the excess storage would be a minimum of 50,000 characters.

By default, when records are printed there is one space between columns. You should not leave spaces in the fields of a record to format report columns. There are other, more efficient means for accomplishing this.

STARTING dBASE IV

This section assumes that dBASE IV has been properly installed for your particular system. The instructions given here are for a stand alone system with a hard disk drive. The instructions also assume that dBASE IV has been installed in a subdirectory on drive C named DBASE. If you are using a different subdirectory name or drive label, there may be some minor differences in the commands needed to start dBASE. If you should have any trouble, consult your local computer expert.

With DOS C> prompt visible, type

cd \dbase
◄┘   Enter key. This DOS command moves you to the DBASE subdirectory. At the next prompt (either C> or C:\DBASE>)
dbase   dBASE, the name of the program to be loaded

◄┘   Enter key. After a short wait while the dBASE program is loading, the dBASE IV copyright screen appears and a message about the license agreement appears at the bottom of the screen.

◄┘   Enter key, to assent to the license agreement and to enter the Control Center

Normally, dBASE puts you in the Control Center and you see the screen shown in Figure 1-2. dBASE can be programmed to escape from the Control Center when dBASE is loaded. If your dBASE has been programmed to escape from the Control Center, you will only see a dot above the highlighted status line. To get to the Control Center menu from the dot prompt, now or at any time, type and enter "assist." To see this, leave the Control Center by entering

F10   F10 Function key

→   Right arrow key, twice to highlight the <Exit> option. Note that <Exit to dot prompt> is already highlighted

◄┘   Enter key, to exit from the Control Center. Notice the absence of the menu and the presence of the dot prompt in the lower left corner

. assist   The dot command to return to the Control Center

◄┘   Enter key, to execute the short, but complete command line

The Control Center Menu

A user can operate dBASE IV from either the dot prompt, which is the command mode, or from the Control Center, which is the menu mode. The Control Center is actually the first in a series of menus which allow a user to perform most dBASE IV features. The Control Center is designed to make dBASE features more accessible for a beginner. Upon re-entering the Control Center, the menu again looks like Figure 1-2. The top line of the screen is called the menu bar and contains the names of several menus and a clock. Notice that <create> under Data is highlighted. On the row that begins with Data and ends with Applications are six types of files that can be created with the Control Center Menu: Data, Queries, Forms, Reports, Labels, and Applications. The area directly under each heading is referred to as a panel. The types of files identified by each panel are described in Figure 1-3. A user can move from panel to panel with the Right and Left arrow keys or the Tab and Shift-tab keys.

```
┌─────────────────────────────────────────────────────────────────────────┐
│ Catalog   Tools   Exit                                        9:37:54 am  │
│                         dBASE IV CONTROL CENTER                           │
│                                                                           │
│                     CATALOG:  C:\DBASE\SAMPLES.CAT                         │
│                                                                           │
│    Data        Queries       Forms       Reports      Labels   Applications│
│  ┌─────────┐ ┌─────────┐ ┌─────────┐ ┌─────────┐ ┌─────────┐ ┌─────────┐ │
│  │<create> │ │<create> │ │<create> │ │<create> │ │<create> │ │<create> │ │
│  │         │ │         │ │         │ │         │ │         │ │         │ │
│  │         │ │         │ │         │ │         │ │         │ │         │ │
│  │         │ │         │ │         │ │         │ │         │ │         │ │
│  │         │ │         │ │         │ │         │ │         │ │         │ │
│  └─────────┘ └─────────┘ └─────────┘ └─────────┘ └─────────┘ └─────────┘ │
│                                                                           │
│  File:        New file                                                    │
│  Description: Press ENTER on <create> to create a new file                │
│                                                                           │
│                                                                           │
│  Help:F1  Use:◄┘  Data:F2  Design:Shift-F2  Quick Report:Shift-F9  Menus:F10│
└─────────────────────────────────────────────────────────────────────────┘
```

Figure 1-2. The Control Center.

TYPE	DESCRIPTION
Data	Database files that store information about people, objects, events, etc.
Queries	Files that store instructions for manipulating data files.
Forms	Files that store customized screen displays for entering or viewing data.
Reports	Files that print reports on databases with customized headings, totals, and subtotals and other printing instructions.
Labels	Files that format and print labels.
Applications	Files that store complex programs for difficult tasks.

Figure 1-3. Types of dBASE IV Files.

At the bottom of the Control Center screen, is the message line. This line gives a list of currently available options. This is a very helpful line. At the far right end of the message line is "Menus:F10." This choice gives you access to the commands Catalog, Tools, and Exit found at the top of the screen. Type

F10   Function key F10, and the first choice on the menu bar is highlighted

The choices in the box below such as "Use a different catalog" and "Modify catalog name" comprise the submenu associated with Catalog. To see the submenus for the other menu bar choices, use the Right and Left arrow keys to move the cursor block over them. To move to an option on a submenu use the Up and Down arrow keys or type the first letter of the desired option. Typing the first letter of an option both highlights and executes that option.

Esc   Escape key, to return to the dBASE IV Control Center menu

Additional information on the Control Center includes the Catalog Name line (in some cases, C:\DBASE\SAMPLES.CAT, but this name may be different) and the File Name and Description lines (in this case, New file and **Press ENTER** on <create> to create a new file). The <create> option on the Data panel is highlighted. To select, or activate, a highlighted option use the Enter key.

◄┘   Enter key, to move to the database structure creation screen shown in Figure 1-4

Note the menu bar at the top of the screen changes as does the message line at the bottom of the screen. Three lines up from the bottom of the screen, you see the status bar (highlighted), followed by the navigation line. The status bar is divided into five sections. The first section tells you that you are using the Database screen of the Control Center. The second section shows the current, or default disk drive, directory path, and file name. The third section (currently Field 1/1) describes the location of the cursor. The fourth section (currently blank) shows which database file or view is the source of the underlying data. The last section (also blank) reflects the status of the Ins, Caps Lock, and Num Lock keys. The navigation line gives information about moving around the screen and selecting options.

Esc   Escape key. A box pops up with the prompt "Are you sure you want to abandon operation?"
Y   Y key, to return to the Control Center
F10   Function key F10, to move up to the menu bar

Use the Left and Right arrow keys to move around the menu bar. Observe how the information at the bottom of the screen, as well as the location and contents of the menu boxes change. Some of the menus are not available until there is a database file in use. These are not highlighted and cannot be invoked. Whenever dBASE displays choices with low intensity, those choices cannot be selected. Monochrome monitors whose contrast and brightness are not adjusted properly may not show differences in intensity.

If the Num Lock key is on, the arrow keys (cursor keys) do not work. So, if these keys do not cause the highlighted area to move in the expected direction, press the Num Lock key once to toggle Num Lock off.

NOTATION

As will be seen, several options from several menus may appear on the screen and may be highlighted at the same time. It is important that you have all the correct choices highlighted before pressing the Enter key. To ensure clarity, the following notation shall be used. The option to be highlighted is surrounded by < and >. When the Enter key must be pressed, it is denoted by ◄┘ . Thus,

<Catalog>

means highlight the menu choice Catalog using the cursor keys, but do not press the Enter key.

<Catalog>
<Use a different catalog>
◄┘

means highlight the menu choice Catalog and the submenu choice Use a different catalog, and then press the Enter key. Do not press this now. If you did press the Escape key to return to the Control Center.

CHANGING THE DEFAULT DRIVE

You are probably accessing dBASE from a hard disk drive on your own system or on a file server. Often system managers attempt to reserve as much hard drive storage as possible for applications programs and require that user files be stored on floppy disks. If you are to save your files on a floppy disk, you have to change the default drive. Do this by entering,

F10   Function key F10, to access the menu
<Tools>
<DOS utilities>
◄─┘   Enter key, to obtain a new menu
F10   Function key, to access the new menu
<Files>
<Change drive:directory>   {C:}
                       The Change drive option displays the default drive as being drive C(:). The default drive
                       designation may differ for computers on a network
◄─┘   Enter key, to obtain the prompt,

                              Drive:Directory:<u>C</u>:
A   Change to drive A
◄─┘   Enter key. The Status line now displays A: as the default drive
F10   Function key F10, to access the menu
<Exit>   Exit the Tool menu
◄─┘   Enter key, to return to the Control Center

CREATING A DATABASE STRUCTURE

The development of a database is an operation initiated under the Data panel of the Control Center. Execute the following to begin this operation:

<Create>   On the Data panel
◄─┘   Enter key

After several seconds delay, the screen shown in Figure 1-4 appears.

This screen enables you to describe the structure of the records to be held by the database which is temporarily called NEW on the status line. The structure of a record consists of a complete list of field names composing each record within the database, the type of data that can be entered in that field of the record, the width of the field, including decimal places, if any, and a note to indicate whether the field is to be used as an index field. A programmer's identification number and a programmer's rank are examples of two fields. As the fields are filled with data, a complete record is created. The records that are stored together form a database.

Note that the status line indicates that the database panel is in use. The navigation line tells you that a field name is to be typed. This line changes as the cursor is moved. The message line changes to tell you what type of data can be entered.

```
 Layout    Organize    Append    Go To    Exit                    9:48:18 am

                                                       Bytes remaining:    4000
 ┌─────┬───────────┬───────────┬───────┬─────┬─────────┐
 │ Num │ Field Name│ Field Type│ Width │ Dec │ Index   │
 ├─────┼───────────┼───────────┼───────┼─────┼─────────┤
 │  1  │           │ Character │       │     │    N    │
 │     │           │           │       │     │         │
 │     │           │           │       │     │         │
 │     │           │           │       │     │         │
 │     │           │           │       │     │         │
 │     │           │           │       │     │         │
 │     │           │           │       │     │         │
 │     │           │           │       │     │         │
 │     │           │           │       │     │         │
 │     │           │           │       │     │         │
 └─────┴───────────┴───────────┴───────┴─────┴─────────┘
 Database B:\<NEW>                      Field 1/1
          Enter the field name. Insert/Delete field:Ctrl-N/Ctrl-U
 Field names begin with a letter and may contain letters, digits and underscores
```

Figure 1-4. Data Structure Definition Screen.

Create the database in the following manner:

Caps Lock	Put Caps Lock on. If you did not, dBASE would automatically put the characters typed into uppercase anyway.
PROGR_NAME	The first field name. If you make a typing error, the Delete, Backspace, and arrow keys can be used to delete characters and to move the cursor. The text completely fills the 10 spaces allowable for a field name. A beep is heard to signify that the space is filled and the cursor automatically moves to the Field Type area.
Space Bar	Pressing the Space Bar steps you through the valid choices for field types. You can select the correct choice by finding the choice you want and then pressing the Enter key, or you can simply press the first character of the choice you wish to make. For example, you would press an N for numeric, an M for memo, etc.
C	To designate PROGR_NAME as a character field
15	The field width
◄⌐	Enter key. Since the field is of type character, the decimal request is bypassed.
◄⌐	Enter key. This leaves an N in the Index area. Typing a Y in this Index area causes dBASE to create a Production Index file. Indexes are discussed later in this chapter.
CLIENT_ID	The second field name. This field name does not fill the block, so the cursor does not automatically advance to the field type block.
◄⌐	Enter key, to accept the field name
C	Select the type as character
4	Select the width as 4
◄⌐	Enter key, to accept the 4 as the field width

◄┘   Enter key, to avoid decimal places
◄┘   Enter key, to leave the N in the Index area

Continue by entering four additional fields in the same way. The fields are:

JOB_ID, Character, 4 characters in width
JOB_TITLE, Character, 18 characters in width
HRS, Numeric, 4 characters in width, 1 decimal place
COMPLETED, Logical, 1 character wide (automatic default)

When you are finished, the screen appears as it does in Figure 1-5.

```
 Layout    Organize    Append    Go To    Exit                    9:48:18 am

                                                     Bytes remaining:    3954
 ┌──────┬────────────┬────────────┬───────┬─────┬───────┐
 │ Num  │ Field Name │ Field Type │ Width │ Dec │ Index │
 ├──────┼────────────┼────────────┼───────┼─────┼───────┤
 │  1   │ PROG_NAME  │ Character  │  15   │     │   N   │
 │  2   │ CLIENT_ID  │ Character  │   4   │     │   N   │
 │  3   │ JOB_ID     │ Character  │   4   │     │   N   │
 │  4   │ JOB_TITLE  │ Character  │  18   │     │   N   │
 │  5   │ HRS        │ Numeric    │   4   │  1  │   N   │
 │  6   │ COMPLETED  │ Logical    │   1   │     │   N   │
 │  7   │            │ Character  │       │     │   N   │
 └──────┴────────────┴────────────┴───────┴─────┴───────┘
 Database C:\<NEW>                      Field 7/7
         Enter the field name. Insert/Delete field:Ctrl-N/Ctrl-U
 Field names begin with a letter and may contain letters, digits and underscores
```

Figure 1-5. Completed Structure Definition Screen

MODIFYING THE DATABASE STRUCTURE

Cursor Movements

The arrow keys can move the cursor nondestructively. That is, they move the cursor without changing any of the contents of the fields. Similarly, the Control-Right and Control-Left arrow keys move the cursor to the beginning or end of a field. If the cursor is already at the edge of the field it advances to the next field. The Home and End keys pan the screen. In a database with a large number of fields, you may not be able to see all of the fields and it may take too long to move the cursor from one field to the next by moving one field at a time. Panning moves the cursor in larger jumps. Practice the movement keys.

Changing Entries

The Insert key functions as it does in WordPerfect. Normally, dBASE is operating in overwrite mode. If you type characters or numbers, what you type replaces the characters and numbers that the cursor passes over. The pressing of the Insert key changes dBASE to insert mode and the characters are inserted at the location of the cursor. Characters to the right are pushed to the right and may be deleted if there is inadequate space to contain all of the characters entered.

The Delete key deletes characters above the cursor. The Backspace key deletes characters to the left of the cursor.

Change the field name COMPLETED to DONE and HRS to HRS_WORKED.   Alter the width of PROGR_NAME to 13.

Addition of New Fields

If you press Control-N, a new field is added between the field above the cursor and the field that contains the cursor. Move the cursor so that it is on the field name DONE. Add two other fields with

Ctrl-N	To insert a new field between HRS_WORKED and DONE
WORK_DATE	The new field's name
◄┘	Enter key
D	To select the **Date** field type. A width of 8 is inserted by default
◄┘	Enter key, to leave an N in the Index area

Move the cursor to the field name HRS_WORKED and enter

Ctrl-N	To insert a new field between HRS_WORKED and JOB_TITLE
JUNK	The new field's name
◄┘	Enter key
C	To select the **Character** field type
7	The field width
◄┘	Enter key, to complete the field
◄┘	Enter key, to leave an N in the Index area

Since Ctrl-N inserts a field between two other fields, it cannot be used to append a ninth field behind the last field. The appending of a field is easily accomplished by pressing the Down arrow until a vacant ninth field is displayed. Do this and enter

NOTES	The new field name
◄┘	Enter key
M	To select the **Memo** field type. A width of 10 is displayed by default, but the actual contents of the memo field can be much larger.

Deletion of Fields

As long as you have not saved the structure, you can change the contents of each field's definition by typing over characters which are shown. Control-U would remove the field that the cursor is seen in. Eliminate the field called JUNK by placing your cursor on the field name JUNK and pressing

Ctrl-U	To delete the field

If you make an error, remember to use Control-N to reinsert a field that can be used to replace the deleted field. You cannot recall a deleted field. All of the values for name, type, and width have to be re-entered.

Control-Y would clear a field space. It does not delete the entire field. Delete one field name and replace it by retyping the entry.

The field definitions should now look like those in Figure 1-6 (though the line form filed number 9 may not appear on your screen).

```
 Layout    Organize    Append    Go To    Exit              9:48:18 am

                                                    Bytes remaining:    3938

 ┌─────┬────────────┬────────────┬───────┬─────┬───────┐
 │ Num │ Field Name │ Field Type │ Width │ Dec │ Index │
 ├─────┼────────────┼────────────┼───────┼─────┼───────┤
 │  1  │ PROG_NAME  │ Character  │  13   │     │   N   │
 │  2  │ CLIENT_ID  │ Character  │   4   │     │   N   │
 │  3  │ JOB_ID     │ Character  │   4   │     │   N   │
 │  4  │ JOB_TITLE  │ Character  │  18   │     │   N   │
 │  5  │ HRS_WORKED │ Numeric    │   4   │  1  │   N   │
 │  6  │ WORK_DATE  │ Date       │   8   │     │   N   │
 │  7  │ DONE       │ Logical    │   1   │     │   N   │
 │  8  │ NOTES      │ Memo       │  10   │     │   N   │
 │  9  │            │ Character  │       │     │   N   │
 └─────┴────────────┴────────────┴───────┴─────┴───────┘

 Database C:\<NEW>              Field 9/9
        Enter the field name. Insert/Delete field:Ctrl-N/Ctrl-U
 Field names begin with a letter and may contain letters, digits and underscores
```

Figure 1-6. Completed Structure Definition Screen

Exiting

When your database structure has been correctly defined, it is saved by pressing the Control-End key combination. If, for some reason, you decide not to save the structure, you can press the Escape key. The Escape key cancels the operation and forces you to start over.

Save the structure for the JOBS database by entering

Ctrl-End   To exit the Definition screen. You are now asked to supply a file name for the database. You receive the prompt "Save as: "
JOBS   The name of the Database file to contain the billing records
◄┘   Enter key, to name and save the structure

ADDING RECORDS

Immediately upon saving a database structure, dBASE prompts you with

Input data records now? (Y/N) _

Respond with Y. The database structure definition screen disappears and a form for data input appears. Each of the field names appears in the order that they appear in the database structure. Highlighting that is precisely as wide as the field's width also appears. The cursor is in the first field. In the third section of the status line, the display Rec 1/1 appears, which means you are adding the first record to the database. As records are added the display changes, for example, to Rec 12/12, which means that dBASE is working on record 12 out of 12 records. It might also show Rec EOF/24 which means that you are at the end-of-file, perhaps adding records, and that there are already 24 records in the database.

Text and numbers can now be entered. As you enter data, if the data completely fills the field, dBASE beeps and automatically advance the cursor to the next field. You only have to press the Enter key if the field entry is shorter than the field width. With the cursor at the beginning of the first field, enter the following information inside of the fields. Do not type the brackets or the slashes. The NOTES field already shows the word memo. Do not enter it again.

```
PROGR_NAME          [Jones, M.   ]
CLIENT_ID           [ 127]
JOB_ID              [1502]
JOB_TITLE           [Accounts Payable  ]
HRS_WORKED          [7.5]
WORK_DATE           [05/01/90]
DONE                [N]
NOTES               [memo]
```

When you press the Enter key in the last field, dBASE automatically enters the record into the database and provides a new form for completion. This and future records are inserted in the database when you do the following:

1.   press the PgDn or PgUp keys;
2.   enter data in the last column of the last field, if it is not a memo field;
3.   press the End or the Enter key anywhere in the last field.

Character fields left-justify their contents, while numeric fields right-justify their contents. A date field automatically provides two slashes to separate the numbers for the month, day, and year. Pressing the Enter key on a blank numeric field automatically inserts a zero. The memo field will not be used now.

If you make any mistakes during data entry, you can edit the contents of the fields in much the same way that you made changes when you created the database structure. The Home, End, and arrow keys allow you to move the cursor. The Delete and Backspace keys delete characters above or to the left of the cursor, while Control-Y and Control-U delete the contents of the field and mark the record for deletion, respectively. The Insert key toggles the editor between insert and overwrite mode. If you have not yet done so, press

◄┘   Enter key, to enter the record and to receive the next blank entry form.

Continue by adding the next record.

```
PROGR_NAME  [Jones, M.    ]
CLIENT_ID   [ 127]
JOB_ID      [1502]
JOB_TITLE   [Accounts Payable ]
HRS_WORKED  [8.0]
WORK_DATE   [05/02/90]
DONE        [N]
NOTES       [memo]
```

If there are any errors, edit the record to make it correct. Whenever you finish and wish to enter more records, press the PgDn or Enter key. The information for the remaining nineteen records is displayed in tabular form, not as screen entries. Each row of data contains the entries for a complete record.

It is easy to accidentally exit from adding records. Pressing the Enter key on an empty first field of the new record transfers control back to the Control Center. The pressing of the Escape key also aborts the operation. If you exit the append operation, to continue where you left off, read the Appending Records section below. Make the following field entries:

PROG_NAME	CLIENT_ID	JOB_ID	JOB_TITLE	HRS_WORKED	WORK_DATE	DONE
Doe, F.	115	1436	Property Managemnt	7.6	05/02/90	N
Doe, F.	115	1436	Property Managemnt	7.3	05/03/90	Y
White, Q.	142	1601	Income Statement	3.5	05/10/90	Y
Grey, Y.	131	1575	Software Install	6.8	05/08/90	N
Brown, R.	135	1575	Software Install	3.2	05/15/90	N
White, Q.	118	1440	Lease Managemnt	5.7	05/17/90	N
White, Q.	127	1502	Accounts Payable	5.8	05/21/90	N
Jones, M.	135	1585	Labels Program	3.5	05/14/90	Y
Jones, M.	142	1595	Depreciation Prgm	2.3	05/21/90	N
Doe, F.	127	1502	Accounts Payable	3.6	05/09/90	N
Doe, F.	127	1503	Accounts Receiv.	4.7	05/16/90	Y
Doe, F.	118	1440	Lease Management	4.7	05/09/90	Y
Grey, Y.	131	1575	Software Install	5.2	05/09/90	Y
White, Q.	127	1502	Accounts Payable	5.8	05/23/90	N
White, Q.	142	1596	Employee Database	8.0	06/04/90	N
Grey, Y.	115	1435	Maintenance D.B.	8.0	05/23/90	Y
Grey, Y.	115	1435	Maintenance D.B.	3.8	05/31/90	Y
Doe, F.	115	1436	Property Managemnt	7.0	06/02/90	Y
Jones, M.	135	1586	Amortization Sched.	5.3	06/01/90	Y

When you have completed entering the 21 records, the status line displays Rec 22/22 and you receive another empty form. If you have the need to, you can return to earlier records by pressing the PgUp key. Without moving the cursor past the first character position in the first field, press

↵   Enter key, to stop entering records and to return to the Control Center. Notice that the file name line displays JOBS.DBF as the database that is in use.

QUICK REPORT

Viewing Records

Having created the database, you now can have dBASE list the records as confirmation that the database has, in fact, been created. With the filename JOBS highlighted in the Data panel of the Control Center, type

Shift-F9   The shift key and the F9 function key, for Quick Report
<View report on screen>
◄┘   Enter key, to create a report

The Quick Report is too long to fit on one screen. Press the Space bar several times to see all the records. When the report is complete you are returned to the Control Center.

Printing Records

Once the records scroll by, their data can only be read by issuing the viewing records command again. You must print the records to see all of the information entered. To print the report you would have selected <Begin Printing> instead of <View report on screen>.

Shift-F9   The shift key and the F9 function key, for Quick Report
<Begin Printing>
◄┘   Enter key, to create a report. This procedure takes time to complete

The fields are still wrapped around. You can see that the Quick Report totaled all numeric fields. Portions of the report are shown in Figure 1-7.

```
Page No.    1
12/01/90

PROGR_NAME    CLIENT_ID  JOB_ID   JOB_TITLE              HRS_WORKED   WORK_DATE   DONE NOTES

Jones, M.          127     1502    Accounts Payable          7.5      05/01/90     N
Jones, M.          127     1502    Accounts Payable          8.0      05/02/90     N
Doe, F.            115     1436    Property Managemnt        7.6      05/02/90     N
Doe, F.            115     1436    Property Managemnt        7.3      05/03/90     Y
*************************************************************************************

*************************************************************************************
Grey, Y.           115     1435    Maintenance D.B.          3.8      05/31/90     Y
Doe, F.            115     1436    Property Managemnt        7.0      06/02/90     Y
Jones, M.          135     1586    Amortization Sched        5.3      06/01/90     Y
                                                           117.3
```

Figure 1-7. Quick Report Format

Another method of seeing the records is to go to the dot prompt and use the LIST command.

F10   Function key F10, to call the menu
<Exit>
<Exit to the dot prompt>
◄┘   Enter key, to move to the dot prompt
LIST

◄┘   To list the records. See Figure 1-8 for sample output.

```
Record#  PROGR_NAME    CLIENT_ID  JOB_ID  JOB_TITLE              HRS_WORKED  WORK_DATE  DONE  NO
     1   Jones, M.          127    1502   Accounts Payable            7.5   05/01/90   .F.   mem
     2   Jones, M.          127    1502   Accounts Payable            8.0   05/02/90   .F.   mem
     3   Doe, F.            115    1436   Property Managemnt          7.6   05/02/90   .F.   mem
     4   Doe, F.            115    1436   Property Management         7.3   05/03/90   .T.   mem

*************************************************************************************

*************************************************************************************
    19   Grey, Y.           115    1435   Maintenance D.B.            3.8   05/31/90   .T.   mem
    20   Doe, F.            115    1436   Property Managemnt          7.0   06/02/90   .T.   mem
    21   Jones, M.          135    1586   Amortization Sched          5.3   06/01/90   .T.   mem
```

Figure 1-8. List Command Format

As the records are listed, the fields for each record are printed horizontally and the data for each field's data appears in the same column. Since the amount of space required for the fields and for spaces between columns is greater than eighty character columns, the width of your screen, there is a wrap-around effect that makes records take up more than one line on your screen. A printer with wide paper could print out the records on one line.

In addition to the data which you entered, notice that the first column includes a record number maintained by dBASE. The next to last column displays periods around the T or F in the field because the Y and N that you entered were converted to either true or false. The final field is a memo field which, even if data had been entered would not be printed out. If the memo field contained any information the word memo would be printed in uppercase and appear as MEMO.

        Enter

assist
◄┘   Enter key, to return to the Control Center

LISTING TO THE PRINTER

Obtain a printed copy of the database by returning to the dot prompt and executing the last set of commands but replace the LIST dot command with LIST TO PRINT. The LIST command does not total the numeric fields.

APPENDING RECORDS

Records can be added through the function key menu choice, Design: Shift-F2. New records are placed at the end of the file, not in the middle of the database. The ordering of records can only be accomplished by sorting and indexing, not by manually attempting to insert them at certain locations in the database.
        To reach the dBASE Append menu, use the following commands:

Shift-F2   To call the design menu
<Append>
<Enter records from keyboard>

        The screen appears as shown in Figure 1-9.

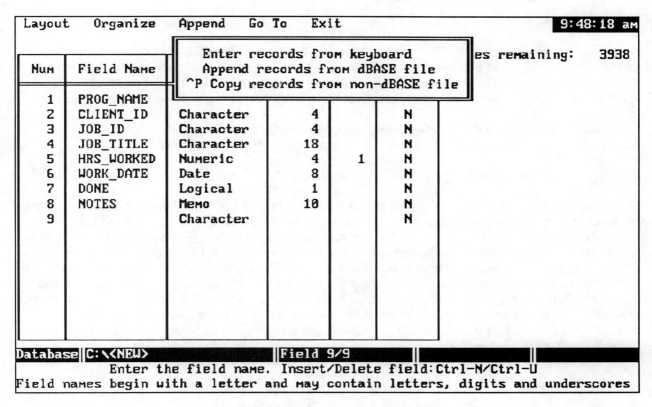

Layout	Organize	Append	Go To	Exit			9:48:18 am

```
┌─────────────────────────────────────────────┐
│          Enter records from keyboard         │
│          Append records from dBASE file      │  es remaining:    3938
│       ^P Copy records from non-dBASE file    │
└─────────────────────────────────────────────┘
```

Num	Field Name				
1	PROG_NAME				
2	CLIENT_ID	Character	4		N
3	JOB_ID	Character	4		N
4	JOB_TITLE	Character	18		N
5	HRS_WORKED	Numeric	4	1	N
6	WORK_DATE	Date	8		N
7	DONE	Logical	1		N
8	NOTES	Memo	10		N
9		Character			N

Database C:\<NEW>   Field 9/9

Enter the field name. Insert/Delete field:Ctrl-N/Ctrl-U
Field names begin with a letter and may contain letters, digits and underscores

Figure 1-9. The Append Menu

◂┘   To call up the data entry screen

The status line reflects that you are appending records to the JOBS database. 22/22 means that a pointer into the database is at record number 22, which is below the bottom of the existing database file. This is the default entry screen. dBASE allows the user to customize the screen for entering and editing records (see Customizing the Screen). Now add five records to the database. Remember that pressing Enter on the NOTES field automatically advances dBASE to the next empty form. Check and correct your entries before pressing Enter (or return to entered records with the PgUp key).

PROGR_NAME	CLIENT_ID	JOB_ID	JOB_TITLE	HRS_WORKED	WORK_DATE	DONE
Doe, F.	131	1434	Spreadsheets	4.5	06/04/90	Y
Jones, M.	135	1586	Sort Routine	5.2	06/01/90	N
Jones, M.	142	1587	Rolling Stock Inv	8.0	06/10/90	Y
Grey, Y.	131	1585	Payroll D.B.	6.8	05/30/90	N
Grey, Y.	131	1585	Payroll D.B.	5.2	06/02/90	Y

When you have received the empty entry form for another record, press

◂┘   Enter key, to avoid entering a blank record into the database and to return to the
           Append menu
<Exit>
<Save changes and exit>
◂┘   Enter key, to save changes and return to the Control Center

EDITING RECORDS

Frequently, it is necessary to change the data in individual records after they have been entered. Changes may be required because field entries were entered incorrectly and because the information may change over time. For instance, in a telephone directory, a person's address and telephone number may change when he or she moves. Editing is initiated from the function key menu choice, Data:F2.

Change some of the data in the existing records to illustrate how to edit the contents of record fields. With the filename JOBS highlighted in the Data area of the Control Center enter

F2   Function key F2, the Data:F2 choice to call the Edit screen

Note the presence of Edit on the left end of the status line. If the word Browse is displayed at the left end of the status line, pressing the F2 key again switches to the Edit screen. Once the Edit screen has been called, pressing F2 toggles back and forth between the Edit and Browse screens (the Browse feature is discussed in Chapter 3: Changing Records with Browse). Press F2 until the status line of the entry screen says EDIT and the current record is displayed. The current record is the record that the file pointer is positioned on. If the pointer is at the bottom of the file, the last record number is displayed. Keys function the same way in Edit as they do in Append. If you use the PgDn while on the last record or the Enter or Down arrow key while in the last field of the last record, you see a prompt "Add new records? (Y/N)." If you respond with a Y, a blank record appears. If you respond with an N, you return to the first field of the last record.

Use the PgUp and PgDn keys to locate and then to change the following records:

1. Record 4: Change JOB_ID to 1437; JOB_TITLE to Tenant List;
2. Record 10: Change HRS_WORKED to 5.3; JOB_TITLE to Mailing List
3. Record 15: Change PROGR_NAME to Doe, F.; HRS_WORKED to 5.7
4. Record 20: Change CLIENT_ID to 7; JOB_ID to 1502; JOB_TITLE to Accounts Payable; HRS_WORKED to 3.6; WORK_DATE to 05/09/90; DONE to N.

Correct any other data that was incorrectly entered in your database.

Ctrl-End   To return to the Control Center

MARKING RECORDS FOR DELETION

Often whole records in a database must be removed. For instance, if a car is sold, its record would be removed from an inventory database. If a duplicate record is entered, one of the copies must be removed.

The deletion of records in dBASE is a 2-step process. In Edit, or in Browse, you mark a record for deletion. dBASE does not actually delete any records until specifically told to do so. That way, if you should accidentally mark a record for deletion, you can recall it as long as you haven't completed the second step and erased the marked records. Once the marked records are erased they are gone and cannot be recalled.

Record 20 was edited. It is now a duplicate of record 12. One of the records should be deleted so the programmer is not paid twice for the same hours. To delete record 12 make sure the data file name JOBS is highlighted and press

F2   Function key F2, to call the Edit screen from the Data choice on the function key menu

PgUp or PgDn	Until the pointer is positioned on record number 12. Watch the record number on the status line.
F10	Function key F10, to call the Records menu

\<Records\>
\<Mark record for deletion\>

◄┘	Return key, to mark record and return to edit screen. Notice the Del indicator appear in the sixth section of the status line. The presence of Del shows that this record is marked for deletion.
PgUp	PgUp to move to record number 11
F10	Function key F10, to call the records menu
F10	Function key F10, to execute the \<Mark record for deletion\> choice. Record 11 is now marked for deletion.
F10	Function key F10, to recall the records menu. Note that now the \<Clear deletion mark\> is highlighted.
F10	Function key F10, to execute the \<Clear deletion mark\> choice

A second way to mark records for deletion is by pressing **Ctrl-U**.

Ctrl-U	Ctrl key and U key, note that record number 11 is again marked for deletion
Ctrl-U	Ctrl key and U key, a second time and unmark record 11

To return to the Command Center press

F10	To call the menus

\<Exit\>
\<Exit\>

◄┘	Enter key, to return to the Command Center

PACKING THE DATABASE

If you were to list the database as described under the Listing the Records section (and you are encouraged to do so), record 12 would continue to be displayed. An asterisk would appear next to the record number, however, to indicate that it has been marked for deletion. To remove the record, enter

\<Shift F2\>	To call the design menu

\<Organize\>
\<Erase marked records\>

◄┘	Enter key, a prompt appears asking "Are you sure you want to erase all marked records?"
Y	Y key, to answer Yes. The database is packed, removing all records marked for deletion. A message, "25 records copied," shows how many records remain. You are returned to the database structure definition screen.
F10	To call the menu

\<Exit\>
\<Save changes and exit\>

◄┘	Enter key, control is returned to the Control Center

PRINTING THE DATABASE

List the database to the printer.

Shift-F9   Quick report
<Begin printing>
◄─┘   Enter key, to begin printing

      To list the database from the dot prompt

F10
<Exit>
<Exit to dot prompt>
◄─┘   Enter key, to move to the dot prompt
list to print
◄─┘   Direct the listing to the printer. Notice that the listing is routed to the screen as well as to
                the printer. The dot prompt appears when the listing is complete.
F2   Function key F2, to return to the Command Center

EXITING dBASE IV

To leave dBASE IV, press

F10   Function key F10, to get the function key menu
<Exit>
<Quit to DOS>
◄─┘

dBASE closes all open files and transfers control back to DOS. Do not just turn off the machine to exit
since information could be lost if the files are not properly closed.

BACKING UP YOUR FILE

Database records are stored to a file one at a time, unlike WordPerfect and Lotus which replace an
entire file when the file is saved. There is no single file save procedure. Backup your database files by
using the DOS copy command. Move to the directory where your database file is stored. Place your
backup diskette in drive A.

copy jobs.* a:
◄─┘   Enter key

This action saves the database file JOBS which has had the extension .DBF assigned by dBASE. It also
saves a file JOBS.DBT which contains any memo filed entries that have been or will be entered in the
NOTES field. To copy all files in your data directory to drive A (but be sure that you want all of the files
in this directory to overwrite those on drive A), enter

copy *.* a:

EXERCISES

A. A central services department for a small corporation is responsible for carrying out services that are charged back to departments. These services are putting postage on mail, distributing the telephone charges that are sent on the monthly bill, duplicating charges for printing, xeroxing, mimeographing, etc., and distributing supplies of varying types. Create a database called SERVICES and enter the following records:

```
Numeric, width 4, 0 decimal places
|       Numeric, width 3, 0 decimal places
|       |       Numeric, width 4, 0 decimal places
|       |       |       Character, width 17, 0 decimal places
|       |       |       |               Numeric, width of 7, decimals 2
|       |       |       |               |
|       |       |       |               |
INV     DEPT    CODE    DESCRIPT         CHARGE
```

INV	DEPT	CODE	DESCRIPT	CHARGE
1940	101	1100	Postage	55.39
1941	102	1100	Postage	27.80
1942	103	1100	Postage	32.70
1943	104	1100	Postage	19.75
1944	104	1200	Telephone (Base)	278.23
1945	102	1200	Telephone (Base)	125.19
1946	103	1200	Telephone (Base)	99.56
1947	104	1200	Telephone (Base)	156.27
1948	101	1400	Duplicating	23.19
1949	101	1400	Duplicating	19.80
1950	102	1400	Duplicating	17.90
1951	103	1400	Duplicating	89.95
1952	101	1400	Duplicating	27.80
1953	102	1400	Duplicating	95.45
1954	102	1400	Duplicating	52.00
1955	101	1300	Telephone (LD)	79.34
1956	102	1300	Telephone (LD)	377.10
1957	103	1300	Telephone (LD)	95.45
1958	104	1300	Telephone (LD)	47.01
1959	104	1500	Supplies	55.55
1960	104	1500	Supplies	98.50
1961	101	1500	Supplies	67.77
1962	102	1500	Supplies	34.56
1963	101	1500	Supplies	33.45
1964	103	1500	Supplies	145.66
1965	103	1500	Supplies	90.30

1. After you have created the database, print it out. Return to the Control Center. Use the Append menu to add the following records:

INV	DEPT	CODE	DESCRIPT	CHARGE
1966	101	1400	Duplicating	27.80
1967	102	1500	Supplies	113.45
1968	104	1300	Telephone (LD)	54.55

2. Modify record number 5 by changing the department to 101. Modify record number 10 to have a
    CODE of 1100 and a description of POSTAGE. Mark record number 7 and the record with
    INVOICE number 1961 for deletion . Erase the marked records. Display the revised database on
    the screen. List it to the printer.

    This database is used again in the exercises of later chapters.

B. A principal of a small school has had a roster of the school's faculty typed up. After reviewing the
    roster, the principal decided to have the list put into a database so that the list could be analyzed
    and updated regularly. Create a database called ROSTER with the following records:

Character, width 25
| Character, width 10
| | Character, width 10
| | | Character, width 1
| | | | Numeric, width 10, 0 decimals
| | | | |
NAME   RANK   DEPARTMENT   SEX   SALARY

NAME	RANK	DEPARTMENT	SEX	SALARY
Nabbort, Nathan	Associate	Humanities	M	35000
Bartone, Barry	Professor	Humanities	M	36700
Raster, Ronald	Associate	Humanities	M	31200
March, Marcia	Associate	Humanities	F	39800
Yarrow, Yancy	Associate	Humanities	M	35600
Franelly, Fred	Lecturer	Humanities	M	20050
Abell, Ana	Associate	Humanities	F	38200
Dyson, Diana	Associate	Math	F	36500
Wilke, Warren	Lecturer	Math	M	23450
Jonesburgher, Jack	Lecturer	Math	M	21400
Quarren, Quinella	Associate	Math	F	35900
Smitty, Samuel	Assistant	Phys. Ed.	M	24550
Lochner, Louise	Associate	Phys. Ed.	F	32500
Orran, Ophelia	Assistant	Phys. Ed.	F	28400
Harberson, Harold	Professor	Science	M	37120
Cransmann, Carlita	Assistant	Science	F	29500
Zarronne, Zelda	Professor	Science	F	40200
Parsons, Paul	Assistant	Science	M	23500
Walters, William	Assistant	Science	M	23200
Arbor, Alan	Instructor	Social Sci.	M	31250
Michelson, Maria	Instructor	Social Sci.	F	27100
Garber, Gretel	Professor	Social Sci.	F	41050
Valour, Valerie	Instructor	Social Sci.	F	23400
Teather, Terry	Assistant	Social Sci.	F	31500
Kristiane, Katherine	Professor	Social Sci.	F	40500

1. Print the database. Add the following records:

NAME	RANK	DEPARTMENT	SEX	SALARY
Beasley, Brenda	Associate	Social Sci	F	36500
Tefford, Thomas	Professor	Science	M	37700
Sedge, Samantha	Associate	Humanities	F	33300

2. Modify Ronald Raster's record by increasing his salary to 32600 and change Quinella Quarren's name to Quinella Harberson.
3. Mark record number 5 and the record with the NAME, Terry Teather, for deletion. Erase these records from the database.
4. Display the revised database. This database is used again in later chapters.

C. A small distributor of software obtains its software from a variety of small companies. It sells this software to computer stores. It has a small inventory that is to be kept on a computerized database. Create the database in a file named SOFTWARE, with the following data:

PRODUCT	MFR	PRCH_PRICE	NUM_BOUGHT	LAST_PRCH	REORDER
Mouser	XYZ Software	18.75	41	03/10/90	N
Space Flier	Barton Inc.	15.75	35	04/01/90	Y
Wood Drill	Daisy Products	19.00	17	02/14/90	Y
Cross Word	Barton Inc.	15.00	20	02/20/90	Y
Accounts Receiv.	QR Bookkeeping	49.00	20	12/30/89	Y
Mail Labeler	QR Bookkeeping	49.00	41	12/30/89	N
Space Squad	XYZ Software	17.00	70	04/01/90	N
My Money Mgr.	Daisy Products	22.50	22	10/11/89	N
Fast Spreadsheet	Cybernetics	27.00	11	01/02/90	N
Accounts Payable	QR Bookkeeping	52.00	49	03/19/90	N
Atom Smasher	Frank Assoc.	12.75	61	04/15/90	N
Expert File	Mountain Inc.	75.00	12	01/15/90	N
Time Scheduler	Mountain Inc.	32.00	79	02/02/90	N
Appointment	Keyboard Inc.	30.50	15	01/02/90	Y
Keeper	Wild Daisy Inc.	21.00	7	02/10/90	Y
Word Analizer	XYZ Software	16.25	16	03/19/90	N
Caves and Captors	Barton's Mfr.	15.60	20	04/01/90	Y
Sea Captain	QR Bookkeeping	58.50	19	02/02/90	Y
Report Writer III	Programmer's Inc.	78.00	51	12/15/89	N
Fast Coder	XYZ Software	17.50	20	11/15/89	N
Whale Hunter	Programmer's Inc.	59.00	12	03/09/90	Y
Program Generator	Graff Maker	23.50	50	02/20/90	N
Font Styler	Graph Maker	43.45	13	11/10/89	Y
Picture Book	Phillips Ltd.	225.90	52	11/10/89	N
Grid Display	H.D.T. Software	122.50	93	01/10/90	N
Card Filer	The Associates	305.00	42	04/01/90	N
Maxitext	C & I Associates	255.00	81	04/01/90	N
Data Works					

1. After the database has been created, print it. Display it to the screen. Then print it in its entirety.
    Add the following records.

Maxicalc	The Associates	196.78	20	03/15/88	Y
The Projector	S & S Associates	225.00	56	01/10/88	N
Text Editor	Jony Associates	98.99	19	03/19/88	N

2. Modify the spelling of Graff to Graph. Change the price of Data Works to 225.00 and the
    manufacturer of Sea Captain to Garage Data Inc.
3. Mark record number 13 as well as the record for Caves and Captors for deletion. Mark record 10
    and the record with the PRODUCT displayed as Card Filer for deletion. Erase these records from
    the database.
4. Display the database to the screen. List the revised database to the printer. This database is
    reused in the exercises in later chapters.

Chapter 2

More on Databases

Chapter Outline

In this chapter you extend your knowledge of how to create and manipulate databases. The database you construct in this chapter offers the opportunity for you to

1. Create a second database;
2. Locate records in the database by using the contents of record fields, by using record numbers, and by moving to the top and bottom of the database;
3. Create a file of sorted records;
4. Locate records in a sorted file using uppercase searches, multiple conditions, and scope conditions;
5. Index a file and use the seek search technique to find a record rapidly;
6. Employ complex expressions.

INTRODUCTION

Computer Software Associates needs to keep a master list of its client companies. It could then produce mailing lists and, eventually, integrate this database with the jobs database to produce billings for the clients. The new database is to include the data that is now kept on a telephone card file. The hand-kept forms look like

Client Id <u>115</u>

Client Name <u>Acme Realty</u>

Street Addr. <u>100 Elm Street</u>

City <u>Wellston</u>

State <u>Nv</u>

Zip Code <u>19870</u>

Figure 2-1. Fields on the File Card

Computer Software Associates currently has fifteen active clients, but the list has periodic additions and deletions.

CREATING THE DATABASE

After booting your computer move to the directory where dBase is installed and enter

dbase	The command to begin loading dBASE
◄┘	Enter key, to execute the command
◄┘	Enter key to acknowledge the dBASE copyright. The Control Center menu appears.
<Create>	Select Create in the Data panel
◄┘	Enter key. The structure definition screen appears.

Review the procedure for creating a database structure in the preceding chapter. Proceed to define the following fields and field lengths.

CLIENT_ID, Numeric, 4, 0 decimal places, Not an index field
CLT_NAME, Character, 20, Not an index field
STREET, Character, 15, Not an index field
CITY, Character, 10, Not an index field
STATE, Character, 2, Not an index field
ZIP, Numeric, 5, 0 decimal places, Not an index field
TELEPHONE, Character, 8, Not an index field

Check the definitions you have entered. If any of the field names, types, and lengths are incorrect, correct them. When all the fields have been properly defined, type

Ctrl_End	To complete the creation of the database structure

The "Save as:" prompt appears

CLIENTS	The file name
◄┘	Enter key, to confirm the completion of the structure definition
Y	Yes, to enter records immediately. The empty entry form appears.

ADDING RECORDS

As you enter the telephone numbers in the records that compose this database, you enter the last character of the last field. This automatically enters the record and give you a new, empty form to fill in. Therefore, you must check for the accuracy of the record before entering this character. Remember, you may check the records for accuracy later as well.

Using upper and lowercase letters as shown, create the database with records that follow:

```
CLT_ID  CLIENT_NAME          STREET          CITY       STATE    ZIP     TELEPHONE

   115  Acme Realty          100 Elm Street  Wellston    NV     19870    765-4000
   118  Riverside Properties 20 Oak Lane     Wellston    NV     19870    765-3580
   127  Fast Accounting      77 Washington   Newtown     NV     19801    376-3010
   131  Green Auto Sales     3583 Riverside  Paradise    UT     29875    885-9002
   135  Direct Marketing Inc.12 First Ave.   Newtown     NV     19801    376-2756
   139  Sheet Metal Works    101 Center St.  Paradise    UT     29875    885-9111
   116  Tonal Music Co.      55 Center St.   Paradise    UT     29875    885-0101
   101  Joe's Haberdashery   95 Madison Dr.  Wellston    NV     19871    675-3691
   110  Quick Trucking       26 Circle Dr.   Wellston    NV     19870    675-3620
   123  Alice's Restaurant   19 Star Lane    Paradise    UT     29875    885-1785
   124  Hart's Breaker Motel Paradise Road   Wellston    NV     19870    675-4120
   133  Pat's Hair Styling   15 Veterans Ln. Wellston    NV     19870    675-4500
   140  Druggist's Distrib.  191 Mill Rd.    Newtown     NV     19801    376-9101
   141  Eagle Markets        27 Liberty St.  Wellston    NV     19871    675-4700
   142  Wellston Holding Co. 1 Lunar Lane    Wellston    NV     19871    675-2725
```

When you have entered the telephone number for Wellston Holding Co., you have completed the database. When you receive a blank entry form, to stop the addition of records to the client database and to return to the Assistant, press

◄┘   Enter key

LOCATING RECORDS IN AN UNORDERED DATABASE

dBASE appends new records to the end of the database. The location of a record in the database only tells you that this record was entered after records that precede it, and before records that come after it. Generally, the use of the PgUp and PgDn keys are inefficient means by which to locate records. A database of a thousand records would, for instance, require an average of 500 keystrokes to move from one record to a particular target record if you had to randomly search for the next record. This average could be reduced if the list is ordered, but the search is essentially visual and inefficient. dBASE provides some quicker means of moving about the database.

The record pointer can be positioned at the first or last record with the Go To option on the menu (Figure 2-2). Press

F10   Function key F10, to call the menu
< Go To >

<Top record>

◄┘   Enter key, to move the record pointer to record 1

To move to the last record, press

F10   Function key F10, to call the menu. Note that the <Go To> and <Top record> choices are remembered.

<Last record>

◄┘   Enter key, to move the record pointer to the last record

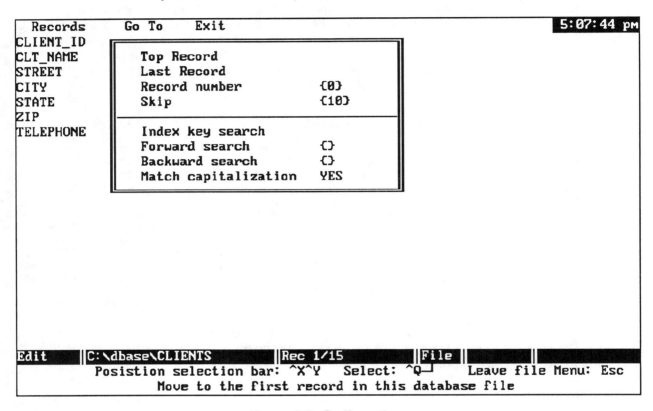

Figure 2-2. Go To options

Locate By Search Condition

dBASE can locate records by searching through the entire database looking for records with specified contents in specific fields. The default approach to searching used by dBASE compares the string of characters you enter with the starting characters in the field being searched to see if they are the same. In order for you to locate a record, you must know in which field a number or character string is found and you must know the precise spelling of any characters used. The Go To option on the menu that appears at the top of the Edit and Browse screens has three options that you can use to find named items in a database. **Forward search** searches those records that follow the highlighted record, **Backward search** searches those records that precede the highlighted record. The **Match capitalization** ensures that the capitalization in the string that you are searching for and the capitalization in the record are an exact match. For example, with Match capitalization set to YES, to locate a record in which the CLT_NAME field contains Acme Realty you must use that spelling, not ACME Realty. With Match capitalization set to OFF, dBASE IV ignores the capitalization.

Locate the Eagle Markets entry in the following manner. First move to the Top record.

F10	Function key F10, for the menu
< Go To >	
< Top record >	
◄┘	Enter key, to move to the Top record. Note that the cursor is in the CLIENT_ID field. The cursor must be in the field that you want to search.
F10	Function key F10
< Go To >	The menu for locating records
< Forward search { } >	
	Search from the current location of the record pointer toward the bottom of the database. The absence of any characters between the braces shows that there is no default search string.
◄┘	Enter key. The prompt "Enter search string: " appears
141	The CLIENT_ID for Eagle Markets
◄┘	Enter key, to begin the search for the Eagle Markets entry
F10	Function key F10, for the menu
< Go To >	
< Top record >	
◄┘	Enter key, to move to the top record
F10	
< Forward search { } >	
◄┘	Enter key. The prompt "Enter search string: " appears along with the remembered search string.
14?	The search string with the ? wildcard
◄┘	Enter key, to begin the search. The record pointer moves to record number 13 and the Druggist's Distrib. record is displayed.
F10	Function key F10, note that the < Go To >, < Forward search >, and the 14? search string are all remembered
◄┘	Enter key, to see the search string
◄┘	Enter key, to begin the search. The record pointer moves to record number 14, the next record that matches the 14? search string, and the record for Eagle Markets is displayed.

This search could have been conducted from outside the Control Center by typing a command at the dot prompt. In this case the command would have been LOCATE FOR CLIENT_ID = 141. If you were searching for a client by name, the command would be LOCATE FOR CLT_NAME = "Eagle Markets." The quotation marks are necessary in this command because the search string is character, rather than numeric, data.

The Continue Command

In the foregoing efforts to locate records, you identified records that were unique. Only one record, for instance, had the CLIENT_ID of 141 and only one record had the CLT_NAME of Eagle Markets. The Shift-F4 keys continues the previous search in the forward direction and the Shift-F3 keys return to one of the records already found. Try this by entering

◄┘	Enter key three times, to move to the CITY field. The cursor must always be in the field that is to be searched.
F10	Function key F10
< Go To >	

\<Top record\>
◄⅃   Enter key, to position the record pointer at the top record
F10
\<Forward search   {}\>
◄⅃   Enter key
Newtown   The search string
◄⅃   Enter key. The search is carried out and the action line displays Record = 3, the record
                             number of the record with the contents, Newtown, in the CITY field.

         To continue the search

Shift-F4   The Shift and F4 function keys. The renewed search locates record number 5 as the
                             next record with the contents, Newtown, in the CITY field.

         To search backward

Shift-F3   The Shift and F3 function keys. The renewed search returns to record number 3.

         By using the Shift-F4 and Shift-F3 commands, you could work your way through the file without
having to locate records visually. Continuing forward searches ribbon from the bottom of a database to
the top if necessary. Backward searches ribbon from the top to the bottom. Visual identification can be
very difficult, especially if the last printed listing of a database is no longer up to date because records
have been deleted.
         A search that has been conducted from the dot prompt can be continued with the **CONTINUE**
command. To see this you need to exit the Control Center menus. To exit the Edit screen type

F10   F10 function key, to go to the menu
\<Exit\>
\<Exit\>
◄⅃   Enter key, to return to the Control Center screen
F10   F10 function key, go to the Control Center menu
\<Exit\>
\<Exit to dot prompt\>
◄⅃   Enter key, to go to dot prompt

         The dot prompt command for locating the first record with Newtown stored in the city field is

LOCATE FOR CITY = "Newtown"
◄⅃   Enter key, to begin the search. You receive a message "Record =   3" and the status
                             line indicates that the pointer is positioned on Rec 3/15.
CONTINUE
◄⅃   Enter key, to resume search. The message "Record =   5" and the status line indicate
                             that the pointer is positioned on record number 5.

Correcting Errors in Dot Commands

People who use dot prompts, from time to time, make errors in entering commands. There are two
methods of making changes. When an error has been made in the structuring of a dot command,
dBASE highlights the command in a box in the center of the screen. The box contains the choices
cancel, edit and help. Cancel returns the dot prompt. You can retype the command if it is short. Edit
returns the command line entered for correction. When the command is recalled, you can edit the line

and when it is correct, the Enter key executes the command. Other keys such as the Delete and Insert keys can be used to facilitate the making of changes to the command line. Help provides assistance in seeing the syntax for a command.

In addition, dBASE remembers many of the previous commands that have been issued. Pressing the Up arrow at the dot prompt recalls the last command issued even if the command was incorrectly typed. Multiple Up arrows recall commands that were issued farther back in the session. Recalling a command with the Up arrow allows you to make changes to the line in the same way that Edit does.

Try the Skip command by entering

F2	Function key F2, to return to the Control Center
F2	Function key F2, to go to the Edit screen
F10	Function key F10, to go to the menu
\<Go To\>	
\<Skip\>	
◄┘	Enter key, the prompt "Enter number of records to skip" appears
5	The number of records to advance
◄┘	Adjust the record pointer. The status line now displays Rec 10/15 .

Move in the opposite direction now.

F10	Function key F10, to go to the menu

Note that \<Go To\> and \<Skip\>, your last choices, are still highlighted

◄┘	Enter key
-5	The number of records to advance
◄┘	Adjust the record pointer. The status line returns to Rec 5/15.

In addition to the skip command, there   To go directly to Quick Trucking's record, enter

F10	Function key F10, to go to the Browse menu
\<Go To\>	
\<Record number\>	
◄┘	Enter key. You are prompted with "Enter record number."
9	The record number of Quick Trucking
◄┘	Enter key, to locate record number 9 and to return to the Browse screen

Location By Scanning

Often you do not know the exact spelling of an entry in a field, but you do know part of the spelling. dBASE enables you to scan the field to see if it contains the search string that you are sure of. For instance, if you wished to search the CLIENTS file to see which records contained the string "ST." so you could display the records that contained Center St. and Liberty St., you would do so by entering

Esc	Escape key, to exit the Edit screen
Esc	Escape key, to exit the Control Center
Y	Yes, to exit the Control Center and to obtain the dot prompt, next to which you should enter
display all for 'St.'$STREET	The dot command that says display all of the records for which the character string St. appears somewhere in the field STREET

◄◄┘   Enter key, to execute the command and to see three records that meet this condition
ASSIST   The dot command for returning to the Control Center
◄┘   Enter key

SORTING

The CLIENTS database is unorganized since none of the fields has been used to order the records. Generally, some order is helpful. dBASE provides two approaches to organizing databases: sorting and indexing. The sorting procedure creates a second copy of a database: it clones it. A database such as CLIENTS could be sorted on several fields: by ZIP; by CLT_NAME; and by CLIENT_ID. Each of these fields when used for sorting provides the user with the data that is effectively ordered for some purposes, yet any one order may not be helpful for other purposes. The sorting of records in dBASE is easily accomplished, but it is a process that should be undertaken with forethought. There are several reasons for this.

1.   dBASE does not simply sort the existing database; it produces a clone of the original database. Every record is recreated in its entirety, albeit in a new location relative to the other records. When a large database is involved, the replication of every record takes a considerable period of time.
2.   The sorting process creates two versions of the same data. A change made to one database is not automatically reflected in the second database. Consequently, the maintenance of accurate data is doubled by the existence of two databases.
3.   The creation of duplicate databases uses up disk space. Each database takes up the same amount of room on the disk. Therefore, if you have a 360 Kb diskette with a database file that uses 190 Kb of space, the sorted file cannot be put on the same disk.
4.   These problems are compounded by the creation of each additional database. If you had a main file which had 10,000 records and took up 1 megabyte of disk space, three additional files for holding differently sorted data would take up an additional three megabytes of disk space. Instead of having to change one record to acknowledge new information, you would have to alter four records.
5.   Sorted files may not stay sorted. If you make changes to the records or if you add records (which are appended to the bottom of the file), the once sorted file may become less than 100% sorted, perhaps without your being aware of the problem.

These problems notwithstanding, there are occasions when a sorted file is desirable. Sort the CLIENTS database on the basis of CLIENT_ID by entering

Shift-F2   Shift key and F2 function key, to go to the design menu
<Organize>
<Sort database on field list>
◄┘   Enter key. A new pop up menus appears. Under the heading Field order it is expected that you type in the field name that you want to sort on.
Shift-F1   Shift key and Function key F1, to call a second pop up menu. This menu contains a list of field names in the current database.
↓   Down arrow key, to highlight
<CLIENT_ID>
                The field on which to sort
◄┘   Enter key, to select the sort-field name. The field list menu disappears. If you wanted to sort on additional fields so that if there is a tie in the preceding fields, the ties can be broken, you could continue to add fields to the field order list.
◄┘   Enter key, to move to the Type of sort column. The type of sort can be changed by pressing the space bar but for now leave the type at Ascending ASCII.

Ctrl-End	Ctrl key and End key. A prompt appears asking "Enter name of sorted file:."
IDFILE	The name of the new database file to store the sorted records. Again, the command SORT ON CLIENT_ID TO IDFILE could be typed in at the dot prompt without the use of the Control Center.
◄┘	Enter key. The sorting process takes time. Shortly, you see that the file is 100% sorted and that fifteen records were sorted. Notice that the status line continues to show that the file in use is CLIENTS, not IDFILE. IDFILE was created, but it has not been selected for use. You are returned to the database structure definition screen.
Esc	Escape key, to avoid changing the structure
Y	Y to return to the Control Center

Note that IDFILE is now listed in the Data panel of the Control Center. To view the file IDFILE, you must direct dBASE to use a new file. In accessing the new file, dBASE closes the file currently in use. Do this by highlighting the name of the new file and entering

<IDFILE>	
◄┘	Enter key, a pop up menu appears
<Use file>	
◄┘	Enter key, to close the present file and to select a new file. The filename, IDFILE, appears on the status line.

Listing the Sorted Records

Now you can view the sorted records with the Quick Report option. Enter

Shift-F9	Shift key and Function key F9, for the Quick report
<View report on screen>	
◄┘	Enter key, the file is listed. The list is in order of the contents of the CLIENT_ID field.
Space bar	Space bar, to see all of the records
Esc	Escape key, to return to the Control Center

Printing the Sorted Records

Shift-F9	Shift key and Function key F9, for the Quick report
<Begin printing>	
◄┘	Enter key, to begin printing

A quick way to check the order of the records is to press the F2 function key to go to the Browse screen. If the first F2 causes the Edit screen to appear, pressing F2 a second time toggles to the Browse screen. Note that the records are in CLIENT_ID order. Press the Esc key to return to the Control Center.

Displaying the Sorted Records

You could have listed the records in the IDFILE database by going to the dot prompt and typing the LIST command however, the listing of files has a major problem. When the output is large, the records listed scroll off the top of the screen. When the output is sent to the printer, this is no problem, but there is often little point in printing large numbers of records when you only wish to see one or if you just wish to confirm that the sort process was correctly carried out. In such a case, you might choose to use the DISPLAY command which functions much like list but when the screen is full, the display stops until you press a key to display another screen full of records. From the Control Center, use this method of viewing records by entering

Esc   Escape key
Y   Yes, to go to the dot prompt
. GO TOP   To position the pointer at the top of the file
◄⌐   Enter key
. DISPLAY ALL
◄⌐   Enter key, to display a screen of records. (The default of the display command is to display one record; the record pointed to by the record pointer.) Note that the third section of the status line displays, 1/15. The record pointer is pointing to the location past the last record, so no record would be displayed by DISPLAY without ALL.
◄⌐   Enter key, to display the remaining record. The status line now displays EOF/15.

The Search Condition Command

In the exercise above, the scope was set to be All, so you saw every record. The List command defaults to a similar scope. The ability to specify the scope of the command enables you to be selective in the output to just those records that you wish to examine. For instance, you may wish to see just those records that have a zip code of 19870, or just those records which have a CLIENT_ID between 120 and 130. Produce a display of all of the records with a CLIENT_ID less than 120 by entering

DISPLAY ALL FOR CLIENT_ID < 120
◄⌐   Enter key, to display the five records in the file that have CLIENT_IDs less than 120

Next

The searches conducted here were made of the entire database since it was small. In some large databases, this is time-consuming. You may know that the records you are looking for is found in a definable group of records that occur immediately after the location of the first record in the group. If that is the case, you can position the record pointer at the first record in that group and instead of using All as the search condition, use Next which allows you to search a specific number of records. You might, for example, build up the dot command

     . display next 10 for zip = 19870

which would cause the search to be applied only to the next ten records. The search begins at the location of the current record pointer. If EOF is reached first, the display would stop at the last record found. Try the Next command by entering

go top
◄⌐   Enter key
display next 5 Display the next five records beginning at the default record
◄⌐   Enter key

Using the Uppercase Search

Sometimes you do not know whether character data has been entered in uppercase, lowercase, or a combination of the two. Was the company name, Apex, APEX, or apex? Visual searching may be prohibitively time consuming. You can search by asking dBASE to temporarily convert the contents of a field to uppercase with the UPPER() function, so that you can search for an uppercase string.

You could do this by building up the command,

. DISPLAY ALL FOR UPPER(CLT_NAME) = 'ACME REALTY'

It would not be productive to enter

. DISPLAY ALL FOR UPPER(CLT_NAME) = 'Acme Realty'

since this compares all of the uppercase entries in the CLT_NAME field with Acme Realty. Note also that the use of acme realty would mean that no records would be found since acme realty is all lowercase. There is a function LOWER() which is similar to UPPER(), that converts all of the fields' contents to lowercase. With this function, you could enter

. DISPLAY ALL FOR LOWER(CLT_NAME) = 'acme realty'

to locate the correct records.

Multiple Conditions

More complex search conditions can be used to define the scope of the Display and List commands through the use of multiple conditions. In the next exercise list all of the records with a CLIENT_ID between 120 and 130 by using multiple conditions. Do this by entering

DISPLAY ALL FOR CLIENT_ID > = 120 .AND. CLIENT_ID < = 130
◄─┘   Enter key, to display the 3 records in the file that have a CLIENT_ID greater than or
                    equal to 120 and less than or equal to 130

This process used two conditions, was the CLIENT_ID less than or equal to 130, and was the CLIENT_ID greater than or equal to 120. Multiple conditions can be framed in many other ways. Different field names might be used. Examples of other multiple conditions using different field names that could be used with a display all command are:

CLIENT_ID > = 130 .AND. CITY = 'Wellston' (lists 3 records)
STATE = 'NV' .AND. STREET = 'Paradise Road' (lists 0 records)
CLT_NAME = 'Acme Realty' .AND. CITY = 'Wellston' (lists 1 record)

Another variation would involve the use of the .OR. operator. In the previous examples, both of the conditions would have to be true in order for a file to be displayed. The .OR. operator would permit the listing of a file if only one of the conditions was evaluated as being true. Examples of the use of the .OR. operator are:

CLIENT_ID > = 130 .OR. CITY = 'Wellston' (lists 12 records)
STATE = 'NV' .OR. STREET = '55 Center St.' (lists 12 records)
CLT_NAME = 'Acme Realty' .OR. CITY = 'Wellston' (lists 8 records)

A third operator is .NOT. which reverses the truth or falsity of the condition that follows. If the dot command

. LIST FOR .NOT. CITY = 'Wellston'

was issued, the listing would not include any record that contained Wellston in the CITY field.

dBASE permits the use of three, four, and more conditions in a command. You are not limited to two conditions, although the logic may become confusing. Be ready to use more conditions when it is appropriate, but always check your results to be sure that you are extracting the records you intended.

Locating On Logical Fields

In the JOBS database, there is a field named DONE which is a logical field. If you enter a Y or a T in this field, the value of DONE is true, or in dBASE's representation, .T. If you enter an N or an F, the value of DONE is false, or in dBASE's representation, .F. Logical conditions can be used in search and scope conditions just as numeric and character fields can be, but a different syntax is allowed. Compare the use of a numeric field in display command with that of a logical field. With a numeric field HRS_WORKED, the statement might look like

. DISPLAY ALL FOR HRS_WORKED > 7.0

which would cause dBASE to display each of the records that have a number greater than 7.0 in the HRS_WORKED field. While examining records, dBASE is determining whether HRS_WORKED is greater than 7.0. If this condition is true, the record is displayed. If the condition is false, the record is not displayed. In the current database, there are no records that meet this condition.

When using a logical field, the field is already true or false. The evaluation has already been made and no comparison is needed. An example of a correctly formulated dot command for the DONE field is

. DISPLAY ALL FOR DONE

dBASE determines that done is either true or false by examining its contents. More to the point, the contents do not have to be compared with anything. It would be incorrect to give the command as:

. DISPLAY ALL FOR DONE = Y

You could type

. DISPLAY ALL FOR DONE = .T.

but everything after the field name DONE is unnecessary.

How would you list records for which DONE was false? The .NOT. operator comes into play here, as in

. DISPLAY ALL FOR .NOT. DONE

or

. DISPLAY ALL FOR DONE = .F.

in which the dBASE would look at the contents of DONE and if it determined that the value of DONE was false, the .NOT. would negate false, to produce true so the record would be displayed. If the value of DONE was true, the .NOT. would negate true to produce false so the record would not be displayed.

Locating By Scope Condition

The searches conducted thus far have been exhaustive searches. That is, in order to complete successfully, they search the entire database looking for records that meet your criteria. The scope condition search used in this section is much more limited. It is intended to identify records that meet some criteria, but as soon as a record is found that no longer meets the criteria, the search is terminated.

To locate all of the people in a telephone book who have the name Sean would require an exhaustive search since a first name may appear next to any last name in the book. If you were looking for someone whose last name was Harris, you could find the first such last name and then you would start searching for the first name that you were looking for. You would stop the search, though, if you encountered a last name that was not Harris. All of the Harrises are found in the same area of the book. The latter search is a search by scope condition.

The List and Display commands allow you to conduct a search of records from the location pointed to by the record pointer up to some other location that is determined through the use of a logical condition. This requires the building of a scope condition. A scope condition such as WHILE STATE = 'NV' does not list all of the records that have 'NV' as the entry for STATE. It only lists the current record if that is the entry for its STATE field and as many subsequent records with 'NV' in the STATE field until a record is encountered that has any other contents in the STATE field. The listing stops at that point, unlike a search condition which continues to seek records meeting the condition. If the current record pointed to by the record pointer does not meet the specified condition, no records are listed. To see how this works you need to open the CLIENTS database and be positioned at the top of the file. You can retrieve the file from the Control Center as previously shown or you can open the file from the dot prompt type

USE CLIENTS

When a database file is opened you are placed at the top of the file. Note that the third section of the status line displays Rec 1/15. If you are not at the top of the CLIENTS database, move to the top by typing

GO TOP
◄┘   Enter key

Now enter the LIST command with a scope condition

LIST WHILE CITY = "Wellston"
◄┘   Enter key, which lists 2 records with Wellston in the CITY field. A record is encountered that does not contain Wellston and the search stops.

Constructing a Field List

A dBASE record can have up to 255 fields. The wrap-around effect can make listings to the printer, as well as listings to the screen, quite difficult to comprehend. If you plan to use three out of twenty-five fields, it is desirable to only see those three and to avoid printing the others. You can restrict the listing to particular fields by constructing a field list. Suppose that you only wished to see the CLIENT_ID, CLT_NAME, and TELEPHONE fields. You could do so in the following fashion:

DISPLAY ALL CLIENT_ID, CLT_NAME, TELEPHONE

◄┘   Enter key, to see the display of the record numbers and the three fields for the entire
                file. Note that the field names in the dot command are separated by commas.

F2   Function key F2, to return to the Control Center

Sorting in Descending Order

dBASE's sorting operation defaults to ascending order. The lower values sort first. A sort based on a
numeric field, displays the lower numbers (i.e., 0, 1, 2 ..., etc.) first and higher numbers later. Character
fields have a similar ordering scheme. The uppercase characters appear first in the order A, B, C, ...,
etc. Lowercase letters appear afterwards, again in the order a through z. Create a list of the records
sorted in descending order by entering

Shift-F2   Shift key and Function key F2, to move to the Control Center
<Organize>
<Sort database file on field list>
◄┘   Enter key
Shift-F1   Shift key and Function key F1, for a field list
<ZIP>
◄┘   Enter key, to select the ZIP field
◄┘   Enter key, to move to the Type of sort area
Space   Space bar. There are four different sort types. Ascending ASCII sorts from A to Z but
                puts an uppercase letters before lowercase letters. To sort on a field regardless of case,
                choose ascending dictionary as the sort type. The remaining two sort types are
                descending ASCII and descending Dictionary.
Space   Space bar as necessary, to make the type descending ASCII
◄┘   Enter key, to select Descending ASCII and to return to the Field order area
◄┘   Enter key, on the blank Field order area. This is equivalent to the Ctrl-End used earlier.
                The prompt "Enter name of sorted file:" appears.
ZIPFILE
◄┘   Enter key, to create the sorted file
Esc   Esc key
Y   Y key, to return to the Control Center

        The file ZIPFILE has been added to the list of databases in the DATA area of the Control Center.
You also could have created this file from the dot prompt with the command

        .SORT ON ZIP DESCENDING TO ZIPFILE

LISTING THE SORTED RECORDS

Now you can view the sorted records with the Quick report option. Enter

<ZIPFILE>
◄┘   Enter key, to go to the pop up menu
<Use file>
◄┘   Enter key, to open the database
Shift-F9   Shift key and Function key F9, to go to the Quick report menu
<Begin printing>

◄⌐   Enter key, to send the output to the printer. The file is listed and it can be seen that the
          list is in order of the contents of the ZIP field.

INDEXING

As noted above, the sorting of files has some severe limitations. Generally, it is not necessary to
sort files in order to see them in an organized manner. dBASE makes an indexing operation available
that is preferable from many points of view. Unlike the sorting operation, indexing does not create a
clone of the original database, although it does create a new file. An index file is quite different from the
original database file, however. This file is like a lens through which the disorganized file can be seen in
an organized manner.

Shortly, you will reuse the file CLIENTS that is not well organized. The records in the sorted file
IDFILE are identical to those in the file CLIENTS, but the organization of the two databases is different.
They even have the same extension, .DBF. When you create an index file, the index file is much smaller
since it only contains information pertinent to the way in which the index file was created and a list of
pointers to the original records.

An index file is small and is loaded into RAM so it can be searched very quickly when records are
to be located. Multiple index files, up to ten, can be in use simultaneously. Most importantly, when a
record is added or edited, the production multiple index file is automatically updated. Therefore, the
problem of having to maintain multiple databases is avoided. Working with several indexes and a very
large database can slow down editing operations. However, these problems are considerably easier to
deal with than are multiple sorted files.

Creating an Index File

The first step in creating an index is to select a database with which to work. The database need not be
sorted, or can be sorted on some basis that is unrelated to the index being created. To create a
production multiple index file you need to check the Index area on the database design screen. This
causes dBASE to create a multiple index file that has the same name as the database but with an .MDX
extension. The production multiple index file is automatically opened and updated each time you use
the associated database.

To create a production multiple index file for the CLIENTS database

<CLIENTS>	The name of the database on the DATA panel of the Control Center
◄⌐	Enter key
<Use file>	
◄⌐	Enter key, to select CLIENTS
Shift-F2	Shift key and Function key F2, to go to the design screen
Esc	Escape key, to remove the pop up menu
v	Down arrow key to highlight CLT_NAME
Tab	Tab key three times, to move to the index area of the CLT_NAME field
Y	Y key, to change index area from N to Y
Ctrl-End	Control key and End key, to create the index
◄⌐	Enter key, to answer Yes to the menu question

A production multiple index file named CLIENTS.MDX has been created. It contains one index
Tag, CLT_NAME. CLIENTS.MDX is automatically opened each time CLIENTS.DBF is used and all index
Tags in the .MDX file are automatically updated. To check the order of the records in CLIENTS press

F2	F2 function key, to go to the Browse screen which shows the last record

PgUp   PgUp key, to see the remaining records. The records appear in CLT_NAME order.

New indexes, or Tags, can be added to the production multiple index files. You must identify an expression which dBASE can use to build the index. An expression in this context can be as simple as a field name. dBASE can order fields alphabetically or numerically. For instance, an index for the CLIENTS database could be constructed from CLT_NAME or CLIENT_ID.

An expression could include a combination of field names of the same type. The + operator is used to concatenate, or append end to end the contents of character fields to make up a continuous string of characters. The expression, CITY+STATE, for example, would create strings like, "Wellston NV" on which to alphabetize the file. Thus, if a file had records with a city of Wellston in Nevada, as well as records with a city of the same name in Washington, the indexed file would keep the two groups of records separate. More than two field names can be concatenated if that is necessary.

A third possibility is that an expression can contain fields with different types if functions are used to convert the fields to the same type. An example of such a function is the STR function which converts numerical data into character data. The STR function might be used in an expression such as STREET+CITY+STATE+STR(ZIP,5), which would organize a file in a comprehensive way. The STR function would convert numerical values in the ZIP field, like 13445 with a length of five, to characters like 13445 that would combine with the characters in the other fields.

CLIENTS.DBF is already in use. Create an index file at the Control Center in this manner:

Shift-F2   Shift key and Function key F2, for the design menu
<Organize>
<Create new index>
◄┘   Enter key, to pop up menu shown in Figure 2-3

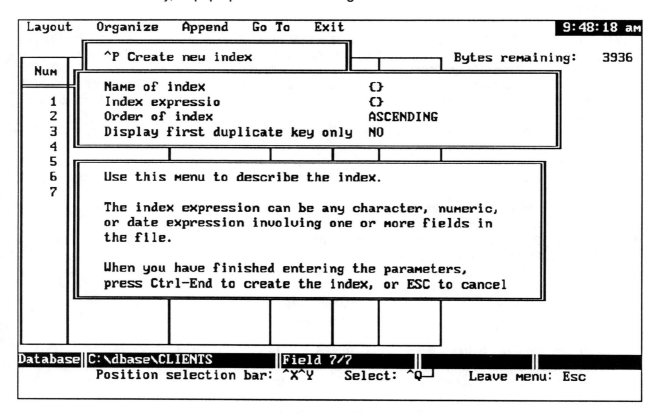

Figure 2-3. Create New Index Prompt

◄⌐	Enter key, to give the index tag a name
IDFILE	The name of the new index tag
◄⌐	Enter key
<Index expression>	
◄⌐	Enter key, to enter an expression on which to index the file
Shift-F1	Shift key and Function key F1, to call the index expression menu. A three column, pop up menu appears. The first column lists field names on which you can build the index. The second column lists the operators that you could use to combine fields and the third column lists functions that can be used to build complex indexes.
<CLIENT_ID>	
◄⌐	Enter key, to select the CLIENT_ID field as the index field
◄⌐	
Ctrl-End	Control key and End key, to create the index
Esc	Escape key
Y	Y key, to return to the Control Center
F2	Function key F2, to go to the Browse screen. The beginning of the list is displayed in the order of the CLIENT_ID field. Remember that you are not looking at the sorted file; you are looking at the unsorted file through the use of an index file.
Esc	Escape key, to return to the Control Center

Seeking a Record

In addition to the LOCATE, SKIP, and GOTO commands for finding specific records, an indexed file can utilize the SEEK command. In a SEEK, dBASE is directed to find a number or a character string expression in the field or fields on which the index file is based. Since the CLIENTS file was indexed on the CLIENT_ID, you can seek numbers that represent a client. If you SEEK for a client's identification number and that number does not exist, you receive a message "Find not successful." Try this with

F2	Function key F2, to go to the Browse screen
F10	Function key F10, to go to the menu
<Go To>	
<Index key search {}>	
◄⌐	Enter key
123	The CLIENT_ID number for Alice's Restaurant
◄⌐	Enter key

Note that you have returned to the Browse screen and the cursor is on the record for Alice's Restaurant.

Now try this from the dot prompt

Esc	Esc key, to return to the Control Center
F10	Function key F10, to go to the menu
<Exit>	
<Exit to dot prompt>	
◄⌐	Enter key, to go to the dot prompt
SEEK 123	The client identification number for Alice's Restaurant
◄⌐	Enter key. No response is seen. The record pointer has been set to the found record, however.

To see the record that was found type

DISPLAY

◄⌐   Enter key, to display one record, the record pointed to by the record pointer

Remember that SEEK functions correctly command only with respect to the fields on which the index was created. You cannot SEEK for a ZIP entry, for example. Seeking a record in a database that is using several indexes, can only be accomplished with the major index, the first index used. You cannot use SEEK to locate a record based on any of the other indexes.

Using a Complex Expression

Create another index file that is based upon the CITY and STATE and ZIP fields. This index organizes the records for display so that zip code areas within cities, as well as the cities themselves appear in the groups.

F2	Function key F2, to go to the Control Center
Shift-F2	Shift key and Function key F2, for the design menu
<Organize>	
<Create new index>	
◄⌐	Enter key
<Name of index>	
◄⌐	Enter key
ZIPFILE	The name of the new index file
◄⌐	Enter key
<Index expression>	
◄⌐	Enter key
Shift-F1	Shift key and Function key F1, for pop up menu
<CITY>	The first field on which to build the index
◄⌐	Enter key
+	Plus sign, to concatenate CITY with the second field
STATE	The second field name. A field name can be typed in directly, you do not need to use the Shift-F1 keys to call up a field list.
+	Plus sign, to concatenate CITY+STATE with the third field
STR(	The start of the function to convert the numeric, ZIP field to a character string
ZIP,5	The third field, followed by its length, to be used
)	A closing parenthesis, to close the expression
◄⌐	Enter key

By default, the order of the index is ascending. Pressing the Enter key while Order of index is highlighted would change the order to descending.

Ctrl-End	Ctrl key and End key. After a period of time during which the index is being constructed, a message appears to advise you that the process has been completed. dBASE automatically puts the index into use.
Esc	Escape key
Y	Y key, to return to the Control Center
F2	Function key F2, to go to the Browse screen. The beginning of the list is displayed in the order of the CITY+STATE+STR(ZIP,5) expression.
Esc	Escape key, to return to the Control Center

EXITING dBASE IV

You can move to the Control Center menu by using the F10 function key but dBASE provides a shortcut for making menu selections. When the **Alt** key is pressed at the same time as the key for the first letter of a menu selection, that selection is highlighted. Try this by typing

Alt-T	Alt key and the T key, to move to the Tools option on the Control Center menu
Esc	Esc key, to return to the Control Center

To leave dBASE IV

Alt-E	Alt key and the E key, for the Exit option on the Control Center menu
< Quit to DOS >	
◄┘	Enter key

dBASE closes all open files and transfers control back to DOS. Do not just turn off the machine to exit since information could be lost and the files can be corrupted if the files are not properly closed.

BACKING UP YOUR FILE

Backup your dBASE IV files by using the DOS copy command. Move into the directory where the dBASE IV files are stored. Place a diskette in drive A. Then type

copy clients.* a:	
◄┘	Enter key. This operation backs up all of the files that have the filename CLIENTS, regardless of their extension.

EXERCISES

A.   Retrieve the central services' charges database, SERVICES. Add ten records to the database as follows:

INVOICE	DEPT	CODE	DESCRIPTION	CHARGE
1970	101	1400	Duplicating	13.11
1971	101	1400	Duplicating	22.80
1972	102	1400	Duplicating	10.50
1973	102	1400	Duplicating	13.45
1974	102	1400	Duplicating	7.77
1975	102	1400	Duplicating	50.45
1976	103	1400	Duplicating	12.00
1977	101	1300	Telephone (LD)	88.24
1978	102	1300	Telephone (LD)	100.05
1979	103	1300	Telephone (LD)	42.55

1.   Experiment with the techniques for locating records in an unordered database with the search condition. Locate, for instance, all records that have 1400 in the CODE field and all records for department 101.
2.   Use a multiple condition search to locate all records that have both of these conditions.
3.   Use a multiple condition to locate all records that have one, but not necessarily both, of these conditions.

4. List to the printer all records that have a CHARGE greater than 50.00. List to the printer all records for DEPT 103.
5. Sort the records by DEPT to a file called DEPTLIST. Print the list.
6. Use the multiple condition feature to display all records with a CODE of 102 and a CHARGE of less than 25.00.
7. Display a listing for the DEPT numbered 101 that shows only the fields INVOICE and CHARGE.
8. Create an index file of the file named SERVICES(.DBF) based on the CHARGE field and call it SERVICES. Use the database and the index file to display the records which are less than 100.00.
9. Using the index file, locate the record with a charge equal to 50.45. Use the scope condition to display all records whose charges are less than 100.00.

B. Retrieve the school roster database, ROSTER. Add nine records to the database as follow:

NAME	RANK	DEPARTMENT	S	SALARY
Pasquale, Peter	Associate	Science	M	33300
Harpsner, Hildegard	Professor	Science	F	37700
Tucker, Trisca	Assistant	Phys. Ed	F	24200
Eardman, Eliza	Associate	Humanities	F	36800
Barriston, Bob	Lecturer	Humanities	M	35600
Dieson, David	Assistant	Humanities	M	22150
Abuhl, Abraham	Associate	Humanities	M	32200
Pascal, Parker	Instructor	Math	F	31500
Baritone, Bart	Instructor	Social Sci	F	24950

1. Display to the screen, all associate professors. Display all humanities assistant professors.
2. List to the printer all records for faculty whose salaries are greater than 25000.00.
3. List to the printer all records for DEPARTMENT equal to Science.
4. Sort the records by NAME to a file called NAMELIST. Print the list.
5. Use the multiple condition feature to display all records with a DEPARTMENT of Math and a SALARY less than 30000.00.
6. Display a listing of the science faculty which shows only the fields NAME and RANK.
7. Create an index file of the file named ROSTER(.DBF) based on the DEPARTMENT field and call it DEPT. Use the database and the index file to display the records for the Humanities Department.
8. Using the index file locate the first record for the mathematics department. Use a scope condition to list all of the mathematics department's records.

C. Retrieve the file SOFTWARE. Add the following 6 records:

PRODUCT	MFR	PURCH_PRICE	NUM_BOUGHT	LAST_PRCH	REORDER
Maxitext	The Associates	305.00	42	06/12/88	N
Two-D Plan	C & I Associates	55.50	34	06/19/88	N
Chart-It!	Sane Screens	122.50	50	07/13/88	N
File Controller	S & S Softwear	59.59	7	04/10/88	Y
Map Designer	QXR Inc.	234.00	15	07/05/88	N

1. List to the printer all records that have a NUM_BOUGHT greater than 30. List to the printer all records for PRCH_PRICE less than 75.00.
2. Sort the records by MFR to a file called MFRLIST. Print the list.
3. Use the multiple condition feature to display all records with a PRCH_PRICE greater than 50.00 and a NUM_BOUGHT of less than 35.
4. Display a listing MFR equal to C & I Associates which shows only the fields PRODUCT and NUM_BOUGHT.

5. Create an index file of the file named SOFTWARE(.DBF) based on the PRODUCT field and call it PRODUCT. Use the database and the index file to display the records whose PRCH_PRICE is less than 50.00.
6. Using the index file, locate the record with a PRODUCT named Caves and Captors. Use the scope condition to list all of the records whose PRODUCT's starting letter is less than N.

Chapter 3

Changing Records with Browse

Chapter Outline

The use of editing as a means of updating records is most useful when you have rapid means of identifying, locating, and recalling to the screen those records that need to be altered. Editing is also useful because the edit screen presents up to twenty-four fields of data within a record. Sometimes it is more useful to see many records at a time. The browse command displays a group of records, one record per line. Data contained in a single field is seen in a column. Consequently, the display is somewhat like that of a spreadsheet. In this chapter you:

1. Use the browse technique for locating records;
2. Learn which keys move the cursor and modify data in fields while in browse;
3. Learn how to look at selected records and how to limit the fields in which changes can be made;
4. See how to add records while in browse.

RETRIEVING A DATABASE

In this chapter the CLIENTS database is used. Boot your computer and run dBASE. When you have received the Control Center menu, enter

< CLIENTS >	The database name under the Data panel of the Control Center
◄┘	Enter key
< Use file >	
◄┘	Enter key

ENTERING BROWSE

Enter the browse mode of record updating with

F2   Function key F2, to go to the Browse screen. Pressed a second time, this key takes
                    you to the Edit screen. If you are at the Edit screen, press the F2 function key again
                    and the Browse screen is toggled on.

```
┌──────────────────────────────────────────────────────────────────────────────────┐
│ Records  Organize    Append    Go To    Exit                        9:48:18 am    │
│                                                                                    │
├──────────┬──────────────────┬──────────────────┬──────────┬──────┬─────┬──────────┤
│ CLIENT_ID│ CLT_NAME         │ STREET           │ CITY     │ STATE│ ZIP │ TELEPHON  │
├──────────┼──────────────────┼──────────────────┼──────────┼──────┼─────┼──────────┤
│       115│ Acme Realty      │ 100 Elm Street   │ Wellston │ NV   │19870│ 765-4000 │
│       118│ Riverside Properties│ 20 Oak Lane   │ Wellston │ NV   │19870│ 765-3580 │
│       127│ Fast Accounting  │ 77 Washington    │ Newtown  │ NV   │19801│ 376-3010 │
│       131│ Green Auto Sales │ 3583 Riverside   │ Paradise │ UT   │29875│ 885-9002 │
│       135│ Direct Marketing Inc│ 12 First Ave. │ Newtown  │ NV   │19801│ 376-2756 │
│       139│ Sheet Metal Works│ 101 Center St.   │ Paradise │ UT   │29875│ 885-9111 │
│       116│ Tonal Music Co.  │ 55 Center St.    │ Paradise │ UT   │29875│ 885-0101 │
│       101│ Joe's Haberdashery│ 95 Madison Dr.  │ Wellston │ NV   │19871│ 675-3691 │
│       110│ Quick Trucking   │ 26 Circle Dr.    │ Wellston │ NV   │19870│ 675-3620 │
│       123│ Alice's Restaurant│ 19 Star Lane    │ Paradise │ UT   │29875│ 885-1785 │
│       124│ Hart's Breaker Motel│ Paradise Road │ Wellston │ NV   │19870│ 675-4120 │
│       133│ Pat's Hair Styling│ 15 Veterans Ln. │ Wellston │ NV   │19870│ 675-4500 │
│       140│ Druggist's Distrib.│ 191 Mill Rd.   │ Newtown  │ NV   │19801│ 376-1901 │
│       141│ Eagle Markets    │ 27 Liberty St.   │ Wellston │ NV   │19871│ 675-4700 │
│       142│ Wellston Holding Co.│ 1 Lunar Lane  │ Wellston │ NV   │19871│ 675-2725 │
│          │                  │                  │          │      │     │          │
├──────────┴──────────────────┴──────────────────┴──────────┴──────┴─────┴──────────┤
│ Browse  ║C:\dbase\CLIENTS        ║Rec 1/15       ║File║         ║                 │
├────────────────────────────────────────────────────────────────────────────────┤
│                           View and edit fields                                   │
└──────────────────────────────────────────────────────────────────────────────────┘
```

Figure 3-1. Sample Browse Screen

MOVING THE CURSOR

The Arrow Keys

The Right and Left arrow keys move the cursor one character at a time and moves the cursor across
fields. The Up arrow moves the cursor up to the next record and leaves it in the same field that it was in
the previous record. The Down arrow moves the cursor down to the next record. The Control key and
the Right arrow move the cursor one word to the right until the end of a field is reached. The Control
key and the Left arrow key move the cursor one word to the left until the left edge of a field is reached.

Other Keys

The Home key moves the cursor to the starting character of the first field, whereas the End key moves
the cursor to the starting character of the last field. If the cursor is moved beyond the limits of a record,

it moves to the next record and places the cursor in the first field of the previous or following record. The tab key moves one field to the right, the Shift key and Tab key moves one field to the left.

PgUp and PgDn

The PgUp key moves the display up one screen full of records with an overlap of one record. PgDn moves the display down one screen full of records with an overlap of one record.

Panning

A record in the CLIENTS database can be seen entirely on one line. Many databases have considerably more fields to display. For long records, in browse, it is not possible to see the entire record at one time. Any movement command (Tab or Shift-tab, for example) that moves into a field which was not originally displayed on the screen causes that field to scroll into view and one of the previously displayed fields disappears off the opposite edge of the screen.

Positioning the Cursor with the F10 Key

Function key F10 places a menu at the top of the screen that can be used to position the cursor and the attendant highlighted bar on a record. Press

F10	Function key F10, to turn on the menu

Practice moving the cursor with

< Go To >
< Last record >

◄┘	Enter key, to move to the end of the file
F10	Function key F10, to recall the positioning menu. Note that the last selections, < Go To> and < Last record> are remembered.

< Top record >

◄┘	Enter key, to move to the top of the file
F10	Recall the positioning menu

< Record Number >

◄┘	Enter key, to move to a specific record number
9	Record number 9
◄┘	Enter key. The status line reflects that the record pointer is at record 9.

If you call up the menu with the F10 key, you can remove it without taking any of the actions by pressing the Escape key.

F10	Function key F10, to recall the positioning menu
Esc	Escape key, to exit the positioning menu

Finding a Record

The F10 key, positioning menu, can be used to find a record based on the contents of the field(s). First position the cursor in the CLIENT_ID field, then

F10	Function key F10, to recall the positioning menu

< Go To >

\<Forward search\>

◄◄┘	Enter key
124	The identification number for Hart's Breaker Motel is the search string
◄◄┘	Enter key. The record which was sought is now highlighted. The record pointer has been moved to 11.

CHANGING THE RECORDS

In browse, as in edit, changes to records are made as soon as you move the cursor to a new record, not at the end of an editing session.

Deletion

The Backspace key deletes characters to the left of the cursor. The Delete key deletes the character above the cursor.

The contents of a field from the location of the cursor can be deleted with the Control and Y keys. Place the cursor in the space between Hart's and Breaker in the CLT_NAME field of the record the cursor is currently located on. Press

Ctrl-Y	To delete the field's contents from the space on. Hart's remains since it was to the left of the cursor.

Then move the cursor to the first character in the same field and press

Ctrl-Y	To delete all of the field's contents

Control and U marks a record for deletion just as it does in edit.

Insertion

The Insert key toggles the entry of characters between insert and overwrite, again, just as it does in edit. Restore part of the previous CLT_NAME entry for this record with

Hart's Inn	The name to start with. Now place the cursor on the blank space between Hart's and Inn.
Ins	Insert key, to turn insert on. Ins appears on the status line.
Space	Space bar, to insert a space after the word Hart's
Breaker	The inserted word with a space between it and the word Inn
Ins	Insert key, to turn insert off and over-write on. Ins disappears from the status line.
Motel	The final word in the field to return the entry to Hart's Breaker Motel. With insert off, the word Motel overwrites the word Inn.

Freeze

The Freeze option of the Browse menu limits your changes to a designated column. Assume that the telephone company had been forced to renumber all of the telephone entries for Wellston. You have to modify all of the TELEPHONE entries for your clients. Without using the lock option, you would find that the cursor constantly moved into fields that are not to be changed. The lock option prevents this.

F10	Recall the positioning menu

\<Fields\>
\<Freeze field\>
◄┘   Enter key, which produces the pop up prompt,

　　　Enter field name: _____

TELEPHONE   The field whose contents are to be altered
◄┘   Enter key. The cursor is placed in the TELEPHONE field. Change the telephone
                      number.
987-4555   The new number. The cursor automatically moves to the start of the next telephone
                      number. Try to move the cursor with the arrow keys. It does not leave the
                      TELEPHONE field.

　　Change two more telephone numbers of your choosing. When you are finished, remove the freeze
option by

F10   Function key F10, to recall the Positioning menu
\<Fields\>
\<Freeze field\>
◄┘   Enter key. The field name TELEPHONE is displayed.
Backspace   Backspace key, to erase the word TELEPHONE
◄┘   Enter key, to toggle freeze off. The cursor is now free to move into any field.

Memo Fields

Memo fields can be edited from either the Browse or Edit screens. The use of Memo fields is discussed
in the next chapter.

ADDING RECORDS

Additional records can be placed into the database while you are in browse. Before beginning activate
the index tag IDFILE which causes records to be displayed in CLIENT_ID number order. From the
Control Center press

Shift-F2   Shift key and Function key F2, for the design menu
\<Organize\>
\<Order records by index\>
◄┘   Enter key
\<IDFILE\>
◄┘   Enter key, to select the IDFILE tag
F10   Function key F10, for the design menu
\<Exit\>
\<Save changes and exit\>
◄┘
◄┘   Enter key, to return to the Control Center

F2   Function key F2, for the Browse screen. The records are displayed in CLIENT_ID
                      number order. You may need to use the Up arrow or PgUp key to see this. Place the
                      cursor on the last record in the database.

↓   Down arrow. The prompt,

= = = >   Add new records? (Y/N) appears. Respond with

Y   Yes, add a new record. A blank record line is displayed into which data can be added.

Enter the following information but remember that when the last number in the telephone number is entered, the record is entered into the database.

CLIENT_ID: 128
CLT_NAME: Heros Sandwiches
STREET: 16 Oak Place

Notice that the CITY, STATE, and ZIP for this record are the same as the CITY, STATE, and ZIP in the preceding record for Wellston Holding Co. Instead of reentering the data one key at a time, you can copy the data a field at a time. Put the cursor in the CITY field, if the cursor is not already there, and press

Shift-F8   Shift key and F8 function key, to copy Wellston from the last record
◄┘   Enter key, to enter Wellston into the CITY field and move the cursor to the STATE field
Shift-F8   Shift key and F8 function key, to copy NV
◄┘   Enter key, to enter NV
Shift-F8   Shift key and F8 function key, to copy 19870
◄┘   Enter key, to enter 19870
987-4240   The telephone number cannot be copied from the previous record so enter the number
               987-4240 in the TELEPHONE field
◄┘   Enter key

When a new record is added, it is automatically appended to the end of the database file as you would expect. In addition, however, the master index files are also updated to include the new record. The records are being displayed in the order determined by the tag IDFILE. When the record is entered with an Up or Down arrow, the IDFILE tag is updated and the record appears where it belongs according to the IDFILE. If you press an Up arrow to enter the record, the cursor does not be put into the Wellston Holding Co. record. It appears in the Fast Accounting record. Try this by pressing

↑   Up arrow, to enter the record. The cursor appears in the Fast Accounting record.

CHANGED INDEX FIELDS

Any time that the field on which an index file is built is altered, the record is automatically reindexed into the database. Leaving the cursor in the CLIENT_ID field of Fast Accounting, type

138   A new CLIENT_ID for Fast Accounting
◄┘   Enter key, to complete the replacement of the 138
↑   Up arrow, to enter the record in a new location in the IDFILE index. The physical
               location of the record in the database has not changed, however.

EXITING BROWSE

You can return to the Control Center at any time you wish. The Escape key can be used to abort the editing of the current record only. This leaves the record unchanged. The normal exit process is

Ctrl-End   The Exit command

EXITING dBASE IV

To leave dBASE IV, choose Exit from the Control Center menu:

F10
<Exit>
<Quit to DOS>
◄⌐   Enter key

     dBASE closes all open files and transfers control back to DOS. Do not turn off the machine to exit since information could be lost and the files can be corrupted if the files are not properly closed.

BACKING UP YOUR FILE

Backup your file by using the DOS copy command. Make sure that the default directory is the one in which your database files are stored and place the backup diskette in drive A. Then type

copy clients.* a:
◄⌐   Enter key. This operation saves the CLIENTS.DBF and CLIENTS.MDX files. Copy *.* can be used for copying all files residing in the directory to drive A.

EXERCISES

Set up the CLIENTS file using the index tag IDFILE for use by dBASE before beginning the exercises.

A.   Enter browse. Turn the browse menu on and off with the F10 and Esc keys. Use the arrow keys, the PgUp, PgDn, Home, and End keys to move the cursor around in the database.

B.   Place the cursor on the blank between Riverside and Properties. Delete the word Properties with the Control and Y keys. Delete the entire field entry with Control and Y by placing the cursor under the R in Riverside. Enter Waterview Realty as the revised field contents.

C.   Change the address 77 Washington to 573 Brook St. for Fast Accounting.

D.   Mark the record for Joe's Haberdashery for deletion.

E.   Append two records as follows:

CLIENT_ID	CLT_NAME	STREET	CITY	ST	ZIP	TELEPHONE
150	Walsh's Diner	100 Elm Street	Hardy	CA	26788	435-2700
152	Capital Laundry	4720 Mills Ave.	Wellston	NV	19870	765-4211

F.   Use the Go To menu associated with function key F10 to move the cursor to the top and last records of the database. Move directly to record number 4 with the same menu.

G.   Freeze the cursor in the CLT_NAME field and change Tonal Music Co. to Harmony Instruments. Change Pat's Hair Styling to Pat's Motorcycles.

H.   Freeze the cursor in the CLIENT_ID field and change the identification number for Joe's Haberdashery to 146, and for Quick Trucking to 147.

I.   Use the Go To and Forward search menu to find the records with the CLIENT_ID's of 118, 116, and 140. Try finding a CLIENT_ID of 100.

J.   Practice the same commands described above on the SERVICES, SOFTWARE, and ROSTER databases constructing your own data for replacements of field data and appended records.

K.   Print the database as it now stands.

Chapter 4

Forms Design

Chapter Outline

You have now used many of the basic features of dBASE IV for creating, changing, and manipulating databases. dBASE offers a considerable number of additional features that permit you to customize dBASE to better meet your needs. In this chapter, you make use of the Forms Design Screen , a feature that lets you construct input and edit screens that can be used in place of the default form screens that normally appear. You will

1. Use the Form Design Screen to develop an input screen with which you append records;
2. Learn how to add information to a memo field;
3. Back up the format screen file;
4. Enter text in a memo field.

FORMS DESIGN

dBASE IV assists in the addition of database records by offering you an entry screen that employs the field names as prompts and entry blocks that are of the width and type that the fields were defined as being. This is the basic Edit screen. Despite the rapidity with which the entry screen is created, the default appearance of this screen can present some problems. These could include:

1. Abbreviations must be used since field names are restricted to ten characters. Field names such as WHSL_COST and EC_OR_QUAN must be used even though WHOLESALE_COST and ECONOMIC_ORDER_QUANTITY are much more helpful to people who must use dBASE to enter their data. Names that seem adequately descriptive when first developed can lose the meaning you thought they had when they are shown to another person or when you come back to them after several months.

2.   The field names are shown in a compact, vertically-oriented format that may not look like the form from which data entry is made. If the visual format on the screen does not look like the form from which data is taken, both efficiency and accuracy during data entry suffer.

3.   The data entry blocks do very little error checking or data correction and editing. A person can enter lowercase letters when uppercase letters are required, and numbers that are not within an expected range are not rejected.

The Form Design Screen is a feature of dBASE IV that allows you to design a data entry form that addresses these limitations. Format screens can expand the prompts, can make the screen look like a business form, can improve on the error checking capabilities of the normal entry screen, and can alter the display of data in edit mode.

In this chapter, you create a new entry screen for the JOBS database. Recall that the dBASE-constructed entry form looks like

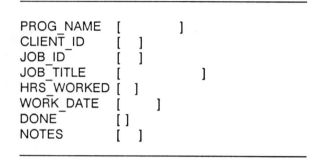

```
PROG_NAME   [         ]
CLIENT_ID   [   ]
JOB_ID      [   ]
JOB_TITLE   [         ]
HRS_WORKED  [   ]
WORK_DATE   [       ]
DONE        [ ]
NOTES       [   ]
```

Figure 4-1. JOBS Database Entry Form

while the form collected by the manager of Computer Associates looks like Figure 4-2.

Set Up

To create the new screen with **Form Design Screen,** boot your computer and load dBASE.

```
        ┌──────────────────────────────┐
        │    Computer Associates        │
        │    Jobs Data Form             │
        └──────────────────────────────┘

   Date 06/12/90            Job ID  1502

   Prog. Name     Jones, M.

   Client ID      127

   Job Title      Accounts Payable

   Hours Spent  7.50        Completed   Y

   Notes: Should the client ask, 4.5 hours of work
   were completed on a home computer.  Three hours were
   completed at customer site.
```

Figure 4-2. Computer Associates Jobs Information Form

Create

Earlier, the Create option on the DATA panel was used to create a database. In this chapter, the Create option on the FORMS panel is be used to create a format file with the Form Design Screen. Continue by entering

<JOBS>	The name of the database file for which a screen is to be created
◄⌐	Enter key
<Use file>	
◄⌐	Enter key, to activate the database
<Create>	Move to the Create option under the Forms panel on the Control Center
◄⌐	Enter key. The status line now shows that you are in the Form screen, that you are creating a <NEW> form, and that the form is based on the database named JOBS.

Quick Layout

At this point, dBASE needs to know which fields are to be used in the data entry screen. Not all of the fields contained in a database need to be included in a format screen, but in this chapter they are all be used so you can use the Quick layout option. In many situations, data is entered into records at different times and with different screens, so several forms may be needed.

<Quick layout>	
◄⌐	Enter key, to load all the fields in the database on the form screen

The Form Design Screen

The field names and the entry blocks are displayed as

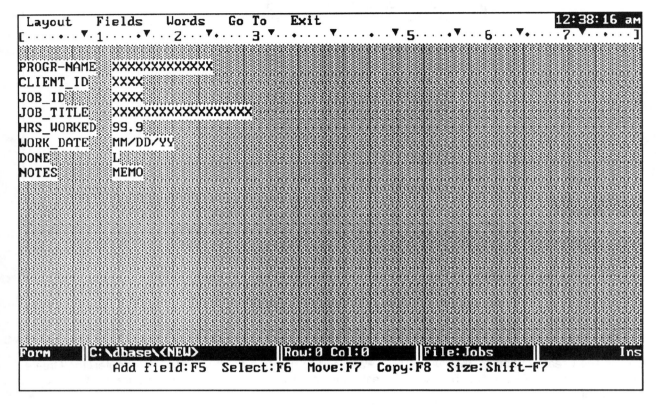

Figure 4-3. The Form Design Screen

in which the X's signify that any character can be entered. A 9 signifies that only numbers can be entered at those locations. Periods and slashes appear in the entry screen when the form is eventually used for data entry. The L identifies a logical field and MEMO identifies a memo field. These letters are called picture templates.

Picture Templates

dBASE's fields default to entries such as 99/99/99, for date fields and L for logical fields. These entries are called picture templates since they control which types of responses can be entered and how the data entered is to be displayed. Picture templates can be changed by typing selected characters across the width of the field. The options that can be entered are summarized in Figure 4-4.

TEMPLATE	EFFECT ON THE DISPLAY
A	Permits the entry of alphabetic characters only
L	Permits the entry of T, F, Y, and N only
N	Permits the entry of numbers or alphabetic characters
X	Permits the entry of any character including mathematical operators, punctuation marks, alphabetic characters, and numbers
Y	Permits the entry of Y or N only
#	Permits the entry of numbers, spaces, periods, and the plus and minus signs only
9	Permits the entry of numbers, signed and unsigned
!	Permits the entry of any character, but alphabetic characters are converted to uppercase
*	Display leading zeros as *
$	Display leading zeros as $
.	Position of decimal point
,	Show comma for large numbers

Figure 4-4. Picture Template Options

Picture templates are not be used in this exercise. If you wish to create an entry screen for the CLIENTS file, enter the option, (999)999-9999 for the telephone field which would automatically include the parentheses and the hyphen in edit and append displays. The template !XXXXXXXXXXX allows the entry of a lowercase letter in the first position, but the letter is automatically converted to uppercase before being stored in the record.

Editing Keys

Within the Form Design Screen, there are a variety of keys that serve different functions. The functions of these keys are summarized in Figure 4-5.

KEY	PURPOSE
←,→,↓,↑	Moves cursor one character
End	Moves cursor to the end of the line
Home	Moves cursor to the beginning of the line
↵	Moves cursor to next line and insert a line if insert is on
PgDn	Moves cursor down 18 lines
PgUp	Moves cursor up 18 lines
Del	Deletes the character above the cursor
Backspace	Deletes the character to the left of the cursor
Ctrl-Y	Deletes the line the cursor is on
Ctrl-U	Deletes the field the cursor is on
Ctrl-T	Deletes the remaining letters in the word that the cursor is on
Ins	Toggles insert on and off
Ctrl-N	Inserts a new, blank line
F10	Toggles between blackboard and menu operations

Figure 4-5. Form Design Screen Editing Keys

TEXT ENTRY

Characters can be typed on to the Form Design Screen at any location. You can type on prompts for field entries, titles that match those on paper forms, and directions for filling out the form. Before proceeding, put the Screen editor into insert by pressing the Ins key. This should place Ins on the status line. The row and column number position of the cursor is displayed on the status line. Some screens may involve so many fields that multiple pages are needed for the form. This is not the case in this exercise. Begin to revise the screen to look as it does in Figure 4-2 by placing the cursor on the row 0, column 0 position with the arrow keys, and

Ins	Insert key, if necessary, to display Ins on the status line
◄┘	Enter key ten times to insert ten blank lines. Using the numbers on the status line as a guide, move the cursor to row 2, column 23 with the arrow keys.
Computer Associates	The first line of the form title. With the arrow keys, not the Enter key, move the cursor to row 3, column 25.
Jobs Data Form	The second line of the form title. Three spaces precede the word Jobs.

Moving Fields

The field blocks that appear next to the field names are moved next. Each block is recognized by dBASE as containing data for a specific field regardless of the prompt that is typed to the left of the field. That allows you to change the prompt to make it meaningful to you. It also permits you to repeat a prompt word or words in several places and dBASE would continue to recognize the fields. The procedure for moving a field is:

1.   place the cursor in the field to be moved
2.   press the F6 function key
3.   press the Enter key, to select the field
4.   move the cursor to the new location for the field
5.   press the F7 function key
6.   press the Enter key, to move the field

The first field to be moved is the WORK_DATE field. Place the cursor in the WORK_DATE field and enter

F6	Function key F6, to select the field for movement
◄┘	Enter key, to select that field
↑,→	Up and Right arrow keys to move the cursor to row 6, column 10. You can see the cursor's row and column coordinates on the status line.
F7	Function key F7, to move the field to this location
◄┘	Enter key, to complete the moving of the field. The field is moved, but the prompt associated with this field is not.

Fields can be moved again at any time and in the same manner.

Retyping Prompts

The prompts for the fields can be retyped the way they appear or they can be changed to be consistent with a paper data entry form or to make the prompt more descriptive. Place the cursor in position row 6, column 5, and, if you are not in overwrite mode, press

Ins   Toggle to overwrite so the field stays in place. If you insert characters in error, use the Delete key to move the field back to its original position.

Continue by entering

Date   The new prompt, which does not include WORK_, and which uses lowercase letters as well as an uppercase letter.

Deleting a Line

The original prompt, WORK_DATE, remains and should be deleted. Do this by placing the cursor on the line with this prompt and entering

Ctrl-Y   Delete the entire line. The line is removed and the lines below the cursor are moved up.

Continue by moving each of the fields and re-entering the prompts. You have to make numerous adaptations to the screen as you do so because the field blocks that are moved and the prompts that are entered may interfere with the text brought in by the Quick Layout command. Use the Ctrl-Y key combination to delete lines. To insert blank lines, turn insert on and use the Enter key. You can overwrite existing text with new text if insert is off. Move the fields, but not the prompts to the following locations:

FIELD	ROW	COLUMN
JOB_ID	06	48
PROGR_NAME	08	16
CLIENT_ID	10	29
JOB_TITLE	12	15
HRS_WORKED	14	18
DONE	14	37
NOTES	16	11

Toggle Insert off with the Ins key and add the following prompts at the locations given:

FIELD	ROW	COLUMN
Job Identification #	06	27
Programmer	08	05
Client Identification #	10	05
Job Title	12	05
Hours Worked	14	05
Completed	14	27
Notes	16	05

Your Form Design Screen should look like Figure 4-6 before proceeding.

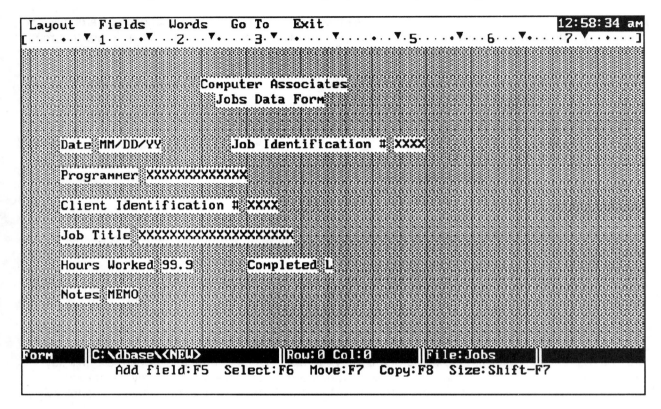

Figure 4-6. Jobs Data Entry Screen

Line Drawing

Although the fields and prompts have been placed correctly to match the form from which data is retrieved, the lines around the form and the double lines around the company name and form name have not been entered. dBASE allows this kind of entry to make forms as understandable and as close to the original as possible. Place your cursor on the row 0, column 0 position and enter

F10   Toggle to the menu
<Box>
◄┘   Enter key, to draw a box
<Single line>
◄┘   Enter key, to select single line. The following prompt appears:

Position upper left of box with cursor keys, complete with ENTER

At this point you would, if the cursor were not in the location where you wanted to begin a box, move the cursor with the arrow keys. Since the cursor is already in the correct location, do not move the cursor.

◄┘   Enter key, to mark the starting position (Row 0, Column 0) from which to begin to draw. The prompt changes to

Stretch box with cursor keys, complete with ENTER

directing you to find the opposing corner of the box that is being drawn.

PgDn   PgDn key, to place the cursor in row 19, column 0
→   Right arrow seventy-five times, to place the cursor in row 19, column 75. The cursor is now in the opposite corner.
◄┘   Enter key, to produce the desired box around the form

   If the line did not come out as you intended, it can be erased by placing your cursor anywhere on the line and pressing the Del key. Sometimes a line may appear to overwrite text in the form. The text is still there but it cannot be seen. Erasing the line brings it back into view. Similarly, the addition of text lines to a form may push some text beneath a drawn line. This text can be retrieved with the removal or addition of other text lines.
   Create the double line box around the company and form name by moving the cursor to row 1, column 19, and

F10   Toggle to the menu
<Box>
◄┘   Enter key, to draw a box
<Double line>
◄┘   Enter key, to select double line
◄┘   Enter key, to mark the starting position from which to begin to draw
↓   Down arrow key three times, to place the cursor in row 4, column 19
→   Right arrow twenty-six times, to place the cursor in row 4, column 45
◄┘   Enter key, to produce the desired box around the two heading lines

   Your completed format screen looks like that shown in Figure 4-7.

Saving Your Screen

To save the entry screen you have created, press

F10   To switch to the menu
<Exit>
<Save changes and exit>
◄┘   Enter key. A prompt appears asking for a file name.
JOBS   The file JOBS.SCR is saved. This generates a JOBS.FMT file, that is used for reproducing the screen you created, and a JOBS.FMO file that is a compiled version of the FMT file.
◄┘   Enter key, to complete the saving of the files. The Control Center reappears.

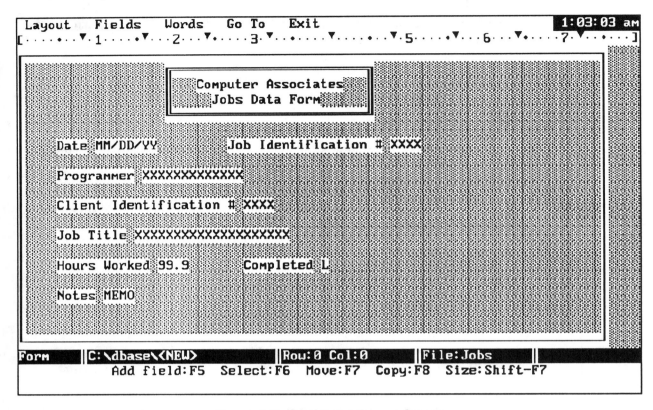

Figure 4-7. Completed Format Screen

USING THE FORMAT SCREEN

The format screen saved in JOBS.FMT can be used when you Update/Edit existing records and when you Update/Append new records. JOBS.FMT should be used in place of the default screen otherwise presented by dBASE. To see the form screen in use:

F2   Function key F2. The JOBS.FMT is automatically in use because it was just created.

     Usually, you to activate a screen format. To do this enter

Esc   Escape key, to return to the Control Center
<JOBS>   Highlight the database name JOBS on the Data panel
◄┘   Enter key
<Close file>
◄┘   Enter key, to close all files

    Put the screen in use by entering

<JOBS>   The database name on the Data panel
◄┘   Enter key
<Use file>
◄┘   Enter key, to use JOBS
<JOBS>   The form name on the Forms panel

◄┘   Enter key, to use the form JOBS.FMT
<Display data>
◄┘   Enter key, to go to the Edit screen

   To add records press

F10   Function key F10, to retrieve the Edit menu
<Add new records>
◄┘   Enter key, to append new records

   Enter the following records for two programmers:

```
┌─────────────────────────────────────────────────────────────┐
│                   ┌──────────────────────┐                    │
│                   │  Computer Associates  │                    │
│                   │    Jobs Data Form     │                    │
│                   └──────────────────────┘                    │
│                                                                │
│      Date 06/10/90            Job Identification # 1455        │
│                                                                │
│      Prog. Name     DOE, F.                                    │
│                                                                │
│      Client ID      135                                        │
│                                                                │
│      Job Title      AUTOMOBILE D.B.                            │
│                                                                │
│      Hours Worked   3.5        Completed   T                   │
│                                                                │
│      Notes   memo                                              │
│                                                                │
└─────────────────────────────────────────────────────────────┘
```

and

```
┌─────────────────────────────────────────────────────────────┐
│              ┌──────────────────────────────┐                │
│              │      Computer Associates      │               │
│              │       Jobs Data Form          │               │
│              └──────────────────────────────┘                │
│                                                               │
│     Date 06/15/90            Job Identification # 1456        │
│                                                               │
│     Prog. Name    DOE, F.                                     │
│                                                               │
│     Client ID     131                                         │
│                                                               │
│     Job Title     SALES LIST                                  │
│                                                               │
│     Hours Worked  7.0         Completed  F                    │
│                                                               │
│     Notes   memo                                              │
│                                                               │
│                                                               │
└─────────────────────────────────────────────────────────────┘
```

Exit at the third screen by pressing the Control and End keys.

USING THE MEMO FIELD

The JOBS database has a structure that includes a memo field which has not been used to this point. A memo field, as noted earlier, need not be used for every record. Unlike other fields, a memo field is a field that actually belongs to another file and can include data of variable length and construction. Memo fields are used to store data in a way that eliminates allocating large blocks of space to records that have no need for any space.

Assume that you wished to add to the information contained in record 22 which pertains to the development of the rolling stock inventory by M. Jones by using the NOTES field. Bring the record into view by

<F2>	F2 function key, to go to the Edit screen
<F10>	F10 function key, to call the Edit menu
<Go To>	
<Record number>	
◄┘	Enter key
22	The number of the record for M. Jones
◄┘	Enter key, to call up record number 22
↓	Down arrow key, to move the cursor to the NOTES field
Ctrl-Home	To open the memo field.

About half of the time spent on this project was used for data entry. Although I told the client that it would be cheaper for the company to use its own staff for entering data, they requested that I put the data in for them.

	Information entered into the memo field
Ctrl-End	To close the memo field. The edit screen reappears.

Ctrl-End   To exit from update/edit. Notice that memo is now displayed as MEMO, indicating that a memo has been written for this record.

        Memo fields are not normally printed out when a database is being listed or displayed. Since memo fields can contain up to 5,000 characters, this is a good thing. If you wish to print the contents of this field, you can do so by specifically identifying this field in a constructed field list.
        The record searching techniques described earlier cannot be used on memo fields.

EXITING dBASE IV

To leave dBASE IV, enter

F10
<Exit>
<Quit to DOS>
◄┘   Enter key

BACKING UP YOUR FILES

Backup your files by using the DOS copy command. Place the backup diskette in drive A. Then type

    copy jobs.* a:

Press Enter. This operation copies all of the files with the filename JOBS found in the dBase directory to the diskette in drive A. This copies the files, JOBS.DBF, JOBS.SCR, JOBS.FMO, and JOBS.FMT to drive A.

EXERCISES

A.   Retrieve the SERVICES database. Create a format screen with screen painter with which to enter two new records with data of your choice. Use the screen to edit existing records.

B.   Retrieve the ROSTER database. Create a format screen with screen painter with which to enter two new records with data of your choice. Use the screen to edit existing records.

C.   Retrieve the SOFTWARE database. Create a format screen with screen painter with which to enter two new records with data of your choice. Use the screen to edit existing records.ft of the company earnings in the database. This data, if stored, would take up a considerable amount of disk space unnecessarily.

Chapter 5

Enhancing Output with the Report Design Screen

Chapter Outline

The printing of reports is another aspect of dBASE IV that gives the user a substantial opportunity for customization in data manipulation. In this chapter, you will

1. Create and save well-formatted reports using the Report Design Screen;
2. Apply the Report to definable subgroups of records within the database;
3. Alter the report.

INDEXING

In earlier chapters, you created lists of records. Some of these lists were complete lists of a database's contents: all its fields and all its records. In some listings, you restricted the listing to records sharing some characteristic(s) and you limited the printing to selected fields. You relied on dBASE to construct the lists for you. The Quick Report command is not the best way to produce many reports, however, since the listings are often unsophisticated. Listings:

1. Rely on the field names as column headings in much the same way as dBASE relies on field names as prompts in entry screens.
2. Print the text, or numbers, in the fields without formatting them in any way.
3. Do not add columns that calculate results dynamically. For instance, in a listing, you cannot multiply the hours worked by an hourly rate to produce a gross salary column.
4. Cannot produce totals and subtotals for numeric columns.
5. Cannot produce summary reports, or break a report up into subsections. You could not, for example, put the records for each programmer in the JOBS database onto a separate page.

In this chapter you use a feature called the Reports Design Screen. The Reports Design Screen addresses all these shortcomings and allows you to produce professional-looking reports in a minimum of time.

The Reports Design Screen, to be most useful, should be used to print from files that have either been sorted or indexed. By grouping the records on some basis, dBASE IV can print related records as a group and can print subtotals for each group. Before proceeding, then, a database you have already used, the JOBS database, should be indexed in anticipation of producing reports that take advantage of the organization of the records. Two indexes are needed. Create these by booting your computer, loading dBASE IV, and entering

\<JOBS\>	The name of the database on the Data panel of the Control Center
◄┘	Enter key
\<Use file\>	
◄┘	Enter key, to use JOBS
Shift-F2	Shift key and the Function key F2, for design screen in order to create the first index
\<Organize\>	
\<Create new index\>	
◄┘	Enter key, to which dBASE requests a name for the index file.
\<Name of index {}\>	
◄┘	Enter key, to name the index
PROGFILE	The name of the index file.
◄┘	Enter key
\<Index expression {}\>	
◄┘	Enter key. dBASE now expects the entry of an index key expression. An expression requires knowledge of the database structure: its field names and field types.
Shift-F1	Shift key and the Function key F1, to list the field names with a pop up menu.
\<PROGR_NAME\>	The first field to be used in the index key expression.
◄┘	Enter key
+	Plus sign, to concatenate the first field with the second field
\<CLIENT_ID\>	The second field (numeric), to be used in the index key expression
◄┘	Enter key, to select the CLIENT_ID field
+	Plus key, to concatenate the third field with the previous fields
\<JOB_ID\>	The third field (numeric), to be used in the index key expression
◄┘	Enter key. The complete index expression is now PROG_NAME+CLIENT_ID+JOB_ID
◄┘	Enter key
Ctrl-End	Ctrl key and the End key, to execute the command. Indexing is carried out on the three-field expression
F10	Function key F10, to return to the Design menu
\<Exit\>	
\<Save changes and exit\>	
◄┘	Enter key. dBASE asks for confirmation that the database structure has not changed and that it can append the old records to this structure. The structure is still correct
◄┘	Enter key, to confirm and to return to the Control Center

Repeat the indexing procedure using the two numeric fields, CLIENT_ID and JOB_ID, and creating the index file, BILLFILE. The STR() function should be used with both fields because they are numeric.

THE REPORT DESIGN SCREEN

Computer Associates' management desires that the first report to be created be a listing of the jobs worked on by each programmer. The report should look like the one pictured in Figure 5-1. In addition to displaying data such as the number of hours worked and the identification numbers of the jobs worked on, the report should calculate how much the programmer should be paid for each job and for the pay period. Each programmer is paid at a rate of $22.50 per hour. A column indicating how much the programmer earned for the company is based on the number of hours worked multiplied by the client charge of $35.00 per hour.

```
03/20/89
Page    1
                           Computer Associates
                             Payroll Report
                      Carole T. Cyberner, Controller

CLIENT JOB
IDENT. IDENT.                   WORK      HOURS      GROSS     GROSS
NUMB.  NUMB.    JOB TITLE       DATE      WORKED       PAY   EARNINGS
===================================================================

Programmer  Brown, R.
 135   1575    Software Install  05/15/90    3.2     72.00     112.00
                                             3.2    $72.00    $112.00
Programmer  Doe, F.
 115   1436    Property Managemnt 05/02/90   7.6    171.00     266.00
 115   1437    Tenant List        05/03/90   7.3    164.25     255.50
 118   1440    Lease Management   05/09/90   4.7    105.75     164.50
 127   1502    Accounts Payable   05/09/90   3.6     81.00     126.00
 127   1502    Accounts Payable   05/23/90   5.7    128.25     199.50
 127   1503    Accounts Receiv.   05/16/90   4.7    105.75     164.50
 131   1434    Spreadsheets       06/04/90   4.5    101.25     157.50
                                            38.1   $857.25   $1333.50
```

Figure 5-1. Partial Sample Pay Report

Set Up

dBASE is using the last index created, BILLFILE, with the JOBS file. Switch to the PROGFILE index instead with the Design option.

Shift-F2	Shift key and F2 function key
<Organize>	
<Order records by index>	
◄┘	Enter key
<PROGFILE>	The index file to be used
◄┘	Enter key
Esc	Escape key
Y	Y key, to return to the Control Center

Create a Report

To create the report desired, follow these steps:

<Create>	Select "create" from the Reports panel of the Control Center
◄⅃	Enter key
Esc	Escape key, to remove the popup menu because you are creating a complete report. The screen changes to that pictured in Figure 5-2.

```
 Layout   Fields   Bands   Words   Go To   Print   Exit          12:29:04 am
[····•··▼·1····•▼···2···▼•····3·▼··•····▼····•···▼·5····•▼···6··▼•···7·▼··•····
Page      Header   Band─────────────────────────────────────────────────────
░░░░░░░░░░░░░░░░░░░░░░░░░░░░░░░░░░░░░░░░░░░░░░░░░░░░░░░░░░░░░░░░░░░░░░░░░░░░░░░
Report    Intro    Band─────────────────────────────────────────────────────
░░░░░░░░░░░░░░░░░░░░░░░░░░░░░░░░░░░░░░░░░░░░░░░░░░░░░░░░░░░░░░░░░░░░░░░░░░░░░░░
Detail             Band─────────────────────────────────────────────────────
░░░░░░░░░░░░░░░░░░░░░░░░░░░░░░░░░░░░░░░░░░░░░░░░░░░░░░░░░░░░░░░░░░░░░░░░░░░░░░░
Report    Summary  Band─────────────────────────────────────────────────────
░░░░░░░░░░░░░░░░░░░░░░░░░░░░░░░░░░░░░░░░░░░░░░░░░░░░░░░░░░░░░░░░░░░░░░░░░░░░░░░
Page      Footer   Band─────────────────────────────────────────────────────
░░░░░░░░░░░░░░░░░░░░░░░░░░░░░░░░░░░░░░░░░░░░░░░░░░░░░░░░░░░░░░░░░░░░░░░░░░░░░░░




Report   ║C:\dbase\<NEW>           ║Band 1/5        ║File:Jobs    ║        Ins
          Add field:F5   Select:F6   Move:F7   Copy:F8   Size:Shift-F7
```

Figure 5-2. Report Screen

The work surface of the screen shown in Figure 5-2 is divided into bands which divide the report into logical pieces. These bands can contain fields from the current database (JOBS), special fields created just for the report, text for titles or, boxes and lines. There are six types of bands, five of which appear automatically when you first enter the Reports Design Screen. The six bands are:

1. **Page Header**   This represents the area at the top of each page that often contains information like page numbers, dates, running titles, report author's name and other documentation.
2. **Report Intro**   This represents the space at the beginning of the first page of the report and often contains titles. This could contain from one line of title to a cover letter explaining the data which follows.
3. **Detail**   This band contains the actual data from the records in the database.
4. **Report Summary**   This represents the space at the end of the report that usually contains the concluding remarks or final totals.
5. **Page Footer**   This represents the area at the bottom of each page and could contain the same information found in the Page Header area.
6. **Group bands**   This is the sixth type of band. It does not appear automatically but you can add it to the screen. These bands organize a report's data by collecting them in groups specified by the report's designer. In this report, for example, the records are to be grouped on the programmer's name (see Figure 5-1).

Figure 5-3. Six Types of Report Bands

Notice that as the report was created, what you saw on the Reports Design Screen was the way the actual, printed report appeared. For this reason, this is often referred to as a "What You See Is What You Get" (WYSIWYG) report generator.

Page Header

Begin with the **Page Header**.

↓   Down arrow key, to move the cursor down one line. Notice that the third section of the status line shows "Line:0 Col:0". The status line always shows where the cursor is on the work surface.

The F10 function key activates the menu at the top of the screen. As a shortcut, you can always move the cursor to a choice on the Report menu by pressing the **Alt** key and the first letter of the menu item. Move to the fields menu by pressing

Alt-F
<Add field>
◄┘   Enter key, for the "Add fields" pop up menu. There are four types of fields to choose from. You want the "Predefined" **Date** field.
<Date>
◄┘   Enter key
Ctrl-End   Ctrl key and the End key, to place the field on the work surface.

Now add the page number

◄┘   Enter key, to open a second line in the Page Header.
Alt-F
<Add field>
◄┘   Enter key
<Pageno>   Select "Pageno" from the Predefined Panel
◄┘   Enter key
<Template>   A picture of how the page number is to look

◄┘   Enter key
Page 999   To insert the word "Page" in front of the page number. The page number appears at the
                      left margin of the page.
◄┘   Enter key
Ctrl-End   Ctrl key and the End key, to place the field on the work surface.

Page Title

Now put the page title on the "Report Intro" band.

↓   Down arrow key, twice to move the cursor to line 0 of the Intro band
→   Right arrow key to move the cursor to column 30
Computer Associates
◄┘   Enter key, to open another line in the Intro band

    Move the cursor to Column 32 and enter

Payroll Report
◄┘   Enter key, to open another line in the Intro band

    Move the cursor to Column 30 and enter

< Your Name >, Controller
                      You may adjust the placement of the name and title with the Delete, Space bar and
                      Backspace keys

Printing Existing Fields

Later some Column headings will be added to the Intro band. Now, move the cursor to the Detail band
and load the fields to be used in the report by entering

↓   Down arrow key, to move the cursor to the Detail band
Home   Home key, to move the cursor to Column 0

    First add the CLIENT_ID number

Alt-F
<Add field>
◄┘   Enter key, to see the fields from the current database.
<CLIENT_ID>   The desired field
◄┘   Enter key
Ctrl-End   Control key and the End key, to accept the default template for CLIENT_ID and to place
                      the field on the work surface.

    If, at some other time, this field needs to be moved on the work surface, the F6 Select and F7
Move keys would be used as they were on the Format Design Screen described in an earlier chapter.

→   Right arrow key, to move the cursor to column 7 and load the JOB_ID number.
Alt-F
<Add field>
◄┘   Enter key

\<JOB_ID\>	The second field to be selected
◄┘	Enter key
Ctrl-End	Control key and the End key, to accept the default template for JOB_ID and to place the field on the work surface.
→	Right arrow key, to move the cursor to column 14 and load the JOB_TITLE field
Alt-F	
\<Add field\>	
◄┘	Enter key
\<JOB_TITLE\>	The field to be selected
◄┘	Enter key
Ctrl-End	Control key and the End key, to accept the default template for JOB_TITLE and to place the field on the work surface.
→	Right arrow key, to move the cursor to column 27 and load the WORK_DATE field
Alt-F	
\<Add field\>	
◄┘	Enter key
\<WORK_DATE\>	The field to be selected
◄┘	Enter key
Ctrl-End	Control key and the End key, to accept the default template for WORK_DATE and to place the field on the work surface.
→	Right arrow key, to move the cursor to column 38 and load the HRS_WORKED field
Alt-F	
\<Add field\>	
◄┘	Enter key
\<HRS_WORKED\>	The field to be selected
◄┘	Enter key
Ctrl-End	Control key and the End key, to accept the default template for HRS_WORKED and to place the field on the work surface.

All the data that have been placed in the report thus far come from fields that are contained in the database structure.

Printing Calculated Fields

A feature of the Reports Design Screen is that you can include columns for which data is created, "on the fly," as it were. In this report you create two columns of data dynamically, a gross pay column and a gross company earnings column. Since the programmers are paid a fixed rate, there is little reason to store either the gross pay or the company earnings in the database. This data, if stored, would take up a considerable amount of disk space unnecessarily.

→	Right arrow key to move the cursor to column 45
Alt-F	
\<Add fields\>	
◄┘	Enter key
\<create\>	Select "create" from the "CALCULATED" panel
◄┘	Enter key
\<Name {}\>	
◄┘	Enter key, to give the new "created" field a name
PAY	The new field name
◄┘	Enter key
\<Expression\>	Specify the display attributes of this field

◄┘	Enter key
Shift-F1	Shift key and F1 function key, for a fields list
<HRS_WORKED>	
◄┘	Enter key
*22.50	Asterisk and 22.50, to calculate the actual gross pay
◄┘	Enter key, to enter the expression
<Template>	
◄┘	
Home	Home key, to move the cursor to the beginning of the 9999999.99
Del	Delete key, until the display shows 9999.99
◄┘	Enter key, to accept the template
Ctrl-End	Ctrl key and the End key, to place the expression on the work surface

Move the cursor to column 55 and using the same procedure described above, create a field called EARNINGS which will be HRS_WORKED multiplied by 35 and a template of 99999.99. Now that all the columns have been placed on the work surface, return the cursor to the Intro band and add column titles.

↑	Up arrow key, to move the cursor to the last line of the Intro band
End	End key, to move the cursor to the end of the line
◄┘	Enter key, to add a blank line
◄┘	Enter key, to add a second blank line

Notice that the cursor is directly above the 9999 displayed in the CLIENT_ID number column of the Detail band. Enter the three lines of column heading:

CLIENT
◄┘
IDENT.
◄┘
NUMB.
◄┘

Move the cursor to line 4, column 7 of the Intro band

JOB

Move the cursor to line 5, column 7 with the arrow keys (not the Enter key) and enter

IDENT.

Move the cursor to line 6, column 7 and enter

NUMB.

Put titles over the remaining five columns as shown in Figure 5-1. When you are finished, move the cursor to the end of line 6 and enter

◄┘	Enter key, to create a seventh title line
=	Sixty-five equal signs to underline the title

Groups

This file (JOBS) is indexed with PROGFILE. Recall that this index file used the expression PROGR_NAME+STR(CLIENT_ID,4)+STR(JOB_ID,4) to create the index. First level breaks can be made on the PROGR_NAME field and, if desired, second level breaks for subgroups can be made on either the CLIENT_ID field or the combined CLIENT_ID and JOB_ID fields. This database is small so breaks will be limited to the first level. To produce a separate report on each programmer, you need to add a Group band. Group bands must always be outside the Detail band. Move the cursor to the start of the last line of the Report Intro band (the status line should show "Line:7 Col:0") and enter the following:

Alt-B	Alt key and B key, to call the "Bands" menu
<Add a group band>	
◄┘	Enter key
<Field value {}>	
◄┘	Enter key, for a pop up menu with the choice of fields
<PROGR_NAME>	The field name on which to create subtotals
◄┘	Enter key to retrieve PROGR_NAME

Notice that two new bands appear on the work surface - a "Group 1 Intro Band" and a "Group 1 Summary Band". Move the cursor to Line 0, Column 0 of the Group 1 Intro Band and enter

Programmer	This is the group heading

Move the cursor to Line 0, Column 12 and enter

Alt-F	Alt key and F key, for the Fields menu
<Add field>	
◄┘	Enter key
<PROGR_NAME>	
◄┘	Enter key
Ctrl-End	To place the field on the work surface.

Move the cursor to Line 0, Column 0 of the Group 1 Summary band. To add the total for the HOURS WORKED column, move the cursor right to Column 38 and enter

Alt-F	Alt key and F key, to call the Fields menu
<Add field>	
◄┘	Enter key
<Sum>	Choose the Sum option from the "SUMMARY" panel of the Add field menu
◄┘	Enter key
<Name {}>	
HOURS	The name of subtotal
◄┘	Enter key
<Field to summarize on {}>	
◄┘	Enter key
<HRS_WORKED>	
◄┘	Enter key
<Template>	
◄┘	Enter key
Home	Home key, to move the cursor to the start of the line
Del	Use the Del key to change the template to 999.9

◄┘	Enter key
Ctrl-End	To place the subtotal on the work surface

Add a subtotal for the GROSS PAY field. Move the cursor to Column 44 and enter

Alt-F	Alt key and F key, for Fields menu
<Add fields>	
◄┘	Enter key
<Sum>	Sum option under the Summary panel
◄┘	Enter key
<Name {}>	
◄┘	Enter key
PAYSUM	Name of the PAY subtotal
◄┘	Enter key
<Field to summarize on {}>	
◄┘	Enter key
<PAY>	Name of the field in the calculated panel to summarize
◄┘	Enter key

Data can be displayed in reports using any of several different "Picture functions". For example, these picture functions allow a user to display all characters as upper case or a numeric field as currency. To display the PAYSUM subtotal as currency,

<Picture functions {}>	
◄┘	Enter key, a menu appears listing the available picture functions
<Financial format $>	
◄┘	Enter key, to have subtotals printed with dollar signs
Ctrl-End	Ctrl key and End key, to save financial format
<Template>	
◄┘	Enter key
Home	Home key, to move the cursor to the start of the entry
Del	Del key, to change the Template to 99999.99
◄┘	Enter key
Ctrl-End	Control key and End key, to place the subtotal on the work surface

In the same manner, add a subtotal for the GROSS EARNINGS column at line 0, column 54 of the Group 1, Summary band. Call it EARNSUM and use the financial format with a 99999.99 template.

Subgroups

A subgroup could be defined if there was a field that was ordered inside of the main field. This is, in fact, the case with the CLIENT_ID field since it was part of the expression that was used to build the index. You could add another Group band, inside the Group 1 bands but outside the Detail band. The number of entries in these subgroups is small, however, and management does not need this breakdown, so a Group 2 band is not used.

Saving The Report File

The creation of this report is now complete. The screen should look like Figure 5-4.

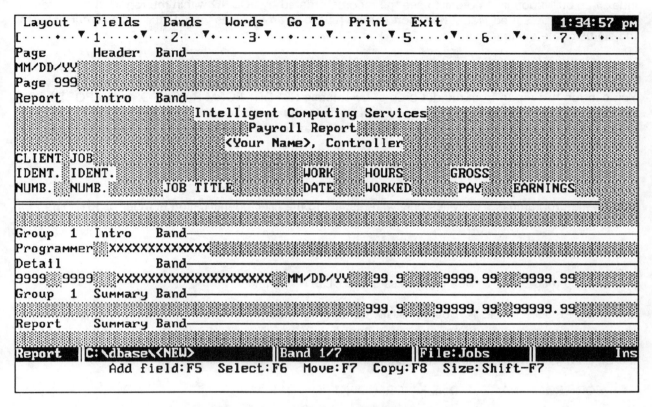

Figure 5-4. Completed Reports Design Screen

Save the report by entering

Alt-E	Alt key and E key, to go to the Exit menu
<Save changes and exit>	
◄┘	Enter key, for the "Save as:" prompt
PAYREPOR	
◄┘	Enter key, to name the report PAYREPOR

Retrieving The Report File

In order to use the report file which you created, you must retrieve it first. If you were retrieving the file immediately after you entered dBASE, you would first have to use the correct database and index files.

<PAYREPOR>	The name of the report from the Reports panel of the Control Center
◄┘	Enter key
<Print report>	
◄┘	Enter key
<Begin printing>	
◄┘	Enter key, to send the report to the printer

If you had selected "View report on screen" the report would have been sent to your screen. The report is printed in the same format as shown in Figure 5-1. The report displays all the records which were indexed on the programmer's name. The job identification number is not used even though the index was built upon it. In order to see the records ordered by JOB_ID within the report, the records would have to be sorted first. The report can be reused at any time as long as the index is current with the status of the database file.

Using a Search Condition

You can run this report from the dot prompt by entering REPORT FORM PAYREPOR or REPORT FORM PAYREPOR TO PRINT to send it to the printer. When entering commands from the dot prompt you can enter a search condition in much the same way as it was used in the listing and display of files. For instance, the search condition,

FOR CLIENT_ID = 131

prints each programmer's activities only with respect to the client identification number of 131. The search condition,

FOR PROGR_NAME = 'Doe, F.'

prints all the records for F. Doe regardless of the CLIENT_ID, and,

FOR PROGR_NAME = 'Doe, F.' .AND. CLIENT_ID = 131

only prints the records for which it is true that the PROGR_NAME = 'Doe, F.' and it was also true that the CLIENT_ID was 131. The search condition,

FOR PROGR_NAME = 'Doe, F.' .OR. CLIENT_ID = 131

lists all of F. Doe's records regardless of CLIENT_ID, as well as every other programmer's records for which it is true that the CLIENT_ID was 131. It would not list records for which both conditions were held to be true twice.

Using a Scope Condition

Similarly, if the record pointer is positioned at the first record for PROGR_NAME = "Grey, Y." the scope condition could be used. The scope condition,

WHILE CLIENT_ID = 131

prints Y. Grey's activities only with respect to the CLIENT_ID of 131, and this only if the record pointer is already pointing to a record that had a CLIENT_ID of 131. The scope condition,

WHILE PROGR_NAME = 'Grey, Y.'

prints all the records for Y. Grey regardless of the CLIENT_ID, and

WHILE PROGR_NAME = 'Doe, F.' .AND. CLIENT_ID = 131

prints records while it is true that the PROGR_NAME = "Doe, F." and it is also true that the CLIENT_ID was 131. The scope condition,

WHILE PROGR_NAME = 'Doe, F.' .OR. CLIENT_ID = 131

would either list all of F. Doe's records regardless of CLIENT_ID or all the records for which it was true that the CLIENT_ID is 131.

EXITING dBASE IV

To leave dBASE IV, choose Exit from the Control Center menu,

Alt-E
< Quit to DOS >
◄┘   Enter key

BACKING UP YOUR FILES

Backup your files by using the DOS copy command. Place the backup files diskette in drive A and then type

copy payrepor.* a:
◄┘   Enter key. This operation only saves the report form file.

EXERCISES

A.   Retrieve the SERVICES database. Create an index file DEPTS based on the DEPT field.   Create a report with the Report Design Screen that shows a breakdown of charges to each department. Include detail lines for each department. Produce a report that shows the expenses for department number 103. Produce another report that displays each department's expenses if the expenses were greater than $75.00.

B.   Retrieve the ROSTER database. Use the previously created index file DEPT that is based on the DEPARTMENT field.   Create a report with the Report Design Screen that shows which faculty are in each department. Generate subtotals for the amount of salary spent annually in each department. Modify the report to include a column that calculates the monthly salary for each faculty member. Produce a report that shows the salaries for the entire Science department. Produce another report that displays the records for each department's faculty only if the faculty member's annual salary is $27,000 or greater.

C.   Retrieve the SOFTWARE database. Create an index file, MFR, that is based on the MFR field. Create a report with the Report Design Screen that shows which software packages have been acquired from each manufacturer and their purchase price. Generate totals and subtotals for the number of packages acquired from each source. Include detail lines. Modify the report to include a column that calculates the investment made in buying software from each vendor (NUM_BOUGHT * PURCH_PRICE). Produce a report that shows the number of packages by manufacturer that must be reordered.

Chapter 6

Using Dot Commands

Chapter Outline

Thus far, most of your work with dBASE IV has involved the Control Center. Many people who use dBASE actively hardly know that the Control Center exists. They use commands at the dot prompt and in programs to perform many of the functions in a different, and some think, faster, way. This chapter

1.   shows you how the function keys can issue commands and how the commands that they issue can be changed
2.   provides you with an overview of the most commonly used dBASE dot commands and their options
3.   gives you practice in issuing dot commands

WHY USE THE DOT COMMANDS?

The Control Center is a useful means of becoming quickly familiar with dBASE's operations. Many people who use dBASE IV can use the Control Center almost exclusively. Other people find that they prefer to work in the dot command mode, however. This is because:

1.   it is faster and often less cumbersome to type out a dot command on the action line than it is to work through a series of menus
2.   there are dot commands available that are not found on the Control Center
3.   dot commands can be stored in files as programs that can be executed many times.

In this chapter, you explore the use of dot commands. The chapter is not intended to be an exhaustive description of all of the commands available, or of all of the options that can be used with those commands that are discussed. Most of the dot commands will not be executed. Many of the commands described duplicate those which were created in the Control Center, and others are for illustration only. Only execute commands that you are specifically directed to. Experiment with the other commands in the last part of the chapter, in the exercises, and on your own. The dot commands described here are also detailed in the dBASE IV Manual.

Load dBASE.

EXITING FROM AND RETURNING TO THE CONTROL CENTER

If you are at the Control Center, you can exit to the dot prompt by pressing

Esc   Escape key
Y   Y key

You can return to the Control Center from the dot prompt by entering

assist
◄⅃   Enter key

This time exit from the Control Center with the

Alt-E   Alt key and E key, to choose Exit from the menu
<Exit to dot prompt>
◄⅃   Enter key, to exit to the dot prompt

THE FUNCTION KEYS

The function keys, marked F1 through F10, are preprogrammed to enter common dBASE commands on the command line. For instance, watching the screen, press function key

F2   To see the command ASSIST automatically entered on the command line

Each of the function keys has a default command function assigned to it. These operations are summarized in Figure 6-1. By pressing a function key, the corresponding command is entered and executed.

KEY	DEFAULT ASSIGNMENT
F1	help
F2	assist
F3	list
F4	dir(ectory)
F5	display structure
F6	display status
F7	display memory
F8	display
F9	append
F10	edit

Figure 6-1. Function Key Assignments

If you have not opened a .DBF file for use before issuing a command with a function key dBASE will prompt you with

No database is in use. Enter filename: _

Respond by entering the database filename you wish to use.

IMMEDIATE COMMANDS

Immediate commands are commands that can be carried out without reference to a particular database. Return to the dot prompt mode

Esc   Escape key
Y   Yes, escape to the dot prompt

Try out these examples of immediate commands:

. ? 22*34   Calculates the result of multiplying 22 by 34. The question mark is an operator that causes dBASE to display the results of the command that follows. If the printer has been set on, the result is also sent to the printer.

. ? date()   Displays the system date

COMMAND ABBREVIATIONS

As commands are described, they will be spelled out completely. Any dBASE command, function, or other reserved word, can be abbreviated to the first four characters. For instance, CREATE can be entered as CREA and the reserved word STRUCTURE can be abbreviated to, STRU. You cannot abbreviate filenames.

COMMANDS

Directory

You can obtain a listing of database filenames by pressing function key F4, or by entering

. dir   The directory command

Although the spelling of the command is the same as the DOS command, the two commands do not produce the same results. The DOS command lists the names of all directory and filenames regardless of their extensions. The dBASE command, by default, only lists database filenames; filenames with the extension .DBF.
Wild cards, the * and the ? symbols, also work in dBASE. Examples of other dBASE dir commands you can try are

. dir *.*   To list the names of all files with any extension
. dir *.fmt   To list the names of files with the extension .FMT
. dir jobs.*   To list the names of files with the filename JOBS, regardless of their extension
. dir a: To list the names of all .DBF files on drive A

Try executing these commands, but be sure that the files diskette is in drive A.

Use

USE is equivalent to highlighting a file name on the DATA panel of the Control Center. Its purpose is to place a database into use for all subsequent commands. It also places index files into use. Examples of this command are:

. use jobs
          Closes any previously open database or index files and places the database file JOBS into use
. use jobs index progfile
          Closes any previously open database or index files and places the database file JOBS and the index file PROGFILE into use.
. use jobs index progfile, billfile
          Closes any previously open database or index files and places the database file JOBS and the index file PROGFILE and BILLFILE into use. PROGFILE is the master index file.
. use   USE without a filename closes any previously open files without opening any other files. This is similar to the close command described below.

Execute the command shown for using JOBS.

Create

The create dot command offers the same options as the Create options on the Control Center panels. This command is used to establish new files of various types. As soon as the commands are executed, you enter the same development environment that you accessed through the Control Center. Do not execute these commands.

. create jobs
> Presents a new structure definition screen with which to build a new database if the database JOBS does not already exist. Otherwise dBASE prints an error message.

. create screen jobsrepo
> Presents a Form Design Screen with which to construct a new screen for data entry and editing. The screen format filename will be JOBSREPO.SCR.

. create report billing
> Presents a Report Design Screen with which to construct a new report. The file created will be named BILLING.FRM.

Append

The append command is used to add records to a database file that is in use. If a database is not in use, the user will be prompted for a database filename to place into use.

. append   Places an empty entry form into use with which to add records. Additional forms are displayed as records are entered.

. append blank
> Places one empty record at the bottom or end of the database. Entry is completed with the addition of that record.

. append from xyzfile
> Appends records found in the file XYZFILE, to those of the database currently in use. If the two files do not have the same structure, only the data from matching field names will be appended. Thus some fields in the default database may be empty if they are not found in XYZFILE, or the data transferred from XYZFILE may be truncated if a field in the default file is shorter than the field of the same name.

The append from command can be modified to include a search condition.

. append from xyzfile for deleted
> Adds to the default file, perhaps named OLDLIST, all of the records which have been marked for deletion.

. append from xyzfile for name = 'Grey, Y.'
> Adds to the default file, perhaps named GREYTOTL, all of the records that have Grey, Y. in the NAME field

Average, Count, Sum

The average command computes the arithmetic mean for all, or for specified numeric fields, in the default database. Assume that a database had three numeric fields named GROSS_INC, NET_INC, and COSTS.

. average   Produces the headings for the three fields and displays the average for each field
                  immediately beneath the column heading.
. average net_inc
                  Produces the heading NET_INC and displays the average beneath the heading.

    A scope condition can be added to the **average** command.

. average costs for supplr = 'Acme'
                  Displays the average of the entries in the field COSTS for records with Acme in the field
                  SUPPLR.

    Execute the **average** command with reference to the field names HRS_WORKED and CLIENT_ID
(equal to 135) in JOBS.
    The **count** command counts how many records there are in a database, or how many records in a
database meet a specified condition. The **sum** command totals the values in numeric fields in the same
ways that averages can be determined. Since these commands are so similar to the average command,
examples are not be given.

Browse

The **browse** command offers the spreadsheet-like, full-screen view of records in the database

. browse   Displays the current database with all of the fields in view, or available through the
                  panning commands
. browse fields progr_name, hrs_worked
                  Displays only the fields PROGR_NAME and HRS_WORKED in the default database,
                  making it easier to change data without excessive searching. Execute this command.

    Exit browse with Control and End

Close

The **close** command is used to close files that are currently in use

. close all   Closes all files of all types

Copy

The dBASE **copy** command does not have the same syntax as the DOS copy command. It is used to
duplicate files. When issuing a copy command, be sure to include the extension to the filename.

. copy file clients.dbf to newlist.dbf
                  Replicates the file CLIENTS.DBF and gives the new file the name, NEWLIST.DBF. This
                  command copies any type of file. Notice the presence of the reserved words FILE and
                  TO in the command line.
. copy structure to nxtlist
                  Replicates the structure of the database currently in use in order to create a new
                  database file with the name NXTLIST(.DBF). The new file has no records. This is a
                  useful command with which to start new databases. For instance, a school might have
                  a personnel database for the art department. The same structure could be used for the

biology department, the chemistry department, etc. There is no need to go through the definition of structure step for each department.

. copy to templist

This command uses the currently active database. It replicates database files only. In this example, the currently active database is cloned to produce an identical database called, TEMPLIST(.DBF).

. copy to finished for done

DONE can be assumed to be a logical field since there is no relational operator with which to compare the contents of the field with a specified value. A new database file, FINISHED(.DBF) is created that has the same structure as the database currently in use, but its records are limited to those for which the DONE field contains .T. or Y.

Execute this command with the JOBS database.

. copy to jobs type wks

This command creates a file called JOBS.WKS that can be read by Lotus 1-2-3. The extension .WKS is the extension used by version 1A of Lotus 1-2-3. This file can be read by version 2. Fields are converted to columns and records are converted to rows.

Execute this command with the JOBS database.

. copy to wpfile type sdf

This command creates a text (ASCII) file called WPFILE (no extension) in which each record occupies one line in the file.

Execute this command with the JOBS database.

. copy to active for .not. done fields progr_name,client_id,job_id

Using the currently active database, all records that have a .F. or N in the field DONE are duplicated in a new database, ACTIVE. Unlike the original record, the ACTIVE record structure only has the fields PROGR_NAME, CLIENT, and JOB_ID.

Delete, Recall

Often records are marked for deletion while the user is in either edit or browse. The Ctrl-U key combination marks the record for deletion, or, if the record is already marked for deletion, Ctrl-U removes the deletion marker. In addition to this approach, a record can be deleted by a dot command and in the <Records> submenu of the Browse or Edit screens. So, too, can records be recalled (i.e., unmarked). Sample commands are:

. delete record 10

Marks record number 10 for deletion. If the record has already been marked for deletion, dBASE reports that no records have been deleted.

. delete for recno() > 100

Marks all records from record 100 on for deletion. RECNO() is a dBASE function that returns the dBASE maintained record number.

. delete for progr_name = 'GREY, Y.'

Searches through the database and deletes all records in which Grey, Y. is contained in the field PROGR_NAME

. recall record 10

Unmarks record 10 for deletion

. recall for recno() > 100

> Unmarks any records whose record number is greater than 100 and which has been previously marked for deletion, but does not affect any other records that had not been marked for deletion

The third example shown demonstrates the use of a search condition. If the file is indexed, the scope condition can also be used with either the delete or the recall commands.

Edit

The edit command allows you to alter the contents of one or more records.

. edit

> The default record number is the current value of the record pointer. If the record pointer referenced record number 12, the edit would be carried out on record 12. With the pressing of the PgUp and PgDn keys, you can continue to edit other records.

. edit record 12

> Changes the record pointer to reference record 12 and begins editing there.

. edit for job_id = 1575

> A search condition that locates the first instance of a record with 1575 in the JOB_ID field. As the PgDn key is pressed, other records with 1575 in that field are retrieved for editing regardless of their location in the database.

. edit while job_id = 1575

> A scope condition that only allows you to continue editing records until the JOB_ID field no longer contains 1575. Other records with this value may exist, but if they are not immediately behind the current record, they will not be edited.

Erase

The erase command is employed to delete a file while the delete command marks records for deletion. The complete filename must be given.

. erase myfile.dbf

> This would eradicate the file MYFILE.DBF. It would not eliminate MYFILE.FMT or MYFILE.NDX since the extensions do not match that file specification in the command.

The erase command cannot erase the file that is currently in use (open). If you were using the file, TEMP, in order to erase it, you would use the close command to close it first. Then you could issue the erase command to remove it.

Find

Applicable only to an indexed file, the find command locates the first record that meets the search condition. The index must have been constructed around the field in which the search string is located. For instance

. find 'Wells'   Would locate the name 'Wells' in the field on which the index was constructed, perhaps a field containing city names

Index, Reindex

The index command creates .MDX files that order database records. If an index file is corrupted (no longer current with the database), the reindex command rebuilds the index based on the command used to construct the original index.

. index on last + first tag alphlist
> Builds an index for the database file currently in use. If there is no file in use, a prompt for a file is displayed. The index is based upon the combination of characters in the LAST and FIRST fields, in that order.

. index on city + str(zip,5) tag citylist
> Builds an index for the database file currently in use. The index is based upon the combination of characters in the field CITY and on the field ZIP which is converted to character data, in that order.

. reindex
> Rebuilds any of the currently active indexes set for use with the database that is open

List

The list command has many variations that go well beyond the listing of records in the database, but most of these are not be described here. Samples similar to those already used are:

. list
> Lists all of the records in the database by scrolling

. list for .not. done
> Lists only those records for which the entry to the logical field DONE is N or .F

. list fields progr_name, job_id, client_id
> Lists the PROGR_NAME, JOB_ID and CLIENT_ID field contents for each record

. list field progr_name, hrs_worked for progr_name = 'Doe, F.'
> Lists only the contents for the PROGR_NAME and JOB_ID fields for anyone with Doe, F. in the PROGR_NAME field

. list to print
> Sends a complete listing of the database to the printer

. list field progr_name, job_id, client_id to print
> Sends the contents of the three fields for every record to the printer

. list structure
> Reports the structure of the database to the screen. This enables you to determine the precise spelling and type for fields.

. list structure to print
> Reports the structure of the database to the printer

Locate

The locate command positions the record pointer to the location of a record which meets a specific condition. This command works on unindexed databases; unsorted and sorted. The search is exhaustive and potentially time-consuming if the database is large.

. locate for job_title = 'Lease Management'
> Searches for the first record with the contents, Lease Management in the JOB_TITLE field

. locate for zip = 12201
> Searches for the first record with the number 12201 in the ZIP field

Modify

The modify command has many variations. It can be used to modify database file structures, query, report, screen, and view files.

. modify structure
>Enables you to alter the structure of the database currently in use. You could add or delete fields and you could change field types, field lengths, and field names. Changes of this type may destroy data. If a database is not in use, you will be prompted to name one. Make, at most, one change per field during a single use of this command. Try this command.

. modify screen
>Enables you to enter the Form Design Screen and to alter the screen

Pack

The pack command is used to physically remove the records that have been marked for deletion from the database. Once the pack command has been executed, the records cannot be retrieved. If any indexes are in use, they are updated. If an index file built on this database is not in use, it has to be reindexed.

. pack   Removes all records in the current database marked for deletion

Quit

This command is used to return to DOS. It should be used whenever you are finished working in dBASE. Quit closes all databases, index and other files properly. Do not simply turn off the machine.

. quit   Exits from dBASE

Rename

Rename is used to change the name of a database. It cannot be used to change the name of the database currently in use. If you wish to rename the database currently in use, close it with the close command first.

. rename fileone.dbf to filetwo.dbf
>Notice the presence of the reserved word TO in the command

Replace

Replace changes the contents of specified fields in a database.

. replace job_title with upper(job_title)
>Changes the contents of the JOB_TITLE field to uppercase for the record currently pointed to by the record pointer. UPPER() is a function that converts all lowercase characters into uppercase.

. replace all job_title with lower(job_title)
>Changes the contents of the JOB_TITLE field to lowercase for the entire database

. replace all job_id with **131** for job_title = **'Accounts Payable'**
> Replaces the contents for JOB_ID field for all records with the entry 131 if Accounts Payable is found in the JOB_TITLE field

Set

The set command has many variations, not all of which are described here. The set command can be entered with

. set
> To produce a menu of changes that can be made to the dBASE programming environment. Changes can be made to the screen, to function key assignments, to the default drive and the search path for finding files, to the default files, to print characteristics, and to the display of decimal places.

You can enter the set command as shown above, or, if you need only to change one characteristic of the environment, you can enter a single command line. Sample command lines using the set command are given below.

Set Bell On/Off

When you enter data in edit, append, and browse, the default is to sound a bell when you enter the last character in the last column of a field. The command

. set bell off   suppresses the bell, and

.set bell on   returns the signal.

Set Default To

When you wish to change the default drive on which to have dBASE read and write files, use this command:

. set default to B   Changes the default to drive B

You can specify pathnames when you want to reference files that are not on the default drive. That is, if the default drive is B, you can copy a file to drive C with

. copy to c:\work\payrecs

Set Exact On/Off

In searching on character fields, dBASE defaults to an inexact search. If a search is made for Johns in a last name field, for instance, dBASE not only locates people whose name is Johns, it also locates persons whose name is Johnson and Johnsen. The command

. set exact on   Causes dBASE to restrict its discoveries to records which are spelled exactly like the search string

Set Fields

By default, whenever you use commands that display or edit the file, you will see the contents of all of the fields in the records. Often this makes visual searching and actual changes in the records awkward and time-consuming. This command limits the number of fields that are displayed.

. set fields to name, balance
> Sets the display of fields to two: NAME and BALANCE; if set fields is on

. set fields on
> Actuates the SET FIELDS TO command

. set fields off
> Returns displays to the full range of fields

Set Function n To

The function keys have default values that were described earlier in the chapter. The default values are not always the most commonly used commands for a given user. SET FUNCTION assigns different values to the function keys.

. set function 10 to "set bell off"
> Changes the command that function key 10 enters from EDIT to SET BELL OFF

Set Print On/Off

Generally, the printer is turned off. When you produce a listing, you can send it to the printer with the command

. list to print
> At times you may wish to capture unformatted output on the printer. The output can include characters you type as well as data produced by dBASE. With the command

. set print on
> the printer prints every character that is subsequently sent to the screen, while

. set print off
> restricts output to the screen.

Set Status On/Off

You can remove the status line from the base of your screen with the command

. set status off
> It can be returned with

. set status on

Sort To

The sort command creates a clone of the database currently in use. The clone is different from the original database because it has been ordered on one or more fields. Some of the variations of this command are as follows:

. sort to newlist on progr_name
>Creates a file, NEWLIST, which has its records in ascending order based on the field PROGR_NAME. Ascending, low to high, order is the default order.

. sort to second on hrs_worked /d
>Creates a file, SECOND, which has its records in descending order based on the HRS_WORKED field. The /d option causes the sort to be in descending order.

. sort to vips on salary for salary > 100000
>Creates a file, VIPS, which has its records in ascending order based on the field SALARY. The records in VIPS may be less than the default database since the search condition limits which records are included.

Up and Down Arrows

When using the dot commands, the Up and Down arrows can play a very useful role. Pressing the Up arrow returns the previous command line to the dot prompt. Pressing the Up arrow additional times returns earlier commands. It is quite common that a minor error in the spelling of a command or field name results in syntactic and semantic errors (i.e. errors in structure and errors in meaning, respectively). It is also quite common that a perfectly well formulated command must be executed again. Instead of retyping the entire command, simply use the Up arrow to find the command, edit it if necessary, and press the Enter key.

If the Up arrow is pressed too often and you need to return to a command that came later than the command currently displayed, the Down arrow can be used to return to these commands.

The command line that is returned to the dot prompt can be edited. The arrow, Home, and End keys move the cursor without changing the line. The Insert key allows you to overwrite or insert characters on the line. The Delete and Backspace keys remove characters on the line. When the line has been edited, the Enter key executes the command.

EXERCISES

The first section of this chapter was intended primarily as a reading assignment. You may have tried some of the commands, but others could not be executed. In this section, all of the commands can be executed. These commands do not encompass all of the examples described above, but enough of the commands are called for to give you a knowledge of how dot commands can be executed.

A.   The DIR command. List the names of the database files. List all of the filenames on drive A. List all filenames on drive A with the extension .NDX.

B.   The USE command. Use the file CLIENTS. Use the file CLIENTS along with the indexes ZIPFILE and IDFILE.

C.   The LIST command. List the records in CLIENTS. List the structure of CLIENTS. List the structure to the printer.

D.   USE the file JOBS.

E.   The COPY command. Copy those records in the JOBS file for CLIENT_ID equal to 131 into a file called GREEN. Copy the structure of CLIENTS to a database file called TEMP. Do not copy any records into TEMP. Also copy the .dbt files for each .dbf file.

F.   The APPEND command. Use TEMP and with the append command, add one record.

G.   The CLOSE command. Close the file TEMP.

H.   The RENAME command. Rename the file GREEN to NUJOBS.

I.   The APPEND FROM command. Use the JOBS file. Append to JOBS the three records that compose the NUJOBS database.

J.   The ERASE command. Remove the file NUJOBS.

K.   The SORT command. Sort from the JOBS file on the basis of the contents of the programmers' names to a file called NAMELST.

L.   The REPLACE command. Use ZIPFILE and replace all of the CLT_NAME entries with the lowercase characters. Replace them with uppercase characters. Replace all of the ZIP fields' contents with 19860 for a CITY name of Wellston. List the records.

M.   The SET command. Set the fields list to CLIENT_ID, CITY and ZIP. List the fields. Use the edit and browse commands to see the effect of limiting the number of fields to be used.

N.   The function keys. Press F5, the List Structure key. Notice that the three fields used in the set fields command, CLIENT_ID, CITY, and ZIP, are preceded by a greater than sign. Set fields to off. Press F5 again.

O.   The SET FUNCTION command. Use the set function command to change the command for function key F5 to LIST FIELDS CLIENT_ID, CLT_NAME and press F5.

P.   Use the CLIENTS file. Create an sdf file called CLIENTS(.TXT).

Q.   Use the SERVICES file. Create an sdf file called SERVICES(.TXT).

R.   Use the ROSTER file. Create an sdf file called ROSTER(.TXT).

S.   Use the SOFTWARE file. Create an sdf file called SOFTWARE(.TXT).

Chapter 7

dBASE Functions

Chapter Outline

You have already used some of dBASE's functions such as upper(), date(), and str(). Recall that a function is a procedure that carries out a complex operation on a number, a series of numbers, a character, or a character string. dBASE IV has a wide variety of functions described in the dBASE manual, many of which will not be dealt with in this book.

Users of dBASE can utilize functions in the dot command mode and in programming. This book does not cover dBASE programming. Suffice to say that dBASE does have a programming language associated with it that gives it the capabilities of languages like BASIC, FORTRAN and Pascal. dBASE functions and dot commands can be stored in files called program files that greatly extend the utility of dBASE IV. In this chapter, you will

1. Learn what functions, arguments, and expressions are.
2. Review the functions that beginning users of dBASE are likely to use.
3. Practice the use of some of these functions in the chapter's exercises.

SET UP

Boot your computer and load dBASE. Use the file, JOBS.DBF. Enter the dot command mode of operation and enter,

. copy to testfile.dbf

create a duplicate of JOBS.DBF called TESTFILE.DBF. Because JOBS.DBF has a memo field that has been used, the command also copies the file JOBS.DBT. Use the database TESTFILE in this chapter. Issue the list structure dot command to recall that the structure of this file is

Record	Field name	Type	Width	Dec
1	PROGR_NAME	Character	13	
2	CLIENT_ID	Character	4	
3	JOB_ID	Character	4	
4	JOB_TITLE	Character	18	
5	HRS_WORKED	Numeric	4	1
6	WORK_DATE	Date	8	
7	DONE	Logical	1	
8	NOTES	Memo	10	

Remain in the dot command mode of operation. All of the commands given below can be carried out on TESTFILE.DBF.

EXPRESSIONS

Functions carry out specialized operations on expressions that they receive. Consider the lower() function. In the command,

. replace progr_name with lower(progr_name)

the function lower() converts to lowercase any uppercase characters in the field PROGR_NAME of the record pointed to by the record pointer. In order for the function to make the conversion, PROGR_NAME must be a field that stores character data. Lower() would also function properly if you entered any of the following dot commands:

. ? lower('UPPERCASE LETTERS')
. ? lower(progr_name + job_title)
. ? lower(progr_name + 'ABC')

In the first example, lower() converts an actual string of characters to lowercase. To be recognized correctly, character strings must be enclosed in matching apostrophes or matching quote marks. The name of a field that contains character data does not have to be enclosed in quotes. In the second example, the plus sign concatenates - unites - the contents of two fields, PROGR_NAME and JOB_TITLE. Lower() then converts the resulting character string entirely to lowercase. In the third example, the plus sign concatenates the contents of the field PROGR_NAME with three letters: "A," "B," and "C."

In each of the three cases, lower() operated on character expressions. A character expression can be:

1.   one, or a concatenation of two or more, fields that have a type defined as character
2.   one, or a concatenation of two or more, character strings
3.   a concatenation of two or more fields of type character, and of one or more character strings

In a similar fashion there are numeric expressions that are composed of numbers, fields that contain numbers, and expressions that can be converted to numbers. There are date expressions that contain dates, fields that contain dates, and expressions that can be converted to dates.

Expressions can be used in many contexts. They can be used in searches with a command such as find, in indexing commands, and in search and scope options for commands such as list and display.

Expressions are also acted upon by functions. When an expression is "passed to" a function, it is called an argument. Functions are designed to work on arguments that are a specific type of expression. Putting the wrong type of expression in a function leads to syntactic errors.

Functions always produce the same type of output. Upper(), for example, not only always uses character expressions as input, it also produces character expressions as output. Other functions produce date expressions, while others produce numeric expressions.

DATE AND TIME FUNCTIONS

Character to Date   **CTOD(< character expression >)**

The CTOD function changes a character string that looks like a date to a date. A date cannot be entered directly on the command line. This function is useful in conditions that are used to select out records with date fields that occur in specific ranges of dates. Examples of usage of CTOD are:

. ? ctod('12/25/90')
> Produces the date, 12/25/90. Note that the date returned is not enclosed in quotes and that the date has a numeric meaning that allows dBASE to compare one date with another to determine which is earlier, later, or whether they are equal to one other.

. list for work_date > ctod('5/15/90')
> The field WORK_DATE is a date field. The command will list all records for which the WORK_DATE field contains a date that is greater than May 15, 1990.

. sum(hrs_worked) for work_date > = ctod('6/1/90') .and. work_date < = ctod('6/30/90')
> WORK_DATE is a date field. The hours worked in June are totaled from dates in the WORK_DATE field that are between June 1 and June 30, 1990.

Date to Character   **DTOC(< date expression >)**

The dtoc() function is the reverse of the ctod() function. It changes a date expression to a character expression. Examples of its use are:

. ? dtoc(work_date)
> Displays the character expression for the WORK_DATE field of the record pointed to by the record pointer. If the record pointer is at EOF, dtoc will return " / / ." Use the "skip -1" command to move back to the last record and repeat the dtoc() command.

. copy to junelist for dtoc(work_date) > = '06/01/90'
> Converts the contents of the WORK_DATE field to a character expression and then compares this expression with the character expression '01/01/90.' If the WORK_DATE-based expression matches or is greater than the criterion expression, the record is copied to a file, JUNELIST.

Date   **DATE()**

The date() function does not operate on an expression. Use of the date() function causes dBASE to get the system date maintained by DOS and to return that date. If the system date was not entered correctly, date() will report the incorrect date.

. ? date()   Returns the system date
. list for work_date < date()
> Lists the records for which the WORK_DATE is lower than (earlier than) the system date

CHARACTER FUNCTIONS

Convert to Uppercase   **UPPER(<character expression >)**

The upper() function takes a character expression and changes all lowercase characters to uppercase, while leaving uppercase characters alone. Nonalphabetic characters are also unchanged.

. ? upper('My Word!')
> Produces "MY WORD!"

. replace job_title with upper(job_title)
> For the current record only, converts the contents of the JOB_TITLE field to uppercase

. replace all job_title with upper(job_title)
> Converts all contents of the JOB_TITLE field to uppercase throughout the database

Convert to Lowercase   **LOWER(<character expression >)**

The lower() function takes a character expression and changes all uppercase characters to lowercase, while leaving lowercase characters alone. Nonalphabetic characters are also unchanged.

. ? lower('My Word!')
> Produces "my word!"

. replace progr_name with lower(progr_name)
> For the current record only, converts the contents of the PROGR_NAME field to lowercase

. replace all job_title with lower(job_title)
> Converts all contents of the JOB_TITLE field to lowercase throughout the database

Trim Leading Blanks   **LTRIM(<character expression >)**

The ltrim() function removes blanks that may occur before the first visible alphabetic or numeric character. This is a useful function for making sure that blanks have not been entered in error.

. ? ltrim('   Bob')
> Produces "Bob" at the left margin of the screen. The leading blanks were stripped.

. replace all job_title with ltrim(job_title)
>   Checks every record and removes any unwanted blanks in front of the entries in
>   JOB_TITLE

Trim Trailing Blanks   RTRIM(< character expression >)

The rtrim() function removes blanks that may occur after the last visible alphabetic or numeric character.
This is a useful function for removing blanks from words that are smaller than the field they are stored in.

. ? rtrim('Mary   ') + ' ' + 'Female'
>   Produces "Mary" at the left margin of the screen, strips the trailing blanks, adds one
>   blank and adds the word "Female"

. ? rtrim(progr_name) + ', ' + rtrim(job_title)
>   If the PROGR_NAME field of the current record was of width 15 and contained 'Grey, Y.
>   ' this command would concatenate the first eight letters with a comma and a blank
>   and then would concatenate the "trimmed" contents of the JOB_TITLE field. If
>   JOB_TITLE contained "Payroll D.B.   " the display would be, "Grey, Y., Payroll D.B."

MATHEMATICAL FUNCTIONS

Absolute Value   ABS(< numeric expression >)

The abs() function returns a number that is the absolute value of the numeric expression. If a number is
negative, it removes the minus sign.

. ? abs(-10)   Displays 10
. ? abs(10)   Displays 10
. replace all hrs_worked with abs(hrs_worked)
>   Replaces all of the field contents of HRS_WORKED for all records in the database with
>   positive numbers

Integer Value   INT(< numeric expression >)

The int() function truncates real numbers so that only the whole part of the number is returned.

. ? int(45.32) Displays 45
. ? replace all hrs_worked with int(hrs_worked)
>   Replaces the contents of the SALARY field for all of the records in the database with the
>   whole number of contents previously held in that field

Maximum Value   MAX(< numeric expression list >)

Max() returns the higher value of two numeric expressions.

. ? max(12,35) Displays 35
. ? max(hrs_worked, client_id)
>   Assume that CLIENT_ID is numeric instead of character, lists the contents of the larger
>   of the two fields

Minimum Value   **MIN(** <numeric expression> **)**

Min() returns the lower value of two numeric expressions.

. ? min(12,35) Displays 12
. ? min(hrs_worked, client_id)

> Assume that the CLIENT_ID is numeric instead of character, lists the contents of the smaller of the two fields

Rounded Value   **ROUND(** <num. expression1, num. expression2> **)**

The round() function rounds off numbers in numeric expression1, to the level indicated by numeric expression2.

. ? round(45.32,1) Displays 45.30
. ? round(45.32,4) Displays 45.32
. ? round(1345.34,-3)

> Displays 1000.00. The negative, numeric expression2 rounds the whole portion of the number

Do not execute the following command since it uses fields that are not found in the current database.

. ? replace all salary with round(salary,-1)

> Replaces the contents of the SALARY field for all records in the database with the salary closest to a $10 break point

OTHER TYPE CONVERSION FUNCTIONS

Value to String   **STR(** <num. express1> , <num. express2> , <num. express3> **)**

The str() function is particularly valuable in combining fields of dissimilar types for indexing, sorting, and searching operations. A numeric expression is either a number, a formula returning a number, a field with numeric contents, or a combination of these expressions. The first expression is the number to be converted. The second expression is to indicate the resulting string length (10 is the default for some operations). The third expression is to indicate how many of the decimal places, if any, are to be carried into the string. For the following examples, assume that the ZIP field is of type numeric.

. ? str(178,3)

> Displays the character expression equivalent of 178 which is "178." The 3 inside the parentheses is the string length

. list for str(hrs_worked,4) = '8.0'

> Equivalent to ". list for HRS_WORKED = 8.0

. index on job_title + str(hrs_worked,4) tag jobfile

> Converts the HRS_WORKED number to a character expression which is then concatenated to the JOB_TITLE character expression to create a single character expression to be used to build the index tag JOBFILE.

String to Value   VAL(<character expression>)

The val() function is used to convert character expressions to numeric expressions.

. ? val('178')
>   Displays the numeric expression equivalent of "178" which is 178
. list for val(client_id) = 131
>   Equivalent to ". list for client_id = 131"

>   Do not execute the following command since it uses a field that is not in your database.

. index on val(zip) tag zipfile
>   converts the ZIP number to a numeric expression which is then used to build the index

RECORD POINTER FUNCTIONS

Beginning Of File   BOF()

The bof() function is primarily used in programming. It is a boolean function that reports whether or not the record pointer is at the beginning of the file (the first record).

. ? bof()   Displays .T. if it is true that the record pointer is at the beginning of the file, or .F. if it is
>   at any other location

End of File   EOF()

Also primarily used in programming, the eof() function is a boolean function that reports whether or not the record pointer is at the end of the file (beyond the last record). Issue the list command which will leave the record pointer at the end of the file.

. ? eof()   Displays .T. if it is true that the record pointer is at the end of the file, or .F. if it is at any
>   other location

Check for Deleted Records   DELETED()

The deleted() function determines whether the record pointed to by the record pointer has been marked for deletion.

. ? deleted()
>   Displays .T. if it is true that the record pointer is pointing to a record that has been
>   marked for deletion, or .F. if the record is not marked for deletion
. list for deleted()
>   Lists the records in the database file in use that have been marked for deletion
. list for .not. deleted()
>   Lists the records in the database file in use that have not been marked for deletion

Record Number   RECNO()

The recno() function returns the value stored by the record pointer. It is used to determine the current record number.

. ? recno()   Displays 9 (or some other number) that indicates the number held by the record pointer
. **list for recno() > 10**
                     Lists all of the records that have a dBASE-maintained, record number greater than 10

EXERCISES

A.   Retrieve the database JOBS. Duplicate (copy) the file to JOBSLIST. Use JOBSLIST. Create an index file called JOBIDS based on the JOB_ID field.

B.   Replace all programmer names (PROGR_NAME) with their lowercase equivalents. For records with a CLIENT_ID of 127, replace the PROG_NAME with its uppercase equivalent.

C.   List all programmer names, and only the programmer names, followed by the character string, " - programmer." A typical line might print as "Doe, F. - programmer."

D.   List to the printer all jobs with a WORK_DATE on or after June 1, 1990. List all jobs with a WORK_DATE between May 10, 1990, and May 15, 1990.

E.   Using the Up arrow, find the command that printed jobs conducted after June 1, 1990, and modify it to print all jobs begun before June 1, 1990.

F.   Display the system date.

G.   List all records with a CLIENT_ID of 127 and a WORK_DATE after May 15, 1990.

H.   Convert and replace all HRS_WORKED for programmer R. Brown to negative numbers (by multiplying by -1).

I.   Set fields to CLIENT_ID, JOB_ID, JOB_TITLE, and HRS_WORKED. List the records. List the records and display the HRS_WORKED as absolute. Set fields off.

J.   List the PROGR_NAME and HRS_WORKED to the closest integer. Use the Up arrow to retrieve the command. Modify it to list the same fields, but print the HRS_WORKED rounded to the nearest whole integer.

K.   Create an index file based on PROGR_NAME (character) and CLIENT_ID (numeric).

L.   With the dot command "delete record," mark records 6 and 13 for deletion. List the records marked for deletion. Copy the records marked for deletion to a file called BADONES. List the records in JOBSLIST that have not been marked for deletion.

M.   List all records for programmers with dBASE-maintained record numbers greater than 10. With record numbers between 5 and 10.

APPENDIX A

dBASE IV COMMANDS

?	Displays an expression or expression list followed by a line feed and a carriage return.
??	Displays an expression or expression list without a line feed or carriage return.
???	Sends a printer code.
@ <row>,<col>	Places the cursor at a specified row and column. Used with SAY, GET, CLEAR TO, FILL TO, COLOR, DOUBLE, and PANEL.
ACCEPT	Prompts for user input of a character string.
ACTIVATE MENU	Places a defined menu bar into use.
ACTIVATE POPUP	Places a defined popup menu into use.
ACTIVATE SCREEN	Reestablishes use of the full screen.
ACTIVATE WINDOW	Places a defined window into use.
APPEND [BLANK]	Adds records to the end of the database.
APPEND [FROM]	Copies records from another database, adding them to the end of the current database.
APPEND FROM ARRAY	Adds records by accessing information in an array.
APPEND MEMO	Imports a file into a memo field.
ASSIST	Recalls the Control Center from the dot prompt.
AVERAGE	Determines the arithmetic mean of a numeric expression.
BEGIN TRANSACTION	Begins a transaction, records changes and terminates with END TRANSACTION.
BROWSE	Calls up the full screen, table-oriented editor.
CALCULATE	Calculates financial and statistical functions.
CALL	Loads binary files.
CANCEL	Terminates execution of a command file.
CHANGE	Calls up an record editor.
CLEAR	Clears all or parts of the screen including GETs.
CLOSE	Closes files of all types.
COMPILE	Converts a dBASE IV source code file into object code.
CONTINUE	Activates the next record meeting a LOCATE condition.
CONVERT TO	Affixes a field to a structure user for record lock detection.
COPY TO	Replicates all or some of a database. Options permit the creation of other than .DBF files.
COPY FILE	Replicates any type of file.
COPY INDEXES	Creates production .MDX file from .NDX files.
COPY MEMO	Replicates memo field files.
COPY STRUCTURE	Replicates a database structure.
COPY TO	Replicates records in a database in a new database file.
COPY TAG	Creates .NDX files from production .MDX files.
COPY TO ARRAY	Stores record contents in an array.
COUNT	Counts the number of records meeting specified or default conditions.
CREATE STRUCTURE	Constructs a database structure.
CREATE APPLICATION	Constructs an complete application with the Applications Generator.
CREATE <fname> FROM	Constructs a database structure from that of another database.

CREATE QUERY/VIEW	Constructs a query design screen.
CREATE REPORT	Constructs a report.
CREATE SCREEN	Constructs a forms screen.
DEACTIVATE MENU	Removes an activated menu.
DEACTIVATE POPUP	Removes an activated popup menu.
DEACTIVATE WINDOW	Removes an activated window.
DEBUG	Accesses the debugger.
DECLARE	Creates arrays and memory variables.
DEFINE BAR	Specifies an option in a popup menu.
DEFINE BOX	Specifies a text box.
DEFINE MENU	Specifies a menu bar.
DEFINE PAD	Specifies a pad in a menu bar.
DEFINE POPUP	Specifies a popup menu.
DEFINE WINDOW	Specifies a window.
DELETE	Marks records for deletion.
DELETE TAG	Removes an index tag from a production .MDX file.
DIRECTORY	Displays filenames with/without wildcards.
DO	Executes a command file.
DO CASE	Selection control structure. Terminated with ENDCASE.
DO WHILE	Conditional loop control structure. Terminated with ENDDO.
EDIT	Activates the record editor.
EJECT	Advances the printer to the next page.
EJECT PAGE	Activates output to top of page with ON PAGE feature.
ERASE (DELETE)	Removes a file from the directory.
EXPORT TO	Replicates a database in a file format for some other application programs.
FIND	Searches on a specified condition for a record in an indexed file.
FUNCTION	Identifies a user-defined functions.
GO/GOTO	Repositions the record pointer.
HELP	Accesses the help system.
IF	Conditional processing of commands. Combined with ELSE and terminated with ENDIF.
IMPORT FROM	Creates database files from other application programs' files.
INDEX ON	Creates .NDX files for ordering a database.
INPUT	Prompts a user for input of a number.
INSERT [BLANK]	Inserts a new record into a database.
JOIN WITH	Merges fields from two databases into a new database.
LABEL FORM	Places a label form into use.
LIST/DISPLAY	Displays the contents of records in current database.
LIST/DISPLAY FILES	Displays directory information.
LIST/DISPLAY HISTORY	Displays most recently issued commands.
LIST/DISPLAY MEMORY	Offers information about RAM usage.
LIST/DISPLAY STATUS	Offers information about dBASE IV status.
LIST/DISPLAY STRUCTURE	Displays the current database's fields.
LIST/DISPLAY USERS	Displays the users logged into a networked version of dBASE IV.
LOAD	Brings a binary file into memory.
LOCATE	Searches for records on specified conditions.
LOGOUT	Exits from a networked version of dBASE IV.

MODIFY COMMAND/FILE	Invokes the full-screen editor to create or change command files, or other files.
MOVE WINDOW	Repositions a defined, activated window.
NOTE/*/&&	Comment designators.
ON ERROR	Executes a correcting program if an error is encountered.
ON PAD	Connects a popup menu with a menu bar pad.
ON PAGE	Inserts headers and footers when page breaks are initiated by ON PAGE.
ON READERROR	Traps and recovers from errors.
ON SELECTION PAD	Indicates the action upon selection of a menu bar choice.
ON SELECTION POPUP	Indicates the action upon selection of a popup menu choice.
PACK	Removes records marked for deletion.
PARAMETERS	Associates local variable names with data passed to a subprogram from a calling program.
PLAY MACRO	Makes a macro library available.
PRINTJOB	Activates a printing commands file.
PRIVATE	Creates localized memory variables.
PROCEDURE	Designates the beginning of a procedure in a procedure file.
PROTECT	Provides security.
PUBLIC	Creates global memory variables.
QUIT	Terminates dBASE IV and closes all open files.
READ	Obtains all GETs not previously cleared or read.
RECALL	Unmarks records marked for deletion.
REINDEX	Reconstructs .NDX and .MDX files.
RELEASE	Removes memory variables.
RENAME	Renames files.
REPLACE	Alters fields' contents.
REPORT FORM	Uses a report form file to print a report.
RESET	Removes an integrity flag from a file.
RESTORE FROM	Reactivates memory variables and arrays previously saved.
RESTORE MACROS FROM	Reactivates macros saved in a macro library.
RESTORE WINDOW	Reactivates a saved window specification.
RESUME	Resumes execution of a suspended program.
RETRY	Reexecutes a series of commands that led to an error condition.
RETURN	Returns control from a subprogram to a calling program.
ROLLBACK	Restores .DBF, .MDX and .NDX files to the state they were in prior to a transaction.
RUN	Executes a DOS program.
SAVE TO	Saves all or some of the current memory variables in a file that can be restored at a later time.
SAVE MACROS TO	Saves the current set of macros to a file.
SAVE WINDOW	Saves window specifications to a file.
SCAN	Conditional loop control structure. Terminated with ENDSCAN.
SEEK	Searches on a specified condition for a record in an indexed file.
SELECT	Changes the work area, thereby changing the currently active file.
SHOW MENU	Displays, but does not activate, a menu bar.
SHOW POPUP	Displays, but does not activate, a popup menu.
SKIP	Changes the current record by incrementing or decrementing the record pointer.

SORT TO	Creates a new .DBF file in ascending or descending order.
STORE	Creates and initializes memory variables and array elements.
SUM	Totals numeric expressions, placing the results in memory variables.
SUSPEND	Suspends the execution of a command file, returning the dot prompt and permitting dot command execution. The program is restarted with RESUME.
TEXT	Displays blocks of text as typed
TOTAL ON	Totals numeric fields, placing the results in another .DBF file.
TYPE	Displays the contents an ASCII file.
UNLOCK	Releases a record or file lock.
UPDATE ON	Updates the information in one .DBF file with the data from corresponding records in another file.
USE	Opens .DBF files with or without index files and index tag files.
WAIT	Pauses command program operation pending user input.
ZAP	Deletes all records in the active file.

Appendix B

dBASE IV FUNCTIONS

&	Macro substitution symbol.
ABS()	Returns the absolute value.
ACCESS()	Returns the access level of the current user.
ACOS()	Returns the angle size in radians from the cosine.
ALIAS()	Returns the alias of a work area number.
ASC()	Converts characters to ASCII representations.
ASIN()	Returns the angle size in radians from the tangent.
AT()	Substring search.
ATAN()	Angle size in radians from the tangent.
ATN2()	Angle size in radians from the sine and cosine.
BAR()	Returns the last number chosen from a popup menu.
BOF()	Evaluates whether the record pointer is at the beginning of the file.
CALL()	Executes binary programs.
CDOW()	Returns the day of the week in a date.
CEILING()	Returns the smallest integer greater than or equal to the value in a numeric expression.
CHANGE()	Evaluates whether a record has been changed.
CHR()	Changes a numeric expression to a character string.
CMONTH()	Changes a character string to a month.
COL()	Returns the cursor's column position.
COMPLETED()	Evaluates whether a transaction has been completed.
COS()	Angle size in radians from the cosine.
CTOD()	Changes a character string to a date.
DATE()	Returns the system date.
DAY()	Returns the day of the week in a date.
DBF()	Returns the active database name.
DELETED()	Evaluates whether a record is marked for deletion.
DIFFERENCE()	Determines the difference between 2 strings.
DISKSPACE()	Returns the space available on the active drive.
DMY()	Changes a date expression to form DD/MM/YY.
DOW()	Returns the day of the week via a number held in a date expression.
DTOC()	Changes a date to a character string.
DTOR()	Changes degrees to radians.
DTOS()	Changes dates to character strings.
EOF()	Evaluates whether the record pointer is at the end of the file.
ERROR()	Returns the ON ERROR condition number.
EXP()	Returns the value of a constant raised to a power.
FIELD()	Returns the field number of a field name in the active database.
FILE()	Determines whether a file exists.
FIXED()	Changes floating point numbers to binary coded decimal numbers.
FKLABEL()	Returns the name of the specified function key.
FKMAX()	Returns the number of programmable function keys

FLOAT()	Changes binary coded decimal numbers to floating point numbers.
FLOCK()	Locks files.
FLOOR()	Returns the largest integer less than or equal to a numeric expression.
FOUND()	Evaluates whether the last FIND, LOCATE, SEEK, or CONTINUE succeeded.
FV()	Future value.
GETENV()	Returns DOS environmental variable contents.
IIF()	Intermediate IF.
INKEY()	Returns an integer symbolizing the last key pressed.
INT()	Returns the integer value of a numeric expression.
ISALPHA()	Evaluates whether a string starts with a alphabetic character.
ISCOLOR()	Evaluates whether a computer has a color monitor/adapter.
ISLOWER()	Evaluates whether a string starts with a lowercase alphabetic character.
ISMARKED()	Evaluates whether a file is marked as undergoing change.
ISUPPER()	Evaluates whether a string starts with a uppercase. alphabetic character.
KEY()	Returns the expression used in an index file.
LASTKEY()	Returns the ASCII value of the last key pressed.
LEFT()	Returns a substring from a specified location begun at the right of a character string.
LEN()	Returns the number of characters in a string.
LIKE()	Carries out wildcard comparisons.
LINENO()	Returns the line number of the line to be processed in a command or procedure file.
LKSYS()	Returns the login name of the user locking a record or file.
LOG()	Natural logarithm.
LOG10()	Common logarithm to base 10.
LOOKUP()	Retrieves a value from a field in a designated record in a database.
LOWER()	Returns the lowercase of a character string.
LTRIM()	Removes leading blanks.
LUPDATE()	Returns the date a file was updated last.
MAX()	Selects the larger of 2 numeric expressions.
MDX()	Returns the .MDX filename for a file.
MDY()	Converts a date to the format MM/DD/YY.
MEMLINES()	Returns the number of lines in a memo field.
MEMORY()	Returns the amount of free random access memory.
MENU()	Returns the active menu name.
MESSAGE()	Returns the message associated with an ON ERROR number.
MIN()	Selects the smallest of 2 numeric expressions.
MLINE()	Returns a specific line from a memo field.
MOD()	Returns the remainder from a division of 2 numeric expressions.
MONTH()	Returns the month by number represented by a date expression.
NDX()	Returns the name of a .NDX file.
NETWORK()	Evaluates whether a the system is networked.
ORDER()	Returns the primary .MDX tag filename.
OS()	Returns the operating system name.

PAD()	Returns the name of the most recently used pad.
PAYMENT()	Calculates a payment for a loan.
PCOL()	Returns the column position of the print head.
PI()	The ration between the circumference and diameter of a circle (3.14159).
POPUP()	Returns the name of the popup menu in use.
PRINTSTATUS()	Evaluates whether the printer is ready for output.
PROGRAM()	Returns the name of the command or procedure file in operation when an error took place.
PROMPT()	Returns the prompt selected from the last popup menu.
PROW()	Returns the row position of the print head.
PV()	Present value of an annuity.
RAND()	Generates a random number.
READKEY()	Returns a number for a key typed in response to a full-screen command.
RECCOUNT()	Returns the number of records in a named .DBF file.
RECNO()	Returns the default record number.
RECSIZE()	Returns the size of records in a .DBF file.
REPLICATE()	Reproduces a character a specified number of times.
RIGHT()	Returns a substring from a specified location begun at the right of a character string.
RLOCK()	Locks a record(s).
ROLLBACK()	Returns true if a rollback command succeeded.
ROUND()	Rounds a numeric expression.
ROW()	Returns the row number of the cursor.
RTOD()	Converts radians to degrees.
RTRIM()	Removes leading blanks.
SEEK()	Returns true if the index key is found.
SELECT()	Returns the work area number for the highest unused file.
SET()	Returns the current setting for a SET option.
SIGN()	Returns the sign of a numeric expression.
SIN()	Returns the sine from an angle in radians.
SOUNDEX()	Returns four characters used in soundex searches.
SPACE()	Expands to a specified number of blanks.
SQRT()	Returns the square root of a number.
STR()	Converts a numeric expression into a character string.
STUFF()	Replaces one substring in a character string with another substring.
SUBSTR()	Returns a specified substring.
TAG()	Returns tag names from .MDX files.
TAN()	Returns the tangent from an angle in radians.
TIME()	Returns the system time.
TRANSFORM()	Formats data similar to that possible with PICTURE.
TRIM()	Removes trailing blanks.
TYPE()	Returns a single character identifying the field type.
UPPER()	Returns the uppercase of a character string.
USER()	Returns a users login name when PROTECT encrypts files.
VAL()	Converts character strings to numbers.
VARREAD()	Returns the name of the field being edited.
VERSION()	Returns the dBASE version number.
YEAR()	Returns the year held by a date expression.

GLOSSARY

? The DOS wildcard for matching single characters in command line parameters. In dBASE, the symbol to display a list of character strings or expressions followed by a carriage return and line feed.

+ The dBASE and DOS concatenation symbol.

* The DOS wildcard for matching multiple characters in command line parameters. In dBASE, this symbol at the beginning of a line causes the line to be treated as a comment statement.

A

Active directory See Current directory.

Alignment The placement of a label in a spreadsheet cell or database field. A label can be left- or right-justified or centered. Alignment is determined by label-prefix characters.

Alphanumeric characters Any combination of letters, numbers, symbols, and spaces.

Append The process of adding records to a database file.

Application The product of a generalized application program such as a document from a word processor, a budget projection from a spreadsheet, or an inventory from a database manager.

Application program A program that allows users to produce specific applications of the computer to a particular area or need.

Arithmetic operators The arithmetic signs /, *, +, -, ^.

Ascending order Arranging data so that lower values come first and higher values come last.

ASCII American Standard Code for Information Interchange; the coding scheme whereby every character, number, or symbol is represented by an integer code between 0 and 255.

ASCII files (Text) Files saved in a format specified by the American Standard Code for Information Interchange. Files saved in this format often can be used by other programs or transmitted by modem because they have a standard format.

Assist The dBASE command for loading the Assistant in dBASE III Plus, and the Control Center in dBASE IV.

B

Back copy A version of a file that is saved if extensive revisions or changes are going to be made. dBASE, EDLIN, and some other programs automatically create back copies.

Backup A process of making a second copy of a file to avoid loss of data. Backups may be created automatically by some applications programs.

Backup copy A duplicate of a file or disk that is saved in case the original file or disk is damaged.

Beep An audible sound notifying a user of an error.

Browse The viewing and editing of dBASE records in a tabular format.

Bug A program error.

Built-in functions Software-provided operations to carry out specific computational activities.

C   **Calculating fields** Fields in a database that can calculate numbers that are entered into other fields.

Cancel To abort a program or command. In dBASE, to return control to the dot prompt.

Catalog A group of logically associated dBASE files.

Character A symbol (numeric, alphabetic, punctuation, or mathematic) represented by one byte.

Character field A component of a database structure that holds character strings.

Character string See String.

Close In dBASE, the command used to close files.

Closing files To take a file out of use so that it cannot be read or written.

Command An instruction to a computer that can be executed.

Commercial software Software that has been copyrighted and licensed, is supported by the developer, and that must be paid for in advance of its usage.

Compiler A computer program that converts an entire source code program into machine-executable form.

Compound condition A logical condition composed of two conditions united with an AND or an OR operator.

CONFIG.DB The file containing dBASE default settings.

Concatenation The process of uniting two or more strings.

Configuration The currently active default values for an operating system or for an applications program. These values may be modifiable during operation.

Constants Values or strings that do not change when they are entered in cells or that are contained in formulas.

Context sensitive Describes the ability of a help system to offer assistance relevant to the status of the system at the point assistance is requested.

Control Center The menu-driven mode of access to dBASE IV.

CPU Central processing unit; the unit that processes data and supports random access memory (RAM).

Current directory The default DOS directory. The directory that is employed first when DOS searches for files and executable commands unless otherwise directed.

Current drive The drive containing the disk on which DOS looks for a directory or file unless otherwise instructed.

Current record The record in a database pointed to by the record pointer.

Cursor The underscore character that indicates where characters will be entered or where commands will be carried out.

Cursor block Reverse video blocks that highlight choices on menus.

Data Alphanumeric and graphic input or output.

Data disk The disk used to store files.

Data file A file that contains the data used by an applications program.

Database An organized collection of related records containing data suitable for manipulation by a database program.

Database field One element in a database structure that is defined by a field name, a length, and a type.

Database management system Software that facilitates the creation, querying, and manipulation of databases.

Database record The fields that make up an entry in a database.

Database structure The order and definition of fields that make up a record.

Date arithmetic The representation and manipulation of dates as values rather than as character strings.

Date field A component of a database structure that holds dates.

DBMS Database management system.

Debug To discover and correct syntactic and semantic errors in a program, function, macro, batch file, or subroutine.

Default configuration The initial defaults used to establish the operating characteristics of an operating system or applications program.

Default directory See Current directory.

Default drive See Current drive.

Default value The value used or the action taken when an acceptable alternative has not been specified.

Default record In dBASE, the record pointed to by the record pointer; the active record.

Descending order Arranging data so that higher values come first and lower values come last.

Destination The target location for data or files transferred from a source location.

Directory A logical grouping of files and subdirectories on a disk. A directory's filenames, extensions, and subdirectory names are displayed together along with each file's size, creation time, and date.

Directory hierarchy The treelike, logical structure holding subdirectories. Subdirectories of root have subdirectories created under them, and so on.

Disk drive The device that reads and writes files to disks.

Diskette A secondary storage medium for a computer. Diskettes come in floppy, rigid, and semi-rigid cases.

Dot prompt The command line-driven mode of access to dBASE.

Double-density disk A disk with 360 Kb of storage.

Double sided A diskette with two surfaces on which to store files.

Drive name The two characters (a letter and a colon) that identify a disk drive. Examples include C: and A:.

E   **End of file** In dBASE, the condition of having the record pointer identifying the location just past the last record.

Error message A warning that a command cannot be performed as requested.

Expression A legal combination of operators, constants, and variables.

Extension Up to three characters that are added to a filename to identify the contents of the file.

F   **Field** A subunit of a record to hold the smallest unit of data. A record is composed of fields.

Field length The maximum number of characters that can be entered in a field.

Field name Individually identifiable subunits of record structure.

Field type The class of data that can be stored in a dBASE field (character, date, float, logical, numeric, memo).

File A collection of data stored in a named and dedicated portion of a disk. Files can contain graphs, documents, databases, worksheets, programs, and other collections of data.

File extension See Extension.

File locking A technique for preventing more than one user from accessing the same file at a time.

File sharing A technique for allowing more than one user to access the same file simultaneously.

File specification The complete specification of a file including a drive letter, a pathway, a filename, and an extension. Also, abbreviated to filespec.

Filename The identifier that uniquely describes a file. Consists of from one to eight characters.

Floppy disk Diskettes that allow some physical flexibility, especially of the 3 1/2" and 5 1/4" size.

Freeze To lock in place; in dBASE to lock some columns or rows in place while panning to view other areas of the worksheet or database.

Full screen editor A text editor that enables full movement of the cursor. Commands are carried out and text is inserted with reference to the location of the cursor, not an editor-maintained line number.

Function A subroutine that performs a limited action on values and character strings.

Function keys Keys marked F1 through F10 (or F12) that carry out specialized macro operations in DOS and in applications software.

G   **Groups** Subdivisions of a dBASE report identifying break points for subtotals.

H   **Hard disk** Secondary storage devices with a rigid disk(s).

Help An on-line program for providing assistance.

Help key The key that recalls help screens (F1 in dBASE).

High density disk See Quad-density disk.

Home key The key that returns the cursor to the head of the previous field in dBASE.

I   **IBM-compatible computer** A computer capable of executing identically to an IBM computer. Also called a clone.

Immediate command A dot prompt command that can be carried out without relation to a database.

Index file In dBASE, a file that provides access to a database file such that it appears to be a predefined order. Also called an inverted file.

Indexing In dBASE, the process of creating a file that is used to organize the appearance of records in a database file.

Information Data to which meaning has been assigned.

Initialize To set up a diskette, a program, or a device with default values and conditions.

Input The data that a program can process.

Insert mode A mode of data entry in which new text is inserted into existing text rather than overwrites it. Opposed to overwrite mode.

Installation The process of tailoring the default values for an applications program to the hardware available and to the user's priorities for initial program parameters such as screen colors, margins, and so on.

Installation program The program that installs the program, driver, and text files needed to operate an applications program.

Interpreter A computer program that converts a source code program into machine-executable form on a line-by-line basis.

K   **Key expression** In dBASE, a combination of fields used to locate, index, or sort a database.

Key field A field in a database used for sorting.

Keyboard, extended 101 keys.

Keyboard, standard 80 keys.

Keyword A word that is reserved by an applications program for special meaning and that often cannot be used in an application.

Kill Terminate an executing program.

L   **Literal** A value that is not to be interpreted; a character string.

Lock In dBASE, to freeze specified fields at the left of the screen, allowing fields to the right to pan.

Logical condition A condition that evaluates to either true or false, or alternatively to yes or no.

Logical fields Also called Boolean fields. Fields in a database whose values are either true or false, or alternatively yes or no.

Logical operator An operator that tests the truth or falsity of a comparison: The logical operators commonly available are $=$, $<>$, $<$, $<=$, $>$, and $>=$.

M   **Memo fields** dBASE fields that contain unstructured comments for a record. Memos are stored in .DBT files.

Memo file See Memo fields.

Memory variable In dBASE, a variable in RAM that is created upon execution of a program and that is not a field in a record.

Menu A series of choices from which the user is to make selections.

Menu bar In dBASE, the menu at the top of the Control Center and other command-based screens.

Merging The operation by which data from a data or secondary file is merged with a primary file (a document) to produce a series of unique documents.

Message line In dBASE, a line at the bottom of the Control Center and other command-related screens offering assistance with highlighted menu choices and with error messages.

Mode The state of an operation.

MS-DOS Abbreviation for Microsoft-Disk Operating System. The operating system used on IBM PC-compatible computers.

N   **Navigation line** In dBASE, a line that offers information about the cursor movement keys.

Null string An empty character string.

Numeric field A component of a database structure that holds numbers.

Numeric functions In dBASE, the SUM, COUNT, and AVERAGE functions.

Numeric keypad The block of ten keys holding numbers as uppercase and cursor movement keys as lowercase.

Num Lock key The key used to toggle the numeric keypad between lowercase and uppercase.

O   **Opening files** To place a file into use so it can be read and written.

Operator A symbol to indicate the action to be performed on operands or to test the relationship of the operands.

Order of precedence The sequence in which operators in a formula are evaluated.

Output Data transferred to an output device.

Output device Any device receiving data from a computer. Common output devices are the monitors, printers, and plotters.

Overwrite mode The mode of data entry in which typed characters type over and replace existing text. Opposed to insert mode.

P   **Padding** Placing blanks (space characters) in the portion of a database field that was not occupied by user-entered characters.

Panning Moving fields that are not currently in view into view.

Parameters Values that are consistent with a command's syntax and are needed for correct execution, or that change the effect of a command.

PC Abbreviation for personal computer.

PC-DOS Abbreviation for Personal Computer--Disk Operating System; the operating system used on IBM personal computers. Comparable to MS-DOS.

Picture An option in dBASE for customizing and controlling input and output.

Popup menu A menu that appears with selections listed vertically.

Primary key Also primary field. The field (key) on which a database is sorted first.

Production file (.MDX) In dBASE, the file that holds dBASE-maintained indexes.

Program A sequence of instructions that a computer can execute to accomplish a task.

Program disk The disk that contains the main program for an application. Also called a system disk.

Prompt The signal that control has been passed to the user and that the system is awaiting a command or data entry.

Public domain software Software that is not copyrighted or supported by the developer.

Pulldown menu A popup menu that is coupled to a horizontal menu bar.

Q   **Quad density disk** A disk with 1.2 Mb storage.

Quit In dBASE, the dot command for exiting from dBASE and to return to DOS.

R   **Random Access Memory (RAM)** The portion of the computer's memory that stores the internal DOS commands, programs, and data. Also called main memory or primary memory.

Read The process of copying data from a file into RAM. In dBASE, the command for obtaining data from GET requests.

Record A single entry in a database. Also the collection of related fields that make up a record structure.

Record locking A technique to prevent two users of the same file from accessing the same record simultaneously.

Record number A number unique to each record in a database; an automatically maintained ordering mechanism created by dBASE.

Record pointer An internally maintained record number that a database program uses to identify the currently active record.

Relational operator See Logical operator.

Report generator A fourth-generation language program for producing a report.

S   **Save** To write a file to secondary storage.

Scope condition A FOR condition in dBASE used to limit the effect of a command to specific records.

Scrolling The line-by-line movement of data on the monitor.

Search The automatic location of a user-entered character string.

Search condition The identification of records in a dBASE file by specification of the contents of the fields.

Search string The user-entered character string that is to be located through a search command.

Secondary file A file that stores variable information to be merged into the primary document during a merge printing operation. Also known as a data file.

Secondary key A field (key) that breaks ties in the primary sort key when a file is sorted.

Semantic error An error in the logic of a computer program such that execution is permitted, but the output is different from that intended.

Software Programs used with a computer system. In contrast to hardware.

Software maintenance Testing, correcting, and updating a program to insure that it continues to produce correct results.

Sort To order the records in a database in ascending or descending order according to the contents of one or more fields.

Source code Original program code that is to be processed by a programming language compiler or interpreter.

String One or more connected characters used as a unit for some computer operation.

Structure The organization of fields defining a database record.

Syntax error An error in the construction of a computer command or programming statement.

System disk A disk containing the files needed for booting a booting system. Sometimes used to refer to the main program disk for an applications program.

System files Files such as the input/output and boot record files that are essential for the booting process to be carried out.

T **Tag** In dBASE, a means of placing an index within a production file into use.

Text Readable characters, including the alphanumeric characters, numerals, and punctuation marks. As opposed to nonvisible control codes. Also, the words in a message. In dBASE, a command that allows the user to describe how textual data will appear on a screen or on printed output.

Time arithmetic The representation and manipulation of hours, minutes, and seconds as values rather than as character strings.

Toggle The process of switching between two states. Also, any device, command, or command switch that has two states, on and off.

Typeover mode See Overwrite mode.

U **Unformatted disk** An uninitialized disk. The condition of the disk when first shipped.

Use In dBASE, a command to place a database into a work area with or without related indexes.

User interface The manner in which a computer user accesses a software package's commands and files.

V **Variable** A named location in RAM that stores values used by DOS or by an executing program.

W **Wildcards** Characters used in DOS and dBASE IV commands and in search operations to match one or more characters in the position of the wildcard in the string. Typically, a question mark matches one character, and an asterisk matches any number of characters.

   Write The process of copying data from RAM to a file.

Z **Zero suppression** In dBASE IV and other programs, the hiding of insignificant zeros.

INDEX